Counterdeception Principles and Applications for National Security

DISCLAIMER

All statements of fact, opinion, or analysis expressed are those of the authors and do not reflect the official positions or views of the CIA or any other U.S. Government agency. Nothing in the contents should be construed as asserting or implying U.S. Government authentication of information or Agency endorsement of the authors' views. This material has been reviewed by the CIA to prevent the disclosure of classified information.

For a listing of recent titles in the *Artech House Intelligence and Information Operations Series,* turn to the back of this book.

Counterdeception Principles and Applications for National Security

Michael Bennett
Edward Waltz

ARTECH HOUSE
BOSTON | LONDON
artechhouse.com

Library of Congress Cataloging-in-Publication Data
A catalog record for this book is available from the U. S. Library of Congress.

British Library Cataloguing in Publication Data
A catalogue record for this book is available from the British Library.

ISBN-13: 978-1-58053-935-7

Cover design by Igor Valdman

685 Canton Street
Norwood, MA 02062

10 9 8 7 6 5 4 3 2 1

Contents

Foreword

In the dozen-plus years that I worked foreign denial and deception (D&D) issues in the U.S. Intelligence Community, I came to appreciate the complexity of the problem and frankly worried about our capacity to deal with it. Part of the challenge was persistent advocacy, urging senior management in agencies big and small to take the issue more seriously, then cajoling first-line managers and working levels to put or keep D&D on their radar screens. Another part of the problem was ensuring that qualified people were appropriately assigned and tasked to address the growing D&D challenge. With bona fide D&D experts perennially short of critical mass in the intelligence community, there seemed never to be enough of us to really do it well.

To confront the foreign denial and deception challenge to U.S. intelligence—and therefore to national security policymakers and military customers of intelligence—with even minimal adequacy, we need to address major D&D issues in the intelligence production process: how information is collected and analyzed, how specialists are trained, how we conduct our research and development, and how adequate are our security and counterintelligence support. Seen this way, dealing effectively with foreign D&D is a community-wide, comprehensive challenge of daunting and growing proportions.

The complexity of denial and deception—deception, especially—defies ordinary approaches to conducting intelligence. Intelligence collectors, for example, in all disciplines (human intelligence, imagery, signals intercept, and measurement and signatures intelligence), who do not understand how their collection channels can be denied through effective countermeasures or how they are vulnerable to collecting and disseminating information that has been manipulated, are excellent candidates to be deceived. Analysts who do not comprehend their cognitive vulnerabilities to drawing conclusions that an adversary seeks to induce in them are part of the problem, not the solution. Trainers who lack needed understanding of D&D are ill equipped to prepare intelligence professionals for their enormous responsibilities to produce accurate, valid, timely, and reliable intelligence for policymakers and warfighters. R&D experts who do not conceive and design technologies and systems that have fewer vulnerabilities to D&D than those now operational—indeed, that can effectively counter it—ensure a diminished intelligence capacity for years to come. Finally, counterintelligence and security experts who are unable to protect the classified information that is intended to safeguard sensitive sources and methods, who cannot detect when we are penetrated or when they are being misled or manipulated, and who fail to neutralize and exploit to the United States' advantage the adversaries' deceptive attempts, elevate the exposure of the entire intelligence cycle to manipulation, error, and uselessness. Undetected deception can make intelligence even worse than useless—it can render it actually counterproductive. Countering deception is a tough business.

How do we become better? We need to get smarter. Michael Bennett and Edward Waltz have produced a remarkable study that not only helps us become smarter about denial and deception, but also, more importantly, shows us how to counter it. This is no small achievement.

In a single volume comprised of substantively packed chapters, Bennett and Waltz have produced—one might say discovered, and in some cases, rediscovered—significant principles of deception. These principles enlighten our understanding of the elusive cognitive bias issue, a key determinant in accurate intelligence, and have leveraged the authors' mastery of deception to the next level: principles of counterdeception. The implications are as profoundly practical as they are theoretical.

A major feature of the book is the breadth and depth of the scholarly literature reviewed. Bennett and Waltz have mined the substantial deception literature—rediscovering the classics from Sun Tsu to Whaley, Masterman, and R. V. Jones, to more contemporary contributors such as Jervis, Heuer, Stech, and others. Apart from acquainting the reader with indispensable literature in this arcane field of inquiry, spanning magic and military, biology, and intelligence, Bennett and Waltz exploit and synthesize the literature for insights and inferences that cannot be gotten in any other way.

From this approach, and drawing on extensive historical case studies, the authors derive four universal principles that underlie all deception—truth, denial, deceit, and misdirection. Because this model enables the disaggregation of known deceptions (such as FORTITUDE), it also suggests hypotheses for discovering unknown deceptions—those that the victim has not yet discovered. In alerting the analyst and operator to these essential deception processes, we can now focus our attention on ways to improve the probability of detecting yet-undiscovered deceptions that may disarm intelligence warning and effectiveness, and thus jeopardize the nation's security. For example, a crucial variable that is typically undervalued in intelligence analysis is the impact of adversary denial measures against collection, the second of the four deception principles. As Bennett and Waltz explain, the critical role that denial plays in all deception should highlight to collectors and analysts why understanding denial is so important, and why it is so essential to examine the impact of denial as a necessary component of deception. This is an important practical as well as theoretical insight.

Understanding this interconnected dynamic—the orchestration of truth, denial, deceit, and misdirection, which is close to a general theory of deception—is not only essential to comprehending how deception succeeds, it is a sine qua non of understanding how to counter it. However, deception and counterdeception do not play on a level playing field. The authors warn that: "The adversary's deception planners, armed with a wide array of deception methods honed by hundreds of years of practical experience, do not face a corresponding counterdeception organization armed with a similarly wide range of practical counterdeception tools." Here 0Bennett and Waltz offer a major contribution: Achieving the goal of counterdeception requires, above all, sound knowledge. To succeed, it is crucial that we *know* ourselves, our adversary, our situation, and our channels. Lacking this, counterdeception is impossible. However, even achieving this is only a necessary but not a sufficient condition. A holistic analytical approach to a fully effective counterdeception capability requires a *prepared mind* and a *prepared organization*. Achievable? Yes, but not easily. This book begins the explanation of how to get there.

For a bookshelf on deception, this volume is indispensable. For counterdeception, it stands alone. To begin the long but attainable journey to a counterdeception capability, one must start with the prepared mind. The best first step toward preparing the mind, which the authors do not provide but I can here, is to read this book, starting on page one. However, the reader should be warned: Bennett and Waltz find that the most important counterdeception theme in the literature is *human reasoning capabilities,* confirming Barton Whaley's earlier insight: Successful detection of deception is found to be "largely or entirely intellectual rather than technological in nature." Readers seeking a quick read or a simplistic solution here are bound to be disappointed, but for those seeking a deeper understanding of high-order complexity that bears on the quality of intelligence and thus the security of the nation, they will be handsomely repaid for the intellectual investment this book demands.

James Bruce
RAND Corporation
Arlington, VA
February 2007

Preface

It is now approaching a decade since we first began studying the literature of deception as part of the projects we were both conducting. These projects focused on developing new tools, methods, and information architectures for improving intelligence analysis, given the challenges facing the U.S. intelligence community in the twenty-first century. Along the way, we started assembling personal libraries of the literature of deception and began cataloging the principles, methods, and applications of deception available to the nation's adversaries, and, like many others who begin to study the subtle simplicity of deception and its powerful effects, we too were soon hooked on this fascinating subject. Since then, our aim has been to apply this knowledge in order to make counterdeception an integral part of the tools, methods, and architectures of intelligence.

By working alongside a diverse cadre of analysts, scientists, and engineers in government, industry, and academia, we have come to recognize that the specter of deception in one form or another is always present in intelligence collection and analysis. The ever-present possibility of deception must be considered not only in the clandestine intelligence that is collected, but even in the endless stream of open source information that must be examined and analyzed. We readily admit that we no longer see the study of denial and deception and counterdeception as a specialty discipline within intelligence; we see counterdeception as part of the foundation of the art and science of intelligence and national security analysis itself.

This book is our attempt to fill a gap that we found in the voluminous deception literature we collected—a single comprehensive text that focuses on the principles, methods, and means of countering deception. Our libraries are filled with the classics of deception, yet we found no single volume that focused solely on the works of counterdeception and explained its applications. In writing such a text, we found it necessary to provide a substantial introduction on deception before describing its counterpart. So what began as a small book on counterdeception has grown to a complete and balanced text that we trust thoroughly introduces deception before providing our treatment of counterdeception. We introduce our own approach to the principles and methods of counterdeception, yet we build on the shoulders of the giants in the field, to whom we are indebted: R. V. Jones, Barton Whaley, William Harris, Michael Handel, Richards Heuer, and dozens more whom we meticulously cite throughout.

We recently spent an enjoyable evening with Barton Whaley, the undisputed pioneer and prolific author in the field (and the most oft cited author in our text). Meeting at a restaurant overlooking the sparkling autumn lights of Washington, D.C., we exchanged stories of magic, World War II deceptions, deceptions in computer operations, and the marvelous ways in which basic deception principles give rise to an ever new array of illusory effects. In the midst of our discussion, he reminded us of the simplicity of the basic principles behind deception, yet the seemingly endless ways that these principles can be applied by the deceiver, using rules withheld from the target, to achieve astounding effect. This book is our attempt to clearly explain those principles and the means to mitigate their potentially devastating effects.

We dedicate this book to the new generation of intelligence officers, both civilian and military, who face a deceptive world and are charged with defeating the deception operations that threaten our nation's security.

Acknowledgments

We are indebted to the scholars, researchers, and intelligence officers who have pioneered and written on the subject of deception; their voluminous literature provided the basis for this work. Dr. Dennis Buede's careful review of the manuscript and helpful recommendations were invaluable to achieve accuracy and completeness in coverage. We deeply appreciate the encouragement we have received throughout the course of this project from Dr. Jim Bruce, whom we have long respected for his leadership in promoting denial and deception awareness, research, and training in the U.S. intelligence community. We are also grateful for the many discussions over the past years with our colleagues throughout the intelligence community on the subject of deception, many of whom we cannot identify by name.

Michael Bennett extends special thanks to Hayden Peake, the curator of the Central Intelligence Agency's Historical Intelligence Collection, for his support and assistance. Others that have contributed time and support include David Schum, Myrdene Anderson, Frank Stech, Russ Vane, Doug Griffith, Jon Morris, and Rob Johnston. Finally, there are my family and friends who lived through the project with me: my wife, who patiently read my many draft chapters, Tom Armour, Dennis McCormick, Val Johnson, Al Zaleski, all the gang at the BRG, and, of course, my father who has been patiently waiting to see his son's first book.

Ed Waltz is grateful for the patience and support of his family and the encouragement of his colleagues at BAE Systems: Chuck Morefield, Mark Lazaroff, Woody Spring, and John Paul Parker. Others that have contributed support and encouragement in numerous discussions on the subject of deception in analysis include: Jeffrey Cooper, Aaron Frank, Frank Hughes, Alice Ling, Rebecca Terbergh, Jeffrey White, and Randall Williams; thanks to Stuart Card, Steve Eick, and Bill Wright for permission to illustrate the use of their analysis tools in the counterdeception process. Finally, I dedicate this book to the newest intelligence analyst in the community, my son, Tim.

CHAPTER 1

Deception and the Need for Counterdeception

Deception is rooted in human nature, and as current events illustrate, humans continue to refine the means of deceit. While technology introduces new avenues and mechanisms, the motives for deceit remain the same. Deception is the central tool of secrecy, protection, and evasion; it is the enabler of surprise. It is a tool of both the defender and the attacker. In his books on *The Art of War*, Niccolo Machiavelli recommended [1]: "No enterprise is more likely to succeed than one concealed from the enemy until it is ripe for execution.... When you are aware that the enemy is aquainted with your designs, you must change them. After you have consulted with many about what you ought to do, confer with very few concerning what you are actually resolved to do." Allen Dulles, in his classic, *The Art of Intelligence*, simply notes that deception is as old as history [2].

The process that *denies* access to information, and the counterpart process that *deceives,* or creates misleading information, is used to target individuals, large audiences, sensor systems, computer and communication systems, and the decision-makers of military units, corporations, and national governments. Combining *denial* and *deception* (D&D), magicians appear to saw women in half, computers access unauthorized bank accounts, Americans have been exfiltrated from Tehran appearing as a Canadian film crew, Israeli aircraft have penetrated foreign airspace undetected, and nations have violated nonproliferation treaties in spite of international inspections. While the means of D&D in each of these cases are distinctly different, the principles remain the same. In describing these principles throughout this book, we use the term *deception* as shorthand to refer to the integrated D&D process, because, in most cases, both denial and deception processes are present, coordinated in a scheme or *stratagem* to deceive a target. Even the simplest deception employs a stratagem that includes an operational security (OPSEC) plan to protect the deception itself. Where denial or deception processes are strictly used independently, we will be careful to point that out. Donald Daniel has described the synergy within the stratagem employing D&D [3]: "denial and deception are separate but overlapping and mutually supportive endeavors that governments employ to protect their secrets. Deception requires denial if it is to succeed, and denial may sometimes require deception if it is not to fail. Because of this symbiosis, they are usually referred to as a unit, but they are more like fraternal twins, deception being the more complex and demanding."

Strategist Karl Von Clausewitz pointed out in his classic, *On War*, that deceit in common language implies the deceiver commits a breech of his word—by stating a lie to the target. In stratagem, however, Von Clausewitz observed that the deceiver does not make an assertion of truth; instead it is the target who commits the error of misunderstanding, being led astray not by a direct lie, but by the skillful manipulation of a situation by the deceiver [4].

The categories of denial and deception discussed in this book are largely focused on the intelligence organizations of governments. Intelligence is often described as the business of gathering foreign secrets by secret means [5]. It is the business of intelligence to provide [6] "knowledge and foreknowledge of the world around us—the prelude to decision and action by US policymakers." Yet intelligence organizations are focused on knowledge about the secrets of others; former Director of U.S. Intelligence, George Tenet, noted [7]: "By definition, intelligence deals with the unclear, the unknown, the deliberately hidden. What the enemies of the United States hope to deny, we work to reveal." Whether national intelligence or military intelligence on the battlefield, deception poses a significant threat to the timeliness, accuracy, and relevance of knowledge and foreknowledge required by policymakers.

This chapter introduces the increasing role of deception in the global security environment—and the technological factors that enable its proliferation as well as the sophistication by which it is conducted. As the role of deception is expanding, the importance of implementing methods of countering deception is increasing. This requires a more thorough understanding of deception processes to implement counterdeception methods. Where the role of intelligence is to penetrate the secrets of an adversary, the process of counterdeception is not a niche activity within intelligence; it is at the core. Even where concealment and deceit is at the center of an adversary's operations, counterdeception is a process that has elements spanning the entire organization. As a necessary introduction, this chapter also introduces the basic terminology of the deception and counterdeception disciplines, before reviewing the rich body of literature on the subject of deception.

1.1 The Changing Role of Deception in National Security

While the practice of denial and deception is as old as competition and conflict, the means of carrying out competition and conflict are changing. Technological capabilities enabling transformations in communications, knowledge management, the physical scale of electromechanical machines (nanotechnology), and human-machine symbiosis, are influencing global politics, commerce, and security. These shifts are enabling new and more sophisticated means to conduct the old trade of deception. Not only are the means of deception changing, but the potential scope and scale of the consequences of deception are also dramatically increasing. Individuals and small groups with personal computers and access to global networks can now conduct what was once a trade uniquely carried out by highly organized crime organizations, foreign militaries, and intelligence services.

The role—and therefore the importance—of deception is significantly expanding as technology introduces new avenues to deceive and globalization expands the opportunities for deception and potential adverse impacts. In the following we consider the primary areas in which the deception role is undergoing change.

Information Superiority

As nations have increased the importance of information in maintaining national security and conducting military operations, deception has necessarily become a central component of the asymmetric strategy of any opponent. The cornerstone of the U.S. Joint Vision 2020 is information superiority—enabling decision superiority [8]. The key to achieving this superiority is the access to dominant battlespace awareness and an operational concept to leverage that dominance. Network-centric warfare (NCW) [9] is the "...information superiority-enabled concept of operation that generates increased combat power by networking sensors, decision makers, and shooters to achieve shared awareness, increased speed of command, higher tempo of operations, greater lethality, increased survivability, and a degree of self-synchronization. In essence, NCW translates information superiority into combat power by effectively linking knowledgeable entities in the battlespace." This concept rests on the availability of sustained intelligence. As the United States seeks to gain a competitive advantage from timely and accurate information, adversaries will seek their own advantages through strategies that deny, delay, distort, and disrupt the flow of such information. While the United States has deployed denial capabilities by the development of stealth technologies (e.g., low radar cross-section aircraft, quiet submarines), adversaries have sought low technology deception capabilities to evade U.S. surveillance (e.g., hiding weapons systems in vegetation, disguising military equipment in commercial vehicles, and burying facilities underground). Lasley [10] has identified four categories of vulnerabilities that expose the United States to deception: "ignorance of the foreign D&D threat, security negligence that provides foreign actors with a wealth of information vital to their D&D efforts, intentional release of information to foreign governments that compromises US collection assets, and American hubris that discounts the viability of such a threat." With the increased attention and dependence upon information superiority, the attention to these vulnerabilities must be addressed by D&D awareness, training, enhanced operational security (OPSEC), and a degree of humility.

Strategic Information Operations

Associated with the emphasis on information superiority is the development of information operations (IO) as a key operational component of military operations. IO are those actions taken to "affect adversaries' and influence others' decision-making processes, information, and information systems, while protecting one's own information and information systems ... IO capitalize on the growing sophistication, connectivity, and reliance on information technology. IO target information or information systems in order to affect the information-based process, whether human or automated" [11]. The development of U.S. Joint IO doctrine has introduced at least three influences on the importance of deception. First, it has formally integrated and synchronized deception into offensive operations [12]: "Offensive IO involve the integrated use of assigned and supporting capabilities and activities, mutually supported by intelligence, to affect adversary decision makers and achieve or promote specific objectives. These assigned and supporting capabilities and activities include, but are not limited to, operations security (OPSEC), military deception, psychological operations, electronic warfare (EW), physical attack/destruction, and special information operations (SIO), and may include computer network attack." Second, defensive IO similarly integrates countermeasures to adversary deception [13]: "Counterdeception supports defensive IO by negating, neutralizing, or diminishing the effects of—or gaining advantage from—a foreign deception operation. Activities contributing to awareness of adversary posture and intent also serve to identify adversary attempts to deceive friendly forces." Third, the computer network operations (CNO) component of IO has introduced new forms of deception and counterdeception to the domain of computer-to-computer conflict. This extends the deceptive tactics of traditional electronic warfare (denial, deception, exploitation, and soft destruction) into the domain of computer networks.

Global Proliferation

The proliferation of weaponizable technologies and weapons of mass destruction (WMD) has prompted nations and terrorist groups alike to employ extensive deception measures to hide their activities from surveillance. The protection of development programs (e.g., theater missiles and nuclear weapons development) requires deception to avoid detection by satellite and other forms of surveillance. The 1998 Report of the Commission to Assess the Ballistic Missile Threat to the United States (the Rumsfeld Commission) observed [14]: "We noted in our Report on such [ballistic missile] threats a number of adverse trends in the post-Cold War threat environment affecting the capability of the [intelligence community] to monitor, assess and warn of ballistic missile threats: emerging capabilities in a larger number of hostile states; increased availability of relevant data, technologies and expertise to those states; and, more sophisticated resort to cover, deception and denial by them." Two years later, the scope of this problem to U.S. intelligence was described more explicitly by the Director of the Defense Intelligence Agency [15]:

> Many potential adversaries—nations, groups, and individuals—are undertaking more and increasingly sophisticated *Cover, Concealment, Camouflage, Denial and Deception (C3D2)* activities against the United States. These operations are generally designed to hide key activities, facilities, and capabilities (e.g. mobilization or attack preparations, WMD programs, advanced weapons systems developments, treaty noncompliance, etc.) from US intelligence, to manipulate US perceptions and assessments of those programs, and to protect key capabilities from US precision strike platforms. Foreign knowledge of US intelligence and military operations capabilities is essential to effective C3D2. Advances in satellite warning capabilities, the growing availability of camouflage, concealment, deception, and obscurant materials, advanced technology for and experience with building underground facilities, and the growing use of fiber optics and encryption, will increase the C3D2 challenge.

Asymmetry and Individual Power

Asymmetric war forms have risen to challenge military superiority by adversaries unable to compete symmetrically. The increase in the lethality of individuals and the potential power to be gained by small groups employing WMD has increased the emphasis on countering the deceptive efforts of small operations cells to recruit, train, move materiel, and conduct catastrophic terrorist operations. This has brought increased attention to networked forms of warfare and insurgencies—and the attendant role of deception as an integral activity in all operations.

1.2 Basic Terminology

A complete terminology of the art has developed to distinguish the principles, means, and effects of deception activities. In this section, we introduce the basic terms, based on the accepted U.S. DoD terminology; in subsequent chapters, more specific terms are introduced for the variety of operations conducted [16].

Denial includes those measures designed to hinder or deny the enemy the knowledge of an object, by hiding or disrupting the means of observation of the object.

Deception includes those measures designed to mislead the enemy by manipulation, distortion, or falsification of evidence to induce him to react in a manner prejudicial to his interests. The goal of deception is to make an enemy more vulnerable to the effects of weapons, maneuver, and operations of friendly forces.

Denial and deception (D&D) include the integration of both processes to mislead an enemy's intelligence capability. The basis of denial is *dissimulation*, the concealing of the truth and the basis of deception is *simulation*, the presentation of that which is false. The acronym C3D2 is synonymous with D&D; it refers to *cover, concealment, camouflage, denial, and deception.*

Deception *means* are those methods, resources, and techniques that can be used to convey information to the deception target. The U.S. DoD categorizes means as:

- *Physical means:* Activities and resources used to convey or deny selected information to a foreign power. (Examples are military operations, including exercises, reconnaissance, training activities, and movement of forces; the use of dummy equipment and devices; tactics; bases, logistic actions, stockpiles, and repair activity; and test and evaluation activities.)
- *Technical means:* Military material resources and their associated operating techniques used to convey or deny selected information to a foreign power through the deliberate radiation, reradiation, alteration, absorption, or reflection of energy; the emission or suppression of chemical or biological odors; and the emission or suppression of nuclear particles.
- *Administrative means:* Resources, methods, and techniques to convey or deny oral, pictorial, documentary, or other physical evidence to a foreign power.

The *deception target* is the adversary decision-maker with the authority to make the decision that will achieve the *deception objective*—the desired result of the deception operation.

Channels of deception are the information paths by which deception means are conveyed to their targets.

The relationship of these terms is illustrated in Figure 1.1 to show the typical flow of information and influence from deception objectives, to means, through channels, and ultimately to the targets of strategic deception. In the strategic deception example, the deception objective is translated to a deception story that explains

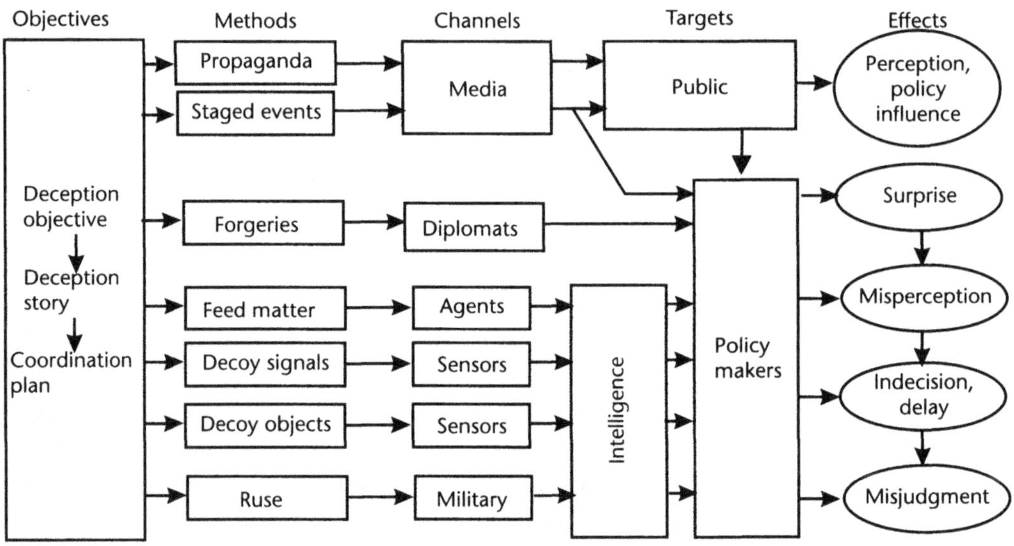

Figure 1.1 A basic deception information flow.

the expected perception to be conveyed to the targets. This, in turn, is translated into a coordination plan or course of action that describes the methods of creating that perception and the avenues that will convey those means to the targets.

Consider how the planners intend to carry out their deception. An event (atrocity) will be staged with supporting media coverage and accompanying deceptive propaganda. This will be fed to through the channels of sympathetic regional media, which will be picked up by the international media. These channels will convey the message to the targeted sympathetic groups within the public to sway public opinion and bring pressure on the targeted government policymakers. The deception planners also create forged documents attributing the atrocity to agents of the target government and leak them through unsuspecting (duped) third-party diplomatic channels. Finally, the planners coordinate the creation of decoyed objects and signals (to be viewed by the targeted government IMINT and SIGINT collectors, respectively) to support the atrocity story. Forged materials are also passed through agent channels to add further credibility to the decoys. These activities are all conducted to convince intelligence analysts that the atrocity story is, indeed, true.

The desired result of these activities is indecision the mind of the policymakers, delay in response in the short period of time that they have to respond, and ultimately misjudgment. The immediate effect of surprise and the pressure from the public outcry will cause the policymakers to misperceive the foreign situation, leading to indecision and delay in response, and ultimately to a misjudgment and policy decision that will serve the long-term objective of the deception planners.

A military *deception course of action (COA)* is the plan developed during the estimate process in sufficient detail to permit decision-making. At a minimum, a deception course of action will identify the deception objective, the deception target, the desired perception, the deception story, and tentative deception means.

Military deception operations, then, are conducted to mislead an enemy, and include activities such as the:

- *Ruse* that involves the deliberate exposure of false information;
- *Demonstration* that presents a show of force on a front where a decision is not sought;
- *Display* that presents a static portrayal of an activity, force, or equipment often involving the use of decoys;
- *Feint* in which an offensive action is conducted involving contact with the adversary conducted for the purpose of deceiving the adversary as to the location and/or time of the actual main offensive action.

Counterdeception includes the intelligence activities to identify denial and deception operations as well as the operational activities undertaken to negate, neutralize, diminish the effects of, or gain advantage from foreign denial and deception operations. (Here, notice, we depart from the DoD definition, which limits the term to operational aspects only: "Counterdeception includes efforts to negate, neutralize, diminish the effects of, or gain advantage from a foreign deception operation. Counterdeception does not include the intelligence function of identifying foreign deception operations.")

Finally, it is important here to identify the U.S. DoD distinction between military deception described earlier and *psychological operations* (PSYOP). PSYOP are the planned operations to convey selected information and indicators to foreign audiences to influence their emotions, motives, objective reasoning, and ultimately the behavior of foreign governments, organizations, groups, and individuals. The purpose of psychological operations is to induce or reinforce foreign attitudes and behavior favorable to the originator's objectives. Note that military deception targets military forces, and PSYOP targets foreign audiences—both civil and military. By U.S. policy, PSYOP and public affairs officers do not deny nor deceive [17]: "PSYOP techniques are used to plan and execute truth projection activities intended to inform foreign groups and populations persuasively. Public affairs (PA) provide objective reporting, without intent to propagandize. As open sources to foreign countries and the United States, PA channels can be used to disseminate international information. *To maintain the credibility of military PA, steps must be taken to protect against slanting or manipulating such PA channels* [emphasis in original]."

Counterdeception activities, however, must include provisions to protect against deceptive PSYOP and public affairs campaigns from adversaries that do not adhere to these standards of truth and objectivity [18]. The term *propaganda* is most often associated with distorted or untruthful dissemination via these channels. *White propaganda* targets a general population while openly acknowledging the source of the information; *black propaganda* targets a general population while attempting to remain covert, hiding the true source (e.g., clandestine radio and Internet broadcast, independent organizations, and agents of influence [19]). Coordinated white and black propaganda efforts, for example, were strategically coordinated by the Soviet Union throughout the Cold War as "active measures" of disinformation (Dezinformatsia) [20]:

> .... for the Soviet Union, active measures constitute a dynamic and integrated array of overt and covert techniques for influencing events and behavior in, and the

actions of, foreign countries. These measures are employed to influence the policies of other governments, undermine confidence in the leaders and institutions of these states, disrupt the relations between various nations, and discredit and weaken major opponents. This frequently involves attempts to deceive the target, and to distort the target's perception of reality.

1.3 Perspectives and Applications of Deception

Throughout this book, we will cover a wide variety of means, channels, and targets of deception. In subsequent chapters, we provide taxonomies to organize the various methods of conducting deception and appropriate countermeasures. It is important, however to place all of these in a larger operational context. The following sections provide a framework for understanding how deception planners, and their counterparts, the opposing counterdeception cells, must view deception at the highest level of abstraction. For this framework, we consider the *levels* at which deception effects are produced and the *domains* in which they are implemented.

1.3.1 Levels of Effects

Deception operations are generally categorized by three the levels of warfare at which they target their effects: strategic, operational, and tactical. *Strategic deception* is aimed at the highest levels of government or the military chain of command. The intended targets are those who formulate strategy, policy, and military plans and operations at national and theater levels [21]. *Operational deception* is conducted at the level of war at which campaigns and major operations are planned, conducted, and sustained to accomplish strategic objectives within theaters or other operational areas. It targets the decision-making of those who plan and conduct major operations. *Tactical deception* operations intend to create effects at the engagement and battle level. Tactical operations include a wide range of methods, for example, physical decoy placements, optical signature suppression, electronic jamming, signal encryption, document forgery, computer attack, and deceptive propaganda. While these distinctions are helpful in symmetric warfare, they are not as clear in asymmetric warfare; for example, the deception activities supporting a single tactical terrorist operation may have a strategic impact on world opinion, entire civil populations, and governments.

1.3.2 Domains of Implementation

Deception operations are also carried out in one of three fundamental realms, or domains of human knowledge based upon the semiotic distinction between physical and cognitive objects, and the symbols by which we relate them. These are not three arbitrary domains; even early philosophers have recognized them as the basic components of our knowledge. Aristotle, an empiricist philosopher, identified these three domains in his *Metaphysics*, written in 350 B.C. He distinguished physical objects, and the abstractions (ideas) that the mind creates once the senses perceive the object. He further distinguished the words that the mind creates to symbolize or represent the abstractions of the mind [22]. We can apply these distinctions to further categorize deception activities [23].

The *physical* domain encompasses the material world of mass, energy, and the laws of physics that regulate them. Deception activities in this domain manipulate the physical signatures of objects and events. The abstract *symbolic* domain of information is conveyed by symbolic transmission between humans using the symbols of words, numbers, and graphics that encode and represent objects perceived in the physical and conceived in the cognitive domain. Deception activities in this domain target computers, communication systems, cryptosystems, and other symbolic channels. The *cognitive* domain is the realm of human thought—the ultimate target of deception, the realm where uncertainties, ambiguities, and well-placed deceptions can cause misperception and ultimately misjudgment. This is the target of direct human-to-human influence as well as deceptions communicated through the physical and symbolic domains to decision-makers [24].

1.3.3 The Operational-Implementation Framework

We can now illustrate the integration of a deception operation (or campaign) in the two-dimensional framework defined by the three domains of implementation and three levels of effects (Figure 1.2) using selected elements of the Operation Fortitude deception plan that protected the World War II Allied invasion plan (code-named

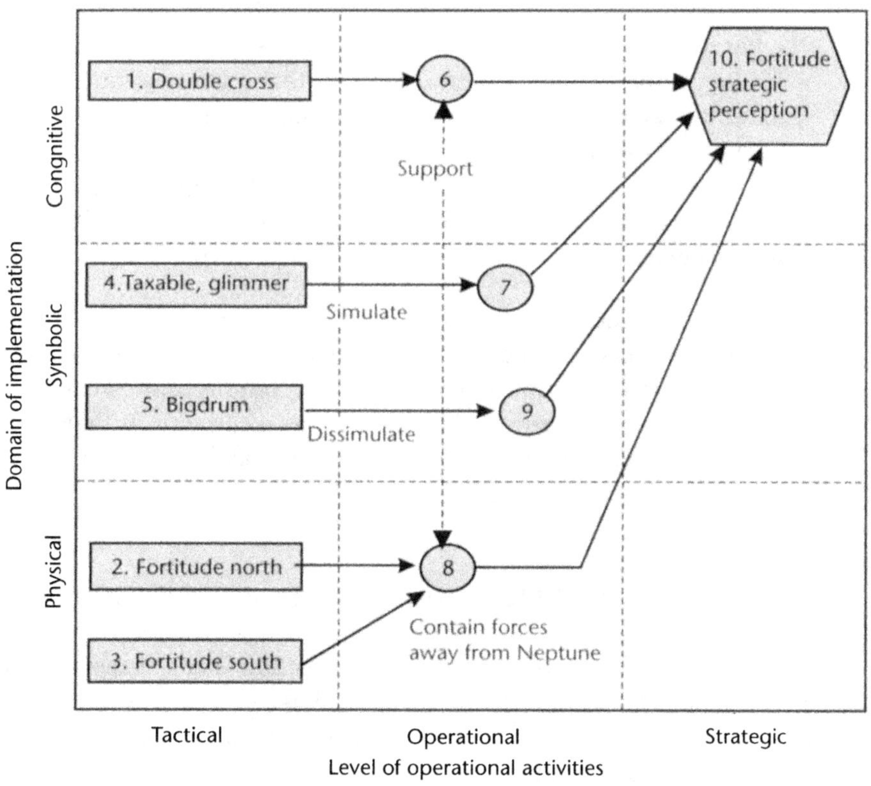

Figure 1.2 An operational-implementation framework for understanding the relationship between deception components.

Neptune) at Normandy on D-Day, July 6, 1944. Fortitude was the European theater deception component of the overall Bodyguard deception plan; Fortitude had a threefold strategic objective (three effects): (1) prior to D-Day, cause enemy planners to position forces away from the planned Normandy landing area; (2) prior to D-Day, cause enemy planners to be deceived about the location and timing of the invasion; and (3) during D-Day and subsequent days, cause enemy planners to retain a belief that Normandy was not the only invasion site. The tactics and channels used by the Fortitude deception team in the figure include the following:

- Double Cross (1) activities included the use of over 100 controlled enemy agents to pass tactical information that supported the operational deception story (6) that an invasion would occur at locations other than Normandy (especially Pas de Calais). This information was passed through trusted human channels to enemy intelligence, and on to strategic planners.
- Fortitude North (2) and South (3) included physical tactical movement of forces to threaten Norway and the Pas de Calais prior to and immediately following D-Day; the operational effect of these visible activities was to keep military forces at a distance from Normandy (8). This effort supported the Double Cross information being fed to enemy planners.
- Operations Taxable and Glimmer (4) employed active electronic countermeasures to simulated radar signal returns, conveying the operational appearance (7) of multiple convoys approaching the coast at locations other than Normandy on days D-1 and D-Day.
- Operation Bigdrum (5) provided tactical support of the actual invasion on D-Day, employing countermeasures to disrupt enemy radars and hide (dissimulate) the actual character of the invading forces, reducing operational effectiveness of the defensive forces (9).
- The focus of all deceptive activities was a desired strategic perception (9), in the minds of enemy planners and decision-makers, which would contain forces away from Normandy up to and even after D-Day.

Notice that synchronized sets of deception actions are created across the domains, with effects focused on the cognitive decisions of intelligence analysts, military planners, and decision-makers (10). The simple framework helps to describe the relationship between the many components of deception that lead to a strategic deception objective, and the desired chain of tactical deception actions required to achieve a desired strategic effect.

1.4 The Development of Deception Theory and Literature

The citation of sixth-century military strategist Sun Tzu's deception doctrine is ubiquitous in the literature [25]: "All warfare is based on deception.... A military leader of wisdom and ability lays deep plans for what other people do not figure on." McCready [26] points out that:

> While Sun Tzu's ideas about using deception are mostly common sense, they are most often tools for the weak to use against the strong. With overwhelming U.S. military power a key factor in the modern world, Sun Tzu's comments on deception operations should be a warning to strategic planners. The sort of deception Sun Tzu talks about does not come from studying manuals. It is a way of thinking and being, a way that is alien to Western intellectual and cultural traditions.... Sun Tzu's army is everywhere and yet nowhere... There are no heavy battalions or massed batteries in this picture. They come into view only if the strategy of indirection and deception fails or is left untried.

The development of deception as a way of thinking proceeded throughout military planning, but since World War I, emerging communication and weapons technologies enabled ever more sophisticated means of its implementation, through new channels to deception targets. Following World War II, a spate of texts were published describing the strategic deception operations of both the Allied and Axis powers, and the methods, operations, and successes of deception campaigns. Historical in nature, a series of books described the planning and operations of strategic deception throughout the war: *The Man Who Never Was* (Montagu, 1953); *The Double Cross System* (Masterman, 1972); *Bodyguard of Lies* (Anthony Cave Brown, 1975); *Practise to Deceive* (Mure, 1977); *Deception in World War II* (Cruickshank, 1979); *Strategic and Operational Intelligence in the Second World War* (Handel, 1987); *Master of Deception* (Mure, 1980); and *The Deception Planners* (Wheatley, 1980).

British intelligence pioneer R. V. Jones described the role of deception from an intelligence perspective in his *Most Secret War: British Scientific Intelligence 1939–1945* (1978) and later in *Reflections on Intelligence* (1989). The effects of surprise in the attack on Pearl Harbor were studied in Wohlstetter's classic study of surprise, *Pearl Harbor Warning and Decision* (1962).

It was not until the closing of the Cold War that more thorough analyses of military and nonmilitary deception operations were published, seeking to articulate the theoretical principles, methods, and effects of strategic deception. Barton Whaley's classic, *Stratagem* (1969), analyzed 168 strategic military operations between 1914 and 1968 and developed a set of principles and effects of deception. The principles and applications of deception were further developed in Daniel and Herbig's *Strategic Military Deception* (1982), and Gooch and Perlmutter's *Military Deception and Strategic Surprise* (1982). Kam's *Surprise Attack* (1982) analyzed the consequences of strategic deception operations in conflicts between 1940 and 1985 and the inevitability of surprise in future warfare. More recently, Godson and Wirtz' *Strategic Denial and Deception: The Twenty-First Century Challenge* (2002) provides a policy-level description of the intelligence challenges posed by strategic deception.

Section 1.6 provides an annotated bibliography of the key texts that are necessary references for those who seek to excel in the deception and counterdeception trade. Although most are out of print, all are worthy of place on the deception or counterdeception planner's bookshelf.

1.5 Book Overview

Chapters 2 through 4 provide a necessary introduction to deception, reviewing the basic principles of deception and illustrating the variety of technical and nontechnical methods that may be integrated in deception campaigns. These chapters build on the classic policy-oriented resources in strategic and tactical military deception, introducing the first principles and practice of deception.

Chapter 2 introduces the fundamental principles of deception, illustrating the implementation of the principles in magic, and then in abstract models of strategic and operational deception. The chapter provides a taxonomy of the methods that derive from the basic principles. Because deception is ultimately an effect in the human mind, Chapter 3 describes the cognitive vulnerabilities that exploited by deception. Chapter 4 then details the technical methods employed to deceive sensors, information channels, and human observers and agents.

Chapters 5 through 9 introduce the principles of counterdeception and the means of implementing them in collection and analysis systems are described. These chapters describe the system-level implementations necessary to counter strategic and tactical deception campaigns. Chapter 5 provides a background on the fundamental thought about the potential approaches, and potential limits of methods to counter deception; in this chapter, we introduce the basic principles of a process of counterdeception. Chapter 6 enumerates the fundamental cognitive and organizational vulnerabilities that enable deception before describing strategies to prepare the individual mind and the culture of an organization to resist deception. Chapter 7 develops a technical approach to implement these counterdeception methods, and Chapter 8 describes the practical implementation in operational and system architecture. Because technology and global trends are changing the role and capabilities of deception and its countermeasures, Chapter 9 provides our speculation on the future of deception and the driving factors that will continue to transform its implementation and impact, as well as the implications for counterdeception.

1.6 Annotated Bibliography of Principal Deception Texts

This brief annotated bibliography describes the essential background texts that are most often cited by the practitioners of deception and counterdeception. We have not included the many historical texts on the subject; rather, we have focused our bibliography on published texts that develop technical principles, analysis, and operations. Throughout this book, we cite more than 100 references to the larger deception literature including monographs, reports, journals, and papers; the following texts form the foundation for that larger body of literature.

- Daniel, D. C., and K. L. Herbig, (eds.), *Strategic Military Deception*, Elmsford, NY: Pergamon Press, 1982. This oft-cited text integrates articles on deception from a variety of perspectives: theoretical, historical, policy, and systems analysis.

- Dewar, M., *The Art of Deception in Warfare*, London, U.K.: David & Charles Publishers, 1989. Introductory text introduces practical principles of deception with illustrations from historical military operations.
- Epstein, E. J., *Deception: The Invisible War Between the KGB and the CIA*, New York, Simon and Schuster, 1989. This provides a historical account of the clandestine intelligence and counterintelligence competitions between U.S. and former Soviet intelligence organizations, focusing on HUMINT deception.
- Godson, R., and J. Wirtz, (eds.), *Strategic Denial and Deception: The Twenty-First Century Challenge,* New Brunswick, NJ: Transaction Publishers, 2002. This edited collection of papers on strategic deception provides a thorough policy-level description of national elements, conditions, and impacts of strategic-level deception and a brief introduction to counterdeception.
- Gooch, J., and A. Perlmutter, (eds.), *Military Deception and Strategic Surprise*, London, U.K.: Frank Cass, 1982. A series of articles (first published in *The Journal of Strategic Studies*) that analyzes deception in German rearmament (1919–1939), in Soviet activities (1955–1981), and in Egypt–Israel (1971–1973) before developing principles of intelligence from intelligence, military, and theoretical perspectives.
- Handel, M. I., (ed.), *Strategic and Operational Intelligence in the Second World War*, London, U.K.: Frank Cass, 1987. This book is a compilation of papers presented at the 1986 International Conference on Intelligence and Military Operations at the U.S. Army Carlisle Barracks. The papers are introduced and organized to provide a scholarly analysis of the operations and effects of deception.
- Heuer, R. J., *Psychology of Intelligence Analysis*, Washington, D.C.: Government Printing Office, 1999. While this book is not on deception, it includes valuable discussions on the cognitive vulnerabilities to deception based on the author's earlier work, "Strategic Deception and Counterdeception: A Cognitive Process Approach," published in *International Studies Quarterly*, Vol. 25, No. 2, June 1981, pp. 294–327. It provides an introduction to the cognitive aspects of misperception and deception from an intelligence perspective.
- Holt, T., *The Deceivers*, New York: Scribner, 2004. Holt provides a comprehensive account of the Allied military deception plans, personnel, operations, and effects in World War II.
- Jervis, R., *Perception and Misperception in International Politics*, Princeton, NJ: Princeton University Press, 1976. Jervis provides a thorough analysis of the psychological causes and effects of misperception by policymakers in international politics; though not directly addressing deception and deceivers, Jervis provides a sound background on the perception vulnerabilities of foreign policymakers.
- Jones, R. V., *Most Secret War: British Scientific Intelligence 1939–1945,* London, U.K.: Wordsworth, 1978. A World War II intelligence pioneer (technical intelligence director for the British Royal Air Force), Jones describes the

development of electronic intelligence and countermeasures, including the considerations of deception of these systems.

- Jones, R. V., *Reflections on Intelligence,* Part One, Section 5: Intelligence and Deception, London, U.K.: William Heinemann, 1989. This book provides commentary on the practical applications of intelligence and the effects of deception.
- Kam, E., *Surprise Attack,* Cambridge, MA: Harvard University Press, 1988. Kam examines the roles of deception and planning and the effects of surprise in a series of military attacks between 1940 and 1985. He assesses the warning analysis process, vulnerabilities, and the inevitability of surprise.
- Whaley, B., *Stratagem: Deception and Surprise in War*, Cambridge, MA: MIT Center for International Studies, 1969. Whaley's classic study analyzes 168 strategic military operations between 1914 and 1968 and develops principles and effects of deception.
- Wohlstetter, R., *Pearl Harbor: Warning and Decision*, Stanford, CA: Stanford University Press, 1962. Though this work only touches on the Japanese deception tactics, it is the classic study of the vulnerabilities of the United States as a deception target and it also provides a thorough analysis of the elements of strategic surprise.

Endnotes

[1] Machiavell, Niccolò, *The Art of War,* originally published 1521, Da Capo Press Edition 2001, translated by Neal Wood, Cambridge, MA: Da Capo, 2001, pp. 202–203.

[2] Dulles, A., *The Craft of Intelligence*, New York: HarperCollins, 1963.

[3] Daniel, D. C. F., "Denial and Deception," in Sims, J. E., and B. Gerber, (eds.), *Transforming U.S. Intelligence*, Washington, D.C.: Georgetown University Press, 2005, p. 136.

[4] von Clausewitz, Carl, *On War,* originally published 1832, Penguin Classic ed., translated by J. J. Graham, London: Penguin, 1968, pp. 274–275.

[5] See Warner, M., "Wanted: A Definition of Intelligence," *Studies in Intelligence*, Vol. 46, No. 3, 2002.

[6] Central Intelligence Agency (Office of Public Affairs), *A Consumer's Guide to Intelligence*, Washington, D.C.: Central Intelligence Agency, 1999, p. vii. For a comprehensive discussion of the range of definitions of intelligence, and its central meaning, see: "Wanted: A Definition of 'Intelligence,'" *Studies in Intelligence*, Washington, D.C.: CIA, Vol. 46, No. 3, 2002, unclassified edition, accessed online October 3, 2002, http://www.cia.gov/csi/studies/vol46no3/index.html.

[7] "Iraq and Weapons of Mass Destruction," remarks as prepared for delivery by Director of Central Intelligence George J. Tenet at Georgetown University, February 5, 2004.

[8] *Joint Vision 2020 America's Military: Preparing for Tomorrow*, U.S. DoD, 2000, p. 8.

[9] Alberts, D. S., J. J. Garstka, and F. P. Stein, *Network Centric Warfare*, Washington, D.C.: National Defense University Press, 1999, p. 2.

[10] Lasley, J., "Denial and Deception: A Serious Threat to Information Superiority?", National Defense University, April 19, 2000, p. 6.

[11] *Joint Doctrine for Information Operations*, JP-3-13, October 9, 1998, p. vii.

[12] Ibid., p. viii.

[13] Ibid., p. III-13.

[14] *Side Letter to the Report of the Commission to Assess the Ballistic Missile Threat to the United States*, ("Rumsfeld Report"), March 18, 1999.

[15] "Military Threats and Security Challenges Through 2015," Statement for the Record by Vice Admiral Thomas R. Wilson, Director, Defense Intelligence Agency before Senate Select Committee on Intelligence, February 2, 2000, p. 12

[16] DoD terms are based upon definitions in the *U.S. DoD Dictionary of Military Terms*, Publication 1-02.

[17] *Doctrine for Joint Psychological Operations*, JP 3-53, July 10, 1996, p. vi.

[18] Note that with the advent of global communications, it is difficult to distinguish between a message targeting foreign audiences and the U.S. population, for example. Any message produced by a government source for a foreign audience can immediately return, translated for its own population. An attempt to deceive a foreign population can also deceive one's own population.

[19] Agent-of-influence operations carry out the subornation (knowing or unwitting) of a person who will use their position, influence, power, or credibility to promote the objectives of a foreign power.

[20] Schultz, R. H., and R. Goodson, *Dezinformatsia: Active Measures in Soviet Strategy*, Washington, D.C.: Pergamon-Brasseys, 1984, p. 16; see also Bittman, L., *The KGB and Soviet Disinformation*, Washington, D.C.: Pergamon-Brasseys, 1985.

[21] See Shulsky, A., "The Elements of Strategic Denial and Deception," in Godson, R., and J. J. Wirtz, (eds.), *Strategic Denial and Deception*, New Brunswick, NJ: Transaction Publishers, 2002, p. 17.

[22] More recently, philosopher C. S. Peirce developed a mathematical theory of signs, or semiotics, that also embraces the three fundamental domains. More explicitly than Aristotle, Peirce's logic distinguished a "triad" of relationships between the physical object, the symbolic sign that represents it, and the cognitive thought in the mind.

[23] The concept of applying the three domains for information operations was introduced in: Waltz, E., *Information Warfare Principles and Operations*, Norwood, MA: Artech House, 1998 (Sections 1.2 and 5.2.). The principle was further applied to intelligence analysis in Waltz, E., *Knowledge Management in the Intelligence Enterprise*, Norwood, MA: Artech House, 2003. See also Alberts, D. S., et al., *Understanding Information Age Warfare*, Washington, D.C.: CCRP, 2001, accessed October 30, 2002, http://www.dodccrp.org/Publications/pdf/UIAW.pdf.

[24] Note that in the DoD terminology physical, technical, and administrative correspond roughly to the more precise (and metaphysically accurate) distinctions of physical, symbolic, and cognitive, respectively.

[25] Griffith, S. B., *Sun Tzu, The Art of War*, New York: Oxford, 1971, p. 17.

[26] McCready, D. M. (Col. USA), "Learning from Sun Tzu," *Military Review*, May–June 2003, p. 87.

CHAPTER 2

Introduction to Deception Principles

2.1 Introduction

Deception has been around for a very long time, probably as long as life itself has existed on this planet. For millions of years, plants, insects, and animals have survived by hiding from predators, trying to be inconspicuous, mimicking other species, or even appearing more fearsome than they really are. Humans, of course, have raised the use of deception to even higher levels of sophistication. Magicians use it to entertain us. Con artists use it to cheat us. It is incorporated into the games and sports we play. As a tool of both generals and diplomats, it can decide the outcome of battles and the fate of nations. It is an integral part of our day-to-day lives, and, in fact, some psychologists think it may be essential to our very mental health.

At the same time, we seem to do a very poor job of counterdeception. As individuals, we do a very poor job of detecting deception in others. In his book *Detecting Lies and Deceit*, Aldert Vrij provides an overview of 39 studies where lay people (mostly college students) were asked to detect lies in people with whom they were not familiar [1]. The mean accuracy rate for these studies was only 57%. This is not much better than simply randomly guessing where the expected accuracy rate should be 50%. In fact, law enforcement officers do not do much better. Vrij cites eight studies where law enforcement officers were asked to detect deception; the mean accuracy rate in these studies was 54%—nearly the same as the college students [2].

Skilled magicians also have no trouble deceiving and amusing us. What is surprising to most people though is that some magicians can also deceive other skilled magicians. Con artists unfortunately seem to have no trouble deceiving us either, but the results are not nearly so amusing. And, of course, this inability to detect deception extends even to the most sophisticated military and intelligence organizations. There is no reason to doubt that anything has really changed since Barton Whaley stated [3], "Indeed, this is a general finding of my study—that is, the deceiver is almost always successful regardless of the sophistication of his victim in the same art."

Before we can address the principles of counterdeception and what we can do to improve our counterdeception capabilities, we need to know something about deception in general, why it works, and how it is implemented. In this chapter, we start our review of deception with an introduction to the history of deception analysis followed by a review of the various conceptual models and theories of deception that have been proposed over the past several years (including models from the disciplines of science and magic). We will also review some of the deception principles and maxims that have been proposed by different authors. We then analyze these models and theories looking for similarities, differences, and the common themes that will lead us to the basic principles of deception that form the foundation of these models and theories. In later chapters, these principles will then act as a basic framework for understanding why humans are vulnerable to deception, categorizing counterdeception approaches, and developing the corresponding principles of counterdeception.

2.2 The History of Deception Analysis

There is a rich but not necessarily voluminous literature in the area of strategic deception [4]. Although the literature extends back into antiquity with the writings of Sun Tzu and Sextus Frontinus [5, 6], formal analysis of deception and its use in international relations and military science did not occur until after World War II. The timeline shown in Figure 2.1 shows that World War I and World War II can be thought of as the *conceptual phase* of deception analysis. In this phase, talented staff officers and operational commanders on all sides of these conflicts began developing the fundamental deception concepts, techniques, and doctrines that still are used to this day. The various mistakes and successes of World War II prompted the *historical analysis* phase of deception literature. Immediately after World War II, a number of military officers and statesmen wrote after action reports and memoirs of their experiences that began to reveal the important role deception played in critical wartime actions. Most of these reports remained classified for years after the war in order to protect sensitive sources. Nevertheless, these documents began to appear throughout the following decades as they were declassified. Examples include *Fortitude: The D-Day Deception Campaign* by Roger Hesketh, *The Man Who Never Was* by Ewen Montagu, *The Double Cross System* by J. C. Masterman, and *Most Secret War: British Scientific Intelligence 1939–1945* by R. V. Jones. The seminal work of the historical analysis phase, though, is Barton Whaley's *Stratagem: Deception and Surprise in War*. Originally published by the Massachusetts Institute of Technology in 1969 and reissued by Artech House in 2007, this is probably the work most often cited by other authors in the field after Sun Tzu. It remains to this day (as far as we know) the only open source empirical analysis of deception's role in strategic and tactical surprise.

The 1970s launched the *theoretical phase* of deception analysis. In this phase, several authors began investigating the basic principles of psychology and sociology and their roles in international relations and military science. The 1973 Middle East War triggered a number of analytical works; for example, Michael Handel's *Perception, Deception, and Surprise: The Case of the Yom Kippur War* is widely cited and provides excellent insights into the role of preconceptions in deception.

The Cold War was also the inspiration for a large number of books and articles on Soviet active measures and maskirovka (e.g., *Soviet Strategic Deception* by Brian Dailey and Patrick Parker). Another major event in deception analysis occurred with the 1981 publication of Richards Heuer's paper "Strategic Deception and Counterdeception: A Cognitive Process Approach," which addressed the role of human cognitive shortcomings in deception.

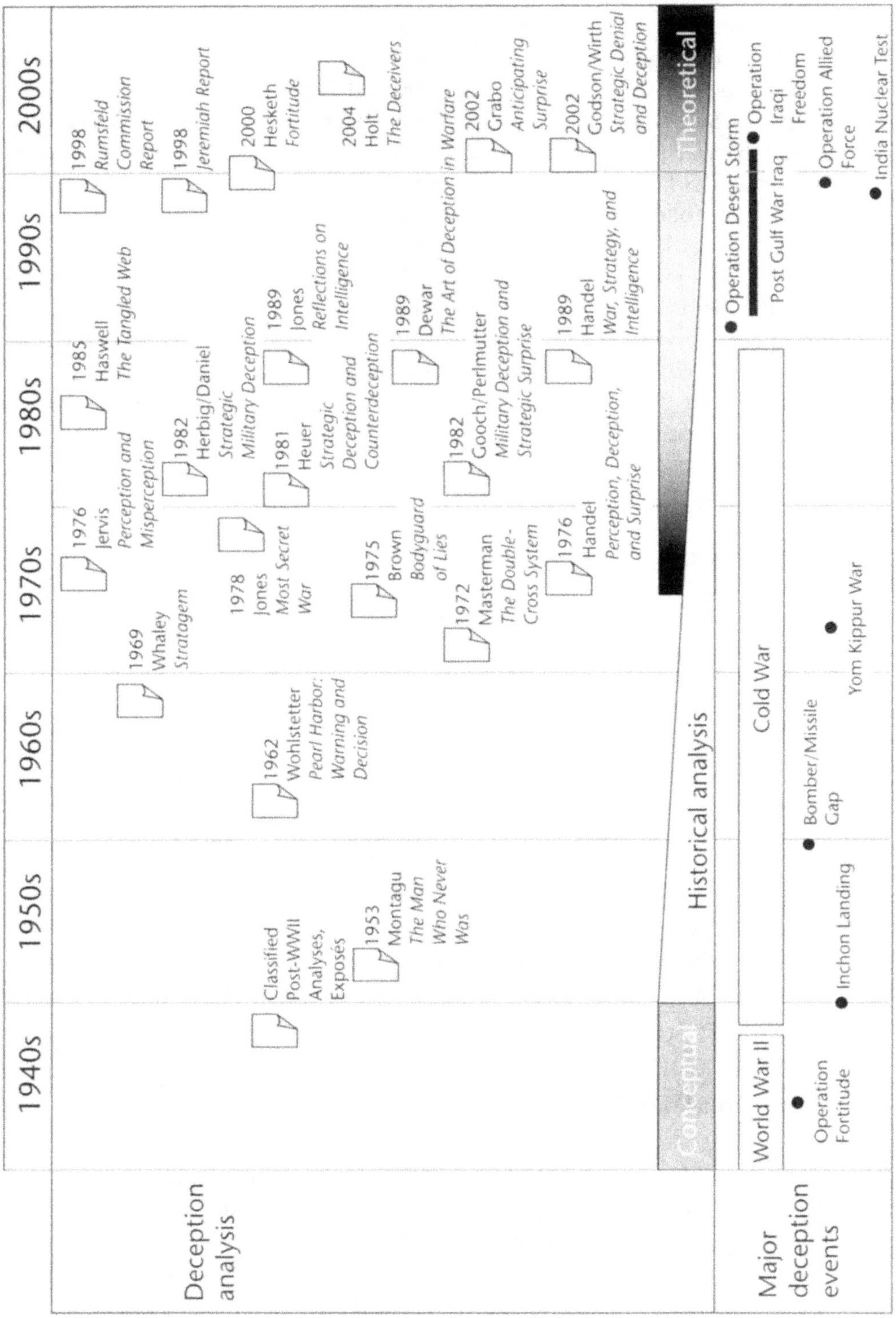

Figure 2.1 Timeline of deception literature.

The end of the Cold War interrupted the theoretical phase. In the general euphoria following the fall of the Berlin Wall in 1989 and the later collapse of the Soviet Union, the well of literature on deception rapidly dried up. However, a number of significant events in the late 1990s proved to be extremely embarrassing to the United States' intelligence community and rekindled interest in strategic deception and how to counter it. In 1991, effective Iraqi deception efforts made finding and targeting their SCUD missiles very difficult during Operation Desert Storm. Revelations after the war about the extent of Iraqi nuclear research facilities, the Indian nuclear test in 1998, and Serbian deception operations aimed at NATO's Operation Allied Force the following year in the Balkans, all prompted new interest in what is now commonly called denial and deception.

It is probably fair to state that, even today, most of the deception literature still falls into the historical analysis category. For example, recent publications include *Hoodwinked: Deception and Resistance (Outwitting the Enemy: Stories from World War II)*, a children's history book, and *The Deceivers: Allied Military Deception in the Second World War*, both published in 2004. Nevertheless, an important subset of the deception literature produced since 1970 focuses on the deception process itself and several authors have made important contributions in this area.

2.3 Conceptual Models and Theories of Deception

Historical accounts of deception operations record and interpret the actions of the individuals and organizations involved in events ranging from specific battles to whole military campaigns. Such historical accounts can help answer a number of questions. Why were deception operations used? How were they planned and implemented? Why did they succeed or fail? Nevertheless, historical accounts do not necessarily help us understand deception itself. As a result, several authors, like their scientific counterparts, have sought to develop models and theories that would help deception practitioners and analysts to understand how deception works, improve deception and counterdeception methods and techniques, guide further investigations on the subject, and generate new ideas. This section summarizes the theories and models developed over the past 30 years by some of the most well-known researchers in the strategic deception field. These summaries are in rough chronological order and permit the reader to see how the study of deception has evolved over the decades.

2.3.1 Barton Whaley

In *Stratagem: Deception and Surprise in War*, Barton Whaley revived the word *stratagem* in order to represent strategic deception used for the purpose of increasing the likelihood that strategic or tactical surprise is achieved on the battlefield. Whaley describes stratagem as being comprised of ruses that he organizes into three main types: *diversions*, *camouflage*, and *disinformation*. According to Whaley [7], "Diversion may be defined as any movement of military units intended to imply a main attack. Its purpose is to divert the opponent's attention and strength away from the real or main operation." Diversions can be further subdivided into two categories: *feints* and *demonstrations*. A feint is a limited objective attack made at a place other than that of the main effort and involves physical contact with the enemy. Demonstrations, on the other hand, are a show of force that threatens an attack at another location but does *not* make contact with the enemy. The demonstration is executed by an actual or simulated massing of combat power, troop movements, or some other activity designed to indicate the preparations for or the beginning of attack at a point other than the main effort.

The second type of ruse is camouflage. The word is derived from the French word *camoufler* meaning "to disguise," and, according to Whaley, has two functions. The first is the concealment of military personnel, equipment, and installations. Whaley refers to this as "negative" or "dissimulative" camouflage. The second is where dummy objects are displayed in order to mislead the enemy. Whaley refers to this as "positive" or "simulative" camouflage and emphasizes it is this function that [8], "...elevates camouflage from security to stratagem."

The third type of ruse is disinformation. Whaley considers this the most important category of ruses and uses the term to include all verbal or written forms of information which are fed to the target's information collection systems for the purposes of deception, whereas camouflage and diversion cover the nonverbal and visual forms of disinformation.

Whaley also introduces his own concept of communication channels and proposes that these information channels can transmit three types of information: relevant and true information (signals), irrelevant information (noise), and relevant but false information (both deliberate disinformation and inadvertent misinformation). He also emphasizes the need for multiple channels for transmitting disinformation in order to increase the likelihood that the target receives the disinformation.

After reviewing the role deception plays in the military doctrines of other nations and the place of surprise and deception in military theory, Whaley introduces his theory of stratagem [9]. The major elements of this theory include:

- The alternative goals or objectives of the deceiver;
- The alternative expectations of the victim;
- The techniques—stratagem—by which the deceiver's goals and objectives are achieved and the victim's expectations are manipulated.

Whaley states [10, 11], "It is much more difficult to find suitable heuristic models for deception, precisely because deception is not made of concrete elements but is rather composed of intangibles that cannot be directly measured or mapped. Some model appropriate to psychological processes is needed. Of the several types available, I have chosen to construct a decision making model, taking as my point of entry Liddell Hart's concept of 'alternative objectives.'" Whaley describes this decision-making model as [12]: "...a simple procedure for designing political-military operations in such a way as to substantially increase the chance of gaining surprise."

This decision-making model comes into play in the first two elements of Whaley's theory of stratagem. First, when the deceiver designs a plan that offers at least two viable alternatives for the victim to deal with, and again when the victim is forced to decide which alternative is the correct one. Even without the use of stratagem, increasing the number of alternative objectives creates uncertainty and forces the victim to divide his resources and attention or to delay his response thereby theoretically increasing the chance of the plan's success. Nevertheless, leaving the target's choice to chance creates two problems. First, there is a diminishing rate of return associated with each alternative added to the deceiver's plans. The likelihood that the target will fail to select the deceiver's real choice does not increase as much as the additional cost of planning and preparing for each alternative. Second, elaborate operations are still likely to be detected by the target's information collectors and analysts. The sheer size and length of time involved in preparations for an operation make it almost impossible for the target to not detect at least some portion of the deceiver's plans and objectives. Successfully achieving surprise goes beyond simply creating alternative objectives. The alternative objectives must be designed in such a way as to take advantage of the expectations of the target and make the target confidently decide on the *wrong* alternative. This is the focus of the third element of Whaley's theory of stratagem.

Whaley describes the technique of stratagem, the third element of his theory, as a two-step process. First, the deceiver must ensure [12] "...that the victim is faced with an ambiguous situation." If the victim is suspected to have knowledge of the deceiver's preferred objective, the deceiver employs the first element of the theory of stratagem in order to supply at least one plausible alternative. This is illustrated in Figure 2.2 where the victim is faced with two possible alternatives, A and B. If the deceiver plans to do A, the target will want to do X in order to hand the deceiver a negative outcome. If the deceiver plans to do B, the target will want to do Y producing the same result. Let's assume that the deceiver's intelligence services have reliably reported that the target believes that both A and B are plausible. The target is therefore faced with the desired ambiguous situation: A or B?

In the second step of the process, the deceiver presents the victim with [12] "...alternative solutions to his predicament." Figure 2.2 shows that the deceiver's highest payoff is realized if the target can be made to think that the deceiver will do A while, in reality, the deceiver actually plans to do B. Ruses (diversions, camouflage, and disinformation) are the means by which the deceiver supplies the data and information that helps the target resolve the ambiguity in favor of A. Whaley summarizes this as follows [13], "In other words, the best stratagem is one that generates a set of warning signals susceptible to alternative, or better yet, optional interpretations, where the intended solution is implausible in terms of the victim's prior

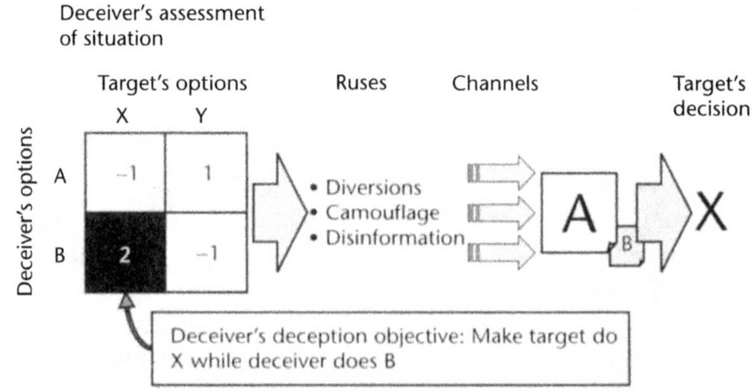

Figure 2.2 Whaley's theory of stratagem.

experience and knowledge while the false solution (or solutions) is plausible. If the victim does not suspect the possibility that deception is operating, he will inevitably be gulled." In Figure 2.2, the target perceives the false alternative, A, as plausible, and the real alternative, B, as implausible. As a result, the target selects option X, the option that most benefits the deceiver.

In summary, Whaley's early model of stratagem introduces several concepts that will appear again and again in other models of the deception process. The first concept is that there must be a deception goal. In Whaley's model, the goal of stratagem is to increase the likelihood that strategic or tactical surprise is achieved on the battlefield. The second concept is the use of alternate goals or objectives to present the target with an ambiguous situation or predicament. The third concept is the use of the ruses (diversions, camouflage, and disinformation) to achieve the deceiver's goal of surprise and to manipulate the victim's expectations and preconceptions. The fourth concept is the use of multiple channels as a means of transmitting disinformation to the target.

There is a final concept that should be mentioned before moving on to the other models of deception. Buried in the last chapter of his book (entitled *Speculative Conclusions*), Whaley introduces what will become the generally accepted model of deception in nearly all of the strategic deception literature that follows: the concepts of *cover-and-deception* or *dissimulation* and *simulation*. As noted in Chapter 1, dissimulation is the concealment of the truth and simulation is the presentation of that which is false. Dissimulation includes both cover and security, while simulation refers to the techniques of stratagem (i.e., deception). Whaley notes that some combination of both is present in most, if not all, of the great historical stratagems. They reinforce each other so that their effect in combination is greater than the effect of either one used alone. In addition, the ineffectiveness of one can be compensated for by the effectiveness of the other (e.g., a good deception operation can compensate for compromises in cover and security). As we will see later in this chapter, Whaley takes the concept of simulation and dissimulation and his theory of stratagem and builds a more detailed model of deception.

2.3.2 Donald Daniel and Katherine Herbig

In the early 1980s, Donald Daniel and Katherine Herbig introduced several new concepts and a simplified model of the deception process [14, 15]. They define deception as "...the deliberate misrepresentation of reality done to gain a competitive advantage" and describe deception as a concept that encompasses the subsidiary concepts of *cover*, *lying*, and *artifice* [16]. Daniel and Herbig use the term cover to mean both secrecy and camouflage and refer to cover as "deception's negative side" because it entails denying access to or the withholding of information [17]. Fundamentally, cover is the very core of deception and is used by the deceiver to hide information not only about the current state of reality but also the deceiver's intentions and plans for future actions. In other words, deception would not be possible without the use of secrecy in one form or another. Daniel and Herbig then introduce an interesting perspective on the next two subsidiary concepts of their deception model: lying and artifice. With regard to lying, they state [18], "To lie is also to withhold information, but it is something more as well: a liar *acts* to deflect his victim away from the truth, and thus highlights deception's positive side. Liars create and perpetuate falsities and seek to fasten a victims' attention to them." Artifice, on the other hand, refers to manipulating the context that surrounds the lie in order to enhance its believability. In this hierarchy of concepts, deception combines cover, lying, and artifice with an awareness of the target's reactions to the lies. This is an interesting way of interpreting the components of deception and one that we will come back to later in this chapter when we introduce our fundamental principles of deception.

Whereas Whaley's goal of deception was surprise, Daniel and Herbig assert that there are three goals to any deception [19]: "The immediate aim is to condition a target's beliefs; the intermediate aim is for the deceiver to influence his actions; and the ultimate aim is for the deceiver to benefit from the target's actions." Whaley's decision-making model emphasized presenting the target with alternative solutions to a predicament. Herbig and Daniel expand this concept by introducing two variants of that concept: *ambiguity producing* deceptions (A-Type) and *misleading* deceptions (M-Type). A-Type deceptions increase the target's ambiguity about a situation by presenting the target with at least two alternatives—one of which may represent the true situation. M-Type deceptions do the opposite. They reduce the target's ambiguity by leading the target to accept the alternative that benefits the deceiver. Herbig and Daniel further decompose the M-Type deception into three categories. The first, M-1, exploits the target's preconceptions by presenting an alternative that the target already is inclined to accept as true or desirable. The M-2 category represents the opposite goal. In an M-2 deception, the deceiver attempts to convince the target to accept an alternative that the target is inclined to doubt or view as improbable The third category, M-3, covers situations where the target's prior predispositions are not directly relevant to or predictive of what the target eventually comes to accept as true.

Finally, Daniel and Herbig introduce two models (see Figure 2.3) of the deception process. The first model (the figure on the left in Figure 2.3) is of the overall

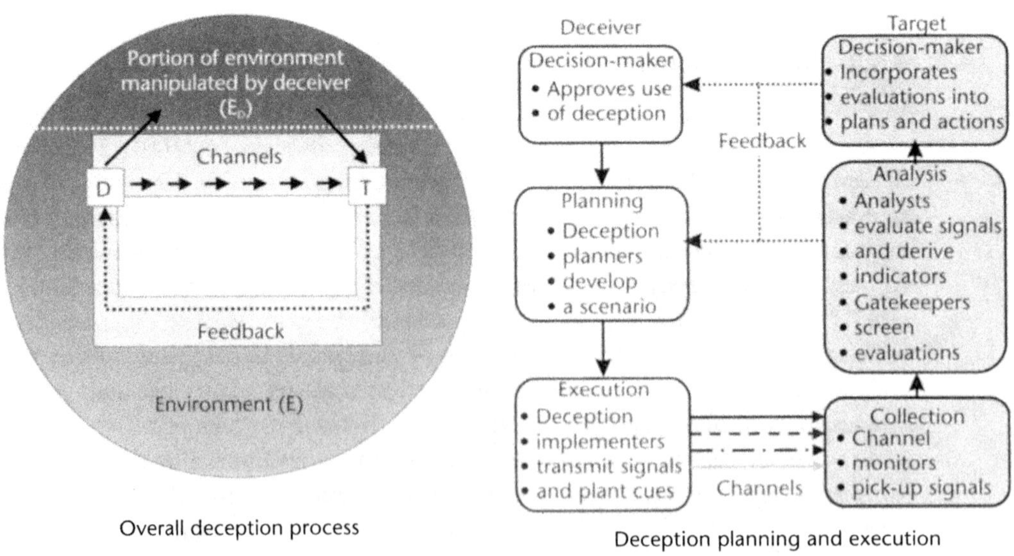

Figure 2.3 Daniel and Herbig's models of deception. (*After*: [14].)

deception process. It consists of an environment encompassing the deceiver, the target, communications channels, and the signals that flow between them. In this model, the deceiver (D) sends signals to the target (T) and receives feedback from the target through the communications channels that link them. In addition, both the deceiver and target are affected by environmental factors (E), some of which the deceiver manipulates (E_D) as part of the deception. The second model (the figure on the right in Figure 2.3) adds further detail to the first and describes the basic steps that occur in planning and executing a deception operation. Note that these models highlight the use of channels to send signals to the target and the flow of feedback from the target to the deceiver regarding the success of the deception plan and giving the deceiver the opportunity to modify their activities. Of course, if the target discovers the deception plan, this feedback channel can be used to deceive the deceiver.

In summary, Herbig and Daniel expand on the concepts found in Whaley's 1969 paper and introduce new concepts for understanding the deception process. First, they broaden the concept of a deception goal from that of achieving surprise on the battlefield to achieving competitive advantage over the target. Second, Herbig and Daniel introduce a new perspective on the concept of deception itself where deception encompasses three ideas: cover, lying, and lying and artifice. Third, they formalize the concept of alternate objectives with their observation that this concept consists of two categories: the A-Type, ambiguity producing, type of deceptions and the M-Type, or misleading, deceptions. Finally, they introduce simple, systems-based models of the deception process that emphasize the flow of signals between the deceiver and the target through communications channels. They explicitly cite the important role that feedback from the target plays in the process. Daniel and Herbig's paper represents an important step towards formalizing the study of deception. Not only do they introduce models that serve as the foundation for many other authors' models of the deception process, but they also provide valuable new insights into the nature of deception itself (e.g., the role of lying and artifice, the different variants of deception, and the factors that affect deception's success or failure).

2.3.3 Barton Whaley and J. Bowyer Bell

The next model we will examine is again the work of Barton Whaley, including work done with J. Bowyer Bell in the late 1970s. Whaley [20] calls this a "preliminary general theory of deception" and presents it as both a "teaching tool" and as an "analytical tool or model for deception operations." Whaley bases this updated theory on additional research he performed in the fields of warfare and magic as well as anecdotal evidence collected from occupational fields that employ or deal with deception to a significant degree. The results of his research led Whaley to conclude [21], "I will go further and assert that deception is the same regardless of whatever field it appears in. It is not a function of technology. All deceptions are applied psychology—the psychology of misperception—and hence are connected by more than one or two analogous points." We will defer examining the psychological aspects of deception until the next chapter. In the meantime we will review Whaley's new general theory.

When we previously examined Whaley's 1969 theory of stratagem, we saw that it consisted of three elements: (1) the creation of alternative goals or objectives by the deceiver; (2) the alternatives perceived or expected by the target; and (3) the techniques—the stratagem—by which the deceiver sought to achieve his goals. These three elements captured the essence of deception's role in achieving surprise: presenting the target with at least two plausible alternatives and using cover and deception to induce the target to select the alternative the deceiver wants him to select (the wrong one). Over a decade later, Whaley's new theory also consists of three major elements, but this theory displays significantly more depth and breadth than the one presented in 1969. Whaley's new theory describes a taxonomy of deception, a structure for thinking about deception, and a process for planning and executing deception operations. The taxonomy is extremely simple. It shows that deception is the result of the target's misperceptions (as opposed to accurate perception, or what Whaley calls "pluperception") and that these misperceptions are the result of deliberate actions on the part of a deceiver (as opposed to unintentional misrepresentation or self-induced misperception).

The next component of Whaley's general theory is a structure for thinking about deception (see Figure 2.4). Here Whaley has significantly expanded on the basic concepts of dissimulation and simulation he introduced in his 1969 book. According to Whaley, dissimulation (hiding the real) and simulation (showing the false) are interdependent and always work in tandem in successful deceptions.

The most obvious change from Whaley's original work is the introduction of six new categories that describe the methods of dissimulation and simulation. In this new structure, dissimulation consists of three methods: *masking*, *repackaging*, and *dazzling*. *Masking* hides the real by concealing most or all of an object's distinctive characteristics, either by screening it from observation or by matching its characteristics with those of its environment, thereby allowing the object to blend in so well that it goes unnoticed. In *repackaging*, an object is disguised by adding or

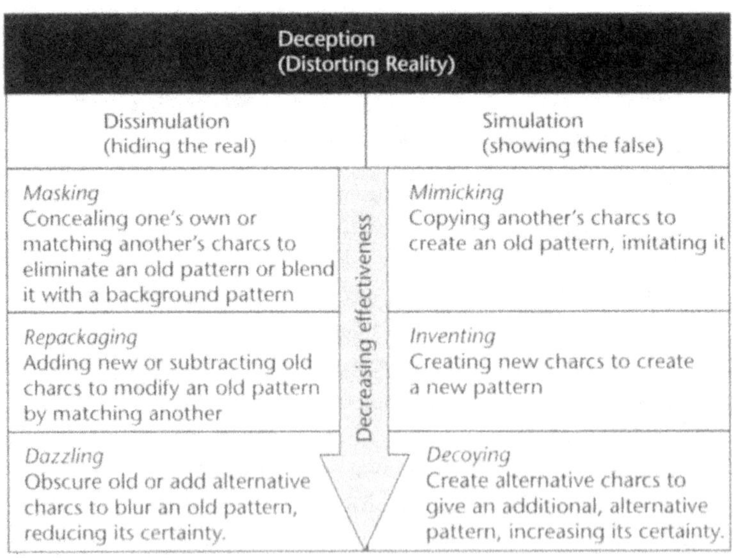

"Charcs" is Whaley's shorthand for characteristics.

Figure 2.4 Whaley's structure of deception.

subtracting characteristics in order for the object to resemble another object. *Dazzling* attempts to hide the real by confusing the observer. The characteristics of the object are changed or obscured in such a way as to blur the object's distinctive pattern and make identification less likely. Likewise, simulation is also divided into three methods: *mimicking*, *inventing*, and *decoying*. *Mimicking* attempts to duplicate enough of the characteristics of another object in order to convincingly imitate it. According to Whaley [22], *inventing* is a method of showing the false by "displaying another reality." New characteristics are created in order to create entirely new patterns that represent a false object. Finally, decoying is defined [22] as creating "alternative false characteristics that give an additional, second pattern." *Decoying* is meant to divert the observer's attention by presenting a pattern that is more convincing than the real one.

Whaley also observes that the effectiveness of each method is arrayed in decreasing order of effectiveness. In general, masking is a more effective means of dissimulation than repackaging which is usually more effective than dazzling. This leads Whaley to hypothesize that the most effective deceptions are likely to simultaneously pair the most effective dissimulation and simulation methods (e.g., masking and mimicking) while the least effective deceptions would combine the least effective methods (i.e., dazzling and decoying). To test this hypothesis, Whaley categorized a sample of 60 magic tricks by which type of dissimulation and simulation they employed. He found that 19 out the 60 magic tricks studied paired masking and mimicking, whereas only one trick combined dazzling and decoying [23]. Whaley's data also clearly demonstrates the critical role that masking plays in deception. Masking was paired with inventing 10 times and paired with decoying another 10 times. The result is that the most effective type of dissimulation—masking—was employed in 39 (nearly two-thirds) of the 60 magic tricks Whaley examined. These figures reinforce the notion that dissimulation (hiding the real) is an indispensable component of deception and combining masking with nearly any other form of simulation has the highest potential of achieving a successful deception.

The third component of Whaley's general theory of deception is an explicit process for planning and executing a deception (see Figure 2.5). The planning phase begins with the clear understanding of the desired *strategic goal*. For example, a dictator might wish to launch a surprise invasion on a neighboring country. The second step in the process is determining how the target should *react* in the situation dictated by the strategic goal. In the case of a surprise attack, the commanding general may want the target to keep its main force deployed on the western front while the general attacks from the south. Once it is determined how the target is desired to react, the deception planners can begin analyzing what they want the target to think about certain observed facts and events. In other words, the deception planners begin determining what it is that the target should *perceive* in order to react in the desired manner.

Manipulating the target's perceptions determines what facts and events must be hidden from the target and what must be simultaneously shown to the target instead. Once this information is determined, the patterns of each fact and event are analyzed in order to identify the distinguishing characteristics that must be changed in order to present a new pattern, either one that hides the distinguishing

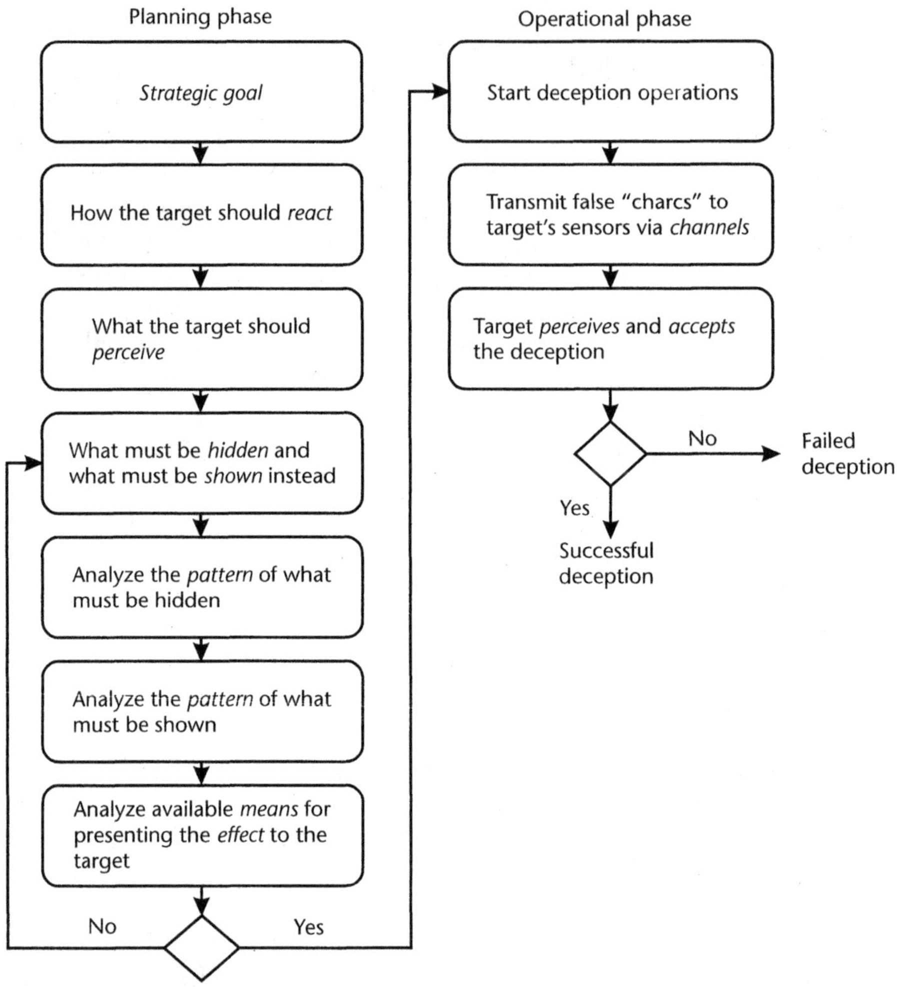

Figure 2.5 The Whaley and Bell deception process.

characteristics or one that simulates false ones. At this point, the deception planners are finished designing the overall effect that they want to achieve, one that will create the desired perceptions and reactions by the target. The plan is reviewed with the intent of determining if the deceiver has the means available by which the deception can be convincingly presented to the target. If the answer is yes, the deception can proceed to the operational phase. If not, the planners must go back to the fourth step and develop a new design.

The operational phase begins with military and intelligence units pulling together and assembling all the parts of the planned deception operation (e.g., instituting security measures, camouflaging facilities and equipment, constructing and deploying decoys, and disseminating disinformation). Once all the various parts of the deception are ready, they are presented to the target's sensors through the *channels* monitored by the target. For example, the deceiver deploys decoys where and when they are sure to be seen by the target's imaging systems, sends false military orders using codes that are known to have been compromised while using frequencies known to be monitored, supplies feed material to the target through double agents controlled by the deceiver, or plants misleading or false stories with news sources monitored by the target. This is a critical aspect of the deception, since disinformation is useless if the target does not observe it.

The final step of the deception process is out of the deceiver's direct control. The deception is successful if the target accepts the deception and acts accordingly. On the other hand, the deception fails if the target fails to detect the intended effects, or detects the deception's effects but judges them irrelevant or misinterprets their meaning or, worst of all, detects the deception itself.

In summary, Whaley's general theory of deception significantly extends his earlier work especially with regard to the concepts of dissimulation and simulation and their interaction. In his earlier theory, Whaley described stratagem as being comprised of three types of ruses (diversions, camouflage, and disinformation) and noted that the effects of dissimulation and simulation (cover and deception) were greater in combination than when employed alone. Now, in this newer general theory, the emphasis is on the methods of dissimulation and simulation and the three ruses have evolved into six categories. The old camouflage ruse is transformed into masking, repackaging, and dazzling, while diversions are mimicking, inventing, and decoying. The disinformation ruse has disappeared, apparently absorbed into the other categories since it is still clearly an essential part of the deception process shown in Figure 2.5, the transmission of false "charcs" (Whaley's shorthand for characteristics) to the target via different channels of communication. Whaley's additional empirical research in the field of magic generally supports his earlier assertion that dissimulation and simulation are more effective when used in combination, and the new research hints that there is a hierarchy of methods (i.e., some combinations are more effective than others). Finally, Whaley introduces a model for the planning and execution of deception operations that complements the one developed by Daniel and Herbig.

2.3.4 Michael Handel

Michael Handel was one of the late twentieth century's foremost thinkers on intelligence analysis, surprise, and deception. In his 1976 monograph, *Perception, Deception, and Surprise: The Case of the Yom Kippur War*, Handel presents two frameworks for thinking about the problems related to the evaluation of intelligence information in order to avoid military surprise. The first framework is relevant to our review of deception models since it describes the flow of information (both signals and noise) through three "noise barriers": the enemy, the international environment, and self-generated noise. In this model, each noise barrier distorts the information flowing through it. As signals travel through each of the three noise barriers, they are weakened and hidden in additional noise to the point where there is little difference between the two. Secrecy and deception play an important role in the first noise barrier; Handel summarizes their contribution this way [24]:

> Secrecy is also [a] problem. With the exception of certain deliberate deception tactics, the enemy is always expected to shroud his capabilities, intentions and plans in a veil of secrecy. Paradoxically, even the simple truth can deceive, for if the enemy's secrets are obtained too often, too easily, they are too good to be believed and deception is expected. The ever-present danger of deception obliges intelligence

> services to examine even definitive signals *as if* they had passed through all three noise barriers, even if they have not. Moreover, correct signals can often *become* self-denying, i.e., can be transformed into noise. As Luttwak and Horowitz so aptly stated, "There is no difference between signals and noise—except in retrospect. There is no true and false data; in a deeper sense, all strategic warning data is noise." The final conclusion is that there is no sure way to prevent deception.

We will return to Handel's framework and his accompanying paradoxes later in Chapter 3.

Handel devotes a chapter to military deception in his 1989 book *War, Strategy, and Intelligence*. He defines deception as, "...a purposeful attempt by the deceiver to manipulate the perceptions of the target's decision makers in order to gain a competitive advantage" and suggests that it takes on three basic "forms" [25]. In the first form, deception is used to misdirect the target's attention in order to cause the target to concentrate his forces in the wrong place. The second is related to the first in that it attempts to make the target waste resources (e.g., manpower, weapons, time, and so forth) on unimportant targets or directions. Finally, the third form of deception is the more familiar objective of surprising the target. These forms emphasize the actions that the deceiver wants the target to take, or in the case of surprise, to induce inaction on the part of the target.

Later, Handel turns his attention to the informational aspects of deception and proposes that deception operations aim to deceive the target with regard to only two categories of information: *intentions* and *capabilities*. The purpose of deception then is to mislead, misinform, or confuse the target regarding the deceiver's intentions and capabilities (see Figure 2.6). In Handel's typology, deceiving the target involves both passive and active modes of deception. According to Handel [26], "Passive deception is largely dependent upon secrecy and camouflage, on hiding one's intentions and/or capabilities from the adversary." He then goes on to emphasize the importance of passive deception when he states [26], "*Moreover, active types of deception are dependent upon the efficacy of the passive operation.* Even more crucial, passive deception can tremendously complicate, and therefore increase the costs of, intelligence work – in terms of time, money, and the like." On the other hand, active deception involves [27] "...a calculated policy of disclosing half-truths supported by 'proof' (verifiable information) and other material evidence." In order to be considered authentic and valuable, the deception information should be well supported by true information and the target should be made to

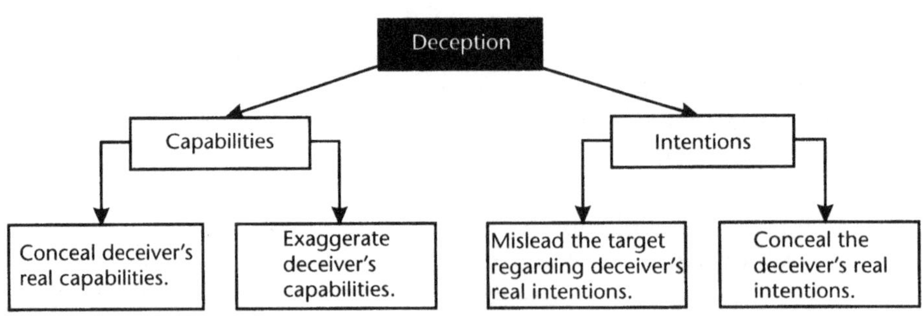

Figure 2.6 Handel's deception typology. (*After:* [25].)

discover the information and feel that he worked hard to obtain it. We will return to this point again in Chapter 3.

In summary, Handel's primary interest in deception is how it affects intelligence analysis and its role in strategic surprise. His noise barrier model and his typology of deception are consistent with these interests. Whereas other authors have proposed general models of deception, Handel's models clearly aim at explaining deception at the strategic level. We will return to Handel's work when we begin to examine why deception works in Chapter 3.

2.3.5 Scott Gerwehr and Russell Glenn

A more recent model of deception is described in a 2002 RAND report titled, *Unweaving the Web: Deception and Adaptation in Future Urban Operations*. In this report prepared for the United States Army, Gerwehr and Glenn investigate a variety of biological deceptions found in nature in order to uncover lessons with application to military deception associated with urban operations. One of the objectives of their report is to [28] "...expand and elaborate upon existing deception theory..." The result is an interesting model that they call "Three Perspectives on Deception."

Figure 2.7 provides an overview of these three perspectives. The first, *level of sophistication*, addresses the degree to which a deception operation takes into account the range of elements including the target's expectations and preconceptions, the target's intelligence, surveillance, and reconnaissance capabilities, and the overall environmental and contextual factors of the situation. Gerwehr and Glenn point out that the level of sophistication is not a value judgment but is intended to be used as a diagnostic measure allowing more precise deception planning as well as

Three perspectives on deception		
Level of sophistication	Effect sought	Means of deception
Static: Deceptions that remain static regardless of the state, activity, or histories of either the deceiver or target.	*Masking:* Concealing a signal. Examples include camouflage, concealment, and signature reduction.	*Morphological:* The part of deception that is primarily a matter of substance or form such as shape, coloration, or temperature.
Dynamic: Deceptions that become active under specific circumstances. Nevertheless, the ruse itself and the associated trigger do not change over time, nor do they vary significantly by circumstance or adversary.	*Misdirecting:* Transmitting a clear and unambiguous false signal. Examples include feints and demonstrations, decoys and dummies, disguises, and disinformation.	
Adaptive: Same as the dynamic category except that the trigger or ruse can be modified with experience. This category covers deceptions that improve through trial and error.		*Behavioral:* The part of deception that is primarily a matter of implementation or function such as timing, location, or patterns of events or behavior.
Premeditative: Deceptions that are designed and implemented on the basis of experience, knowledge of the deceiver's own capabilities and vulnerabilities, and knowledge of the target's sensors and search strategies.	*Confusing:* Raising the noise level in order to create uncertainty or paralyze the target's perceptual capabilities. Examples include voluminous communications traffic, conditioning, and random behavior	

Figure 2.7 Gerwehr and Glenn's perspectives on deception.

suggesting possible strategies for uncovering deception. They view level of sophistication as a spectrum of deceptions that range from the static on one end to the premeditative on the other. *Static* deceptions remain constant and unchanging regardless of the situation. The camouflage paint on an aircraft is an example of this category. *Dynamic* deceptions are more sophisticated. These are deceptions that are activated under certain specific circumstances. The deception and its associated trigger do not change over time, however, nor do they vary significantly across different situations or adversaries. Equipping the camouflaged aircraft with countermeasures that drop flares when the flight crew detects the launch of a shoulder-fired missile would be an example of a dynamic deception.

Adaptive deceptions are essentially the same as dynamic deceptions except that either or both the trigger and ruse can be modified based on the deceiver's experience with both the adversary and the environment. In other words, they are tailored to the circumstances of each situation. Adding radar-jamming equipment such as the ALQ-131 to the aircraft is an example of an adaptive deception. The ALQ-131 pod can be reprogrammed to match the expected threat depending on the circumstances. Finally, the most sophisticated deceptions are *premeditative*. These deceptions are planned and implemented using detailed knowledge of not only the capabilities and vulnerabilities of the target, but those of the deceiver as well. All of the famous historical strategic deception operations fall into this category.

The second perspective on deception is the *effect sought*, that is, the type of effect that the deceiver seeks to create in order to influence the target's perception of the situation. Gerwehr and Glenn propose three categories of effects: *masking*, *misdirecting*, and *confusing*. Masking includes camouflage, concealment, and signal reduction techniques used to reduce or eliminate the real signals produced by objects and events. Misdirecting aims to transmit false signals to the target in order to divert attention and associated actions away from what the deceiver is really doing or intends to do. Confusing effects impair the target's information collection and analysis capabilities in order to create uncertainty and delay or even stop the target from taking effective action. Gerwehr and Glenn cite "voluminous background noise, oversaturation, unpredictability, and the need for haste" as examples of confusing effects [29].

The *means of deception* is the third perspective on deception. Gerwehr and Glenn divide the means of deception into two categories corresponding to form and function. They refer to the form-based category as *morphological*, meaning that part of deception that has material characteristics such as shape, coloration, or temperature. Our earlier example of an aircraft painted in a camouflage to match a certain geographic environment is employs a morphological deception. The functional category is referred to as a *behavioral* means of deception. Behavioral deceptions are characterized by the timing or location of activities as well as by patterns of events or behaviors. An example would be the use of military maneuvers to condition the target to their regular, nonthreatening occurrence and then launching the actual attack under the cover of the maneuvers themselves.

Gerwehr and Glenn make it clear that these three perspectives on deception are merely the first step toward developing a more "comprehensive and useful" deception theory. Such a theory would enable commanders and decision-makers to better understand the costs, benefits, and tradeoffs of deception as well as the interactions between deception and other measures (e.g., speed, lethality, and intelligence). They note that deception methods and the way they are applied can be combined in order to create even more effective tactical and strategic deceptions. This creates at least four ways that more effective deceptions can be created:

- Use multiple, similar deception methods.
- Use multiple, different deception methods.
- Employ the selected deception methods at different points in time.
- Employ the selected deception methods at different points in space.

They also point out that, as the deceiver's knowledge of the target improves, the sophistication of the deceptions employed can also increase yielding a likely increase in deception effectiveness.

In summary, Gerwehr and Glenn both complement and extend our theoretical knowledge about deception. Their three perspectives model is based on their thorough study of deception in nature and they propose that this model can be a valuable tool for evaluating the tradeoffs associated with different deception strategies as well as for developing ways of countering an adversary's deception efforts. They introduce a new concept—level of sophistication—and provide a different perspective on deception effects and means than that of Whaley and other authors. Like Whaley, though, they recognize that combinations of deception methods increase its effectiveness while adding the obvious time and space dimensions to the equation.

2.4 Principles and Maxims of Deception

A number of other authors have also contributed to the historical literature on deception but instead of developing models or theories, these authors propose a number of principles or maxims of deception that they have derived from their research. The following sections focus on several of these sources.

2.4.1 R. V. Jones

Often referred to as "the father of scientific intelligence," Jones played a vital role in World War II as the Assistant Director of Intelligence (Science) in the British Air Ministry. During the course of the war, he was closely involved with the scientific assessment of German military technology and the subsequent development of British offensive and defensive countermeasures. He is well known for his theory of spoof that described the basic methods of confounding German radars—persuading the adversary that you are either where you are not, or not where you really are [30]. The theory of spoof is also where Jones states that [30]: "No imitation can be perfect without being the real thing, but it is surprising what can be done by dexterous suggestion."

In his book *Reflections on Intelligence* [31], Jones devotes a chapter to the topic of intelligence and deception in which he describes a variety of historical deception operations as well as the various technical deceptions that he helped to develop in order to deceive German radars. But it is in his chapter on intelligence and security that we find his advice regarding security and deception. According to Jones, the aim of security is to prevent your adversary from deducing as many as possible of the following pieces of information:

- Where you are and/or where he is;
- What forces and weapons you have at your disposal;
- What you intend to do;
- When you intend to do it;
- How you intend to do it;
- Your knowledge of the enemy's intentions and technique;
- How successful his operations are;
- Where you believe your own most vulnerable points to be.

These are primarily wartime objectives. Jones notes that in peacetime the emphasis should be on protecting intentions, capabilities, and the effects of new technology.

While noting that security is a prerequisite for any successful deception, Jones goes on to provides a set of corresponding deception objectives that aim at leading your adversary to one or more of the following conclusions:

- You are somewhere different from where you actually are.
- The adversary is somewhere different from where he actually is.
- Your weapons and forces are different from those that you actually have.
- You will do something different from what you actually intend.
- Your knowledge of the adversary is either greater or less than it actually is.
- The adversary's operations are either more or less successful than they are.

Jones' security and deception objectives are consistent with concepts related to dissimulation and simulation that we have reviewed previously. Jones refers to security as "...a negative activity, in that you are trying to stop the flow of clues to an opponent..." and makes the point that good security is a prerequisite for any successful deception [32]. Deception is the "positive counterpart" of security and provides the false clues that will be fed to the target through "appropriate" communications channels. Jones also emphasizes the concept of channels by noting that the more channels that are available to the target, the more difficult is the task of deception in that the deceiver must make sure that the information fed to the target in all these channels is consistent.

2.4.2 The Mathtech Deception Research Program

In the late 1970s, the Central Intelligence Agency's Office of Research and Development contracted with Mathtech, Inc., and other consultants [33] to investigate a wide variety of deception topics. The result of this "Deception Research Program" was 10 publications ranging from case studies like *The Meinertzhagen Haversack Ruse* to an extensive bibliography and survey of the literature of misperception. One report of special interest to the field of deception theory was *Deception Maxims: Fact and Folklore* [34]. The intent of this report was to explore and integrate work done in the post–World War II years in a variety of fields, not only deception and surprise in military and political affairs, but also in political science, sociology, and psychology. The hope was to summarize this diverse information about deception, misperception, and cognitive biases into a unified body of knowledge. The result [35] was a set of 10 maxims that would serve as "...hypotheses for further testing and analysis..." Although these maxims do not really represent a formal model of deception, they illustrate a number of common deception concepts that appear in other models and throughout the literature. Figure 2.8 lists the 10 maxims and provides a brief description of each.

Maxims 1 and 2 will be addressed in Chapter 3 since they are related more towards why human beings are vulnerable to deception. The basis for the other

Maxim 1: Magruder's Principle	It is easier to for the target to maintain a preexisting belief even if presented with information that would be expected to change that belief.
Maxim 2: Limitations to human information processing	Several limitations to human information processing can be exploited in the design of deception schemes, including the law of small numbers and susceptibility to conditioning.
Maxim 3: The multiple forms of surprise	Surprise can be achieved in different forms: location, strength, intention, style, and timing.
Maxim 4: Jones' Lemma	Deception becomes more difficult as the number of channels available to the target increases. Nevertheless, within limits, the greater the number of channels that are controlled by the deceiver, the greater the likelihood that the deception will be believed.
Maxim 5: A choice among types of deception	Where possible the objective of the deception planner should be to reduce the ambiguity in the mind of the target in order to make the target more certain of a particular falsehood rather than less certain of the truth.
Maxim 6: Axelrod's contribution: The husbanding of assets	There are circumstances where deception assets should be husbanded, despite the costs of maintaining them and the risk of exposure, until they can be put to more fruitful use.
Maxim 7: A sequencing rule	Deception activities should occur in a sequence that prolongs the target's false perceptions of the situation for as long as possible.
Maxim 8: The importance of feedback	Accurate feedback from the target increases the deception's likelihood of success.
Maxim 9: The Monkey's Paw	The deception may produce subtle and unwanted side effects. Deception planners should be sensitive to this possibility and attempt to minimize them.
Maxim 10: Care in the design of planned placement of deceptive material	Great care must be taken when designing schemes to leak notional plans. Apparent windfalls are subject to close scrutiny and are often disbelieved.

Figure 2.8 The 10 deception maxims.

maxims can be found throughout the literature. Maxim 3 can be found in Whaley's 1969 book that we summarized in Section 2.2.2. Jones' Lemma (Maxim 4) is named for R. V. Jones, as described earlier. We will examine Maxim 4 again later in Chapters 3 and 5 when we address counterdeception. Maxim 5 is derived from the work of Daniel and Herbig that we covered earlier in this chapter. Maxim 6 is based on the work of Robert Axelrod [36] but a similar meaning can be found in Masterman when he writes [37]: "In other words we must keep our eye firmly fixed on time in the future when we should be able to put over large schemes of strategic deception, and we must remember that the gains from smaller pieces of tactical deception or from minor pieces of misinformation passed to the enemy were of small account when compared with the much more important though still distant objects." Maxim 7 has to do with the timing of deception activities. The most blatant activities (i.e., the ones that may be the most inconsistent with the target's preconceptions) should be deferred up until the last possible moment. As we have seen, the importance of feedback (Maxim 8) appears in nearly all of the deception literature. Maxim 9 is intended primarily to sensitize deception planners to the side effects caused by the tight security surrounding deception operations. Units and commanders who are not privy to the deception plan may react in unanticipated ways to the deception and the target's response. The point of Maxim 10 is that deceptive information is more likely to be accepted by the target if the target has to work for it. Handel states [27, 38]: "The deceived party must 'discover' the evidence himself, and he should have to work hard for it to be more convinced of its authenticity and value. Frequently, information that is easily obtained seems to be less credible and of doubtful value."

2.4.3 Haswell, Dewar, and Latimer

Jock Haswell, Michael Dewar, and Jon Latimer are all former British Army officers who have written books on military deception [39–41]. The purpose, principles, and techniques of deception that they describe are all very similar, differing primarily in the historical and contemporary examples of deception in military operations each author uses. Like Whaley, all three authors emphasize that the goal of deception in warfare is surprise, both at the tactical and strategic levels, while Latimer also notes that the general goal of any deception is to gain advantage over one's opponent. All three propose six to seven guiding principles of deception. These principles are described separately or in combination (e.g., centralized control versus centralized control and coordination) and all differ in the order in which they are presented. The five principles common to all three authors are:

- *Preparation:* Successful deception operations require careful intelligence preparation in order to develop detailed knowledge of the target and the target's likely reaction to each part of the deception.
- *Centralized control and coordination:* Uncoordinated deception operations can cause confusion among friendly forces and reduce or negate the effectiveness of the deception. Haswell treats centralized control and coordination as separate principles.

- *Credibility:* The deception should produce information (both real and false) and a pattern of events that are in line with the target's preconceptions and expectations.
- *Multiple information channels:* False information must be presented to the target through as many channels as possible without arousing the target's suspicions that the information is too good to be true. Latimer calls this *confirmation* and combines it with credibility.
- *Security:* Access to the deception plan must be carefully restricted; however, the information approved for release to the target must be revealed in such a way so that the absence of normal security precautions does not arouse the target's suspicions.

Haswell and Latimer include *flexibility* as another principle. Deception plans must have the flexibility to deal with unforeseen development even to the point of abandoning the deception plan if necessary. Dewar adds *timing* to his list of principles, whereas Latimer combines it with preparation. Dewar's view of timing is that the target must be given enough time to react to the deception but not enough time for analysis that would expose the deception and reveal its purpose. Latimer's perspective is similar adding that the timing of the deception should follow a sequence that the target would expect (see Maxim 7 in Figure 2.8). Finally, Latimer includes two additional principles that he calls *focus* and *action*. Focus refers to the focus of the deception operation—the mind of the enemy commander or decision-maker. Action emphasizes that the goal of deception is to make the target act in a way that benefits the deceiver.

In addition to offering principles of deception, all three authors also describe a common set of deception techniques. Haswell and Latimer start by dividing deception into five categories consisting of "countersurveillance" (meaning camouflage and concealment), displays (e.g., decoys, dummy positions, heat sources, and so forth), feints, demonstrations, and ruses. Oddly enough, Haswell [42] defines a ruse as "...any trick, stratagem or artifice designed to deceive the enemy, and therefore can be a display, a feint or a demonstration" which leads one to wonder why he double-counts feints and demonstrations. All three authors describe six or seven ruses as examples of the methods or techniques of deception. These include:

- *The lure:* Presenting the target with what appears to be a sudden desirable opportunity that begs to be exploited, but is in fact a trap.
- *The repetitive process:* This technique lulls the target into a false sense of security through the repetition of seemingly nonthreatening activities.
- *The double bluff:* The true plans are revealed to a target that has been conditioned to expect deception with the expectation that the target will reject the truth as another deception.
- *The unintentional mistake:* The target is led to believe that seemingly valuable information has fallen into his hands through negligence or a failure of security. The information, of course, is false.
- *The piece of bad luck:* This technique is similar to the unintentional mistake but differs in that the target believes the information has fallen into his hands by accident.

- *The substitution:* The target is persuaded that something is false and to continue to hold that belief even after the false has been replaced by the real.

Although all three authors describe what they call "principles of deception," we believe it is more appropriate to consider them as principles for guiding the planning and execution of deception *operations*. Likewise, their descriptions of deception techniques are more likely described as types of deception operations. Nevertheless, they summarize the important features of deception operations clearly and concisely. For example, Cohen [43] comments that, "Dewar reviews the history of deception in warfare and, in only 12 pages, gives one of the most cogent high-level descriptions of the basis, means, and methods of deception."

In summary, all these authors provide some of the best sources of practical advice concerning deception operations. Their principles are based on the lessons learned from a wide range of historical deception operations. In addition, they reinforce several of the concepts previously discussed such as the need for a deception goal, the importance of "sound and thorough preparation," the need for multiple channels with which to feed information and disinformation to the target, and the close coupling between security and deception.

2.5 The View from Science

The social and natural sciences provide another important set of literature focusing on deception going back to the nineteenth century. In 1862, British scientist Henry Walter Bates published his study of South American butterflies, *Contributions to an insect fauna of the Amazon valley: Lepidoptera: Heliconidae*, where he described how nonpoisonous butterflies mimic the bright warning colors of other poisonous or unpalatable species. Such mimicry in animals is known as Batesian mimicry in his honor. At the end of the nineteenth century, both George Romanes and C. Lloyd Morgan addressed the question of deception in their examinations of animal intelligence. Since that time, extensive work on both human and animal deception has been done in fields such as biology, psychology, and anthropology. The next few sections summarize the work of three researchers from those fields aimed at understanding deception in humans and animals.

In *Deception: Perspectives on Human and Nonhuman Deceit* [44], Mitchell defines deception as any phenomenon that which fulfills three criteria. These criteria are:

1. A receiving organism R registers (or believes) something Y from some sending organism S, where S can be described as benefiting when (or desiring that).
2. R acts appropriately toward Y, because Y means X.
3. It is untrue that X is the case.

In the first criterion, registering refers to an organism's ability to perceive and attend to stimuli that are relevant to its goals. Self-deception occurs when S and R are the same organism.

Based on this definition, Mitchell divides deception into four levels where each level is determined by the motivations of the sender and receiver (see Figure 2.9). Each level is represented by different types of emerging phenomena that can be characterized by the level of control over the phenomena by S and R. Nearly all plant and animal deception that occurs in nature can be assigned to one of the first three levels in Mitchell's model. Although human deception clearly falls into Level 4 of this model, the issue of Level 4 deception in animals, especially primates, is still a hotly debated issue and is the subject of continuing research [45].

Mitchell also suggests that deceptions of all sorts, both animal and human, are likely to share a common set of principles. Of the 11 principles he proposed, 5 of them are relevant to the study of strategic deception. These are:

- *All deception requires simulation.* The deceiver produces signals that mimic other signals (either of the deceiver's own behaviors or that of other species) or that distracts or confuses the target. It is interesting to note that Mitchell considers camouflage (i.e., simulated appearance) as a form of simulation.
- *Predictability in the victim's responses favors the occurrence of deception while unpredictability discourages it.* A simple example is parking meters. If the city does not police the system, it is easy to park for free. Random policing by the traffic police discourages cheating.

Level	Basis for deception	Deception rule	Examples
I	Appearance	Always do X.	• Batesian mimicry • Protective coloration and patterns
II	Coordination of perception and action	Do X when Y is registered.	• Aggressive or defensive mimicry in response to a stimulus, (e.g., false visual signals, feigning injury, or bluffing)
III	Learning	Do any X given that X resulted in some desired consequence Y in the past.	• The organism learns (through trial and error, conditioning, or observation) that it benefits from specific behaviors, (e.g., the cat meowing at the door to go out).
IV	Planning	The sender continually changes his strategy in order to be successful. These changes are dependent on both the current states and past behaviors of both the sender and receiver.	• Most prevalent among humans and found in all aspects of activity • Some evidence that primates such as chimpanzees are capable of intentional deception, (e.g., deceiving other chimps about the location of food)

Figure 2.9 Mitchell's levels of deception. (*After*: [44].)

- *All deception works within the context of honesty.* Since most organisms in a system expect a signal to have a particular, honest response, a deceiver can deceive a member of that system when the expected signal has a different result. In a strategic deception context, Handel provides an appropriate paradox [46]: "The more one has a reputation for honesty—the easier it is to lie convincingly. Even more concisely: Honest people/states can deceive the best."
- *Most victims of deception are capable of learning.* In fact, learning makes deception possible. For example, all military commanders learn that a retreating enemy is vulnerable to a counterattack; however, this leaves them vulnerable to the Lure ruse. However, learning aids in countering deception as well. The same military commanders learn about historical battles where the Lure ruse was successfully employed and thereby are theoretically capable of recognizing that deception.
- *Deceivers can develop in their ability to deceive and victims can develop in their ability to detect deception.* This is the age old "good news, bad news" paradox. The good news is that victims can develop their abilities to detect deception (we hope that this book makes a contribution in this regard); the bad news is that the deceivers are also capable of developing their abilities to deceive (just consider the sophistication of modern magic performances).

W. John Smith offers an "informational perspective on manipulation" where information is a property, not an object [47]. It can be possessed and shared, but not given, and it permits predictions to be made, on which the recipient of the information can select future actions. The resulting predictions have three characteristics:

- They are conditional. For example, the sender may signal that it may attack; however, that possibility is conditional on the receiver's subsequent behavior.
- They are probabilistic. The signal does not provide information that something *will* occur if the conditions are right, but only provides the receiver with the ability to assess the likelihood that it will occur relative to other kinds of behavior.
- They differ in the extent to which the information can be used to make a detailed prediction. All signalers withhold information and generally only signal information that, on average, benefits the signaler.

Manipulating the receiver's behavior in order to increase the benefits to the sender at the expense of the receiver can be achieved in two ways. The first way is that the sender can withhold information from the receiver, especially that information that could usually be expected in a certain situation. The second way is that the sender misinforms the receiver. Smith asserts that all misleading signaling depends on mimicry. Misinforming signals either mimic an otherwise reliable signal or mimic the form of other sources of information.

Anthropologist Myrdene Anderson [48, p. 324] uses systems theory to define deception as "simply the sending and/or receiving of misleading information in open cybernetic systems" and to propose that deception includes any "subversion of informational and energetic circuits from one path to another." To put it another way, deception involves the subversion of communications and physical processes. This approach produces a matrix of methods for manipulating information and objects or processes in the real world in order to reveal or conceal either facts or fiction (see Figure 2.10). As we will see later, this matrix will be extremely valuable in our understanding of the relationships between the various concepts we summarized in the previous sections.

Anderson also presents a typology of deception that addresses not only the sender's deception and the receiver's response, but the feedback that occurs between sender and receiver as well (see Figure 2.11). In this typology, deception is the result of the intentional or unintentional distortion or suppression of information. Deception can be nonintentional, especially if the sender is not capable of intention (e.g., plants, insects, and most animals). The receiver decodes the sender's signals and finds the deception either believable or unbelievable (nonbelievable in the case of receivers incapable of belief—animals again). If the deception is believable, the receiver has three possible responses. He can believe it, not believe it, or become suspicious. If unbelievable, the receiver may not believe it or may suspect a completely different meaning. The receiver's positive or negative reactions can be overt or covert. The deceiver's reaction to this feedback can take three forms: he can maintain, stop, or even escalate the deception. If it appears that the sender's signals have been ignored, the deceiver is in the difficult position of having to blindly decide what course of action to take.

As we observed in the introduction to this chapter, deception in nature has been around for nearly as long as life itself has existed on our planet. We have reviewed just a few of the general conceptual models of deception that can found in the scientific literature in order to demonstrate that strategic deception is not merely the invention of generals and politicians. It is, in many ways, the key to the survival of innumerable species including our own, and, in fact [49], "Deception may be more common than truthful communication." Because deception is a ubiquitous element of life itself, there are lessons to be learned from the study of deception in nature, not only with regard to why and how deception itself works, but also with regard to how to detect and counter it.

2.6 The View from Magic

One cannot study deception without also considering the art of magic. By magic we mean [50] "…the ancient art of honest deception, of magicians, who, unlike

	To Reveal	To Conceal
Fact	I: Disclose E: Evince	I: Impose secrecy E: Act stealthily
Fiction	I: Falsify E: Bluff	I: Suppress a lie E: Curb a sham

"I" represents the manipulation of information.
"E" represents the manipulation of "energy" (i.e., physical objects and processes).

Figure 2.10 Anderson's system management matrix. (*After:* [48].)

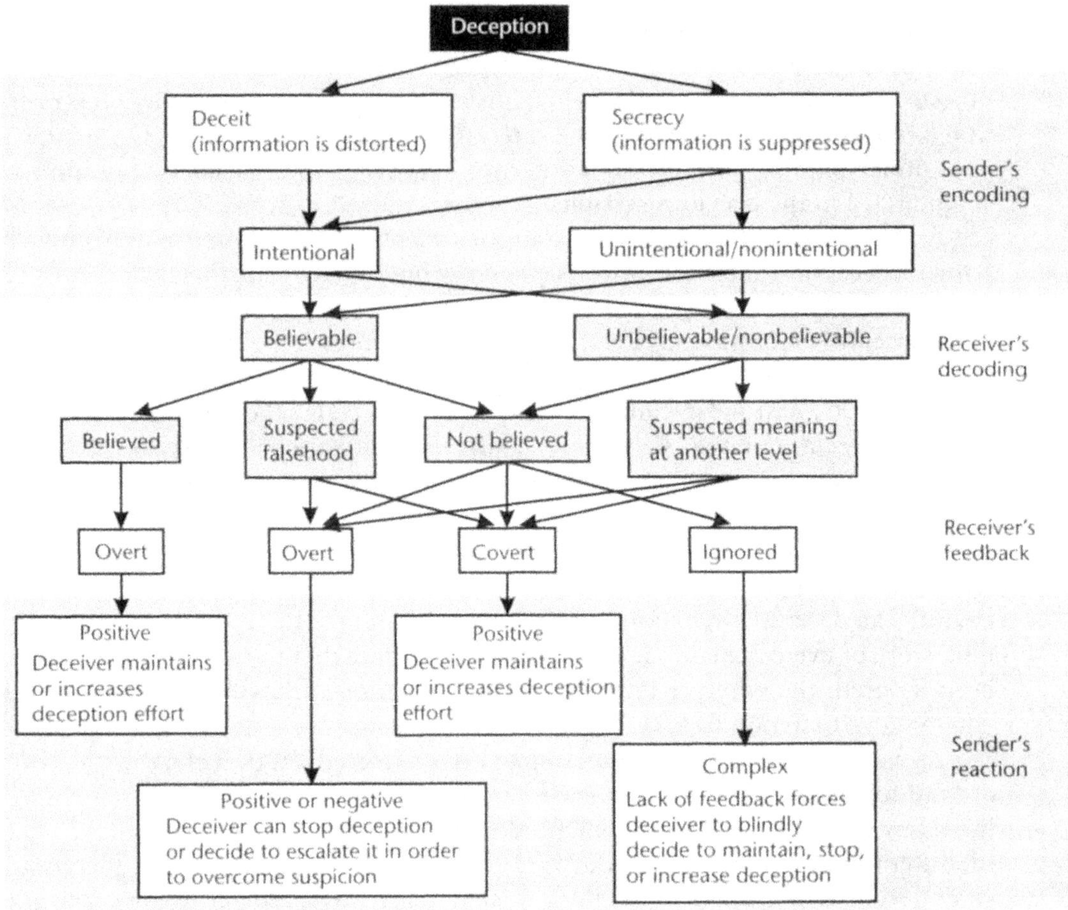

Figure 2.11 Anderson's deception typology. (*After:* [48].)

mystics, soothsayers, and diviners, did not pretend to have supernatural powers." The art of magic is ancient; its literature goes back to some of the earliest documents and inscriptions found by archaeologists. In *The Illustrated History of Magic*, Milbourne Christopher relates that the first-known written account of a magic performance is found in the Westcar papyrus (currently at the State Museum in Berlin) [51]. This papyrus describes a command performance of the magician Dedi for the pharaoh Cheops. Even earlier is a drawing (made around 2500 B.C.) on a wall of a burial chamber in Beni Hasan, Egypt. This drawing is commonly interpreted as depicting a magician performing the cup-and-ball trick for a spectator, although other researchers differ with this interpretation [52]. In addition, scroll paintings show that Chinese magicians were practicing their craft at least 2,000 ago. The first known book on practical magic, *La Première Partie des Subtitles et Plaisantes Inventions*, was published in France in 1584, and shortly thereafter *The Discoverie of Witchcraft* was published in England by Reginald Scot. Scot's book was intended to counteract the witch-hunting craze sweeping Europe and describes a wide variety of conjuring tricks and is still in print [53]. Since that time hundreds if not thousands of books have been written on the art of magic.

But what is a magic trick, and how does it differ from what we call deception? A magic trick consists of an *effect* and one or more *methods* for producing the effect. Lamont and Wiseman [54] describe a conjuring effect as "...what the spectator sees, and includes an event that the spectator regards as incompatible with his view of how the world works." This is what makes magic different from deception. Although both deception and magic are a form of storytelling, in magic the story line leads to amazing, impossible events. Objects appear or disappear. Beautiful women float in the air or are transformed into tigers or are sawed in half. Magicians walk through walls or escape from diabolical apparatus. In deception, however, the story line leads eventually to unexpected, but still real, events (e.g., the German's blitzkrieg through the Ardennes), or, in some deceptions, the victim is totally unaware that he has been deceived. For example, Ferdinand Waldo Demara, the Great Imposter, convincingly fooled many people who never guessed that he was, at various times, a physician, a Ph.D. in psychology, a schoolteacher, and other personas.

There are probably thousands of effects and methods to be found in books and articles about magic. Numerous authors have attempted to categorize this information and have produced taxonomies ranging from one that has only six general categories to another that describes 13 types of effects and 48 methods. In *Hiding the Elephant* [55], Jim Steinmeyer describes 10 categories of effects [56], while Lamont and Wiseman [57] present a classification system with nine effects and describe the methods generally used to produce each effect (see Figure 2.12).

Like the methods of strategic deception, the methods described in Figure 2.12 can be categorized either as dissimulation or simulation with dissimulation playing the dominant role. Dissimulation in magic primarily takes two forms. The first is concealment. Steinmeyer writes [58]: "Conjuring has always been based on techniques of concealment. That's why sleight of hand was built on a foundation of 'palming,' the technical term for concealing a small object in the hand, and stage magic was based on containers with false bottoms, tables with false tops, trapdoors, thin wires or thread." Mirrors play a large role in magic and are used extensively to make objects, people, and apparatus invisible from the spectators. The second form of dissimulation is secrecy. Most sophisticated methods of magic are the closely guarded secrets of the magician that created them. Magicians combine this secrecy with the average individual's lack of both basic scientific and conjuring knowledge to conceal the methods being used to create the effect. Simulation also has a role in magic but seems to mainly take the form of duplicate or disguised objects.

Although concealment forms the basis of most methods, it is misdirection that is absolutely essential to performance magic. Lamont and Wiseman [59] define misdirection as "that which directs the audience towards the effect and away from the method." Their framework for understanding misdirection is shown in Figure 2.13 and the rest of this section will focus on the concepts it contains.

Lamont and Wiseman divide misdirection into two broad categories. In the first, physical misdirection, the magician aims to control the spectator's attention. In the second, psychological misdirection, the magician aims to shape what the spectator thinks is occurring by controlling his suspicions.

Physical misdirection depends on the fact that although our eyes capture tens of millions of bits of information each second that our eyes are open, we selectively

Effect	Description	Typical methods
Appearance	An object appears where it was not.	• Object was already there but was concealed. • Object was secretly put in position. • Object is not actually there but appears to be.
Vanish	An object disappears from where it was.	• Object was not there but appeared to be there. • Object was secretly removed. • Object is still there but concealed.
Transposition	An object changes position in space.	• Object appeared to be at A but was already at B. • Object is still at A but appears to be at B. • Object was secretly moved from A to B. • A duplicate object was used.
Transformation	An object changes form (size, shape, a nd so on).	• Object A was secretly switched for B. • Object B was already there but disguised as A. • Object A is still there but is disguised as B.
Penetration	One object appears to pass through another.	• Employs techniques similar to transpositions and restorations.
Restoration	An object is damaged and then restored to its original condition.	• The object was not really damaged. • The object was not really restored. • A duplicate object was used.
Extraordinary feats	The appearance of extraordinary mental or physical abilities.	• May be faked using techniques relevant to other effects. • May rely in whole or in part on obscure scientific knowledge.
Telekinesis	The apparent ability to control the movement of objects without physical contact.	• Action caused by external force • Action caused by internal force • Action did not take place but appeared to.
Extrasensory perception (ESP)	The appearance of clairvoyance, telepathy, precognition, or mental control.	• Forcing information • Discovering unknown information (e.g., glimpses, cold reading, circumventing blindfolds, and so on) • Revealing information as if known

Figure 2.12 Conjuring effects and methods. (*After:* [54].)

attend to only a minute portion of it and effectively discard the rest [60]. The cognitive psychology term for this is *change blindness*. Magicians exploit change blindness as well as another phenomenon called *inattentional blindness* to distract the audience (i.e., to misdirect their attention) [61].

As Figure 2.13 shows, physically directing the spectator's attention can be done using *passive* or *active* methods. Passive methods rely on the fact that our attention is naturally drawn to an area when certain conditions exist. Lamont and Wiseman [62] define active methods as "the creation of primary and secondary interest through social interaction."

Lamont and Wiseman describe three categories of conditions that contribute to passive physical misdirection. The first of these conditions is *novelty*. Nothing is more novel than something new in the environment and it almost always attracts our attention. We also direct more attention towards unfamiliar objects in the environment than familiar ones. In addition, sudden sounds or showmanship techniques like a change of pace or more intense facial expressions also attract our attention. *Movement* is the second condition that attracts attention. The moving hand in a

<table>
<tr><th colspan="4">Misdirection</th></tr>
<tr><th colspan="2">Physical</th><th colspan="2">Psychological</th></tr>
<tr><td>Directing *where* the spectator is looking</td><td>Directing *when* the spectator is looking</td><td>Reducing suspicion</td><td>Diverting suspicion</td></tr>
<tr><td>*Passive*—the use of natural conditions of primary and secondary interest:
-Novelty
-Movement
-Contrast</td><td>*Reducing attention at the moment of method:*
-Outside the effect
-Inside the effect</td><td rowspan="2">• Naturalness
–Consistency
–Necessity
• Justification
–Familiarization
–Ruse
• Conviction
–Charisma
–Self-conviction
–Reinforcement</td><td rowspan="2">• False solutions
• False expectations</td></tr>
<tr><td>*Active*–the creation of areas of primary and secondary interest using:
-Eyes
-Voice
-Body language
-External source of diversion</td><td>*Increasing attention at the moment of magic:*
-Separating the moments of effect and method
-Reinforcing the moment of effect</td></tr>
</table>

Figure 2.13 Lamont-Wiseman misdirection framework.

sleight of hand trick attracts more attention than the stationary hand. Large or rapid movements also attract more attention than slow, subtle ones. Coordinated movement forces the spectator to divide his attention between the two, thereby reducing the attention that is given to each individual movement. Actions that begin almost simultaneously are also an opportunity for misdirection. In these cases, the movement that begins first will normally attract the spectators' attention. This effect can be so strong that properly coordinated movement will result in secondary movements going absolutely unnoticed (change blindness again). The third condition is *contrast*, that is, any action, object, or event that is perceived as different from the overall background environment. Bright colors against a drab background will attract our attention as will a different colored object among a group that is all the same color, for example, a dime among several pennies. A misaligned object in a line of similar objects will also stand out and attract attention.

The active form of directing the spectator's attention relies on the magician's social interaction with the audience. The most common way for a magician to direct the spectator's attention is to establish eye contact with the person and then look in the direction that he wants the spectator to look, say at a chessboard on a table. The magician also uses his voice, his "patter," to direct the spectator's attention. This patter can be used to reinforce other forms of misdirection (e.g., the magician can mention the chessboard on the table while looking at it), or it can be a means for directing the spectator's attention by itself. For example, the magician may address the spectator by name and ask a question such as "Ed, do you play chess? Would you pick up the white king, please?" The spectator's attention will usually be drawn first to the magician's face and then to the chessboard. An accomplished magician can do just about anything during that time. Body language and body contact are another way for directing a person's attention. Lamont and Wiseman note that increased body tension attracts attention while relaxation tends to relax attention. Pickpockets often use body contact as a distraction and a number of magicians use this means as well.

Magicians also take advantage of the fact that our attention level is not constant, it fluctuates over time. The magician takes advantage of this phenomenon in order to direct *when* the spectator directs his attention to something. In magic this means either reducing attention at the moment of method or to increase attention at the moment of the effect. The primary way of reducing attention outside of the effect is to make the spectator think that the trick has not yet begun or that it has already ended. Reducing attention inside the effect can be done in several ways. Repetition, confusion, or tedium all will reduce someone's attention. Another method is the "off-beat," a single moment of relaxed attention. A well-timed joke or "accident" produces a small surprise and results in a momentary relaxation of attention that allows the magician to execute a method. Increasing attention, on the other hand, allows the magician to separate the moment of effect from the moment of the method thereby preventing the spectator from linking the two.

The essence of physical misdirection is directing what the spectator perceives by controlling his attention. However, controlling perception is not enough to make the magic act work convincingly; Lamont and Wiseman assert that the magician must also control the spectator's suspicions either by reducing or diverting them. The audience's suspicions can be raised in any number of ways. Any irregular actions or behaviors, unnatural movements, and poor or obvious physical misdirection can all create suspicion in the mind of the observer. Since we assume that magicians really don't rely on supernatural magic to achieve their effects, they must use methods that would not be necessary if supernatural magic really did exist (e.g., mirrors, trap doors, and sleight-of-hand). These methods rely on making the apparatus and actions that make up these methods seem completely normal, and making these methods normal means reducing suspicion.

Lamont and Wiseman propose three methods for reducing suspicion in the mind of the observer. The first method is by "maximizing naturalness" where naturalness is characterized by consistency and necessity. Actions and events appear natural to the spectator when they are consistent with the spectator's preconceptions about the real world. Steinmeyer gives an excellent example in *Hiding the Elephant* [63]:

> Our preconceptions include the things that catch our attention and the things we ignore. For example, there are brown paper bags. Most of us have seen a bag boy at a supermarket pick up a bag, snap it in the air with a "crack" so that it opens, and drop it flat on the tabletop, ready to receive groceries. I can depend on the sound and the gesture of opening the bag to suggest that the bag is empty. Every bag handled in that way is empty. Experts in handling bags open empty bags in precisely that manner.

Steinmeyer's example is a way of reducing suspicion through naturalness through both consistency and necessity. Opening a bag in that manner is consistent with our experiences at the supermarket, and it is an accepted necessary action if one wants to open a brown paper bag. Of course, Steinmeyer observes that this method of opening a bag would be suspicious to someone from another culture that did not use brown paper bags and could also be considered suspicious in our own culture where plastic bags are becoming more and more common.

The second method of reducing suspicion is by making the unnatural appear to be natural (i.e., the magician's actions seem justified). This can be done through familiarization or by means of a ruse. Familiarization simply makes the inconsistent consistent. A good example is passing a coin back and forth from hand to hand before performing a false transfer. This familiarizes the observer with the action of the false transfer method so that when it is done it appears normal. Lamont and Wiseman point out that suspicions about an unfamiliar prop or apparatus can be reduced by familiarization. The magician takes some time to demonstrate an apparatus (e.g., using the guillotine to chop a cabbage in half) or to explain its purpose in order to justify its use. Ruses in magic are unnecessary actions that are made to appear necessary. The old "magic dust" ruse is one example. The magician tells the spectator that the magic dust is "necessary" for the trick to work and the ruse allows the magician to place one hand out of sight momentarily in order to bring out the dust.

The third method of reducing suspicion is to raise the spectator's conviction regarding the effect. If the effect is pulling a rabbit out of an empty hat, the spectator's conviction that the hat is empty must be maximized if his suspicions are to be reduced. Conviction can be raised in three ways. The first way is the charisma of the magician himself. If the magician is both authoritative (due to perceived competence) and likable, the magician can more easily direct the spectator towards the effect and reduce suspicion regarding the method. Likeability is especially important because the audience then wants the magician to succeed and their attention and suspicion become easier to control. The second way to raise conviction is the conviction of the magician himself. If the magician appears convinced, the audience is less likely to be suspicious of the method. Levant and Wiseman as well as Steinmeyer quote the famous magician Jean Robert-Houdin that a magician is just "an actor playing the part of a magician." Their use of the quotation means that it is more difficult for a participant to analyze a magic trick than it is for a mere observer. Turning the spectator into a participant requires acting ability. If the magician is doing his job as an actor, he can engage the audience at the emotional level and they become involved in the event and not just observe it [64].

The final way of raising conviction is reinforcement, that is, reinforcing the spectator's belief about the situation in either a direct or indirect manner. Direct reinforcement is simply proof that a given situation is true (e.g., a spectator's suspicion that a coin is in the left hand can be removed by revealing that the coin is, indeed, in the left hand). Indirect reinforcement on the other hand involves a situation that implies that something is true. The magician uses verbal and nonverbal clues (say deliberately miscalling a card as he places it into the deck, which the spectator then corrects) to reinforce the spectator's beliefs (i.e., that the card the magician placed in the deck was really the card the spectator had chosen).

The final piece of the Lamont and Wiseman misdirection framework is diverting suspicion through the use of either false solutions or false expectations. A magician will often deliberately provoke the spectator's suspicion in a manner that will lead the person to believe he has solved the method: the false solution. Again, Lamont and Wiseman quote Robert-Houdin again in this regard: "[I]nduce the audience to attribute the effect produced to any cause rather than the real one." Creating false expectations by misrepresenting the effect to be produced can also divert the spectator's suspicions. Through a combination of verbal and nonverbal clues, the magician leads the spectator to expect one effect, which diverts his attention from the method used to produce the real effect. For example, the magician might set up a trick to select a card the spectator has chosen from a deck of cards. After searching for the card and failing to find it, the magician reveals that the card has been somewhere else.

The study of deception inevitably leads to the study of magic. Although their objectives differ, they are remarkably similar in many ways in their methods, effects, planning, and underlying principles. After all, it was Jasper Maskelyne of the last generation of famous Maskelyne magicians (his grandfather was John Nevil Maskelyne, known as "The Chief") who, with his "Crazy Gang" in a cordoned off area called Magic Valley, designed and built many of the deceptions used by the British in North Africa during World War II [65]. And, as we saw in Section 2.2.2, Barton Whaley used an empirical study of magic tricks to test his and Bell's hypotheses regarding the most effective pairings of dissimulation and simulation methods. In the next section we will examine theses similarities, as well as differences, in our search for a set of fundamental principles of deception that will guide our search for similar principles of counterdeception.

2.7 Searching for Common Themes

It should be clear by now that although there seems to be general agreement in the deception research community on some topics, considerable diversity exists with regard to the structure and vocabulary of deception. There are theories, structures, principles, frameworks, taxonomies, and typologies, all of which attempt to explain deception. All are similar and yet different. A plethora of terms such as camouflage, dazzling, disinformation, masking, and mimicking, as well as decoys, diversions, and ruses are used to describe deception techniques, methods, and effects. Is there any way to sort out all these ideas and concepts? We think the answer is yes and we propose to use a framework of our own in which to place the various concepts summarized in the previous sections and arrive at a set of common themes. These themes can then be used to uncover the fundamental principles of deception that will eventually lead us to a set of corresponding principles of counterdeception.

The framework we propose to use is loosely based on a three-level hierarchy of information described by Waltz in *Information Warfare Principles and Operations* [66]. In this hierarchy, information is a concept that encompasses three levels of abstraction. The lowest level is *data*, which are the individual observations and measurements produced by human communications or physical processes. The next level is *information*, which consists of sets of data that have been placed into context, indexed, and organized. When information has been analyzed and understood, it becomes *knowledge* where it can provide explanations for the data and the processes or behaviors being observed. Knowledge can be applied to implement plans or take action in order to achieve specific goals or end states. Decision-making is basically effectively applied knowledge. This hierarchy of data, information, and knowledge can be discerned in nearly all of the deception research we reviewed earlier in this chapter.

All of the authors we have reviewed have, in one form or another, attempted to describe the deception process. In his original study, Whaley described a process that went something like this: design plans that offer at least two plausible alternatives for the target to deal with, and use stratagem in the form of ruses (diversions, camouflage, and disinformation) to present these alternatives to the target via multiple communications channels in such a manner that the wrong alternative is the one most plausible to the target. Later, Daniel and Herbig described a deception process based on systems theory (see Figure 2.3) that adds a number of steps describing what happens on the target's side of the process as well a feedback loop from the target by which the deceiver can observe the target's reactions to the deception plan. Whaley's early process later evolved into a more detailed one (see Figure 2.5) that emphasizes the planning phase of the deception operation. Haswell, Dewar, and Latimer then described the basic principles they gleaned from historical analysis that apply to running successful deception operations. If we incorporate the concepts described by Handel and Smith, we can create a generalized deception cycle and place it into the context of our information hierarchy (see Figure 2.14). In

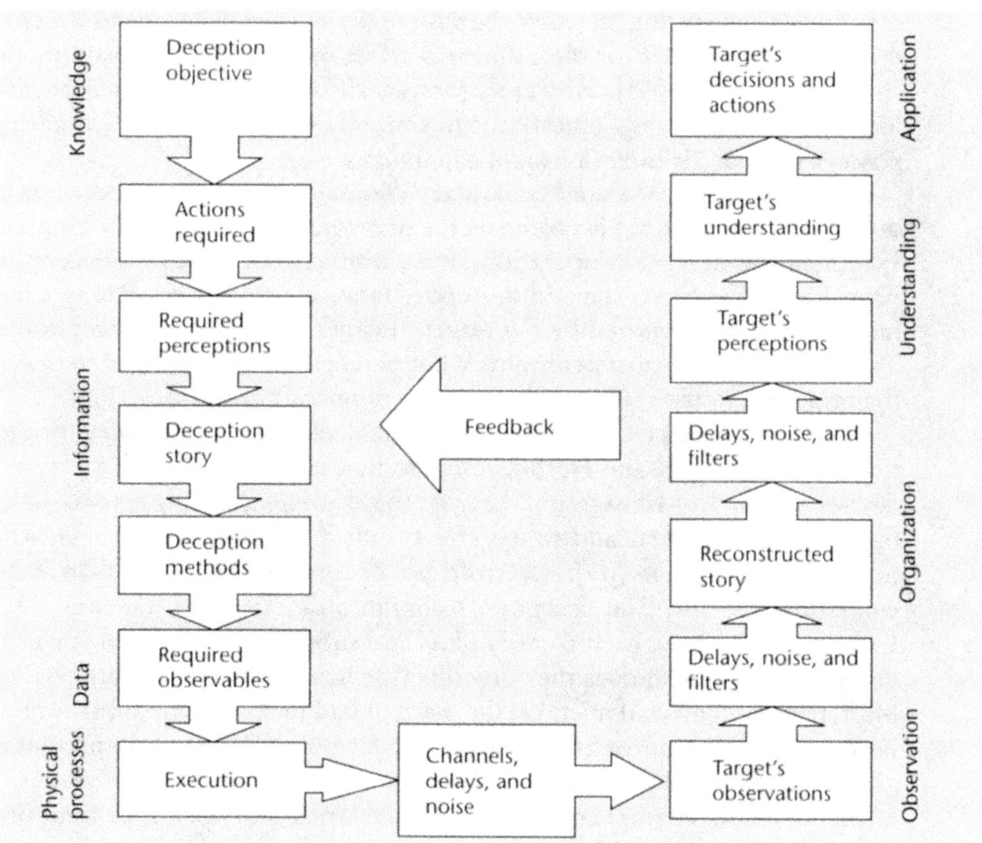

Figure 2.14 Generalized deception cycle.

this cycle, the deceiver transforms knowledge into information and then into data, whereas the target transforms data into information and finally back into knowledge. The goal of the deceiver, of course, is to see that the process distorts the target's knowledge.

This cycle begins with another theme common to all the research we have reviewed: the *deception objective*. In wartime, achieving strategic or tactical surprise has been the objective of nearly every military commander since Sun Tzu and the connection between deception and surprise is a strong one. Whaley found 73% of the strategic operations and 53% of the tactical operations he examined involved both surprise and deception, and most other authors writing about military deception cite surprise as the objective of deception. Nevertheless, surprise is not the only objective. Both the strategic deception and scientific literature describe the objective of deception in terms of competitive advantage.

You find deception in nearly any situation you can think of—nature, business, politics, or personal relationships—anywhere it might provide someone, or something, an edge. In terms of national security however, competitive advantage is best expressed by Handel [67]: "In the final analysis, all types of deception operations can be said to be directed at misleading, misinforming, or confusing an opponent on only two basic categories of information. The first is to deceive him concerning one's own *intentions*; the second is to deceive him concerning one's own *capabilities*." The competitive advantage to be gained is realized in basically three ways: a deceiver (1) intends to secretly grow in strength in order to achieve surprise, (2) exaggerates his capabilities, appearing stronger than he really is in order to deter an enemy, gain prestige and influence, or bluff during a crisis, or (3) seek blackmail or concessions from an adversary [68]. However, putting all of this in terms of our information hierarchy, the deceiver's objective is to conceal or exaggerate the *knowledge* that he possesses about his intentions and capabilities.

Once the political leader or military commander makes the decision to employ deception in pursuit of his objective, the organizations responsible for planning and executing the deception operation swing into action. Whaley's deception process provides the next two steps in our cycle. First, the deception planners must determine the *actions required* by the target in order to realize the deception objective. Then, the planners must determine what perceptions are required in order to make the target act in the required manner: the *required perceptions*.

Creating these perceptions requires a plausible *deception story*. In their deception process, Daniel and Herbig compare this step to the job of a playwright who devises a story and seeks to put it across to the audience using actors, dialogue, costumes, props, scenery, and sound effects, all of which must be presented with the proper coordination [69]. In strategic deception, the story can take several well-known forms. The deception techniques described by Haswell, Dewar, and Latimer can be thought of as story plots and subplots available for use in a strategic deception. The techniques they describe (the lure, the repetitive process, the double bluff, the unintentional mistake, the piece of bad luck, and the substitution) have all been used at one time or another to construct a plausible story to present to the target. Just think of Major Martin in *The Man Who Never Was* (the piece of bad-luck technique) as an example of a subplot in the larger story being written for presentation to the Germans in Operation Husky: the invasion of Sicily.

In our information hierarchy framework, these three steps—identifying the actions required by the target, determining the perceptions that will induce the target to take these actions, and developing the deception story that will lead the target to these perceptions—represent the transformation of knowledge (about the target and the deceiver's own capabilities) into information (a story) that will be presented to an audience: the target's military, intelligence, and diplomatic analysts and decision-makers.

Once the deception story has been developed and approved, the deception planners can begin to identify the *deception methods* to be used to generate the data, the *required observables* that support the deception story. We face a challenge, however, when dealing with the concept of deception methods. As we noted in the introduction to this section, all the authors have their own ideas, concepts, and terminology that they use when discussing how deception is implemented. In his 1969 book, Whaley talked about stratagem being implemented by three ruses consisting of diversions, camouflage, and disinformation. Later, he constructs a structure of deception consisting of dissimulation and simulation and their associated subcategories of masking, repackaging, dazzling, mimicking, inventing, and decoying. Daniel and Herbig use the terms cover, lying, and artifice when describing how deception is implemented. Even though Gerwehr and Glenn use the phrase "effect sought" in their framework, the detailed descriptions for some of the effects are more akin to methods of deception (i.e., masking, decoys, camouflage, signal reduction, and transmitting false signals). Handel talks about "passive" and "active" deception consisting of secrecy, camouflage, misleading, misinforming, and confusing. Finally, in a biological context, Smith [70, 71] states that, "All signalers withhold information" and "...all misleading signaling depends on mimicry." Given this diversity in ideas and terminology, just what are deception methods?

We think the answer can be found in the work of another author we reviewed. We believe that the matrix described by Myrdene Anderson in Figure 2.10 provides the means for organizing the great diversity of ideas regarding deception methods into an easy-to-understand framework. Anderson's matrix is a method for describing ways to reveal or conceal either fact or fiction. Using her matrix as the basis for organizing deception methods helps us to resolve some of the confusion that exists due to overlapping concepts and vocabulary. The deception methods matrix shown in Figure 2.15 consists of four quadrants. Like Anderson's original matrix, the two columns represent the concepts of revealing or concealing something and the rows represent fact and fiction. Each quadrant of the matrix is further divided into two categories: information and physical processes (equivalent to Anderson's "energy").

First, note that two of the quadrants are black and two are white. The two black quadrants correspond to the concepts of dissimulation and simulation. Note that most of the concepts that other authors have called methods, effects, and ruses fall into these two black quadrants. We will come back to these quadrants in a just moment, but first, examine the white, upper left quadrant. This quadrant represents revealing facts—information that is true or events and processes that actually occur. Most of the emphasis, nearly all, in fact, in the deception literature is on dissimulation and simulation; however, the revelation of facts is just as important to deception as is concealing facts or revealing fiction. Several of the authors we have

<table>
<tr>
<td>Reveal facts

• Information:
• Release true information that benefits the deceiver (e.g., the double bluff ruse).
• Physical:
• Display real equipment or facilities (e.g., in order to build a source's credibility).</td>
<td>Conceal facts (dissimulation)
• Information:
• Secrecy (i.e., security clearance programs, physical security, and INFOSEC)
• Withholding information to create a false or misleading impression
• Physical:
• Camouflage, concealment, signal reduction (e.g., stealth designs and materials, spread spectrum communications), disguises, dazzling
• Nonverbal deceit</td>
</tr>
<tr>
<td>Reveal fiction (simulation)
• Information:
• Disinformation
• Includes lying: providing information known to be untrue
• Dazzling (e.g., large volumes of communications)
• Physical:
•Decoys, diversions (feints and demonstrations), duplicates, disguises, dummy positions, equipment, and facilities
• Nonverbal deceit</td>
<td>Conceal fiction

• Information:
• Suppress a lie.
• Physical:
• Hide a sham.</td>
</tr>
</table>

Figure 2.15 The deception methods matrix.

reviewed make this point quite forcefully. For example, Masterman states [72], "Broadly speaking, then, this particular principle amounts to little more than the insistence on the prime necessity for truth whenever truth is possible. A lie when it is needed will only be believed if it rests on a firm foundation of previous truth." Handel also refers to role of the truth in deception several times. In one example he states [73], "Since the deceiver intends to present noise as highly trustworthy information, most successful uses of stratagem are based on the supply of largely accurate and verifiable data to the adversary." Finally, when referring to deception in humans and animals, Mitchell states [74], "All deception works within the context of honesty." We will return to this topic later in Section 2.3.

Now, let's turn our attention back to the two black quadrants representing concealing facts (dissimulation) and revealing fiction (simulation). Starting with concealing facts we find that nearly all authors agree that secrecy is one of the major underpinnings of deception. Secrecy seeks to deny the target factual information about the deceiver's intentions, capabilities, and, of course, the deception plan itself. Keeping information secret depends on security clearance programs, espionage laws, and information security concepts such as cryptography and steganography. Keeping physical objects and processes secret involves camouflage, concealment (e.g., underground facilities in North Korea and mirrors and secret compartments in stage magic), signal reduction techniques (e.g., stealth designs/materials and spread spectrum communications in defense or the darkened wires used to support a levitation act in magic), and physical security measures such as fences, alarms, locks and safes, armed guards, and secure facilities. In face-to-face interactions, nonverbal deceit (minimizing or neutralizing facial expressions and body language) represents another physical means of concealing facts from another person. Overall, the term *masking* is an appropriate way of describing all these methods for concealing facts.

The black quadrant in the lower left of Figure 2.15 represents revealing fiction—something that has been invented but is not true. This quadrant corresponds to the concept of simulation: showing the false. The general term disinformation addresses the informational aspects of revealing fictional information. Disinformation (or *dezinformatsiya* in Russian deception terminology) deals with the dissemination of false or misleading information. Lying, deliberately providing information known to be untrue is, of course, the everyday term for the concept. Any communication channel that transmits true information can be used to transmit disinformation. Fictional physical objects and processes are created using methods that are familiar themes in the work we have reviewed. Decoys, diversions (feints and demonstrations), forgeries, doubles, and dummies (dummy positions, equipments, and facilities) are all methods of revealing fictional (false) physical objects and processes to the target. There is simulation in face-to-face interactions too, such as exaggerating one's emotions or substituting one facial expression for another (e.g., when a smile isn't a smile). The term *mimicking* is an appropriate way of generally describing all these methods for revealing the false.

But where does dazzling as a deception method fit in? Whaley categorizes it as a dissimulation method [75]: "Dazzling hides the real by confusing." This is reasonable if the intent is to hide the true nature of an object, the classic example being the dazzle patterns painted on ships during World War I and World War II. On the other hand, confusion as an effect can also be achieved other ways. Gerwehr and Glen define confusion as, "Raising the noise level in order to create uncertainty or paralyze the target's perceptual capabilities." They cite voluminous communications traffic as an example, which would suggest that dazzling could also be categorized as a disinformation method. In fact, Whaley in his 1969 study suggests that disinformation can be used to overload the target's communication and analysis systems during critical periods causing delays and confusion. For this reason we choose to include dazzling as a method in both quadrants, used either to conceal facts (the precise shape, course, and speed of a ship at sea) or reveal a fiction (fictional levels of communications traffic).

Note that we have not included Whaley's "inventing" and "repackaging" categories in our matrix. This is because it seems to us that both inventing and repackaging are identical to mimicking. Whaley's own examples of inventing and repackaging tend to support this conclusion. One of Whaley's examples for inventing states [76], "Generals create rubber tanks, wooden guns, canvas aircraft, and dummy radio traffic; admirals create dummy warships. Major Frederick Funston dressed his Philippino troops in Moro costume to capture their leader, Aguinaldo in 1901." Another example for repackaging includes [75], "An admiral disguises a warship as a harmless freighter." The rubber tanks, wooden guns, and freighter disguised as a warship are all examples of creating one object that *mimics* another.

The meaning of the last quadrant, concealing fiction, is not as clear-cut as the other three. Anderson uses the terms "suppress a lie" and "curb a sham" in her original figure; however, she does not clearly explain these concepts or give examples. More recently, she has suggested that concealing fiction is related to the concept of *spin* [Myrdene Anderson, personal communication, July 24, 2005]. Equivocal statements from spin doctors are often subject to two or more interpretations and are usually intended to mislead or confuse. Such statements make it possible to avoid revealing that one is lying (suppress a lie) or that one's actions are a hoax (curb a sham). A possible example is the role dual use facilities play in deception. Such facilities make it possible to make equivocal statements like: "Our facilities are part of a nuclear power program." If the sole purpose of such a facility was to develop nuclear weapons, then the statement would be a lie (revealing fiction), but since it can be used to create electricity *and* be used in a weapons development program, the statement avoids telling the outright lie.

Let's now return to the generalized deception cycle and look at the next step: *required observables*. The choice of deception methods determines the observables that will be presented to the target when the deception plan is executed. These observables represent the transition from information to data in our framework. Deception methods aimed at simulation produce physical objects or phenomena that subsequently produce detectable observables such as mass, shape, volume, temperature, motion, reflectivity, amplitude, frequency, and other attributes. We generally know these objects and phenomena in forms such as dummy aircraft and buildings on a decoy airfield, forged documents, verbal and text messages from spies, radar reflectors or chaff, and electronic communications. On the other hand, deception methods aimed at dissimulation seek to deny the target access to observables (e.g., secrecy, concealment, and cryptography) or to reduce or suppress them (e.g., camouflage, stealth materials, and low-probability-of-intercept signals).

Another theme common to all of our authors is that deception requires a means by which the deception story's observables can be presented to the target. This is the channels, delays, and noise box in our deception cycle. Channels are the means by which the deceiver makes the observables (data) available to the target. Channels can exploit all five of our senses—sight, hearing, smell, taste, and touch—and as Haswell points out [77], " It is an axiom of deception that as many as possible of these channels should be used, provided they are complementary and confirmatory. A dubious piece of information is no longer so questionable if other evidence on other channels appears to support it." Common channels used in deception operations include the target's reconnaissance systems (imaging, nonimaging, and electronic intercept systems), diplomats, spies, agents-of-influence, newspapers, radio, and television, as well as nearly any other method that one can imagine. All channels are subject to delays and noise as well and distort the data being transmitted to the target. For example, a false document meant to confirm observations from a reconnaissance aircraft might be delayed in transit because the agent selected to pass the document to the target misses a meeting with the target's case officer, or the target's translator translates an article placed in a newspaper incorrectly. As we shall see, the channels used and their associated delays and noise affect the target's ability to make sense of the observables; that is, to turn data back into information.

Once the deceiver begins to fill the selected channels with data, it is up to the target's military, diplomatic, and intelligence channel monitors to detect it. This leads us to the next step in our process: the *target's observations*. As Whaley aptly observed [78], "The key question is: 'Is anybody listening?'" The deceiver's plan depends on the target picking up the various pieces of data that support the deception story, but what data is actually collected by the target depends on the answers to a wide variety of questions: Are the target's sensors able to detect the observables? Is a target sensor actually pointed at the right place at the right time to observe what the deceiver wants observed? What priorities affect the target's collection efforts? How much data does the target collect? What channels are considered to be more credible than others? The output of this step in the process becomes the raw material for the target's analytical processes and determines both the target's subsequent perceptions and actions.

The next overarching theme that we found in our review of the deception literature is that a successful deception targets the target's perceptions in ways favorable to the deceiver. Common effects described include: an increase or decrease in the target's perceived ambiguity (Daniel and Herbig's A- and M-Type deceptions), the creation of false expectations or solutions in the mind of the target (e.g., Whaley's alternative objectives), directing or diverting the target's attention (Whaley, Handel, and Gerwehr and Glenn), confusion (Gerwehr and Glenn), and, of course, surprise (Whaley, Handel, and most others). Also, as we saw in Section 2.6, increasing or decreasing the target's suspicions is also an effect of the deception. All of these effects are the results of the processes shown on the right-hand side of Figure 2.14—the reconstructed story, the target's perceptions, and, eventually, the target's understanding—each of which is part of the process of organizing data, the target's observations, back into information. Complicating this process are additional delays, noise, and filters that affect each step.

The first step towards achieving the desired effect on the target is the target's reconstruction of the deception story developed by the deceiver. Obviously, this is not as easy as it sounds. Daniel and Herbig extend their playwright analogy by describing three ways that the story reconstruction process can be distorted. First, they point out [69]: "...the deceiver cannot assume that his audience is attending only to his production." This means that the target's attention is usually divided among any number of other situations or items of interest, which affects how well the available data is analyzed. Second, what the target knows about any given situation is not restricted to the data being provided by the deceiver. As Daniel and Herbig state [69], "In other words, the deceiver is putting on a show but he does not fully control the number of actors on stage or all the lines being said." Third, it is more than likely that much of the data being provided to the target will simply not be picked up by the target (even if collected), and may be misinterpreted as well. Imagine trying to reconstruct the plot of a movie if you had to leave the theater every 15 minutes to watch another movie for 15 minutes, the director of the movie had no control over who appeared in the movie or the lines they spoke (some of which are badly translated from a foreign language), and several scenes of the movie are missing. It sounds hopeless, but as history has demonstrated, if the deception has been designed and executed properly, most of the data intended for the target will be detected, noticed, and organized by competent analysts into the important elements of the deception story (i.e., data, the observables made available to the target, are transformed into information).

This might be a good time to revisit just who is the target of the deception operation. Up to this point, the primary recipients of the real and false data produced by the deception operation have likely been the analysts working in the target's intelligence organizations. In most cases, they are the ones who will be finding the pieces

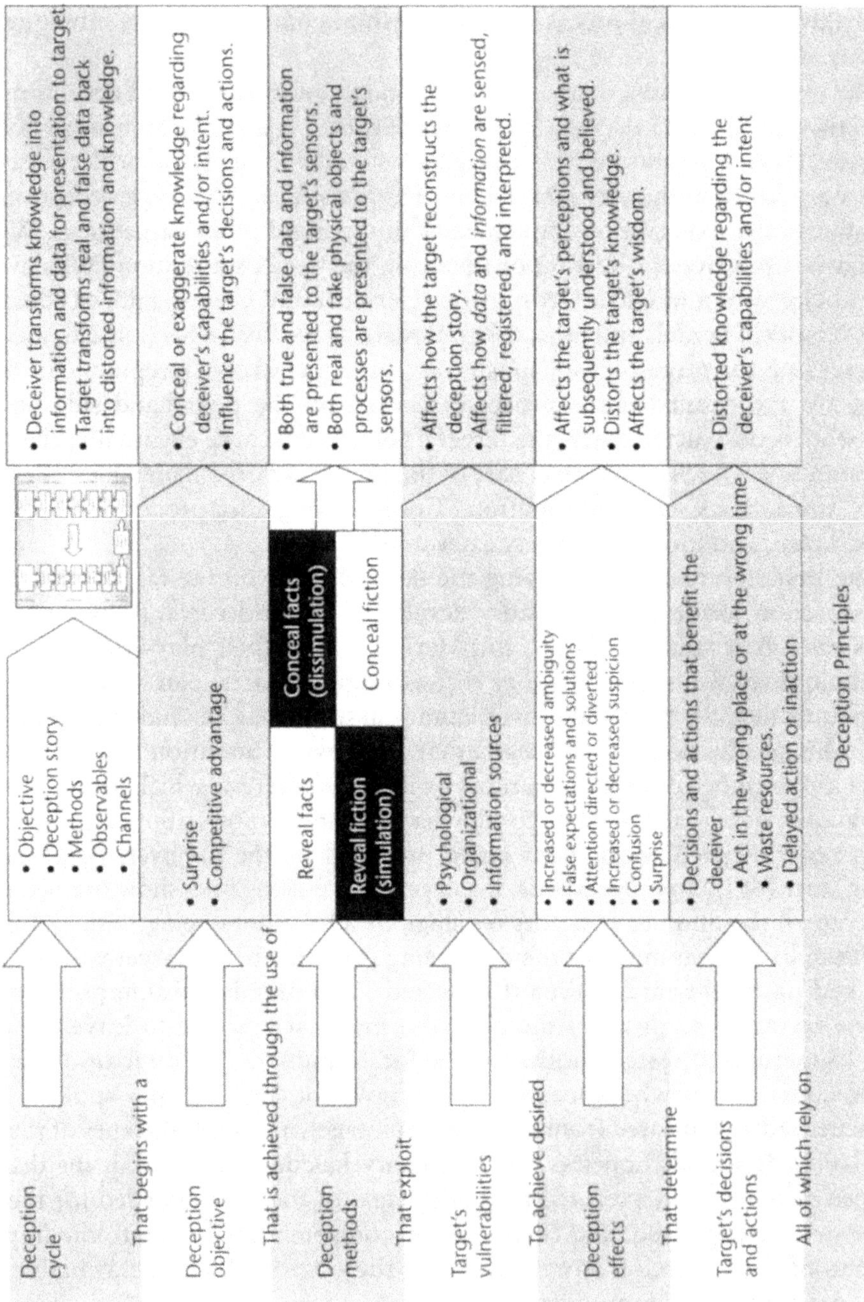

Figure 2.16 Summary of common themes in the deception literature.

of the puzzle and assembling them into a reconstruction of the deceiver's deception story. Along the way they also filter the data and introduce further delays and noise of their own, but remember, in strategic deception the target's political leaders and military commanders are the real targets of the deception. They are the ones whom the deception story is meant to influence; therefore, the next two steps in the process—*target's perceptions* and *target's understanding*—refer to the target's decision-makers.

Information regarding the reconstructed deception story makes its way up to the target's leadership and is subjected to further delays, noise, and filters as it passes through various information gatekeepers (refer back to Daniel and Herbig's process on the right in Figure 2.3). Ultimately the leadership forms their own perceptions (actually, misperceptions if the deception is working) of the information and incorporates the new information into their own understanding of the situation. It is at this point that the effects of the deception we described earlier begin to appear. Perhaps, as intended, the leadership's uncertainty about the situation begins to decrease and the deceiver's feedback sources show that they are latching on to the alternative suggested by the deception story, or perhaps their attention is diverted from the western front to the southern front. In effect, the target is transforming the information they are receiving into knowledge about their situation. This sets up the final step in the process, the *target's decisions and actions*.

It is at this step that all the real and false data presented to the target via multiple channels has been processed and the information incorporated into the knowledge on which the target bases his decisions and actions. Also, this step represents the last major theme of the research we reviewed, that is, the purpose of the deception is to induce the target to *act* in a manner that benefits the deceiver. As Hesketh notes [79], "In order to prove that a deception plan has achieved its purpose, it is not enough to show that it reached the enemy Intelligence and was accepted by them as true. It is also necessary to establish the fact that it influenced the actions of the commander and so changed the course of battle." There are probably countless ways for the target to act that will benefit the deceiver in some way depending on the situation; however, all of these actions can be grouped into three general categories:

- The target decides to act in the wrong place or at the wrong time.
- The target decides to act in a manner that wastes his resources.
- The target delays acting or fails to act at all.

An example of the first category is when the deception causes the target to concentrate his forces in the wrong place. The success of Operation Fortitude in keeping German forces concentrated near Pas de Calais, the expected invasion target, instead of Normandy, is one of the most obvious examples. The second category turns out to be one of Handel's forms of deception. In this case the deception causes the target to waste valuable resources (e.g., manpower, ammunition, fuel, weapons, or time) on unimportant or irrelevant targets or in the wrong direction. The British efforts during the Battle of Britain to decoy the German Luftwaffe away from real airfields and attack dummy targets, the Q- and K-sites, is a good example. The third category of desired target actions, or inaction in this case, can result when the target is surprised. Hitler and the German High Command's delay in ordering the German

15th Army from the Pas de Calais to Normandy is, again, a famous example, and delaying the German response was a major objective of Operation Fortitude South and Fortitude South II. In each of these categories, the target's distorted knowledge about the deceiver's capabilities and intent produces decisions and actions that play into the hands of the target.

Figure 2.16 is intended to summarize the common themes we have been found in our survey of various deception models. Each major theme is a row in the figure and we can see that the deception cycle begins with a clear deception objective. That objective is achieved through the use of deception methods that exploit the target's vulnerabilities. We will address these vulnerabilities in Chapter 3. The deception methods exploit the target's vulnerabilities to achieve the desired *deception effects*, which distort the target's perceptions, understanding, and beliefs about the situation. These deception effects ultimately determine the *target's decisions and actions*, and it is these decisions and actions that determine if the deception objective has been successfully achieved. Did the target act in the manner desired by the deceiver? Note that there is one more row at the bottom of Figure 2.16 and that all the other rows rely on this foundation: a set of basic deception principles. Section 2.8 will examine what we believe these principles to be.

2.8 Fundamental Principles of Deception: Truth, Denial, Deceit, and Misdirection

This chapter has been, so far, an overview of the study of deception in general with particular emphasis on those authors who have taken a theoretical approach to the study of deception or who have attempted to synthesize the basic principles that govern it. Despite considerable diversity in terminology, we were able to uncover several common themes that emerge from this sampling of the deception literature. Yet we are not quite done. What we plan to do in this section is to go one more step and further decompose the different theories, models, and themes we have examined in order to establish a set of fundamental principles of deception. We will use these principles in later chapters as a framework for understanding our own cognitive vulnerabilities to deception and to guide us in the development of a set of corresponding principles of counterdeception.

What do we mean by *principles of deception*? A fairly common definition of the word *principle* is that it is a basic truth, law, or assumption and is usually the basis for further reasoning. In the context of deception, we take this to mean that a principle is a fundamental truth upon which the various theories and models of deception *in general* are based. This is why in Section 2.2.3 we made the statement that the principles of deception described by Haswell, Dewar, and Latimer should be considered principles for guiding the planning and execution of deception *operations*, but not as principles for deception in general. Using the same reasoning, Mathtech's deception maxims can be viewed the same way.

So let us now turn our attention to the four fundamental principles that we believe form the foundation of deception theory in general. These principles are all related to how the target of deception acquires, registers, processes, and ultimately perceives data and information about the world (see Figure 2.17) and can be stated as follows:

1. *Truth:* All deception works within the context of what is true.
2. *Denial:* Denying the target access to the truth is the prerequisite to all deception.
3. *Deceit:* All deception requires deceit.
4. *Misdirection:* Deception depends on manipulating what the target registers.

2.8.1 Truth

Deception is the deliberate attempt to manipulate the perceptions of the target. The first of our four principles, *truth*, recognizes that, if deception is to work at all, there must be a foundation of accurate perceptions that can be manipulated. In other words, deception works because most of what we observe and experience in the real world is nondeceptive. Everything around us—houses, cars, people, trees, and animals—are all usually what they appear to be and act as we expect them to act. If a strange dog that is wagging its tail approaches you, your experiences tell you that you can be almost certain that the dog is friendly. If you are driving along and you are pulled over by a car with police markings and flashing lights, and a uniformed police officer with a badge steps out, you can be pretty sure that it is a real police officer and you are probably going to get a ticket. Perhaps you come home from work and find your spouse to be irritable and sarcastic. Later when you ask what is wrong, the response is: "I just don't want to talk about it." You will likely be correct if you interpret these signals as a sign that your spouse is angry with you. In almost all cases, things are what they appear to be.

This first principle of deception is paraphrased from one of Mitchell's "descriptive and explanatory principles," which states [74], "All deception works within the

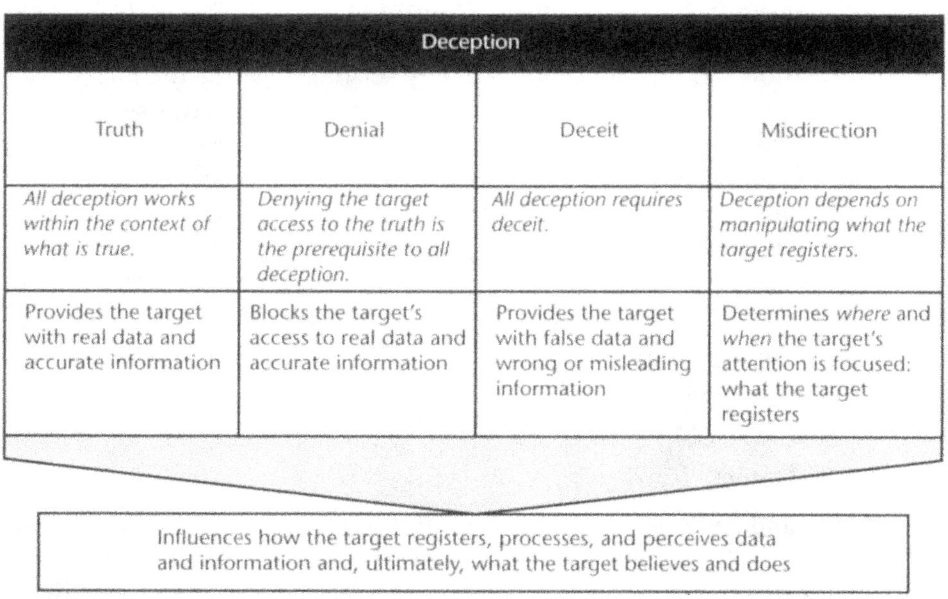

Figure 2.17 Fundamental principles of deception.

context of honesty." It is based on the concept of coadaptation [74], that is, "In the system to be exploited, the appearance or actions of one organism are commonly or functionally connected to a particular response by another organism. A deceiver can deceive a member of such a system because the victim expects a signal to have a particular result or, more generally, because the victim is designed to respond in a certain way to certain signs." An example from nature is the Fang blenny (*Plagiotremus rhinorhynchos*), which mimics the coloration of another species, the Cleaner wrasse (*Labroides dimidiatus*). Cleaner fish have coadapted with larger species that allow the cleaners to approach them in order to pick off parasites. The blenny's markings mimic the cleaner fish's markings and allow it to get in close enough to bite off chunks of flesh from its prey. Humans are preyed upon too in similar ways. Although it is uncommon, there have been incidents where criminals have dressed in a police uniform and used red or blue lights in attempts to pull over a victim driving alone at night. Unfortunately, this deception often works since the criminal knows his disguise in the form of a trusted authority figure is likely to provoke an automatic reaction by the victim even if it overrides the victim's common sense.

Putting this principle into the context of strategic deception, recall that the upper left quadrant of Figure 2.15 addressed releasing facts as a category of deception methods. Making real data or accurate information available to the target is often the most important part of a successful deception. Handel quotes David Mure in this regard [31], "Truths should make up at least 90% of the information fed to the enemy." Handel also provides four rules for providing the deception target real information [31]: "(1) whenever possible, supply the adversary with correct but low grade information, bits of gossip, and 'chicken-feed'; (2) feed him correct information that *he is known* to have already obtained *independently*; (3) pass on correct, important information that will arrive *too late* to be of any real use to him and will not have actual operational value; (4) finally, supply him with information that is actually important if the sacrifice will allow one to reap much greater future benefits *which could not otherwise* be obtained." Rules like these are meant to increase the target's confidence in his sources of information (e.g., recall Haswell and Latimer's principle of credibility described in Section 2.2.3) and help to reinforce the target's expectations and preconceptions. They set the stage for the target's acceptance of false information as if it were true. Handel summarizes this situation as a paradox [80]: "*The more one has a reputation for honesty—the easier it is to lie convincingly.* Even more concisely: *Honest people/states can deceive the best.*"

In summary, much of our day-to-day experience is in the context of real, not deceptive, objects and signals. These experiences form the foundations of our expectations and preconceptions about what is happening at any given moment and for our predictions of what might happen in the future. As we will see in the next chapter, our first principle of deception is related to a number of cognitive biases that make us vulnerable to deception.

2.8.2 Denial

Denial and deception (D&D) is now the nearly universal way for describing the act of strategic deception. Although *denial*, blocking the target's access to real data and accurate information, can be considered a stand-alone concept, it is, in reality, the linchpin of deception. It is no surprise then that our second principle of deception is mentioned in one way or another by nearly every author we have reviewed. With regard to deception in nature, Smith makes the role of denial in deceptive signaling between organisms quite clear when he states [81], "Yet, however much detail it provides, *no* signaling animal ever makes available *all* the information it has. All signalers withhold information." Frans De Waal studies chimpanzees and writes [82]: "Withholding of information about ones' knowledge, impulses or intentions is presumably the most widespread form of deception in primates." He cites an example of a chimpanzee that was able to successfully conceal any reaction at all to the fact he had discovered where some food had been hidden in the enclosure. The chimpanzee was able to maintain this control for over three hours until he calmly went to the spot to dig up and eat the hidden food. Denial plays a critical role in magic as well. Recall Steinmeyer's statement in Section 2.2.5 that conjuring is based on the techniques of concealment.

In strategic deception, every author that we reviewed in Sections 2.2.2 and 2.2.3 emphasizes how the principle of denial makes deception possible. Denial is referred to using terms such as "security," "secrecy," "cover," "dissimulation," "masking," or "passive deception," and yet many authors focus primarily on deception operations and their associated ruses and methods. Nevertheless, the success of a deception operation is ultimately dependent on concealing facts from the target (refer to the upper right quadrant of Figure 2.15). Handel makes this point clear when he writes [26], "Some experts view passive deception as inferior and not likely to succeed against any competent intelligence organization. As we have seen in the preceding text, this is not necessarily true. While measures of secrecy do not have the same aura of romance and intellectual excitement as that associated with active deception, they can frequently be as effective as other more elaborate operations. *Moreover, active types of deception are dependent upon the efficacy of the passive operation.*" Daniel and Herbig also reinforce this point by putting denial right at the center of their conceptual model of deception. They use the term *cover* and state [83], "Cover is at the center of deception because, no matter what his or her other goals, a deceiver wishes to protect the existence of some truth, be it knowledge of an already existing reality (e.g., the capabilities of a weapon) or an intended reality (such as the scenario for the weapon's use)." Denial is also a major component of Whaley's structure of deception (see Figure 2.4) appearing in the form of masking and he showed it to be employed in nearly two-thirds of the magic tricks he studied. Finally, denial in one form or another is cited as an important factor by all the other authors we examined. In the form of secrecy, it is part of the first noise barrier in Handel's signal and noise information flow model. Gerwehr and Glen use the term "masking" for it in their deception framework. Finally, denial in the general form security and "countersurveillance" appears in Jones, Haswell, Dewar, and Latimer.

Denial protects the deceiver's real capabilities and intentions and the results of denial alone can have serious consequences as shown in these examples [84, 85]:

- "For instance, the Japanese attack on Pearl Harbor was immediately preceded by an unexpected change in Japanese naval doctrine. In contrast to the usual cautious behavior of the Japanese military, large numbers of aircraft carriers were concentrated in one task force, despite the risk of the loss of up to a third of their entire carrier fleet in a single operation. This shift in naval doctrine was unknown to American intelligence, which continued to base its assumptions on the old Japanese naval doctrine of caution."

- "Israel intelligence was unaware of some important changes in Egyptian and Syrian military doctrine concerning control of the skies (or its negation) which, combined with lack of information on the performance of new antiaircraft weapons, caused a completely erroneous evaluation of the military capabilities and intentions of both countries."

Lacking access to all the facts, the target must make do with what few real signals he can obtain from the mass of data available and must subsequently rely on previous experience, preconceptions, and, as is often the case, wishful thinking in order to analyze the situation an develop a course of action. As we will see in the next section, denial creates the opportunity to manipulate the target's perceptions by offering the target something highly desirable: *information* that the target considers to be relevant and valuable to his needs and believes to be true.

2.8.3 Deceit

At first, our third principle, *all deception requires deceit*, seems banal. This is probably because the word deception is often defined in terms of the act of deceiving. But to put it another way, all deception requires *lying*. Lying involves knowingly making a false statement with the intent to deceive. The deceiver knows the content of the statement is a lie and uses the lie to deliberately deceive the victim. Without deliberate deceit, the target is only the victim of misperceptions due to misinformation and/or self-deception, not deception. As we learned in Section 2.2.4, deliberate deceit in nature is confined to organisms capable of Level 4 deception (refer to Figure 2.9), that is, certain primates and humans. Although there is considerable controversy with regard to deliberate deceit in primates, there is none whatsoever about its prevalence in humans. We all lie to each other and to ourselves. For example, Ford cites figures showing that 90% of Americans who were polled admitted they were deceitful about things like their true feelings, income, accomplishments, sex life, and age [86]. We lie to attract attention or impress others. We lie to avoid punishment or to preserve our self-esteem. We lie for personal gain or to hurt someone else. In some cases, we lie pathologically as in the case of *pseudologia fantastica* (usually characterized by fantastic descriptions of false events in one's life), and, in the case of strategic deception, nations lie to each other for competitive advantage.

Like the principle of denial, every author we have reviewed has addressed the concept of deceit and its role in strategic deception. Deceit in the form of disinformation is one of Whaley's three categories of ruses that make up stratagem [87]: "The most important single broad category of ruses includes all false information fed into another's information system in order to deceive him." Whaley also makes the distinction between deliberate disinformation and inadvertent misinformation. Later, in his deception taxonomy, Whaley makes it clear that deception is the deliberate attempt by the deceiver to create misperceptions in the mind of the target. In his deception structure, deceit takes the form of simulation [88]: "Its task is to pretend, portray, profess an intended lie."

Deceit, as distinct from deception, plays a major role in Daniel and Herbig's conceptual model of deception as well. In their model lying (deceit) encompasses their concept of cover (denial) and their comments on the differences between lying and deception are worth citing [89]: "Although the terms are often used interchangeably, deception and lying are not exact synonyms. Lying looks primarily to one side of the interaction between liar and audience. It stresses the actions of the teller of falsehoods. Deception is a term of wider scope because it also stresses the reactions of the receiver of those falsehoods. Someone whose false tale is not believed is still a liar, but he has not deceived. One does not fail at lying because the audience is not convinced, but one does fail at deception if the audience does not believe the lie." Deceit appears in Jones' writings as the false clues that are fed to the adversary through a variety of communications channels. Likewise, Jones, Haswell, Dewar, and Latimer advise that credible false information (lies) must be presented to the target through as many channels as possible. Techniques like the "unintentional mistake" and "piece of bad luck" rely on deceit.

The methods of denial (secrecy, concealment, and signal reduction) reduce or eliminate the real signals that the target needs to form accurate perceptions of a situation. The selective use of the truth (supplying the target with real data) can establish the credibility of those channels of communication that the target depends on but that have been compromised by the deceiver. These set the stage for the methods of deceit (disinformation and the associated physical objects that mimic other objects) and allow the deceiver to present the target with what appears to be highly desirable, genuine data; but it is data that has been deliberately fashioned so as to manipulate the target's perceptions to the deceiver's benefit. However, there still remains one more principle that determines the success or failure of the deception.

2.8.4 Misdirection

As we saw in Section 2.2.5, misdirection is beyond a doubt the most fundamental principle of magic. In magic, misdirection directs the audience's attention towards the effect and away from the method that produces it. The key word in this definition is *attention.* Recall that one of the criteria in Mitchell's definition of deception [90] was "An organism R registers (or believes) something Y from organism S...." In this context, the concept of registering something refers to the act of perceiving and attending to some stimuli relevant to the organism's goals, or put another way, paying attention to something. If deception depends on creating misperceptions in the target's mind, then we can see that deception depends on manipulating what the target perceives by manipulating what the target registers (i.e., attends to and finds to be relevant). This is our fourth fundamental principle of deception.

Misdirection is a regular feature of deception in nature. A good example is avian distraction displays which Sordahl describes [91]: "When confronted with a predator, particularly one that threatens their eggs or young but is too formidable to be attacked and driven away, many kinds of birds perform displays which function to divert the attention of the predator to them." One of the authors has had direct experience with this kind of avian misdirection when a pair of Killdeer (*Charadrius vociferous*) built a nest on the side of his driveway. Both adults would use calls as well as crouch-run and wing displays to lead the threat (the author and even the author's car as he entered or left the driveway) away from the nest. Misdirection occurs in many human activities as well such as eye fakes in football or basketball. And, of course, there is magic. We think enough was said about this subject in Section 2.2.5, but we will leave the reader with this quote from magician Jean Hugard [92]: "The principle of misdirection plays such an important role in magic that one might say that Magic is misdirection and misdirection is Magic."

The strategic deception literature, except for a few important exceptions, generally does not explicitly recognize misdirection as a distinct concept. It is often described obliquely or it is imbedded in other deception concepts. For example, the techniques of diversion often represent the concept of misdirection. Whaley does this in his 1969 book; diversion's purpose, he writes [7], "...is to divert the opponent's attention and strength away from the real or main operation." Dewar, in his Glossary of Terms, defines diversion as [93], "The act of drawing the attention and forces of an enemy from the point of principal operation; an attack, alarm, or feint which diverts attention." Haswell and Latimer describe categories of deception that include "displays," "feints," and "demonstrations," all of which are examples of diversions meant to draw the adversary's attention away from the real operation. Daniel and Herbig refer to misdirection indirectly when they write [18], "Liars create and perpetuate falsities and seek to fasten a victim's attention to them." In all these cases, seeking to "fasten" the victim's "attention" to something false can certainly be interpreted as misdirection.

Misdirection as a distinct concept appears in surprisingly few sources. Handel refers to it directly as we saw earlier in Section 2.2.2 when he describes his first type of deception. It specifically states that one aim of deception is to misdirect the enemy's attention. His second type of deception is also based on misdirection although Handel does not specifically use the term. However, he makes it clear that attempts to make the adversary violate the principle of economy of force involve misdirection in the form of decoy equipment and facilities. He refers to misdirection in even broader terms when describing the second noise barrier (the international environment) in his information flow framework. He writes [94], "For example, American attention to Japanese aggressive intentions was in part misdirected or diverted by dangers in the Atlantic and by the conflict in Europe." He then continues that the same effect (misdirection) can be the result of exactly the opposite condition (i.e., a relaxed international environment). In fact, he proposes [95], "Paradox no. 3: The sounds of silence. A quiet international environment can act as background noise which, by conditioning observers to a peaceful routine, actually covers preparations for war." Note the resemblance of this paradox to Lamont and Wiseman's "psychological" method of misdirection by reducing suspicion through consistency and familiarization. In this case, misdirection is achieved by *reducing* the target's attention.

Whaley later directly refers to misdirection; however, he treats it only as one category (decoying) of simulation [76]: "Decoying shows the false by diverting attention. It offers a distracting, misleading option and is therefore a matter of feints and diversions, literally misdirection. Decoying is done by creating alternative false characteristics that give an additional, second pattern. Ideally this alternative carries more conviction, conveys more certainty, than the real one." Although Whaley makes the direct link between decoying and misdirection, this new version does not appear much different than his original description of the use of diversion as a ruse for diverting the adversary's attention. Gerwehr and Glenn also list *misdirecting* as one of the three effects sought in their deception framework (refer to Figure 2.7). Like Whaley, they consider the purpose of these misdirecting techniques to be [96] "...the clear and unambiguous transmission of a *false* signal (often in hopes of diverting attention, resources, or attacks away from real assets or activities)."

In summary, nearly all of the authors in the field of strategic deception seem to treat misdirection simply as a method of deception that consists primarily of displaying false signals to the target. This is not necessarily the case. Recall that misdirection involves redirecting one's attention and that the signal that does this can be either real or false. For example, a feint is a *real* attack, not a false one, which draws the adversary's attention away from where the main attack will occur. We cited another example earlier. The events in Europe that distracted America from Japanese attentions were *real* events. Thus, we believe misdirection has a broad and fundamental role in deception, and that it can involve any combination of the principles we have already discussed along with their associated methods. Used in concert, these principles and methods are put to use by the deceiver in order to control the target's attention and thereby what the target registers and thus what the target perceives.

These four principles are the foundation for influencing how the target registers, processes, and perceives data and information. Ultimately those perceptions directly affect what the target believes and the actions he takes. Before moving on, though, let's finish this section by examining the relationship between the four deception principles and the deception matrix shown in Figure 2.15. First, there is a clear, one-to-one relationship between our first two principles, *truth* and *denial*, and the *reveal facts* and *conceal facts* quadrants of the deception methods matrix (see Figure 2.18). Our third deception principle, *deceit*, is related to the other two quadrants of the matrix, *reveal fiction* and *conceal fiction*. The relationship to the *reveal fiction* quadrant should be obvious; deceit involves providing the target with false data and information. Its relationship to the *conceal fiction* quadrant is based on our speculation that the concept of *spin* is involved. Not only can the deceiver provide the target with false data, but the deceiver can also use spin to further confuse and mislead the target. Finally, there is the *misdirection* principle. Misdirection

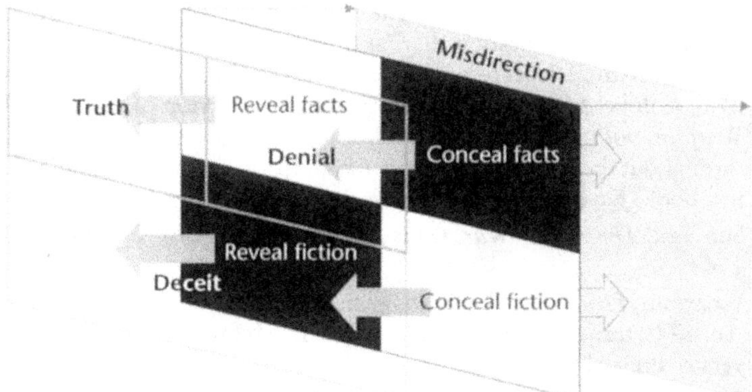

Figure 2.18 Fundamental principles of deception mapped to the deception matrix.

involves both physical methods to misdirect the target's attention and psychological methods to reduce or divert the target's suspicions. This suggests that all four quadrants of the deception methods matrix are available to the deceiver in order to influence when and where the target's attention is focused and subsequently what the target registers and processes. Thus, the four deception principles act as fundamental guides to the deception methods to be employed in achieving the deceiver's objective.

2.9 Summary

The purpose of this chapter has been to derive a set of fundamental principles of deception that could be used as a basic framework for understanding why deception works, categorizing approaches for detecting and countering deception, and developing a corresponding set of counterdeception principles to guide further research. Our strategy for achieving this purpose was to first provide the reader with an overview of the leading conceptual models and theories in the fields of strategic deception, science, and magic in order to identify common themes. This strategy allowed us to develop a general deception cycle and use it to examine the objectives, theoretical methods, and effects of deception. Finally, we then went one step further and proposed a set of four fundamental principles of deception that show how both providing the target with, and blocking the target's access to, real data and accurate information sets the stage for the use of deceit, and how misdirection then can be used to control where and when the target's attention is focused and thereby manipulate what the target actually perceives. In the next chapter we will use these principles to organize our investigation into why humans are so vulnerable to deception.

Endnotes

[1] Vrij, A., *Detecting Lies and Deceit: The Psychology of Lying and the Implications for Professional Practice*, New York: John Wiley & Sons, 2000, p. 69.

[2] Ibid., p. 74.

[3] Whaley, B., *Stratagem: Deception and Surprise in War*, Center for International Studies, Massachusetts Institute of Technology, 1969, p. 146.

[4] In *Anticipating Surprise: Analysis for Strategic Warning*, Cynthia Grabo comments that, "There can be no question that, at least until quite recently, deception has been one of the least understood, least researched and least studied aspects of both history and intelligence." Also, Colonel Michael Dewar starts the introduction of his book, *The Art of Deception in Warfare*, with the statement, "Although the outcome of countless campaigns and battles throughout the history of warfare has hung on the success of a Deception Plan, surprisingly few books have been published on the subject."

[5] Sun Tzu, *The Art of War*, trans. Samuel B. Griffith, New York: Oxford University Press, 1963.

[6] Frontinus, *Frontinus: The Stratagems and the Aqueducts of Rome (Loeb Classical Library, No. 174)*, trans. Charles E. Bennett, M. B. McElwain, (ed.), Cambridge, MA: Harvard University Press, 1997.

[7] Whaley, B., *Stratagem: Deception and Surprise in War*, Center for International Studies, Massachusetts Institute of Technology, 1969, p. 13.

[8] Ibid., p. 16.

[9] Ibid., p. 127.

[10] Ibid., p. 129.

[11] "To be practical, any plan must take account of the enemy's power to frustrate it; the best chance of overcoming such obstruction is to have a plan that can be easily varied to fit the circumstances met; to keep such adaptability, while still keeping the initiative, the best way is to operate along a line which offers alternative objectives." —B. H. Liddell Hart, *Strategy: The Indirect Approach,* 2nd rev. ed., NY: Meridan Penguin Group, 1991. Original edition: B.H. Liddell Hart, *The Decisive Wars of History,* London: G. Bell and Sons, 1929.

[12] Whaley, B., *Stratagem: Deception and Surprise in War*, Center for International Studies, Massachusetts Institute of Technology, 1969, p. 139.

[13] Ibid., p. 142.

[14] Daniel, D., and K. Herbig, "Propositions on Military Deception," in Daniel, D., and K. Herbig, (eds.), *Strategic Military Deception*, New York: Pergamon Press, 1981.

[15] Daniel, D., and K. Herbig, "Propositions on Military Deception," in Gooch, J., and A. Perlmutter, (eds.), *Military Deception and Strategic Surprise*, Totowa, NJ: Frank Cass & Co., Ltd., 1982.

[16] Ibid., pp. 155–156.

[17] Ibid., p. 155.

[18] Ibid., p. 156.

[19] Ibid., p. 157.

[20] Whaley, B., "Toward a General Theory of Deception," in Gooch, J., and A. Perlmutter (eds.), *Military Deception and Strategic Surprise*, Totowa, NJ: Frank Cass & Co., Ltd., 1982, p. 178.

[21] Ibid., p. 179.

[22] Ibid., p. 185.

[23] Ibid., p. 188.

[24] Handel, M., *Perception, Deception and Surprise: The Case of the Yom Kippur War*, Jerusalem: The Hebrew University, 1976, p. 14.

[25] Handel, M., *War, Strategy and Intelligence*, London, U.K.: Frank Cass & Co., Ltd., 1989.

[26] Ibid., p. 327.

[27] Ibid., p. 328.

[28] Gerwehr, S., and R. Glenn, *Unweaving the Web: Deception and Adaptation in Future Urban Operations*, Santa Monica, CA: RAND, 2002, p. iii.

[29] Ibid., p. 37.

[30] Jones, R. V., *Most Secret War*, Hertfordshire, U.K.: Wordsworth Editions Ltd., 1998, p. 288.

[31] Jones, R. V., *Reflections on Intelligence*. London, U.K.: William Heinemann Ltd., 1989.

[32] Ibid., p. 105.

[33] Both Barton Whaley and J. Bowyer Bell participated in this effort. In the introduction to the Transaction Edition of their book *Cheating and Deception,* Bell briefly describes his involvement and the challenges of obtaining the appropriate security clearances. Bell's research into terrorism and insurgency had put him into contact with "gunmen, terrorists, and active revolutionaries" and made the security process longer and more interesting for him.

[34] *Deception Maxims: Fact and Folklore*, Princeton, NJ: Everest Consulting Associates and Mathtech, Inc., April 1980.

[35] Ibid., p. 1.

[36] Axelrod, R., "The Rational Timing of Surprise," *World Politics*, Vol. 31, No. 2, January 1979, pp. 228–246.

[37] Masterman, J. C., *The Double-Cross System*, New York: The Lyons Press, 2000, p. 104.

[38] In the U.S. intelligence community, highly classified information from sensitive sources is usually considered more credible and valuable than open source intelligence even though open source has routinely demonstrated its value on several occasions.

[39] Haswell, J., *The Tangled Web: The Art of Tactical and Strategic Deception*, Wendover, Buckinghamshire, U.K.: John Goodchild Publishers, 1985.

[40] Dewar, M., *The Art of Deception in Warfare*, Devon, U.K.: David & Charles Publishers, 1989.

[41] Latimer, J., *Deception in War: The Art of the Bluff, The Value of Deceit, and the Most Thrilling Episodes of Cunning in Military History, from the Trojan Horse to the Gulf War*, Woodstock, NY: The Overlook Press, 2001.

[42] Haswell, J., *The Tangled Web: The Art of Tactical and Strategic Deception*, Wendover, Buckinghamshire, U.K.: John Goodchild Publishers, 1985, p. 32.

[43] Cohen, F., et al., "A Framework for Deception," 2001, http://www.all.net/journal/deception/Framework/Framework.html.

[44] Mitchell, R. W., "A Framework for Discussing Deception," in Mitchell, R. W., and N. S. Thompson, (eds.), *Deception: Perspectives on Human and Nonhuman Deceit*, Albany, NY: State University of New York Press, 1986.

[45] For an interesting overview of the debate, see M. D. Hauser's September 1998 article in *Discover* magazine titled "Games Primates Play."

[46] Handel, M., *War, Strategy, and Intelligence*, London: Frank Cass & Co., Ltd., 1989, p. 335.

[47] Smith, W. J., "An 'Informational' Perspective on Manipulation," in Mitchell, R. W., and N. S. Thompson, (eds.), *Deception: Perspectives on Human and Nonhuman Deceit*, Albany, NY: State University of New York Press, 1986.

[48] Anderson, M., "Cultural Concatenation of Deceit and Secrecy," in Mitchell, R. W., and N. S. Thompson, (eds.), *Deception: Perspectives on Human and Nonhuman Deceit*, Albany, NY: State University of New York Press, 1986.

[49] Mitchell, R. W., "Epilogue," in Mitchell, R. W., and N. S. Thompson, (eds.), *Deception: Perspectives on Human and Nonhuman Deceit*, Albany, NY: State University of New York Press, 1986, p. 357.

[50] Christopher, M., *The Illustrated History of Magic*, New York: Thomas Y. Crowell Co., 1973, p. 7.

[51] Ibid., pp. 8–9.

[52] Fajuri, G., "Ancient Deceptions: The First Magic Trick," *Magical Past Times*, http://www.illusionata.com/mpt/view.php?id=173&type=articles.

[53] Scot, R., *The Discovery of Witchcraft*, New York: Dover Publications, 1989.

[54] Lamont, P., and R. Wiseman, *Magic in Theory*, Hertfordshire, U.K.: University of Hertfordshire Press, 1999.

[55] Steinmeyer, J., *Hiding the Elephant*, New York: Carroll & Graf Publishers, 2003, p. 241.

[56] Steinmeyer's list includes: making things appear, making things disappear, causing an object to transpose form one place to another, causing an object to be transformed, causing an object to float, restoring an object that has been destroyed, cut apart, or divided, animating an inanimate object, causing one object to penetrate another, demonstrating something that violates a natural law, or simulating mind reading or other psychic phenomena.

[57] Lamont, P., and R. Wiseman, *Magic in Theory*, Hertfordshire, U.K.: University of Hertfordshire Press, 1999, pp. 1–24.

[58] Steinmeyer, J., *Hiding the Elephant*, New York: Carroll & Graf Publishers, 2003, p. 90.

[59] Lamont, P., and R. Wiseman, *Magic in Theory*, Hertfordshire, U.K.: University of Hertfordshire Press, 1999, p. 31.

[60] Koch, C., *The Quest for Consciousness: A Neurobiological Approach*, Englewood, NJ: Roberts and Company Publishers, 2004, p. 153.

[61] Ibid., pp. 155–157.

[62] Lamont, P., and R. Wiseman, *Magic in Theory*, Hertfordshire, U.K.: University of Hertfordshire Press, 1999, p. 42.

[63] Steinmeyer, J., *Hiding the Elephant*, New York: Carroll & Graf Publishers, 2003, p. 117.

[64] Lamont, P., and R. Wiseman, *Magic in Theory*, Hertfordshire, U.K.: University of Hertfordshire Press, 1999, p. 67.

[65] Holt, T., *The Deceivers*, New York: Scribner, 2004, pp. 28–29.

[66] Waltz, E., *Information Warfare Principles and Operations*, Norwood, MA: Artech House, 1998, pp. 1–2.

[67] Handel, M., *War, Strategy, and Intelligence*, London, U.K.: Frank Cass & Co., Ltd., 1989, p. 314.

[68] Ibid., p. 315.

[69] Daniel, D., and Herbig, K. "Propositions on Military Deception," in Gooch, J., and A. Perlmutter, (eds.), *Military Deception and Strategic Surprise*, Totowa, NJ: Frank Cass & Co., Ltd., 1982, p. 161.

[70] Smith, W. J., "An 'Informational' Perspective on Manipulation," in Mitchell, R. W., and N. S. Thompson, (eds.), *Deception: Perspectives on Human and Nonhuman Deceit*, Albany, NY: State University of New York Press, 1986, p. 71.

[71] Ibid., p. 82.

[72] Masterman, J. C., *The Double-Cross System*. New York: The Lyons Press, 2000. p. 20.

[73] Handel, M., *War, Strategy, and Intelligence*, London, U.K.: Frank Cass & Co., Ltd., 1989, p. 236.

[74] Mitchell, R. W., "Epilogue," in Mitchell, R. W., and N. S. Thompson, (eds.), *Deception, Perspectives on Human and Nonhuman Deceit*, Albany, NY: State University of New York Press, 1986, p. 358.

[75] Whaley, B., "Toward a General Theory of Deception," in Gooch, J., and A. Perlmutter, (eds.), *Military Deception and Strategic Surprise*, Totowa, NJ: Frank Cass & Co., Ltd., 1982, p. 184.

[76] Ibid., p. 185.

[77] Haswell, J., *The Tangled Web: The Art of Tactical and Strategic Deception*, Wendover, Buckinghamshire, U.K.: John Goodchild Publishers, 1985, p. 23.

[78] Whaley, B., *Stratagem: Deception and Surprise in War,* Center for International Studies, Massachusetts Institute of Technology, 1969, p. 19.

[79] Hesketh, R. *Fortitude: The D-Day Deception Campaign,* Woodstock, NY: The Overlook Press, 2000, p. 237.

[80] Handel, M., *War, Strategy, and Intelligence,* London, U.K.: Frank Cass & Co., Ltd., 1989, p. 335.

[81] Smith, W. J., "An 'Informational' Perspective on Manipulation," in Mitchell, R. W., and N. S. Thompson, (eds.), *Deception: Perspectives on Human and Nonhuman Deceit*, Albany, NY: State University of New York Press, 1986, p. 77.

[82] De Waal, F., "Deception in the Natural Communication of Chimpanzees," in Mitchell, R. W., and N. S. Thompson, (eds.), *Deception: Perspectives on Human and Nonhuman Deceit*, Albany, NY: State University of New York Press, 1986, p. 226.

[83] Daniel, D., and K. Herbig, "Propositions on Military Deception," in Daniel, D., and K. Herbig, (eds.), *Strategic Military Deception*, New York: Pergamon Press, 1981, p. 4.

[84] Handel, M., *Perception, Deception, and Surprise: The Case of the Yom Kippur War.* Jerusalem: The Hebrew University, 1976, p. 12.

[85] Ibid., p. 13.

[86] Ford, M., *Lies! Lies! Lies!: The Psychology of Deceit,* Washington, D.C.: American Psychiatric Press, Inc., 1995, p. 4.

[87] Whaley, B., *Stratagem: Deception and Surprise in War,* Cambridge, MA: Center for International Studies, Massachusetts Institute of Technology, 1969, p. 17.

[88] Whaley, B., "Toward a General Theory of Deception," in Gooch, J., and A. Perlmutter, (eds.), *Military Deception and Strategic Surprise,* Totowa, NJ: Frank Cass & Co., Ltd., 1982, p. 183.

[89] Daniel, D., and K. Herbig, "Propositions on Military Deception," in Daniel, D., and K. Herbig, (eds.), *Strategic Military Deception,* New York: Pergamon Press, 1981, pp. 4–5.

[90] Mitchell, R. W., "A Framework for Discussing Deception," in Mitchell, R. W., and N. S. Thompson, (eds.), *Deception: Perspectives on Human and Nonhuman Deceit,* Albany, NY: State University of New York Press, 1986, p. 21.

[91] Sordahl, T., "Evolutionary Aspects of Avian Distraction Display: Variation in American Avocet and Black-Necked Stilt Antipredator Behavior," in Mitchell, R. W., and N. S. Thompson (eds.), *Deception: Perspectives on Human and Nonhuman Deceit,* Albany, NY: State University of New York Press, 1986, p. 87.

[92] Leirpoll, J., "Misdirection Resource Center," http://www.leirpoll.com/misdirection/misdirection.htm.

[93] Dewar, M., *The Art of Deception in Warfare,* Devon, U.K.: David & Charles Publishers, 1989, p. 218.

[94] Handel, M., *Perception, Deception, and Surprise: The Case of the Yom Kippur War.* Jerusalem: The Hebrew University, 1976, p. 16.

[95] Ibid., p. 17.

[96] Gerwehr, S., and R. Glenn, *Unweaving the Web: Deception and Adaptation in Future Urban Operations*, Santa Monica, CA: RAND, 2002, p. 36.

CHAPTER 3

The Cognitive Aspects of Deception: Why Does Deception Work?

In Chapter 2, we presented a broad overview of deception with emphasis on the various conceptual models that have been proposed in the fields of national security, magic, and science. Deception, as we saw, is the deliberate manipulation of the target's perceptions and beliefs in order to distort his knowledge of the situation and to affect his decisions and actions in ways that benefit the deceiver. The intended effects of the deception may be to increase or decrease the target's ambiguity with regard to a situation, to direct or divert his attention, to increase or decrease his suspicions, to create confusion, or to surprise the target. The deceiver uses a wide variety of deception methods to both reveal and conceal facts and fictions to the target's sensors (both human and technical) in order to affect how the target senses, registers, and interprets data and information. If the deception is successful, the target uses this data and information to reconstruct the intended deception story and react in the manner intended by the deceiver. In this chapter, we will examine the role biases play in deception and how they contribute to the manipulation of human perceptions and beliefs. Biases in judgment and decision-making can be the result of personal, cultural, organizational, or cognitive factors. Most of this chapter, however, will address the cognitive aspects of human perception, judgment, and reasoning, and we will be using Thomas Gilovich's six determinants of questionable beliefs as our framework for examining the role that these biases play in deception. Finally, we will look at how the deception principles we developed in Chapter 2 contribute to the target's acceptance of the deception story. This analysis will then provide a foundation from which we can explore different counterdeception approaches and develop a set of counterdeception principles.

3.1 Biases Relevant to Deception

In everyday usage, bias generally refers to an inclination to judge others or interpret situations based on a personal and oftentimes unreasoned point of view. In the context of deception, however, biases are the systematic errors in perception, judgment, and reasoning that contribute to the target's distorted knowledge of reality. In their discussion of the cognitive biases of intelligence analysis, Thompson et al. cited three categories of bias that analysts needed to recognize [1]. These categories are:

- Cultural and personal biases;
- Organizational biases;
- Cognitive biases.

Each of these biases can be used to manipulate the target's perceptions and beliefs about reality in order to influence the target's decisions and actions.

3.1.1 The Influence of Cultural Biases on Deception

Cultural bias is the result of interpreting and judging phenomena in terms particular to one's own culture and is influenced by the knowledge, beliefs, customs, morals, habits, and cognitive styles that are acquired as a member of one's specific social environment. For example, take the reaction of an American ambassador in a foreign country when a group of local diplomats arrive 50 minutes late for a meeting [2], "How can you depend on these people when they arrive an hour late for an appointment and then just mutter something? They don't even give you a full sentence of apology." The ambassador's reaction reflects an attitude toward time found in American culture which interprets being 50 minutes late as insulting, whereas in the host country such lateness is interpreted to be just about right for a daytime official visit. Culture does not determine a precise course of action for individuals or groups, but it can limit the range of options one considers, influence the way actions and ideas are defined, and establish the narrative structure that provides meaning to events.

Not only can cultural biases affect perceptions, but they can also influence *how* people go about solving problems and analyzing situations. For example, a 2004 article in *Studies in Intelligence* suggests that the assumptions that underlie U.S. intelligence thinking about China rest primarily on Western linear approaches to information processing and ignore "synthetic" or "complementary" approaches for analyzing nonlinear systems such as international relations [3]. Such knowledge could potentially be exploited by deception planners.

Cultural differences extend to strategic thinking as well. Using China again as an example, we see that the Chinese way of war is strikingly different from that of the West. Since the Greeks, Western civilization, and now especially the United States, has emphasized the use of overwhelming force and superior technological capability. There is a general distaste for deception, sneak attacks, ambushes, and other dishonorable strategies and tactics in the West. On the other hand, Chinese military strategy and diplomacy is influenced by over 2,000 years of a completely different philosophical structure and the teachings of Sun Tzu and other military writings. The differences are expressed in several concepts that are different from Western thinking. Lai cites several notable examples such as *Bing yi zha li* (war is based on deception), *Yi-rou ke-gang* (use the soft and gentle to overcome the hard and strong), and other Chinese four-character proverbs that are strategic and dialectic in nature and bear some character of flowing water [4].

Even our games are different. The Western game of chess is essentially a force on force contest, while the 4,000-year-old Chinese game of Go features simple stones all with equal power and emphasizes fluid movement on multiple battlefronts. It should be sobering reminder to us living in the West that computers now routinely defeat chess champions, but that no computer program has yet been developed that can even defeat an average amateur Go player.

In summary, deception plans require a through understanding of the culture of the target. Godson and Wirtz make the case that [5]: "To be successful, the deceiver must recognize the target's perceptual context to know what (false) pictures of the world will appear plausible. History, culture, bureaucratic preferences, and the general economic and political milieu all influence the target's perceptions. False information should conform to the idiosyncrasies of strategic and even popular culture." As we just pointed out, arrogance and projection play an important role in cultural bias and can increase one's vulnerability to deception. As Dahl notes [6], cultural bias "...can manifest as a national or individual perception. In the extreme case, it foregoes any serious search of alternatives or decision analysis beyond what the decision maker has already decided." Such cultural bias on the part of the Israelis worked to the Arabs advantage in the 1973 war with Israel [7]: "The deception plan that emerged as a consequence was a blend of Israeli and Western tactics. More importantly, it was designed to utilize Western (and Israeli) images of the Arabs, especially those images that stressed the following elements: (1) the Arabs' inability to keep any secrets; (2) the general ineptness of Arab military forces; (3) the Arabs' inability to plan or conduct any sort of coordinated military action."

3.1.2 The Influence of Personal Biases on Deception

Personal biases are the result of personality traits and the firsthand experiences that affect a person's world view throughout the course of their life. Jervis lists four variables that influence the degree to which personal experience affects perceptual predispositions. These are: firsthand experience, whether the experience occurred in the person's early adulthood or career, the importance of the consequences to the person or his nation, and the extent to which the person is familiar with a sufficient range of events that would facilitate alternative perceptions [8].

The deception impact of personal bias is the result of the preconceptions and beliefs that are formed by the individual's personal experiences. Since preconceptions and beliefs are extremely resistant to change, even in the face of large amounts of discrepant information, they can be exploited by deception planners. Stalin's reaction to the intelligence he received regarding the buildup of German forces prior to Operation Barbarossa is a good example of how personality and firsthand experience can have an impact on the success of a deception operation. In the words of Michael Handel [9]:

> Stalin may have deceived himself by imagining that trickery lurked behind many of the moves of other states. Thus when Churchill and the British warned him of the impending German attack in 1941 based on knowledge acquired through Ultra, he refused to believe them and viewed this information as bait to drag the Soviet Union into war against Germany in order to ease the pressure in the West. Given Stalin's communist background and his paranoia, such an attitude is not altogether surprising.

Firsthand experience seems to have also had a role in biasing Hitler's beliefs. Foot relates an interesting anecdote about the FORTITUDE NORTH deception plan designed to convince the Germans of an invasion of Norway. According to Foot, Andrew (Bulgy) Thorne met Hitler at a large diplomatic reception in Berlin in 1933 when Thorne was the British military attaché. Foot describes their meeting [10]:

> Making the rounds, Hitler with his odd eye for detail noticed that Thorne was wearing—after his gallantry decorations—what the army called (after a once famous children's cartoon) Pip, Squeak, and Wilfred, the three main Great War service medals, with the 1914 star. Had he been at Ypres? He had? Where was he on 30 October 1914? It turned out the two of them had been only about five hundred yards apart that day. Hitler, therefore, marked Thorne down as "ein alter Frontkämpfer," his highest praise, and was disappointed when Thorne was posted back to Aldershot to command the Guards Brigade two years later.

Foot suggests that placing Thorne in command of the notional British 4th Army as part of FORTITUDE NORTH may have been one of the reasons that Hitler left over 300,000 troops in Norway to face an invasion that never came.

Simple greed can also be the source of personal biases that affect the success of a deception plan. For example, the German Abwehr officers running agents in Britain and other countries were paid according to how well their particular agents performed. Thus greed became an incentive that undermined the Abwehr's skeptical evaluation of its sources of information and made them more vulnerable to the British Double Cross operation [11].

Personal traits such as risk-taking and overconfidence (hubris) can also lead to disastrous results in situations where deception is a factor. Germany's arrogance resulting from its early successes in World War II is an extreme example; however, the United States is also guilty of hubris on occasion (e.g., on the eve of Pearl Harbor) as were the Israelis in 1973 [12].

3.1.3 Organizational Biases and Deception

The nineteenth century ushered in the era of large armies and corporations as a way of organizing and directing large groups of individuals towards the purpose of unheard-of feats of destruction and production. Concepts like the division of labor made it possible for these large organizations to become both efficient and effective. However, their vastly increased size also created the need for management and coordination (or command and control) systems that also led to the creation of large bureaucracies. Organizational biases are the result of the goals, mores, policies, and traditions that characterize the specific organization in which the individual works. These biases are generally associated with the limitations and weaknessess of large bureaucratic organizations. The problem is made even worse in government which consists of numerous large bureacracies.

Most large organizations depend on formal and informal rules to guide and direct the work of the organziation. Both civilian and military bureaucracies employ standard operating procedures (SOPs) as a means of standardizing processes, again in the name of efficiency, and when everything works, the results can be spectacularly successful. While SOPs make the organization efficient in normal conditions, they are not known for being very flexible or adaptable, and they can bias the organization's collection of information and generation of policy and strategy alternatives. Very large corporations and governments also require extensive coordination between the diffferent bureaucratic organizations that deal with different aspects of the business or mission. This division of labor is intended to make the overall organization more efficient, but it can create additional biases resulting from organizational parochialism and the tendency for a fairly autonomous bureaucracy to focus on its own goals related to increasing its own size and power.

Unfortunately, the evolution of large industrial-era organizations also has resulted in side effects that can be used to the deception planner's advantage. The division of labor and bureaucracies that help to make such large organizations efficient also creates barriers to the flow of information in the form of internal delays, filters, and choke points. These barriers are not necessarily a bad thing. They help to coordinate activities and optimize information flows by making decisions whether or not information is allowed to pass from one level to the next higher level, but they can also be a weak point when they are a target for deception. In their model of deception, Daniel and Herbig [13] describe how the "gatekeepers in intelligence agencies and command staffs...screen the information and analysis, and determine what is actually forwarded to civilian or military authorities—the ultimate deception targets." Sherwin [14] also discusses the role of gatekeepers in deception: "Gatekeepers are supposed to optimize the flow of information needed at the top. Knowing who the gatekeepers are, how they function, and where they are located can be an important element in planning to deceive an organization." For example, Sherwin describes the role of German Vice Admiral Canaris, the head of the Abwehr, as a particularly "intriguing" gatekeeper who allegedly selectively transmitted information to, or withheld information from Hitler in his personal effort to undermine the Nazi regime [14].

Not only does information face barriers such as gatekeepers as it flows through large organizations, but the very nature of the information about a specific topic changes as it winds up flowing through different channels. Jervis addresses the impact this has on perceptions when he writes [15]: "Differences in evoked sets caused by differences in information can lead various parts of a state's bureaucracy to different perceptions of others' actions. Well-known are the consequences of major differences in perspective caused by the division of labor within a government." Differences in information across a collection of large organizations are even more extreme when classified information is involved. The differences in perception due to the uneven distribution of compartmented information contributed heavily to the United States' failure to anticipate the Japanese attack on Pearl Harbor. Roberta Wohlstetter summarizes the effect of the structure of the information channels within the U.S. intelligence and command community had on the transmittal of information, especially the highly controlled MAGIC intercepts of Japanese communications [16]: "As we have seen, only a very few key individuals saw these secret messages, and they saw them only briefly. They had no opportunity or time to make a critical review of the material, and each one assumed that others who had seen it would arrive at identical interpretations. Exactly who those 'others' were was not quite clear to any recipient."

Bureaucratic politics can also have considerable impact on how information is interpreted at the organizational level. Whether such politics are the result of organizational self-interest or a genuine belief that a particular policy is superior to that of a rival organization, such competition between different organizations has the potential to be deliberately exploited by the deceiver. For example, the British were able to manipulate the rivalry between the German military's Abwehr and the Nazi intelligence service, the Sicherheitsdienst (SD), by feeding the Abwehr information that increased its credibility with the Nazi leadership at the expense of the SD.

Two examples of organizational biases should be mentioned before moving on. The first of these is the result of what is known as the *coordination* process in the intelligence community. Handel [17] notes that although this process is a crucial one, it "introduces a number of inevitable biases into the final intelligence product." If military organizations dominate the process, coordination can bias the resulting intelligence estimate towards an exaggerated, military-oriented view of threats. Biases are also introduced if the coordination process comes to reflect the power and prestige of the more powerful agencies at the expense of the best professional judgments available. Finally, consensus may become a goal in and of itself and may deprive decision makers of important information about the basis for the judgments as well as the existence and grounds of alternative views.

The second example, time pressure, is an important one because it exacerbates many of the cognitive biases we will review in the next section. Intelligence analysts have always been under some sort of pressure to provide timely intelligence. Nevertheless, Heuer's observation that [18] "Decision makers' needs for interpretive analysis are greatest within, at most, two or three days after an event occurs" is now probably out of date. More likely, analysis is needed within 24 hours or even less. The result is that the intelligence analysis "requires the analyst to make an almost instant diagnosis before sufficient hard information makes a well-grounded judgment possible" [18].

3.1.4 Cognitive Biases and Deception

Cognitive biases differ from cultural, personal, and organizational biases in that they represent the innate ways that human beings perceive, recall, and process information from the environment. Although cognitive biases do not usually interfere with our ability to accurately perceive and understand the world around us on a day-to-day basis, they do make us vulnerable to optical illusions, magician's tricks, con artists, and, of special interest to us, military and diplomatic deception.

3.1.4.1 General Purpose Heuristics and Biases

In 1971, Daniel Kahneman and Amos Tversky published their first joint paper that examined the systematic errors in the casual statistical judgments of statistically sophisticated researchers [19]. In their paper, they extended the idea of bounded rationality by arguing that intuitive judgment processes are not just simpler than the reasoning processes demanded by rational choice theory, but that they were a different kind of judgmental process that they called *heuristics*. They proposed that people rely on these heuristics in order to reduce complex tasks involving the assessment of probabilities and the prediction of values to simpler judgmental operations, especially under conditions of uncertainty, unavailability, or indeterminacy of important information [20]. Kahneman and Tversky proposed three general-purpose heuristics: *representativeness*, *availability*, and *anchoring and adjustment*. In experiments that continued throughout the succeeding decades, each heuristic was found to be associated with a corresponding set of *biases* (see Figure 3.1). These biases represent the departures from the results predicted by normative rational theory and can result in severe and systematic errors in judgment.

Kahneman and Tversky describe the *representativeness* heuristic as follows [21]: "A person who follows this heuristic evaluates the probability of a certain event, or a sample, by the degree to which it is: (i) similar in essential properties to its parent population; and (ii) reflects the salient features of the process by which it is generated." In other words, likelihood is evaluated by the degree to which A is representative of B, that is, the degree to which A resembles B. Unfortunately, when A is highly representative of B, people often overestimate the likelihood that A is a member of B (where B is a class) or originates from B (where B is a process) [22]. The reverse is also true, where A is not considered to be similar to B; people judge the likelihood that A is a member of B or originates from B to be lower than it actually is.

The *availability* heuristic is another shortcut that people use to assess the likelihood of uncertain events. When using this heuristic, people assess the frequency of a class or probability of an event by the ease with which instances or occurrences can be brought to mind. Unfortunately, what is available to us is often affected more by factors other than the actual frequency of the class or instance, and, like representativeness, relying on the availability heuristic leads to a number of predictable biases.

The availability heuristic also produces biases of imaginability. This bias is associated with situations where instances are not stored in memory; instead, we generate several instances using our imagination and evaluate the desired frequency or probability based on the ease with which they can be constructed. This bias has significant implications for situations such as prediction, assessing the probability of a specified event, assessing conditioned probabilities, counterfactual assessments, and assessments of causality. There are also significant implications related to the development of scenarios for war games and training exercises intended to help commanders and policy-makers plan and assess strategies for dealing with future situations. Tversky and Kahneman caution that the availability heuristic poses the danger that [23], "The production of a compelling scenario is likely to constrain future thinking. There is much evidence showing that, once an uncertain situation

Representativeness	Availability	Anchoring and Adjustment
• Insensitivity to prior probability of outcomes • Insensitivity to sample size • Misconceptions of chance • Insensitivity to predictability • Illusion of validity • Misconceptions of regression	• Biases due to retrievability of instances • Biases due to effectiveness of a search set • Biases of imaginability • Illusory correlation	• Insufficient adjustment • Biases in evaluation of conjunctive and disjunctive events • Anchoring in the assessment of subjective probability distributions

Figure 3.1 General-purpose heuristics and their associated biases.

has been perceived or interpreted in a particular fashion, it is quite difficult to view it in any other way. Thus the generation of a specific scenario may inhibit the emergence of other scenarios, particularly those that lead to different outcomes." Admiral Chester Nimitz touched on this point in 1961 when he addressed the Naval War College [24]: "The war with Japan had been reenacted in the game room here by so many people and in so many different ways that nothing that happened during the war was a surprise—absolutely nothing except the Kamikaze tactic toward the end of the war; we had not visualized those."

Biases of *anchoring and adjustment* occur when people are given an initial conspicuous but uninformative number and are asked to make a numerical estimate of some quantity. For example, is the Mississippi River more or less than 800 miles long? Research has shown that the resulting adjustments from the initial value (the anchor) are typically insufficient and different starting points yield different estimates biased toward the initial values. In addition, even arbitrary values and partial calculations can act as anchors and influence the final value. By the way, the actual length of the Mississippi River is anywhere from 2,300 to 2,500 miles depending on who does the measuring [25]. Was your estimate influenced by the 800-mile figure?

3.1.4.2 Heuer's Cognitive Factors of Deception

In 1981, Richards Heuer published *Strategic Deception and Counterdeception*, one of the most important papers to appear regarding strategic deception [26]. Heuer was the first to apply the results of the early research in heuristics and biases to the analysis of strategic deception and counterdeception. He organized his analysis into four categories: biases of perception, biases in estimating probabilities, biases in evaluating evidence, and biases in attributing causality. He then described the possible implications for intelligence analysis and deception for each category (see Figure 3.2).

Heuer's research into cognitive biases provided strong support for a conclusion that previous deception researchers and historians had already observed, that is, it is easier to deceive a target by reinforcing the target's preconceptions and prior beliefs than it is to convince the target to accept an alternative to which he is not predisposed. Heuer based his conclusion on the effects of three biases: the tendency to assimilate new information to existing beliefs, anchoring, and overconfidence. In addition, Heuer also concludes that [27]: "The human capacity to rationalize contradictory evidence is easily sufficient to outweigh the pernicious effects of security leaks and uncontrolled channels of information that deception planners might otherwise fear are certain to compromise their efforts." In other words, security leaks in the deceiver's organization may be less serious than expected.

Biases related to the availability heuristic are the basis for another important deception method. Heuer suggests that availability makes it very likely that the watch offices of intelligence and military organizations will generally overestimate the probability of whatever they are watching for [28]. Through training and experience they have been primed to detect certain patterns of events. The deceiver can exploit this tendency by provoking the target's watch office to issue false alerts: the cry-wolf syndrome. The deceiver's goal is to influence decision-makers to discount alerts at a time when it is actually an authentic warning.

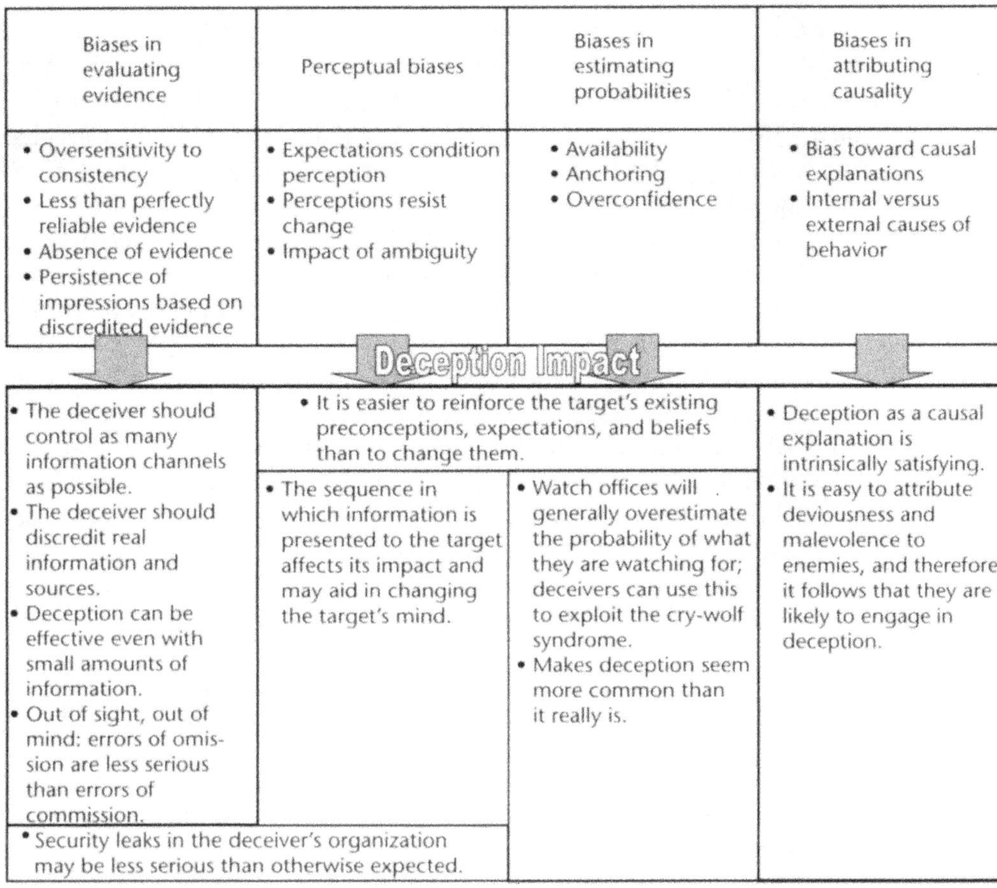

Figure 3.2 Heuer's categories of cognitive factors affecting deception.

Biases of availability may also make it more likely that analysts and decision-makers will believe they see deception when it actually is not present. According to Heuer [29], "Successful cases of deception are far more salient, and consequently more available for recall in memory, than cases in which deception was not employed under comparable circumstances." Biases of causality and attribution also support a tendency to see deception where there is none since deception "...is intrinsically satisfying precisely because it is so orderly and rational" [30]. In addition, the fundamental attribution error can reinforce this tendency since it easy to attribute "deviousness and malevolence" to the enemy and it naturally follows that devious, malevolent enemies would engage in deception [31].

Finally, Heuer addresses several biases related to the evaluation of evidence: oversensitivity to consistency, the effects of the absence of evidence, and the persistence of impressions based on discredited evidence. The first, oversensitivity to consistency, is related to the representativeness heuristic and the illusion of validity. Heuer notes [32]: "The bias in favoring a small amount of consistent information over a large body of less consistent data support the common maxim in deception operations that the deceiver should control as many information channels as possible in order to reduce the amount of discrepant information available to the target."

Heuer also suggests that, in order to achieve maximum consistency, it is also advisable for the deceiver to discredit the truth as well as confirming the deceit. With regard to the absence of information, Heuer suggests that deceptions are unlikely to fail due to information the deceiver does not provide the target. This is a characteristic of the availability heuristic where any information that is not immediately available or imaginable is simply not even considered—it becomes a case of out-of-sight, out-of-mind. In contrast, as Heuer puts it [32], the deceiver's "...errors of omission will be less serious than errors of commission." Finally, the persistence of belief effect that occurs when the source of information or the information itself has been discredited has a major impact on the success of deception operations. Heuer uses the example of an intelligence asset that is discovered to have come under hostile control. The information that the asset has provided has been instrumental in the formation of certain impressions about some situation. It is likely that some of the original impressions formed will persist since [33], "It is easy to rationalize the perseverance of these impressions by arguing that the information was true despite the agent being under hostile control, or by doubting the validity of the report claiming the agent is under control." Masterman describes a real life version of this example that occurred during World War II [34]:

> We assisted on many occasions in creating the threat of an invasion of Norway from this country; we started always with the belief that the agent might succeed but must "blow" himself in the process. Such was not the case... when the deception succeeded the agent was *not*, in our experience, usually "blown," for the Germans had far more credible explanations of what had occurred than the true explanation that the agent was a double cross.

In summary, Heuer's general conclusions with regard to the impact that cognitive biases have on deception are:

- People don't do a very good job at generating a full set of hypotheses.
- There is a strong tendency to view information as either supporting, contradicting, or irrelevant to a hypothesis that is already believed to be the case.
- Analysts can become fixed in a "mental set" that resists discrepant information.

These conclusions support everything that has been generally observed about successful deceptions. In the case of the first conclusion, if the target of deception expects his adversary to do A or B, and the adversary has a deception plan in operation to protect a third alternative C, a wide range of cognitive biases make it unlikely that the target will ever be aware of the third option. In the second case, if the target is aware that his adversary has two likely options, A and B, but expects his adversary to do A, then the adversary's deception plan reinforcing that expectation will likely succeed and the target will not only fit information to his expectation but any information that suggests that the adversary will do B or C will be ignored, rejected, or found irrelevant. Finally, the mental set (or mindset) conclusion should be a familiar metaphor for the preconceptions, expectations, and beliefs that seem to influence all aspects of human information processing.

3.1.4.3 Dual Process Theory and New Heuristics

Continuing research in the heuristics and biases field has both extended earlier work in general-purpose heuristics as well as identifying new processes and special purpose heuristics. A few of these are worth mentioning here.

One important new concept is the idea that human cognition involves two substantially different processes that operate simultaneously. This idea goes back to the 1970s [35], but it was Sloman [36] who first discussed the implications of this idea for judgment and decision-making in 1996. He proposed that reasoning consists of both an *associative system* and a *rule-based system*. The associative system is associated with cognitive functions such as intuition, fantasy, creativity, imagination, visual recognition, and associative memory. The rule-based system is associated with deliberation, explanation, formal analysis, verification, ascription of purpose, and strategic memory. Stanovich and West [37] introduced the labels *System 1* and *System 2* for these processes and characterized System 1 as "automatic, heuristic-based, and relatively undemanding," while System 2 is characterized by controlled processes that employ rules and principles. Kahneman and Frederick also use the System 1 and 2 labels and associate System 1 with intuition and System 2 with reasoning and reflection. Kahneman describes the operations of System 1 as [38], "...fast, automatic, effortless, associative, implicit (not available to introspection), and often emotionally charged; they are also governed by habit and are therefore difficult to control or modify." Likewise, he describes System 2 as [38], "...slower, serial, effortful, more likely to be consciously monitored and deliberately controlled; they are also relatively flexible and potentially rule governed." System 1 and System 2 operate in parallel to form judgments; however, intuitive judgments are those that directly reflect the impressions formed by System 1 that are not modified by System 2. System 2 is often said to monitor the activities of System 1, but this monitoring is quite lax with the result that the individual forms many rapid, intuitive judgments some of which are erroneous. Nearly all of the biases we have reviewed can be thought of in terms of System 1 processes; however, it is important to remember that the intuitive judgments of System 1 can also be very powerful and very accurate.

Another area of research, *support theory*, has shown that people do not attach probability judgments to events but to the *descriptions* of events [39]. In other words, different descriptions of the same event often produce different subjective probability estimates. The judged probability of an event depends on the explicitness of its description, that is, the relative support, or strength of evidence. It assumes that the judged probability of an event generally increases when its description is unpacked into disjoint components. What this means is that by unpacking the description of some event (e.g., a plane crash) into a set of disjoint components (e.g., an *accidental* plane crash, caused by *human error* or *mechanical failure* or *sabotage*) generally increases the perceived support for the event. In other words, we tend to view an accidental plane crash caused by human error as more likely than a plane crash that is not supported by some cause. Support theory also helps explain the errors in probability assessment associated with the *conjunction effect* (also called the conjunction fallacy). In the conjunction effect, the probability of the conjunction, P(A and B), is judged to be higher than the probability of one of the components, say, P(A). Similar effects are seen when people are asked to generate hypotheses and assess their likelihood. Their estimates of the likelihood of a hypothesis depend on the extent to which they mentally unpack the residual hypothesis and thus tend to overestimate the probability of the ones they unpack relative to those left unspecified.

In psychology, the term *affect* is used to describe patterns of observable behaviors that are the expression of a subjectively experienced state or feeling (i.e., emotion). In 2002, Slovic et al. proposed that a growing body of evidence supported the idea of an *affect heuristic* where affect denotes the quality of goodness or badness [40]. Affective reactions of goodness or badness are often our very first reactions to some stimulus. For example, your coworker comes to work wearing a new tie. You don't just see a tie; you tend to see an *attractive* tie or an *ugly* tie. For more complex judgments, people consult an "affect pool" of positive and negative tags associated with objects and events being evaluated. In a manner similar to other heuristics, using the affect pool may be a faster, easier, and more efficient way of weighing the pros and cons of a decision.

Affect plays a role in a wide array of judgment and choice situations. Since affect is a strong conditioner of preference (even if the cause of that affect is not consciously perceived), it is possible to make a judgment that one feels good about but is not necessarily good for the individual (e.g., the decision to smoke cigarettes). Affect is also a factor in the *evaluability* of a choice or judgment: the precision of affective impressions affects judgments (i.e., more precise affective impressions reflect more precise meanings and therefore carry more weight). The concept of evaluability is important because it suggests that even important attributes may not be used unless they can be translated precisely into an affective frame of reference. Probability also appears to map precisely to attractiveness—we innately feel that a high probability of winning is good while a low probability is bad—and the attractiveness of a gamble or other choice is closely related to the attribute of proportion or percentage. These effects are often seen in judgments of risk and benefit for activities such as cigarette smoking, pharmaceuticals, and nuclear power. If people like an activity, they tend to judge the risks as low and the benefits as high. If they dislike it, they judge the opposite. The power of this heuristic is formidable as Slovic et al. note at the end of their paper [41]:

> It is sobering to contemplate how elusive meaning is, due to its dependence on affect. Thus the forms of meaning that we take for granted and use to justify immense effort and expense toward gathering and disseminating "meaningful" information may be illusory. We cannot assume that an intelligent person can understand the meaning of and properly act upon even the simplest of numbers such as amounts of money, not to mention more esoteric measures of statistics, unless these numbers are infused with affect.

3.1.4.4 Gilovich's Determinants of Questionable Beliefs as a Framework for Examining the Role of Cognitive Biases in Deception

In 1991, Thomas Gilovich published a very readable book called *How We Know What Isn't So: The Fallibility of Human Reason in Everyday Life* [42], in which he summarizes much of the social and cognitive psychology research related to what he calls the "determinants" of questionable and erroneous beliefs. Gilovich organizes these determinants into two major categories that capture the essence of the underlying heuristics and biases: *cognitive determinants* and *motivational and social determinants*.

The cognitive determinants category consists of three subcategories. The first subcategory, *something out of nothing*, addresses what Gilovich [43] describes as our ability "...to 'see' order where there is none, and...spot meaningful patterns where only the vagaries of chance are operating." Humans have a powerful ability to explain why the patterns they observe exist and what they mean. As we have already seen, these abilities have been essential to the success of our species. Unfortunately, it is also fairly easy for a person to incorporate a misidentified random pattern into their beliefs about the real world. This biases the person's evaluation and assessment of new information in such a way as to reinforce the original mistaken belief. The *something out of nothing* category includes biases related to the representativeness heuristic, misconceptions of regression, biases related to causality, and hindsight biases.

Too much from too little addresses the *illusion of validity* resulting from judgments and beliefs formed on the basis of incomplete or unrepresentative information. Since we tend to make predictions by selecting the outcome that is most representative of the input, it should be no surprise that our confidence about our predictions depends on the degree of quality of the match (sometimes called goodness of fit) between the input and output. The illusion of validity results in a degree of confidence that is unwarranted by the predictive accuracy of the input and persists even when a person is made aware of the factors limiting the accuracy of the input. Other *too much from too little* biases include errors in detecting covariation, the tendency to seek confirmation (i.e., confirmation bias), the problems of hidden or absent data, and self-fulfilling prophecies (e.g., situations where a person's expectations elicit behaviors that produce the expected results). Errors in covariation make us prone to detecting relationships that are not really there (e.g., illusory correlation) and along with the tendency to seek out confirmatory information, give us an erroneous sense of confidence in our judgments.

Since the *too much from too little* determinant is an important contributor to one's vulnerability to deception, it is worthwhile to explore these last three biases—illusory correlation, confirmation bias, and overconfidence—in a bit more detail. Illusory correlation produces biased judgments about how frequently two events co-occur. The perception of how likely the two events are likely to co-occur is based on the strength of the *associate bond* between them. Strong associations are associated with higher frequencies of co-occurrence. Illusory correlation has been found in clinical settings and is also responsible for many superstitions. A very simple example of this bias is found in word association tests. Words that are highly associated with each other are often seen as occurring more often together than they actually do. For example, test subjects said that the word pairs *bacon-eggs* and *lion-tiger* appeared more often than other pairs (e.g., *bacon-notebook* or *blossoms-tiger*), even though each word pair appeared equally as often as every other [44].

Confirmation bias was compellingly demonstrated in studies performed by Lord et al. in 1979 [45]. In this study, two groups of subjects were given the results of purportedly authentic empirical studies on the deterrent effects of capital punishment. One group had previously indicated their strong belief in capital punishment. The second group felt just as strongly that capital punishment was worthless as a deterrent. The data in one study supported a pro–capital punishment position; the other study supported the opposite position. Both groups rated the study supporting their position as more convincing and better conducted than the study opposing their beliefs. The real surprise was that reading both studies actually polarized the beliefs of both groups even further. Such studies show that information that potentially confirms a person's beliefs is readily accepted, while disconfirmatory evidence is subjected to critical and highly skeptical scrutiny. To matters worse, nearly *any* pattern of ambiguous information—even if it is essentially random—will be seen as supporting the person's initial beliefs.

The word *confidence* refers to the quality or state of being certain. If you ask someone, "How certain are you?" you are essentially asking them if they have any doubts about their answer to the question at hand. Considerable research has been conducted on the question of confidence especially the relationship between level of confidence and level of accuracy. A general conclusion is that there are numerous situations where a person's confidence in his judgment is unwarranted. For example, research shows that people are generally overconfident when tested on general knowledge items of moderate or extreme difficulty. This is not just an effect seen in your typical undergraduate psychology test subject. Over 900 Defense Intelligence Agency analysts and managers were given a general knowledge test [the Subjective Probability Assessment Test (SPATe)] between August 1976 and June 1977, and the results showed that even this group tended to be overconfident [46]. Figure 3.3 shows the DIA SPATe results. Ideally, both the percentage correct and the analyst's estimated probability that the answers are correct should match—the diagonal line in the figure. Data points to the left of the diagonal line indicate overconfidence. Test results for groups of Central Intelligence Agency analysts and managers revealed similar results. In addition, research has shown there appears to be a relationship between the difficulty of the questions and confidence. This has been dubbed

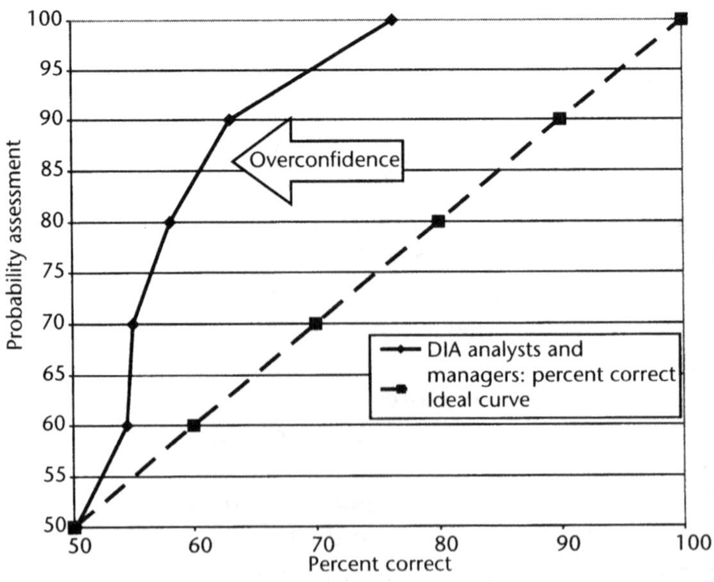

Figure 3.3 DIA intelligence analysts' and managers' SPATe results.

the *difficulty effect*: overconfidence and difficulty are inversely related. Overconfidence tends to decrease as the questions get easier even to the point where the most knowledgeable subjects show significant underconfidence.

What about more realistic situations? How do experts do? Not surprisingly, research has found that experts exhibit significant overconfidence in many situations. For example, Tetlock [47] investigated the reactions of experts to the confirmation or disconfirmation of predictions they had made regarding various world events. The experts participating in the study included graduate students in political science and international relations, postdoctoral fellows in security studies, university professors, think-tank policy analysts, mass media journalists, and even intelligence analysts. Tetlock found that [48]: "Across all seven domains, experts were only slightly more accurate than one would expect from chance (the proverbial dart-throwing, blindfolded chimpanzee who poses such tough competition for financial forecasters)." The margins of error he found were also significantly higher than those usually found in laboratory tests (such as the general knowledge task). Thus, he concludes [48], "Expertise thus may not translate into predictive accuracy but it does translate into the ability to generate explanations for predictions that experts themselves find so compelling that the result is massive over-confidence."

The *seeing what we expect to see* subcategory is again related to the representativeness heuristic as well as to confirmation bias and biases of attribution and causality. The System 1 processes described earlier permit us to rapidly make generally accurate judgments with ease, but can also be responsible for systematic errors. Gilovich notes [49]: "No feature of human judgment and reasoning illustrates this trade-off of advantage and disadvantage better than the tendency for our expectations, preconceptions, and prior beliefs to influence our interpretation of new information. When examining evidence relevant to a given belief, people are inclined to see what they expect to see, and conclude what they expect to conclude." We readily accept ambiguous information and fit it to our preconceptions. Unambiguous information that is consistent with our preconceptions is accepted with little skepticism. Once again, this tendency works to create an erroneous sense of confirmation regarding our preconceptions and beliefs. Inconsistent information is subjected to critical scrutiny and is either found to be flawed and rejected or is given little weight. Inconsistent information can also be redefined and placed in a different category that we believe to be irrelevant to our expectations. Encountering inconsistent information also prompts us to seek out more information until we find information more consistent with our expectations. This category also includes biases related to the selective recall of information consistent with our beliefs due to the availability and of events.

Gilovich also includes the concept of *multiple endpoints* in the *seeing what we expect to see* category. The complexity of many systems (such as human beings) means that any comparison of two entities is likely to produce a certain amount of overlap and thus any prior expectations, especially of similarity, are likely to be confirmed. For example, most of us expect children to bear some resemblance to their parents. This expectation is so strong that similarities are even seen even when the child has been adopted. Multiple endpoints are an important issue in clinical studies where the investigators expectations can lead to erroneous conclusions regarding treatment therapies.

Beliefs are not only resistant to new data, but are also remarkably resistant to information that undermines the original data that formed the basis for the belief in the first place. Belief perseverance after the evidence has been discredited has been demonstrated experimentally. In one experiment [50], a set of test subjects were given the role of observers while other test participants performed a discrimination task. In this task, test subjects had to distinguish authentic suicide notes from fictitious ones. Each test subject received *false* feedback regarding his or her performance. Later, these test subjects were informed, in the presence of the other test subjects who were acting as observers, that the feedback had been fictitious and completely unrelated to their actual performance. Following this discrediting of the feedback, the *observing* test subjects were asked to complete a questionnaire covering the other test subjects' performance and abilities on the task. The results showed the discredited feedback that the subjects in the observer role had formed unmistakable residual effects on their assessment of the subjects' performance and abilities related to the just-completed task. This effect is called *post debriefing perseverance* of personal impressions. Other studies [51] have demonstrated belief perseverance in the formation of an individual's theories (models) about the relationship between variables. These experiments showed that very minimal data (a single pair of firefighters, one successful and one unsuccessful, with suitably discrepant scores of risk-taking preferences) were sufficient to produce strong theories about the relationship. The experiments showed that these theories continued to survive even after it was revealed that the cases were totally fictitious and, in fact, the different firefighters had completely opposite pairings of scores and job outcomes.

Tversky and Kahneman identify prediction and explanation as examples of causal types of inference, while revision represents a type of diagnostic inference [52]. Assuming that people utilize internal models, or schemas, in order to draw inferences about the world, then prediction consists of selecting those outcomes that are most congruent to the person's model. Likewise, the process of explanation consists of identifying features of the model that are most likely to produce the specified outcome. Finally, an individual should revise the model when confronted with new data. Most people would probably agree that the models they rely on can be inaccurate, incomplete, and sometimes incorrect. Unfortunately, as we have seen in previous sections, people confidently make predictions and give explanations that go well beyond that called for by their uncertain models. In addition, if aware that their models are inaccurate and incomplete, they should be ready to revise their models when confronted with new data. In addition, causal data generally have greater impact on our judgments than does diagnostic data. These factors account for our ability to create causal explanations for outcomes that our internal models are not able to predict. It also accounts for the apparent difficulty that people have revising their internal models in the face of new data. Tversky and Kahneman conclude that [53]: "In our view, the subject's response illustrate both the reluctance to revise a rich and coherent model, however uncertain, and the ease with which such a model can be used to explain new facts, however unexpected." This is the very essence of the *seeing what we expect to see* determinant.

The motivational and social determinants category also consists of three subcategories: seeing what we want to see, believing what we are told, and the imagined agreement of others. The *seeing what we want to see* subcategory (not the same as wishful thinking) focuses on many of the egocentric biases found in psychology which show that we tend to adopt self-serving beliefs about ourselves along with comforting beliefs about the world around us [54]. These biases influence what and how much information we consider when making judgments as well as the criteria we use in evaluating it. Research has shown that we tend to form questions in ways that steer us towards information that supports our beliefs and away from information that might contradict our desired conclusion [55]. People also have a tendency to stop the search for information early, especially when the initial search produces supporting information. If the initial evidence contradicts our belief we continue the search for supporting information or for evidence that the earlier, contradictory information was flawed.

Over the past few centuries, the amount of information we obtain about the world firsthand compared to what we receive from secondhand sources has gone steadily down. In fact, it is probably safe to say that most of our knowledge of the world around us is obtained second-hand: from television, radio, newspapers, magazines, the Internet, movies, our friends, coworkers, and on and on. Many of these sources of information are accurate, and the knowledge we derive benefits us in innumerable ways. Nevertheless, this dependence on second-hand sources leaves us vulnerable if we unknowingly incorporate information that is incorrect or distorted into our mental models of the world or our belief systems. The *believing what we are told* subcategory addresses the distortions in accuracy that results from the need or desire to tell a good story and how that same good story can bias our beliefs. For example, distortions in accuracy are often introduced by the person telling a story through the use of sharpening and leveling [56]. Sharpening occurs when the speaker emphasizes what he believes to be the gist of the story's message while simultaneously leveling, or deemphasizing, details that are believed to be less essential or less important. Both are normal processes in human communication and can distort much of what we know from secondhand sources, especially as the distance from the original story increases. Other sources of distortion in stories are simple errors of fact, deliberate errors due to self-interest on the part of the speaker, and by attempts to make the story more informative by making it more immediate, more entertaining, or more plausible.

Finally, *the imagined agreement of others* addresses other egocentric biases such as fundamental attribution error and the false consensus effect [57]. Such biases reflect our tendency to project onto others our own beliefs, attitudes, and predispositions (often known as *mirror-imaging*) and play a role in cultural bias. For example, Jervis [58] quotes William Kaufman's observation that Secretary of State Hull and many of his advisors saw the world "as peopled largely by foreign-speaking Americans." Gilovich also includes inadequate feedback from others in this subcategory. He attributes this to the fact that we tend to associate primarily with those that share our own beliefs and he points to research results that show our general reluctance to voice disagreements—people generally tend to avoid potential conflict with others. One result of this reluctance is the tendency for individuals to suppress their real thoughts and opinions in group situations (i.e., groupthink).

3.2 The Impact of Cognitive Biases on the Deception Story

Heuer's research and insights showed how specific heuristics and biases explain several effects that make deception so effective. We suggested that the categories of cognitive, motivational, and social determinants of beliefs described in the previous section provide a more practical way of thinking about the effects of cognitive biases. In this section we use that framework as we take a more holistic approach to examining the role that cognitive biases have on the development, delivery, and, ultimately, the target's acceptance of the deceiver's deception story.

Stories are a powerful part of nearly all societies and cultures. Records of storytelling exist in numerous languages and go back to mankind's earliest recorded history (recall the Westcar Papyrus mentioned in Chapter 2). It is likely that story telling developed along with human language as a means of explaining the surrounding physical world, communicating experiences to other humans, remembering the history of one's ancestors, entertainment, religious beliefs, and even as a form of art. Stories often have tremendous salience that gives them their power to influence beliefs and actions. The Bible, the Koran, and other scriptural texts include stories (parables and so forth) that tell the tales of gods and prophets, lay down laws, teach codes of behavior, and promise salvation to the faithful. Stories such as folk tales play an important role in transmitting cultural values from one generation to another. Bardic tales chronicle events and memorialize illustrious ancestors or contemporary leaders.

Corporations and the knowledge management community have discovered the power of stories and narrative as well. For example, "war stories" are a common way of learning in organizations and as an effective way of transferring key organizational values and knowledge and building core capabilities. War stories can be regarded as complex forms of examples, filled with many contextual details, insights, surprises, and drama [59]. The same article notes that the case study stories are made memorable by adding drama and complications, which increase the later *availability* of the information, making it more likely to be acted upon when the situation warrants.

Stories can also be just as effective as formal augmentation when it comes to persuasion [60]: "A good story and a well-formed argument are different natural kinds. Both can be used as means for convincing another. Yet what they convince of is fundamentally different: arguments convince one of their truth, stories of their lifelikeness. The one verifies by eventual appeal to procedures for establishing formal and empirical proof. The other establishes not truth but verisimilitude...." The good story's verisimilitude, the *appearance* of truth, is what makes it relevant to deception. The good story has the appearance of truth, it is plausible and believable, but, of course, it is not necessarily true.

It is no wonder that deception researchers have always recognized the power of story and narrative to influence the target. Daniel and Herbig [61] equate the deception planner's task to that of a playwright, "A deception expert has compared his task of formulating and transmitting signals to the work of a playwright. Each devises a story and seeks to put it across to an audience by means of 'scenery, props, costumes, principals, extras, dialogue, and sound effects.' In order to have the story unfold in the intended manner, each must coordinate the timing, tempo, and content of his signals." Narrative psychologist Theodore Sarbin also makes it clear that the deception planner's job is to build a tempting, easily believable story [62]:

> I propose that the planners of strategic interactions, in the course of their work, create a story the elements of which are the bits and pieces of action, some of which are manipulated and some of which are allowed to happen "naturally." The author of a strategy, like any teller of tales, does not string events or happenings together haphazardly, but follows a story line...Like the author of a novel, the author of a strategy emplots a narrative. He fashions a story in which the characters are to play out their roles, influencing each other according to the requirements of the plot.

From Chapter 2 and Heuer's research, we saw that the most successful deceptions were those that exploit the target's preconceptions by presenting a plausible alternative that the target is already inclined to accept as true or desirable and is serious enough to provoke action. A successful deception operation therefore relies on identifying those preconceptions, expectations, and prior beliefs in order to determine what story is congruent with the target's beliefs, that is, what story does the target *want* to hear? Close study of the target is preferred using all the means at the deceiver's disposal, but Daniel and Herbig [63] point out that, "...indirect means of studying the strategic situation will reveal the adversary's expectations clearly enough." In World War II, the compromise of German and Japanese codes gave the Allies the ability to routinely obtain detailed information about German preconceptions, beliefs, and plans, and to subsequently use that information in the development of their deception plans. On the other hand, even the Arabs' indirect knowledge of Israeli and general Western beliefs and preconceptions allowed them to develop a successful deception operation in the 1973 war.

As we pointed out in Chapter 2, deception planners face several problems that playwrights, novelists, storytellers, and magicians don't have. The deception planner does not necessarily have the target's undivided attention, the target's knowledge about the situation is not restricted to the data and information provided by the deceiver, nor can the deceiver be sure that the target will detect and accurately interpret that data and information, and finally, the deceiver does not control all the actors and action that occur. Despite these problems, the target still usually manages to detect, reconstruct, and accept the deception story. Let us now turn our attention to the role cognitive biases might have in helping a deceiver sell a deception story.

We will use Plan BODYGUARD, the overall deception strategy aimed at Germany in preparation for the cross-channel invasion of Europe (Operation OVERLORD), as an example. Although the BODYGUARD deception operation is unique in many ways, it still remains one of the most successful and well-documented deception plans ever created and offers valuable examples of the impact of cognitive bias on the success of the deception.

Anthony Cave Brown [64] described BODYGUARD as "a game plan to mislead the enemy about, and to obscure the truth of, Allied intentions in northwest Europe in 1944." However, instead of a game metaphor, we can also view the overall strategy of the BODYGUARD plan as similar in structure to a challenging mystery story. Good mystery stories actually consist of two stories. The surface story describes what *appeared* to happen while the real story involves what *did* happen.

Mystery stories will often also reveal the story's ending—usually a murder—at the beginning and the reader follows the protagonist's attempts to uncover the truth (e.g., Sherlock Holmes in *The Speckled Band)*. A deception story then is analogous to the surface story of a mystery except that the deception planner does not want the reader to unravel the real story. Like the murder mystery reader, the Germans knew at the beginning of 1944 what the outcome of the story was going to be, in this case, an invasion, not a murder. The Germans were also aware that they were the target of extensive Allied deception operations and yet the Allies' deception still succeeded. The challenge for deception planners is to make sure the target accepts the surface story and fails to discover the real plan.

We will start with the overall plot of the BODYGUARD deception and then examine how cognitive biases played a role in the various elements of the plan. The general objective of BODYGUARD [65] was to "persuade the enemy to dispose his forces in areas where they can cause the least interference with operations OVERLORD and ANVIL and with operations on the Russian Front" and to "deceive the enemy as to the strength, objective and timing of OVERLORD and ANVIL." The broad themes of the deception story are shown in Figure 3.4. The general idea was to convince the Germans that the Allies would continue the peripheral strategy they employed in 1943 and that the cross-Channel attack would not occur before July 1944.

How did the Allied deception planners come up with these particular plot elements? In the case of BODYGUARD, the British were able to gain a remarkably accurate picture of Hitler's mindset from their ULTRA intercepts of German communications and through intercepts of the Japanese Ambassador's diplomatic

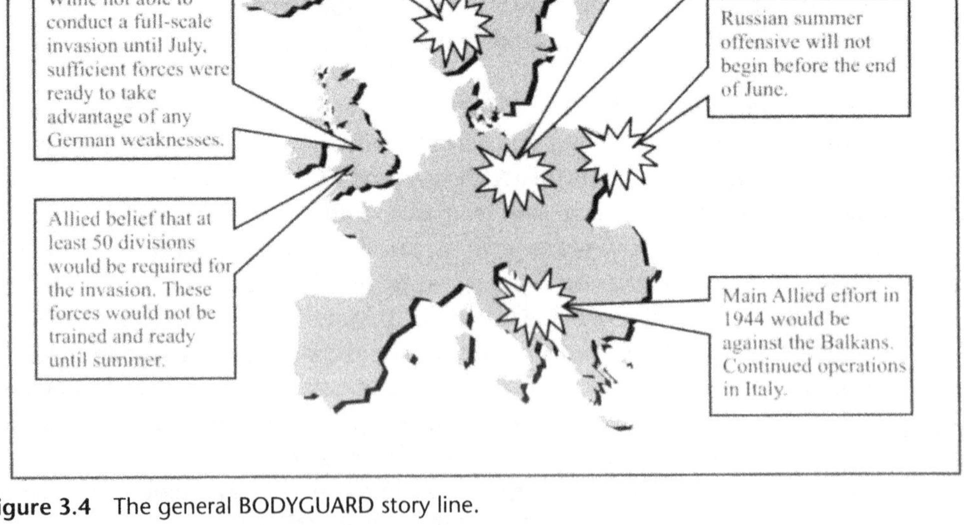

Figure 3.4 The general BODYGUARD story line.

traffic. The British also exploited the Abwehr's deficiencies as well as the dysfunctional command structure that resulted from Hitler's leadership style. This knowledge gave the British a tremendous advantage when scripting the deception story. The overarching themes of BODYGUARD shown in Figure 3.4 then guided the creation of various subplans such as FORTITUDE NORTH, FORTITUDE SOUTH, ZEPPELIN, IRONSIDE, VENDETTA, and so forth. These plans specified the details for acting out the various plot elements and orchestrating the scripts, scenery, props, casting, and special effects that would be put into operation by the various units responsible for implementing each part of the deception story. The end result was a complex mystery story for the Germans to try to unravel—one played out on a stage stretching from Norway to the eastern Mediterranean.

The success of BODYGUARD rested on many factors, random chance playing a major role, of course, but many of its achievements were the direct results of German misperceptions. These misperceptions were for the most part the result of the Germans' personal, cultural, organizational, and cognitive biases when interpreting the information in their possession. Figure 3.5 uses Gilovich's categories as the framework for organizing the various roles that heuristics and biases had in making the BODYGUARD story plausible and ultimately led to its acceptance by Hitler and his generals. The impact of each category on the deception story is shown along with examples taken from the BODYGUARD deception plan.

The *something from nothing* category addresses the human ability to detect seemingly meaningful patterns in random data. The adversary's security efforts, the environment, and distortions in the one's own information processes lead Handel to conclude that [66]: "As a result of the great difficulties in differentiating between 'signals' and 'noise' in strategic warning, both valid and invalid information must be treated on similar basis. In effect, all that exists is noise, not signals." Since noise is, by definition, random, we can see that *something from nothing* plays an important role in deception. *Something from nothing* pretty much ensures that the target is likely to discern patterns in his data. The challenge for the deceiver is for the target to discern the pattern of the deception story, and that is where the too much from too little determinant comes in.

Whereas, *something from nothing* primes the target to detect possible patterns in large amounts of noise, the heuristics that characterize *too much from too little* allow the target to reconstruct the deception story from the fragmentary information that the deceiver feeds into the target's collection channels. The British deception planners knew from experience that they could not just hand masses of disinformation over to the Germans—information that was easily obtained or was too good to be true would likely be disbelieved—instead [67], "It would have to be 'leaked' in bits and pieces in indirect and subtle ways from places far from where the main battle would be fought." At the same time, the British realized that strict security precautions would have to be put into place to ensure that real signals, signals that would contradict the deception story, did not pop up out of the noise and provoke suspicion on the part of the Germans. In the case of the BODYGUARD deception, the Germans did detect and recognize most of the bits and pieces of information and disinformation that were fed to them. By May 1944, Hitler had demonstrated [68] that he had "acquired a thorough grasp of the FORTITUDE SOUTH plot, thus anticipating by more than a week the systematic programme of

	Cognitive heuristics and biases	Impact on the deception story	BODYGUARD examples
Something from nothing	• Bias of representativeness and causality	• Makes it possible for the target to detect patterns even in seemingly random data and integrate those patterns into his beliefs	
Too much from too little	• Errors in detecting covariation • Confirmation bias • Effects of absent or hidden evidence • Overconfidence	• Makes it possible for the target to reconstruct the deception story from even small amounts of information • Alternative story lines are out of sight and out of mind.	• Disinformation fed to the Germans in indirect, subtle bits and pieces • Lack of German access to British Isles • Allied concealment of Mulberry harbors and Pluto pipeline • Air raids against German wireless intercept and DF sites
Seeing what we want to see	• Egocentric biases affecting how people view themselves and what information they consider and how much	• Decision makers are prone to self-serving assessments when apportioning success and failure. • The target tends to search for information that supports his reconstruction of the deception story.	• Hitler saw his military successes as the result of his abilities; any failures that occurred he attributed to those around him.
The imagined agreement of others	• False consensus effect • Reluctance to voice agreement	• Deception planners can exploit the target's tendency to expect an adversary to do what they would do in a given situation. • If the decision-maker accepts the deception story, he is unlikely to hear any information that contradicts that view.	• Increasing reluctance to disagree with Hitler or to be the bearer of bad news • Hitler's withdrawal from those who disagreed with him
Seeing what we expect to see	• Confirmation bias • Overconfidence • Multiple endpoints • Belief persistence and polarization • Prediction, explanation, and revisions	• The deception story is more plausible when it is confirmed by multiple sources: –Ambiguous info is fit to the deception story. –Consistent info is readily accepted with little skepticism and taken as confirmation. –Inconsistent or contradictory info is ignored or subjected to critical scrutiny and rejected or found to be flawed.	• Czar Boris III's death • Recon photos of Mulberry caissons • Double agent "confirmation" of wireless deception • Provocations in Norway and the Balkans • Patton given command of FUSAG • Double agent reports of FUSAG order of battle
Believing what we are told	• Biases of causality, availability, and imaginability • Affect heuristic • Support theory	• The deception story must be salient and plausible to the target. • The deceiver should deny the target access to firsthand info and exploit the distortions resulting from secondhand sources.	• Hitler's preoccupation with Norway and the Balkans • Germany's overreliance on secondary sources (e.g., agents, newspapers and radio reports, "leaks," and rumors)

Figure 3.5 The role of cognitive bias on selling the deception story.

disclosure which the Allied deception staff had set for the performance of the game." In addition, biases related to missing information ensure that alternative story lines, such as the deceiver's real intentions remain out of sight and out of mind.

In addition, two fortuitous conditions ensured that the Germans would be forced to make do with too little information when attempting to decipher the Allies' intentions. The first of these conditions was the lack of any significant German access to the British Isles during the war. The second was the compromise of the entire German spy network in Britain. These two conditions meant that the Germans were cut off from potentially important independent sources of information that might produce data inconsistent with or that contradicted the BODYGUARD story line. For example, lack of access and the compromise of all German agents in England meant that the Allies were able to conceal two critical elements of the NEPTUNE plan (the Normandy landings themselves): the Mulberry harbors and the PLUTO underwater pipeline. The German failure to discover critical information such as this meant that nothing was likely to disturb their belief that the Allies would aim their assault at the Pas de Calais in order to rapidly secure a major port with which to supply the invasion force.

The Allies also took active measures to ensure that the Germans would have to derive *too much from too little.* The British knew and respected the German's expertise at intercepting radio signals and direction finding and exploiting that expertise made up a major part of the FORTITUDE deception program. For example, during FORTITUDE NORTH it did not take long for the Germans to locate and strafe the source of the British 4th Army's wireless deception operations [69]. Later, in order to prevent the Germans from employing those direction-finding skills to delve too deeply into the FUSAG deception, the Allies bombed German intercept and DF sites, as well as their signals intelligence headquarters near Cherbourg, putting them out of commission and preventing any further collection. Once again, the Germans would be left to reconstruct the story from only the bits and pieces that the Allies wanted them to have.

The *seeing what we want to see* category concerns the egocentric biases that affect a person's assessment of their own abilities and explanations for their actions as well as how they search for evidence to support their beliefs. Hitler represents an extreme example of where egocentric biases contributed to the success of a deception plan. Handel [70] describes Hitler's leadership style: "Having developed no habits of cooperation and orderly staff work, Hitler insisted on imposing his ideas on others. Early successes in the face of the opposition of senior military commanders and foreign policy experts convinced him that his intuition was infallible and spurred him on to even more hubristic behavior." Hitler saw his military successes as the result of his abilities, not as the result of complex situational factors. Any failures that occurred he attributed to those around him. Egocentric bias also influences whom people consult when they want opinions or other information and there is a general tendency to selectively search for information in a way that increases the likelihood that a person will hear the opinions that he wants to hear. Once again, Hitler offers an extreme example. By early 1944, Hitler was already becoming more and more withdrawn [71] and deliberately chose his companions "so as not to remind him of his grave and by then insoluble errors." Hitler's egocentric biases, which were generally well known to the British, made him a much easier target for a deception story customized to fit his preconceptions. It is probably impossible to come up with a better extreme example of *seeing what we want to see.*

The deception impact of biases related to *the imagined agreement of others* is seen in two areas. Deception planners know they can often rely on the target's tendency to expect an adversary to do what they themselves would do in the same situation. This behavior is related to the false consensus effect and is generally referred to as mirror imaging. A good example can be found in Brown's description of Rommel pouring over his maps [72], "If he were Montgomery, *he* would invade the Calvados, using his armor to split the 7th and 15th armies and move on Paris." The second area concerns the general reluctance of people to voice disagreement and avoid confrontation. The immediate impact of this inclination in a deception situation is that a decision-maker who is known to have certain beliefs is unlikely to hear any information that contradicts that view or have his beliefs challenged by subordinates. As the war went on and Hitler became increasingly unstable, it became dangerous to disagree with him or to bring him bad news or information that that he did not want to hear. In his section on Intelligence-Leadership Relations, Handel writes [73]: "A look at the leaders and military assistants closest to Hitler—men such as Jodl and Keitel in the OKW, and Ribbentrop, Göring, and Goebbels—reveals that almost all of those with whom he had any contact were sycophants. Ribbentrop and Göring (as well as others in Hitler's coterie) carefully ensured that he received only the reports that confirmed his beliefs and images."

Now we now come to the very linchpin of any deception operation: presenting the target with multiple channels of information that confirm the target's preconceptions and expectations. The German interpretation of the information and disinformation they received in 1944 and their subsequent decisions and actions illustrate all of the different ways that cognitive biases play a role in *seeing what we expect to see.*

As we have seen, one effect of *seeing what we expect to see* is that people have a tendency to interpret ambiguous information as supportive of their beliefs. A good example in our BODYGUARD story is Hitler's reaction to the death of Czar Boris III of Bulgaria who mysteriously collapsed and died in August 1943. Hitler interpreted the ambiguous information regarding the czar's cause of death as evidence of an "enemy plot" by the British and thus a grave threat to his Balkans strategy [74]. Another example involves the Mulberry floating docks referred to earlier. German reconnaissance aircraft had photographed the massive concrete caissons while they were under construction. The photographs were shown to Hitler and although they were direct evidence of some sort of Allied capability, they were ambiguous as to what exactly they were to be used for. As one might expect, Hitler's interpretation of the photographs was consistent with his preconceptions. He thought they were self-propelled quays to replace those in the French port that the Allies planned to seize and which the German engineers had orders to destroy when the invasion started [75].

However, the key to the target's acceptance of the deception story is to play to the cognitive biases that give rise to confirmation bias and belief persistence. The BODYGUARD deception did this in spades. First, the lack of German access to the British Isles, the compromise of the German spy network, and stringent security measures meant that the British were able to effectively put Jones' Lemma (Deception Maxim 4 in Figure 2.7) into effect and control nearly all important channels of information available to the Germans. This gave them the opportunity to ensure that disinformation fed to the Germans through one channel could be confirmed through another. For example, the FORTITUDE NORTH radio deception campaign was carefully coordinated with the British "special means" (their network of double agents) in order to ensure that both means supported the other. Several British double agents provided the Germans with information that confirmed not only the wireless deception activities but other agent reports as well. For example, two days before wireless deception operations began, FREAK provided information about the arrival of the fictitious 2nd British Corps in Stirling, Scotland. A few weeks later, GARBO's notional "deputy," Agent Three, reported that he had seen the British 52nd Lowland Division (a real unit) in Dundee as well as an unidentified military unit whose troops wore an insignia employing a shell on dark background. Later, BRUTUS reported the existence of the notional British 7th Corps at Dundee who used a seashell on a blue rectangle as their insignia. This conveniently confirmed the information provided by Agent Three earlier [76].

Other BODYGUARD examples of feeding the deception target information consistent with his expectations included:

- Provocations in Norway and the Balkans in order to create information that confirmed German expectations that those areas were targets for invasion;
- Giving Patton "command" of the notional First U.S. Army Group (FUSAG) based on known German expectations that Patton would be the spearhead of the invasion;
- Double agent (BRUTUS) reports of the FUSAG order of battle that confirmed German estimates;
- And, of course, once NEPTUNE was underway, there was GARBO's famous message that the Normandy assault was only a feint; thus confirming German beliefs that the real attack would come at Pas de Calais.

The FORTITUDE SOUTH deception plan also illustrates the effects of *multiple endpoints*. The immense scale and complexity of preparations for OVERLORD meant that many observations could be fit to multiple endpoints (i.e., any number of invasion possibilities). The rest of Brown's anecdote about Rommel provides a good example [77]:

> Then with a pair of calipers he would draw arcs from the main air bases in southern and southwestern England—arcs that described the ranges of the enemy's Spitfire and Mustang fighter force. Rommel knew that whatever else they did, the Allies would never land except at a point where their air forces could be deployed to maximum effect. But those arcs embraced all of the beaches of Normandy, as well as the Cherbourg and Breton peninsulas. In short, Rommel did not have the slightest idea where or when the Allies would land.

In the end, however, the Germans fit their observations, both real and false, to their belief in an invasion aimed at Pas de Calais. Even the landings at Normandy fit into their preconceptions since they had expected diversionary landings at Normandy or Brittany. It was clearly a case of *seeing what we expect to see*.

The deception impact of our last category, *believing what we are told*, might seem obvious at first, but is actually a bit more subtle than its literal interpretation implies. All of the categories discussed so far primarily address how we process information and are directly related to the heuristics and biases we reviewed in Section 3.1.2. On the other hand, the errors and biases in belief that are associated with the *believing what we are told* category are related directly to the distorted information that results as people rely more and more on secondhand sources of information. Cognitive biases are likely to play an important, but secondary role; but the real problem is that the information received from secondhand sources may already be distorted. As Gilovich [78] points out, "A person's conclusions can only be as solid as the information on which they are based. Thus, a person who is exposed to almost nothing but inaccurate information on a given subject almost inevitably develops an erroneous belief, a belief that can seem to be 'an irresistible product' of the individual's (secondhand) experience."

The *believing what we are told* category has direct relevance to the problem of deception, since the target of deception, the decision-maker, depends almost entirely on secondhand information. It has been a very long time since a national leader or senior military commander has been able to obtain all the information needed concerning a situation on a firsthand basis. Even in ancient times, leaders had to rely on secondhand sources such as spies, traders, and diplomats for information about an adversary's capabilities and intent. In the information age the problem is even worse. Decision-makers must rely on the reports and summaries from diplomats, all source intelligence analysts, military and political advisors, and the media, all of which, in turn, rely mostly on secondhand sources for their own information. The spy's secondhand verbal report (or possibly even third- or fourth-hand) is summarized by his case officer and sent back to headquarters where it may be further filtered before it reaches the analyst who interprets it and integrates it with other secondhand information before delivering it the decision-maker. Even information that is considered direct evidence such as satellite imagery is transformed into secondhand information. The bulk of imagery that is collected is interpreted by imagery analysts who document their analysis of the picture in a written report. Jervis provides an example of one such photo interpreter report from World War II. The photo interpreter described seeing [79]: "a thick vertical column about forty feet high and four feet thick." Such reports provided accurate but not very useful information until photo interpreters realized that what they were looking at were German V-2 rockets. The possibility for introducing distortions and inaccuracies in this information chain seems almost inevitable even if only due to simple errors and omissions. The situation is made far worse when bureaucratic politics and self-interest enter the picture. For example, it was common practice for the Sicherheitsdienst (SD) to cut by half the Fremde Heere West (FHW; the section of the German General Staff responsible for intelligence estimates about the western Allies) estimates of the Allied order of battle in England before passing them on to Hitler. This was part of the SD's attempt to prove their superiority over the army. As a result of these lower estimates, Hitler began removing units from the West, further weakening the Atlantic Wall. In response, the FHW began doubling their estimates of the order of battle in order to convince Hitler to reinforce the wall, not weaken it, and justified these higher estimates by using all the information at the FHW's disposal, including much of what they considered to be part of the deception efforts of the Allies. When the SD suddenly began accepting and passing on the inflated FHW estimates, the result was general German acceptance of the FORTITUDE order of battle (over 90 divisions, including seven airborne divisions), instead of the original, more accurate FHW estimates [80–82].

When deception is a factor, secondhand information becomes even more distorted. Deception planners love secondhand sources and depend on them heavily to pass disinformation to the target. They are especially effective when the information is difficult, if not impossible, to verify. As we saw earlier, the German's lack of access to the British Isles meant that they were forced to rely almost solely on secondhand sources of information. The British used information leaked to newspapers and radio to provide many of the bits and pieces of the deception. Newspapers reported items such as football matches involving notional army units and the BBC even "spent a day" with the fictional 7th Corps in Scotland. This type of information tipped German radio intercept operators to the existence of Allied units that the British controlled double agents were then later tasked to cover. Secondhand sources can also be used to *confirm* information obtained firsthand from reconnaissance photos or communications intercepts as we saw earlier when British controlled German agents confirmed information from other sources and from each other. The success of the FORTITUDE deception demonstrates that the target's overreliance on secondhand sources of information, combined with overconfidence in the credibility of those sources, can significantly increase the likelihood that the deception story will be believed.

Human sources of information can also often distort information even if they are not controlled by a hostile service. Their stories are not only subject to normal sharpening and leveling distortions, but they may be deliberately distorted (or even fabricated) out of self-interest or just an honest effort to be helpful. For example, an agent might report that he observed an event in person when in actuality he was only reporting a rumor he had heard. Sources might also leave out important qualifiers—the test aircraft made its first flight, but crashed shortly afterwards—or to stretch their facts when they provide information in an effort to make it more valuable to the intended audience.

Increasing the immediacy or entertainment value of a story can also be used to increase the likelihood the target accept its premises. The FORTITUDE deception planners seemed to have had an innate understanding of this aspect to believability. They went to great efforts to give a sense of immediacy to their double agent reports. In fact, Masterman lists this as one of his 12 principles for working with double agents [83]:

> The next principle is that a double agent should as far as possible, actually live the life and go through all the motions of a genuine agent. If, for example, our agent was told by his German masters to inspect and report on factories at Wolverhampton, we arrange, if it was possible, that he should visit the place himself before he replied...As a result his messages appeared to be true, and he did not trip over details of topographical or local observation.

They even made their deception stories entertaining for their German audience. FUSAG radio chatter coming from southeast England included tidbits like [84]

"1/5th Queen's Royal Regiment report a number of civilian women, presumably unauthorized, in the baggage train. What are we going to do with them—take them to Calais?"

In the end, a deception story is only believable because the story itself is plausible. In Chapter 2 we quoted Whaley's proposal that [85], "the best stratagem is one that generates a set of warning signals susceptible to alternative, or better yet, optional interpretations, where the intended solution is implausible in terms of the victim's prior experience and knowledge while the false solution (or solutions) is plausible. If the victim does not suspect the possibility that deception is operating, he will inevitably be gulled." The BODYGUARD deception demonstrates the real power of a well-planned, highly plausible deception story that is designed to exploit the target's biases. Such a story makes it possible for the target to be "gulled" *even when he suspects* that his adversary is running a deception operation against him. As we have seen throughout this section, every aspect of the BODYGUARD deception story was designed to attract the attention of the Germans, make it relevant to their known beliefs and expectations, and, of course, be entirely plausible. After all, given Patton's reputation as a commander, wasn't it entirely plausible, if not completely obvious, that he would be given command of main assault force, FUSAG? The plausibility of all the story elements and the German's unwarranted confidence in their secondhand sources represents a classic case of *believing what we are told*.

3.3 Cognitive Bias and Principles of Deception

The generalized deception cycle we presented in Chapter 2 (see Figure 2.13) showed a process by which the data the target receives through various channels is reorganized into information (the reconstructed story) that affects the target's perceptions, which shape the target's understanding of the situation, which guides the target's decisions and actions. We also noted that additional delays, noise, and filters complicate the process at each step. We also proposed that the methods used to reveal/conceal both facts and fictions to/from the target are based on four basic principles of deception:

1. *Truth.* All deception works within the context of what is true.
2. *Denial.* Denying the target access to the truth is the prerequisite to all deception.
3. *Deceit.* All deception requires deceit.
4. *Misdirection.* Deception depends on manipulating what the target registers.

In this section, we will look at what roles, in concert with the target's cognitive biases, these principles play in the target's reconstruction and acceptance of the deception story (see Figure 3.6). Our assumption is that once the target reconstructs the story and finds it plausible, believable, and *actionable*, it will likely affect his perceptions and understanding in the intended manner and thus prompt the actions and decisions that will give the deceiver some sort of competitive advantage. As you read, keep in mind that both these principles and the various cognitive biases are

	Truth	Denial	Deceit	Misdirection
Something out of nothing	Patterns associated with real objects, phenomena, events, and information	Wrong or distorted patterns because access to real objects, phenomena, events, and information is blocked	Wrong or distorted patterns based on observations of mimics and disinformation	Patterns associated with real or false objects, phenomena, events, and information used to divert attention or reduce suspicion
Too much from too little	Finding relationships between real objects, phenomena, events, and information	Errors in detecting covariation or causality, illusion of validity, and overconfidence due to hidden and absent data	Errors in detecting covariation or causality, illusion of validity, and overconfidence due to judgments based on disinformation or false observations	Errors in covariation and causality as well as overconfidence contribute to diverting attention or reducing suspicion.
Seeing what we expect to see	Ambiguous information fit to expectations and preconceptions Contradictory information ignored or critically scrutinized and given little weight Real objects, phenomena, events, and information imply *multiple endpoints*. Revealing the truth can be used to reinforce the target's preconceptions and expectations.	Out of sight, out of mind	Disinformation and false observations are readily fit to expectations and preconceptions.	Real or false objects, phenomena, events, and information used to reduce suspicion or divert attention
Seeing what we want to see	The search for supporting information continues despite finding information that contradicts beliefs.	Lack of access limits sources and amounts of information used to make judgments and reinforces tendency to search for information that supports beliefs.	Discovery of disinformation that supports beliefs contributes to premature termination of search.	Discovery of disinformation that supports beliefs contributes to reduced suspicions.
Believing what we are told	Real events and information contribute to the informativeness, immediacy, entertainment value, and plausibility of the good story. Real events and information reinforce the target's confidence in his second-hand sources.	Secondhand sources leave inconsistencies and ambiguous details out of the story (leveling). Secondhand sources create deliberate distortions by leaving out important details. Access to firsthand sources cut off or denied	Deliberate distortions used to make the story seemingly more informative, immediate, entertaining, or plausible	Real, distorted, or false stories used to divert attention or reduce suspicion
The imagined agreement of others	Real events and information contribute to the false consensus effect.	Inadequate feedback from others	Others pretend to agree out of self interest.	Others pretend to agree or provide inadequate feedback in order to reduce suspicion or divert attention.

Figure 3.6 Deception principles contribute to every type of cognitive bias.

highly interdependent. All of the cells in the matrix shown in Figure 3.6 represent a holistic system that, taken together, will affect what the target perceives. Deception methods based on one principle might exploit one set of cognitive biases with the result that methods based on another principle are able to more effectively exploit another set of other cognitive biases and so on and so on. Trying to imagine all the possible combinations and permutations is probably impossible so the following discussion concentrates on the relationship between each principle and each of the categories of cognitive biases that we have used so far as our framework.

3.3.1 Truth: The Source of Expectations, Preconceptions, and Beliefs

The heuristics described in Section 3.1.4 produce judgments and decisions that are generally accurate and make our day-to-day lives possible. They use sophisticated cognitive processes to arrive at fast, automatic, and nearly effortless assessments of stimuli in a wide variety of contexts. Most of the stimuli associated with our day-to-day experiences are in the context of real, not deceptive, objects, events, phenomena, and signals and the perceptions associated with them form the basis for our mental models (patterns) of how the world works. They also form the foundation from which many of our expectations, preconceptions, and beliefs are derived. The physical objects, events, phenomena and signals we observe and the information and knowledge that we derive from them constitute the *truth* we refer to in our first principle of deception. Since the truth is the source of so many expectations, preconceptions, and beliefs about the world, it should be no surprise that it is called upon to support the deceiver's deception story and to exploit the target's biases.

In the case of *something out of nothing*, we saw that real but random events are often interpreted to represent patterns that do not really exist (such as the "hot hand" in basketball) and we suggested that this predisposition to detect patterns in even random data makes it possible for the target to pick out the deceiver's signals from a jumbled background of signals and noise. One example of this that is relevant to deception is traffic analysis. This is the process of intercepting and analyzing an adversary's communications network in order to infer intelligence from the *patterns* of messages that are observed flowing over a communications network. For example, analyzing who talks to who can reveal information about an adversary's chain of command and order of battle, while examining the volume and timing of communications traffic can reveal information about operational plans (e.g., large amounts of traffic flowing between specific entities are normally associated with upcoming training exercises). As we will see, the *real* patterns that the target associates with the deceiver's routine behaviors can be exploited by deception methods associated with other deception principles.

The traffic analysis example provides an excellent lead in for considering the role that truth plays in exploiting the next category of biases: *too much from too little*. Recall that this category concerns the inordinate impact that confirmation has on people's ability to recognize relationships between two variables. If both variables are present, people are likely to conclude there is a relationship between them. So, for example, if traffic analysis of intercepts and agent reports show the presence of a unit in a certain geographic area, that might indicate a relationship between it and another unit in that same area. An example can be found in Hesketh [86], "Let us see what the Germans should have discovered by 1st April as a result of these reports. The location of Fourth Army at Edinburgh was confirmed... The 2nd British Corps had just moved to Stirling. It was therefore, not unreasonable to suppose that it might be connected in some way with Fourth Army." In this example, both the Fourth Army and the 2nd British Corps are fictional units; however, the FORTITUDE NORTH plan included real British and American units if they happened to be located in the right places as in the case of the British 52nd Lowland Division in Dundee which helped to establish its relationship to the fictional 7th British Corps also located in Dundee. Including real units in a way that they would be associated with fictional corps and armies contributed to the *too much from too little* errors in the German assessments of the Allied order of battle.

As we stated at the beginning of this section, truth, more often than deception, forms the basis for our expectations, preconceptions, and beliefs. In the context of deception, truth contributes in several ways to the deceiver's exploitation of the *seeing what we expect to see* biases. First, any true but ambiguous information is readily accepted by the target and fit into his expectations as we saw earlier with Hitler's reaction to the news of Czar Boris III's death. Second, the target's *seeing what we expect to see* biases give the deceiver a decided advantage if any pieces of the real plan happen to be revealed since information that contradicts expectations is often ignored or critically scrutinized in an attempt to minimize its impact. Dewar relates a story about the U.S. Secretary of the Navy, Frank Knox, who was quoted in the press that Sicily would be the next target of the Allies (Operation HUSKY). Fortunately the BARCLAY deception was so effective that Joseph Goebbels dismissed Fox's gaffe with the statement [87]: "We pay no attention to these....attempts at camouflage." The truth also supports deception plans thanks to the multiple endpoints effect we have discussed. The real units that made up British naval forces in Scotland ('S' Force) were part of both the FORTITUDE NORTH deception operation as well as the real planning for NEPTUNE. However, the Germans tended to overlook this fact and see 'S' Force only in the role they expected to see, that of supporting an Allied thrust at Norway. Finally, and probably most importantly, revealing the truth can be used to reinforce the target's preconceptions and expectations. Those were real operations (e.g., commando attacks in Norway and the Balkans) that helped to reinforce Hitler's preconceptions. Even the reality of the landings themselves supported Germans expectations that they were only a diversion, as well as further adding to the credibility of the British double agents. Likewise, the truth plays a similar role in the *seeing what we want to see* category. When the target is confronted with real data or information that contradicts his beliefs, he is unlikely to change them but instead will continue his search for information until he finds information that confirms those beliefs.

In the previous section we saw that *believing what we are told* by secondhand sources can contribute to the acceptance of questionable and erroneous beliefs. From the perspective of the deception planner, revealing the truth to the target via secondhand sources is important for two reasons. First, incorporating real events, people, organizations, equipment, and information into the deception story and making that information available to the target is likely to significantly increase its immediacy, plausibility, and even entertainment value, thus making it more believable. As Masterman states [88], "Broadly speaking, then, this particular principle amounts to little more than an insistence on the prime necessity for truth whenever truth is possible. A lie when it is needed will only be believed if it rests on a firm foundation of previous truth." Second, revealing the truth to the target not only makes the deception story more plausible, but it also increases his confidence in his sources of information. In Chapter 2 we gave the example of Handel's four rules for "feeding" the target's intelligence system real information in this regard. The effective use of feed material bolsters the source's credibility and later, when the time is right, the various channels that have proven to be so reliable will be used to funnel the deceiver's disinformation to a target that is already predisposed to accept those sources without question.

Finally, the truth contributes to the false consensus effect and other *imagined agreement of others* biases since real events reinforce these egocentric biases. Because people tend to associate with people who are similar to them, they are exposed to more situations in which others have agreed with them than disagreed. This is particularly typical of authoritarian leaders like Hitler and Stalin where their day-to-day experiences with subordinates were likely to bias their judgment.

3.3.2 Denial: Out of Sight, Out of Mind

If the deceiver has accurately assessed the target and has developed a fairly accurate picture of the target's preconceptions and expectations, then denial is the key to making sure that nothing significant occurs to change the target's mind. As we stated in Chapter 2, the success of the deception operation is highly dependent on concealing the true nature of the situation from target. Denial is a powerful lever for making deception more effective and improves the likelihood that the target will detect and accept the deceiver's deception story.

If the something out of nothing biases produce a strong predisposition to find patterns in random data, than blocking the target's access to real data almost guarantees that the patterns the deception target finds based on his observations will be wrong or distorted. For example, the Allied security measures protecting the NEPTUNE plan included strict radio silence and use of landline communications to conceal the real buildup of forces in southwest England from the German eavesdropping. At the same time, the Allies transmitted phony radio traffic both in code and in the clear in order to give the appearance of an increasing concentration of FUSAG forces in southeast England. Once the target has detected the false pattern of the deception story, the too much from too little category of biases adds to the target's distorted picture of the situation. Without access to accurate information, the target is even more likely to make errors in detecting covariation or causality.

Denial has its greatest impact though on the seeing what we expect to see set of biases. The auto repair fault tree experiment [89] and real-world examples such as the DC-10 cargo compartment decompression disasters [90] demonstrate that people consistently fail to appreciate the limits of the data and information available to them—the famous "But there are also unknown unknowns—the ones we don't know we don't know" quote of U.S. Secretary of Defense Donald Rumsfeld. What is unknown, what is out of sight, is essentially out of mind. Once again, the Mulberry floating harbors and PLUTO underwater pipeline from the BODYGUARD deception provide an excellent example. The Allies success at concealing the purpose of the Mulberries and the existence of PLUTO from the Germans meant that any available information the Germans did come to have, such as the reconnaissance photos mentioned earlier, only reinforced their expectations that the Allies would probably seek to seize a good sized harbor with which to supply the invasion force.

Denial can contribute to the impact of the seeing what we want to see biases as well. Since people tend to search for information that supports their preferences, and to terminate that search once they find it, concealing contradictory information from the deception target helps to ensure that the target will be satisfied with information that he obtains that supports his beliefs. For example, Hesketh notes that [91], "The inadequacy of air reconnaissance was a constant cause of complaint by the German Intelligence Staff." Overland coverage of southern England was nonexistent. What reconnaissance was available to the Germans was limited to coverage of the southern English ports and coast. Given that the Germans were receiving what they saw as high quality information from their British-controlled agents, there seems to have been little pressure on the Luftwaffe to provide more aggressive air reconnaissance.

Denial plays a significant role in distorting the information from secondhand sources. From the perspective of the deception planner, denial is important to the believing what we are told category for three reasons. First, secondhand sources normally tend to leave minor inconsistencies and ambiguous details out of the story anyway. Recall that this leveling introduces distortions to a story that become worse as the distance between the listener and original source increases (i.e., third-hand, fourth-hand, or greater). Second, these distortions are obviously made even worse when secondhand sources, like double agents or agents of influence, deliberately leave out or fabricate important details. And third, denying access to firsthand, uncontrolled sources makes it less likely that the target will be able to verify his secondhand information. The success of the BODYGUARD deception was the result of German lack of access to uncontrolled firsthand sources of information and their mistaken confidence in their most important secondhand sources: their Abwehr agents in Britain. They believed the deception story these sources were telling them.

Finally, denial's role in the imagined agreement of others is different—it is usually not the deceiver who is doing the denial. As we saw in Hitler's case, when it becomes dangerous to bring bad news or information that contradicts a decision-maker's beliefs, those around him are likely to withhold important information out of fear. They are essentially practicing a form of denial that is just as effective as if it was done by the deceiver.

3.3.3 Deceit: Reinforcing the Biases

While denial is the foundation of deception's success, deceit is the means for weaving the fabric of the deception story. Deceit actively distorts the target's perceptions and subsequent understanding of the situation by leveraging the other deception principles and further exploiting and reinforcing the target's biases. Deception planners deliberately design deception methods and observables to reinforce the something out of nothing and too much from too little biases. In the case of the former, deceit increases the likelihood that the patterns of deception the target discovers are not only wrong or distorted but that they are also actually the patterns that the deceiver wants the target to see. The latter exploit the target's tendency to rely too much on instances that seem to confirm the existence of relationships. In the case of BODYGUARD, the fact that so many German divisions were still in Norway, the Balkans, Italy, and southern France on D-Day is convincing evidence that the deceit elements of the deception operation successfully contributed to Hitler's perceived and registered the patterns that the Allies wanted him to see.

If the truth contributes to creating the target's expectations and helps to establish the credibility of the channels controlled by the deceiver, then deceit is the means by which those expectations and channels are fully exploited. The deceiver employs methods of deception in the physical and symbolic domains that is specifically tailored to fit the target's expectations. For example, to reinforce German expectations that the main Allied assault would be aimed at the Pas de Calais, the British constructed a giant dummy oil dock at Dover. Physically, the dock occupied almost three square miles and consisted of fake pipelines, storage tanks, jetties, and all the other details that gave it the appearance of a real oil dock. It was heavily guarded by military police and protected by anti-aircraft guns as well as constant fighter protection overhead. If the Germans shelled the facility with long-range artillery across the Channel, the British would simulate hits with the appropriate fire and smoke. The king "inspected" the dock, as did General Montgomery. Such a sophisticate creation provided the Germans with realistic physical and symbolic evidence that fit their expectations of a major effort aimed at Calais.

Deceit is a factor in the *seeing what we want to see* bias when the target's discovery of information supporting his beliefs causes him to prematurely terminate any further serious search for additional evidence. As we saw in the previous section, the Germans considered the information they were receiving from their agents in England to be both extremely valuable and highly credible. Of course, much of this information was fabricated by the BODYGUARD deception planners to appeal to German beliefs and preconceptions and since it had all the appearance of being authentic, it likely limited any serious attempts to search for other sources of information.

Deceit is probably the first thing one thinks of with regard to the relationship between believing what we are told and deception. After all, it is deceit in the form of double agent intrigue, daring operations like MINCEMEAT, security "leaks," and inflatable tanks, trucks, and landing craft that makes reading about the history of deception interesting. Deceit in day-to-day life varies from blatant misrepresentation to subtle implications and from altruistic little white lies to malicious deceit aimed at gaining advantage over another person. Likewise, deceit in deception ranges from the propagandist's "Big Lie" [92] to the dozens of false details that went into creating "Major Martin" in the MINCEMEAT operation. In all cases, the intent is to create a believable false or misleading perception in the mind of the target. Earlier we made the point that the target of deception, the decision-maker, depends almost entirely on secondhand information and that this dependence makes the decision-maker vulnerable to serious biases and errors, especially if those secondhand sources are providing false or inaccurate information. To quote Gilovich again [93], "... a person who is exposed to almost nothing but inaccurate information on a given subject almost inevitably develops an erroneous belief..." Thus, in the BODYGUARD operation, hundreds of deceits were presented to the Germans, who, relying on a limited number of secondhand sources, reconstructed and accepted nearly all the elements of the overall deception story outlined in Figure 3.5.

Deceit contributes to the biases associated with the imagined agreement of others in two ways. First, pretending to agree with an adversary has been used as a form of strategic deception for most of human history. One side signs treaties, nonaggression pacts, arms limitation or disarmament agreements, and other types of promises with no real intent of abiding by them. In 1939, Hitler signed a nonaggression pact with Stalin in order to forestall having to fight a two-front war only to turn and launch a surprise attack on Russia two years later in Operation Barbarossa. The second way is when those around the decision maker agree with his beliefs out of their own self-interest. No doubt many of the German officers around Hitler made the expedient decision to agree with the Führer, thereby further aggravating his preconceptions.

3.3.4 Misdirection: Diverting Attention and Reducing Suspicion

Magic not only exploits many of our perceptual biases, but it also is likely that it takes advantage of many of the cognitive biases covered in Section 3.1. The way the magician sets up the trick hints at framing effects, the order in which the trick unfolds suggests errors related to causality and covariation, and many of the magician's methods probably exploit many of the biases related to availability biases. Likewise, deception planners use methods that are designed to control the target's attention and suspicions, not to entertain, but to put the target at a disadvantage.

Misdirection relevant to the something out of nothing case typically takes the form of physical misdirection. The deceiver exploits the natural tendency for novelty, movement, and contrast to attract or divert the target's attention. New patterns of activity, changes in personnel, new equipment configurations, or new or upgraded facilities are often quickly detected and attract the attention of observers and analysts in an attempt to understand what the new pattern means. Movement also has the same effect and can quickly capture the target's attention. The Allies always made sure to pass information to the Germans about the movement of real and fictional units related to the FUSAG deception knowing that this would attract their attention and distract them from the real buildup in southwest England. The second relevant form of misdirection is reducing suspicion through the use of consistency and necessity. If the deceiver can create a pattern of activity that is consistent with routine activities, the target is likely to detect the pattern and immediately classify it as representative of normal activity—nothing to worry about—like the military exercises that the Egyptians held along the Suez prior to the 1973 war. The same is true for necessity. For example, part of the BODYGUARD story was that an invasion of France would not occur before July 1944 because the assault forces would not be ready until then. As a result, deception operations were aimed at reducing German suspicions of an earlier assault by reinforcing a pattern that implied that Allied units were still receiving necessary training and equipment.

The fact that Hitler left thousands of troops and tanks spread over Norway, the Balkans, Italy, and southern France instead of concentrating them along the Atlantic Wall attests to the power of misdirection with regard to deception for the rest of our categories. The entire BODYGUARD deception plan was based on misdirection and, as we have seen in previous sections, manipulated a broad range of biases across each category. Too much from too little biases meant that the Germans erroneously accepted the FUSAG order of battle, while seeing what we expect to see biases meant that they erroneously concluded that Patton's assignment to FUSAG meant it would be the main assault force. Such errors diverted their attention to southeast England and reduced their suspicions that Normandy was the real target.

Seeing what we want to see biases kept German attention focused on Norway and the Balkans as well as reducing the likelihood that they would uncover information that might increase their suspicions. The Ultra intercepts and the Double Cross system gave the Allies a unique advantage over the Germans and made it possible to design a deception story that effectively exploited the believing what we are told biases. British-controlled double agents fed the Germans nearly all the important pieces of the deception story diverting German attention from one area while attracting it to another, increasing Hitler's suspicions with regard to one place and reducing them somewhere else.

Finally, misdirection can contribute to *the imagined agreement of others*. One of the misdirection methods we described in Chapter 2 involved reducing the spectator's suspicion by raising his conviction regarding the effect. This method involved charisma, likeability, and the conviction of the magician himself. In the context of deception, a charismatic and likeable leader can often convince others that he agrees with them and is committed to their interests. Such behavior can be a very powerful means of reducing the adversary's suspicions and diverting his attention from his real intent.

3.4 Summary

The purpose of this chapter has been to examine the role biases, and especially cognitive biases, play in deception and how they contribute to the manipulation of the deception target's perceptions and beliefs as well as his acceptance of the deception story. Our strategy for achieving this purpose was to provide the reader with a brief overview of the concepts of personal, cultural, and organizational biases and then to focus on a broader review of cognitive biases, primarily in the area known as heuristics and biases. Our intent was not to cover every aspect of social and cognitive psychology that might be relevant to deception in general, but to concentrate in an area that has already been identified as important to the topic of intelligence analysis and counterdeception. We also introduced Thomas Gilovich's six determinants of questionable beliefs as a simplified framework for thinking about the role cognitive biases play in deception. After briefly reviewing the seminal work of Richards Heuer in this area, we used Gilovich's framework to examine the impact of cognitive biases from a different perspective, that of the impact they have on the reconstruction and acceptance of the deceiver's deception story. Finally, we looked at how the four basic deception principles that we developed in Chapter 2 contribute to the effectiveness of each category of cognitive bias in creating a plausible and believable deception story.

Before moving on, it should be noted that although the picture we paint in this chapter makes it sound like human judgment and decision-making are hopelessly flawed, that is not necessarily the case. As Heuer has noted in 1982 [94], "How humans perceive and process information to arrive at analytical judgments is not fully understood. Although the evidence presented here is persuasive, it is not conclusive. The intention of this paper is not to deliver the last word in psychological theory...The purpose is to describe the current state of knowledge from a perspective that views human cognitive processes as a critical variable in explaining fallible human judgment." Indeed, since Heuer first noted the applicability of heuristics and biases to the study of deception, the field has continued to evolve and is not without controversy [95]. It is also important to note that even the proponents of these theories recognized that people's beliefs do change given the right circumstances [96]. The aim of this chapter has been to make the reader aware of the impact biases have on belief when deception is a factor and to set the stage in Chapter 6 where we will look at what the field of psychology has to say about debiasing and how those ideas can contribute to the development of various approaches to counterdeception.

Endnotes

[1] Thompson, J. R., R. Hopf-Weichel, and R. E. Geiselman, *The Cognitive Bases of Intelligence Analysis,* Arlington, VA: U.S. Army Intelligence and Threat Analysis Center Report No. R83-039C, 1984, pp. 2–9.

[2] Hall, E., *The Silent Language,* New York: Anchor Books, 1990, p. 148.

[3] Kerbel, J., "Thinking Straight: Cognitive Bias in the US Debate About China," *Studies in Intelligence,* Vol. 48, No. 3, 2004, pp. 27–35.

[4] Lai, D., "Learning from the Stones: A *Go* Approach to Mastering China's Strategic Concept, *Shi,*" Strategic Studies Institute, U.S. Army War College, 2004, p. 5, http://www.carlisle.army.mil/ssi/.

[5] Godson, R., and J. J. Wirtz, "Strategic Denial and Deception," in Godson, R., and J. Wirtz, (eds.), *Strategic Denial and Deception: The Twenty-First Century Challenge,* New Brunswick, NJ: Transaction Publishers, 2002, p. 3.

[6] Dahl, A. B., "Command Dysfunction: Minding the Cognitive War," master's thesis, School of Advanced Airpower Studies, Air University, 1996, p. 20.

[7] Amos, J., "Deception and the 1973 Middle East War," in Daniel, D., and K. Herbig, (eds.), *Strategic Military Deception,* New York: Pergamon Press, 1982, p. 322.

[8] Jervis, R., *Perception and Misperception in International Politics,* Princeton, NJ: Princeton University Press, 1976, p. 239.

[9] Handel, M. I., *War, Strategy, and Intelligence*, London, U.K.: Frank Cass & Co., Ltd., 1989, p. 335.

[10] Foot, M. R. D., "Conditions Making for Success and Failure of Denial and Deception: Democratic Regimes," in Godson, R., and J. Wirtz, (eds.), *Strategic Denial and Deception: The Twenty-First Century Challenge,* New Brunswick, NJ: Transaction Publishers, 2002, p. 112.

[11] Daniel, D. C., and K. L. Herbig, "Propositions on Military Deception," in Daniel, D., and K. Herbig, (eds.), *Strategic Military Deception,* New York: Pergamon Press, 1982, p. 19.

[12] Handel, M. I., *War, Strategy, and Intelligence,* London, U.K.: Frank Cass & Co., Ltd., 1989, p. 337.

[13] Daniel, D. C., and K. L. Herbig, "Propositions on Military Deception," in Daniel, D., and K. Herbig, (eds.), *Strategic Military Deception,* New York: Pergamon Press, 1982, pp. 8–9.

[14] Sherwin, R. G., "The Organizational Approach to Strategic Deception: Implications for Theory and Policy," in Daniel, D., and K. Herbig, (eds.), *Strategic Military Deception,* New York: Pergamon Press, 1982, p. 76.

[15] Jervis, R., *Perception and Misperception in International Politics,* Princeton, NJ: Princeton University Press, 1976, p. 209.

[16] Wohlstetter, R., *Pearl Harbor: Warning and Decision,* Stanford, CA: Stanford University Press, 1962, p. 394.

[17] Handel, M. I., *War, Strategy, and Intelligence*, London, U.K.: Frank Cass & Co., Ltd., 1989, p. 201.

[18] Heuer, R. J., "Strategic Deception and Counterdeception: A Cognitive Process Approach," *International Studies Quarterly,* Vol. 25, No. 2, 1981, p. 298.

[19] Tversky, A., and D. Kahneman, "Belief in the Law of Small Numbers," *Psychological Bulletin,* Vol. 76, pp. 105–110.

[20] Tversky, A., and D. Kahneman, "Judgment Under Uncertainty: Heuristics and Biases," in Kahneman, D., P. Slovic, and A. Tversky, (eds.), *Judgment Under Uncertainty: Heuristics and Biases,* Cambridge, U.K.: Cambridge University Press, 1982.

[21] Kahneman, D., and A. Tversky, "Subjective Probability: A Judgment of Representativeness," in Kahneman, D., P. Slovic, and A. Tversky, (eds.), *Judgment Under Uncertainty: Heuristics and Biases,* Cambridge, U.K.: Cambridge University Press, 1982, p. 33.

[22] Tversky, A., and D. Kahneman, "Judgment Under Uncertainty: Heuristics and Biases," in Kahneman, D., P. Slovic, and A. Tversky, (eds.), *Judgment Under Uncertainty: Heuristics and Biases,* Cambridge, U.K.: Cambridge University Press, 1982, p. 4.

[23] Tversky, A. and, Kahneman, D., "Availability: A Heuristic for Judging Frequency and Probability," *Cognitive Psychology,* Vol. 4, 1973, pp. 207–232.

[24] Dunnigan, J., and M. Macedonia, "The Edge: Wargaming the Unexpected," Firestrike.org, April 22, 2005, http://firestrike.org/wargaming.html.

[25] "General Information about the Mississippi River," National Park Service, U.S. Department of the Interior, April 22, 2005, http://www.nps.gov/miss/features/factoids.

[26] Heuer, R. J., "Strategic Deception and Counterdeception: A Cognitive Process Approach," *International Studies Quarterly,* Vol. 25, No. 2, 1981, pp. 294–327.

[27] Heuer, R. J., "Cognitive Factors in Deception and Counterdeception," in Daniel, D., and K. Herbig, (eds.), *Strategic Military Deception,* New York: Pergamon Press, 1982, p. 42.

[28] Ibid., pp. 48–49.

[29] Ibid., p. 48.

[30] Ibid., p. 59.

[31] Ibid., pp. 59–60.

[32] Ibid., p. 54.

[33] Ibid., p. 55.

[34] Masterman, J. C., *The Double-Cross System: The Incredible True Story of How Nazi Spies Were Turned into Double Agents,* New York: The Lyons Press, 2000, p. 30.

[35] Schneider, W., and R. M. Shiffrin, "Controlled and Automatic Human Information Processing: Detection, Search, and Attention," *Psychological Review,* Vol. 84, 1977, pp. 1–66.

[36] Sloman, S. A., "The Empirical Case for Two Systems of Reasoning," *Psychological Bulletin,* Vol. 119, 1996, pp. 3–22.

[37] Stanovich, K. E., and R. F. West, "Individual Differences in Reasoning: Implications for the Rationality Debate," in Gilovich, T., D. Griffin, and D. Kahneman, (eds.), *Heuristics and Biases: The Psychology of Intuitive Judgment,* Cambridge, U.K.: Cambridge University Press, 2002.

[38] Kahneman, D., "A Perspective on Judgment and Choice: Mapping Bounded Rationality," *American Psychologist,* Vol. 58, No. 9, 2003, p. 698.

[39] Tversky, A., and D. J. Koehler, "Support Theory: A Nonextensional Representation of Subjective Probability," in Gilovich, T., D. Griffin, and D. Kahneman, (eds.), *Heuristics and Biases: The Psychology of Intuitive Judgment,* Cambridge, U.K.: Cambridge University Press, 2002, p. 443.

[40] Slovic, P., et al., "The Affect Heuristic," in Gilovich, T., D. Griffin, and D. Kahneman, (eds.), *Heuristics and Biases: The Psychology of Intuitive Judgment,* Cambridge, U.K.: Cambridge University Press, 2002.

[41] Ibid., p. 420.

[42] Gilovich, T., *How We Know What Isn't So: The Fallibility of Human Reason in Everyday Life,* New York: The Free Press, 1991.

[43] Ibid., p. 9.

[44] Chapman, L. J., and J. Chapman, "Test Results Are What You Think They Are," in Kahneman, D., P. Slovic, and A. Tversky, (eds.), *Judgment Under Uncertainty: Heuristics and Biases,* Cambridge, U.K.: Cambridge University Press, 1982, p. 241.

[45] Lord, C., M. R. Lepper, and L. Ross, "Biased Assimilation and Attitude Polarization: The Effects of Prior Theories on Subsequently Considered Evidence," *Journal of Personality and Social Psychology,* Vol. 37, 1979, pp. 2098–2110.

[46] Cambridge, C., and R. Shreckengost, *Are You Sure? The Subjective Probability Assessment Test,* Information Science Center, Office of Training, Central Intelligence Agency, 1978.

[47] Tetlock, P. E., "Theory-Driven Reasoning About Plausible Pasts and Probable Futures in World Politics," in Gilovich, T., D. Griffin, and D. Kahneman, (eds.), *Heuristics and Biases: The Psychology of Intuitive Judgment,* Cambridge, U.K.: Cambridge University Press, 2002, p. 751.

[48] Ibid., p. 752.

[49] Gilovich, T. *How We Know What Isn't So: The Fallibility of Human Reason in Everyday Life,* New York: The Free Press, 1991, p. 50.

[50] Ross, L., and C. A. Anderson, "Shortcomings in the Attribution Process: On the Origins and Maintenance of Erroneous Social Assessments," in Kahneman, D., P. Slovic, and A. Tversky, (eds.), *Judgment Under Uncertainty: Heuristics and Biases,* Cambridge, U.K.: Cambridge University Press, 1982, p. 147.

[51] Ibid., pp. 148–149.

[52] Tversky, A., and D. Kahneman, "Causal Schemas in Judgments Under Uncertainty," in Kahneman, D., P. Slovic, and A. Tversky, (eds.), *Judgment Under Uncertainty: Heuristics and Biases,* Cambridge, U.K.: Cambridge University Press, 1982, p. 125.

[53] Ibid., p. 128.

[54] Gilovich, T., *How We Know What Isn't So: The Fallibility of Human Reason in Everyday Life,* New York: The Free Press, 1991, p. 78.

[55] Ibid., p. 81.

[56] Ibid., p. 91.

[57] The *false consensus* effect refers to another egocentric bias related to the overuse of self-related knowledge in estimating the prevalence of attributes in a population. In other words, we tend to overestimate the extent that others think as we do. For example, in a study by Ross and Anderson, subjects were asked to walk around campus wearing a sandwich board a simple message (e.g., "Eat at Joe's"). Those who agreed to wear the sign estimated that 62% of their peers would do so while those who refused expected only 33% to agree.

[58] Jervis, R., *Perception and Misperception in International Politics,* Princeton, NJ: Princeton University Press, 1976, p. 283.

[59] Crawford, S., et al., "Emergent Issues for Training: The Benefits of Learning from Other People's Mistakes," *Fire Australia,* August 2003, pp. 26–27.

[60] Bruner, J., "Two Modes of Knowing: Abstract and Narrative," *Story Telling: Passport to the 21st Century*, April 26, 2005, http://www2.parc.com/ops/members/brown/storytelling/Intro3-Narrative&abstract.html.

[61] Daniel, D. C., and K. L. Herbig, "Propositions on Military Deception," in Daniel, D., and K. Herbig, (eds.), *Strategic Military Deception,* New York: Pergamon Press, 1982, p. 9.

[62] Sarbin, T. R., "Prolegomenon to a Theory of Counterdeception," in Daniel, D., and K. Herbig, (eds.), *Strategic Military Deception,* New York: Pergamon Press, 1982, p. 157.

[63] Daniel, D. C., and K. L. Herbig, "Propositions on Military Deception," in Daniel, D., and K. Herbig, (eds.), *Strategic Military Deception,* New York: Pergamon Press, 1982, p. 22.

[64] Brown, A. C., *Bodyguard of Lies: The Extraordinary True Story Behind D-Day,* Guilford, U.K.: The Lyons Press, 2002, p. 432.

[65] Hesketh, R., *Fortitude: The D-Day Deception Campaign,* New York: The Overlook Press, 2000, p. 364.

[66] Handel, M. I., *Perception, Deception, and Surprise: The Case of the Yom Kippur War,* Jerusalem: The Jerusalem Post Press, 1976, p. 15.

[67] Brown, A. C., *Bodyguard of Lies: The Extraordinary True Story Behind D-Day,* Guilford, U.K.: The Lyons Press, 2002, p. 436.

[68] Hesketh, R., *Fortitude: The D-Day Deception Campaign,* New York: The Overlook Press, 2000, p. 193.

[69] Brown, A. C., *Bodyguard of Lies: The Extraordinary True Story Behind D-Day,* Guilford, U.K.: The Lyons Press, 2002, p. 465.

[70] Handel, M. I., *War, Strategy, and Intelligence,* London, U.K.: Frank Cass & Co., Ltd., 1989, p. 209.

[71] Brown, A. C., *Bodyguard of Lies: The Extraordinary True Story Behind D-Day,* Guilford, U.K.: The Lyons Press, 2002, p. 424.

[72] Ibid., p. 431.

[73] Handel, M. I., *War, Strategy, and Intelligence,* London, U.K.: Frank Cass & Co., Ltd., 1989, p. 253.

[74] Brown, A. C., *Bodyguard of Lies: The Extraordinary True Story Behind D-Day,* Guilford, U.K.: The Lyons Press, 2002, pp. 446–447.

[75] Ibid., 426.

[76] Hesketh, R., *Fortitude: The D-Day Deception Campaign,* New York: The Overlook Press, 2000, p. 474.

[77] Brown, A. C., *Bodyguard of Lies: The Extraordinary True Story Behind D-Day,* Guilford, U.K.: The Lyons Press, 2002, p. 431.

[78] Gilovich, T., *How We Know What Isn't So: The Fallibility of Human Reason in Everyday Life,* New York: The Free Press, 1991, p. 111.

[79] Jervis, R., *Perception and Misperception in International Politics,* Princeton, NJ: Princeton University Press, 1976, p. 143.

[80] Brown, A. C., *Bodyguard of Lies: The Extraordinary True Story Behind D-Day,* Guilford, U.K.: The Lyons Press, 2002, pp. 493–497.

[81] In his book *Righteous Deception: German Officers Against Hitler,* David Johnson argues that Admiral Wilhelm Canaris, who headed the Abwehr until 1944, persuaded the chief of the German FHW, Colonel Alexis Baron von Roenne, to join the conspiracy against Hitler. Johnson claims that von Roenne was well aware that the FORTITUDE SOUTH deception to invade the Pas de Calais was false, but instead, went along with it in order to persuade Hitler to keep the German 15th Army right where it was not needed for as long as possible.

[82] It is also conceivable that anchoring and adjustment played a role in the German's inflated estimates of Allied forces in southern England. Regarding Roenne estimates Anthony Clive Brown notes that, "He discovered that it was much easier to put Allied divisions on the order of battle chart than it was to get them off..."

[83] Masterman, J. C., *The Double-Cross System: The Incredible True Story of How Nazi Spies Were Turned into Double Agents,* New York: The Lyons Press, 2000, p. 19.

[84] Brown, A. C., *Bodyguard of Lies: The Extraordinary True Story Behind D-Day,* Guilford, U.K.: The Lyons Press, 2002, p. 604.

[85] Whaley, B., *Stratagem: Deception and Surprise in War,* Center for International Studies, Massachusetts Institute of Technology, 1969, p. 142.

[86] Hesketh, R., *Fortitude: The D-Day Deception Campaign,* New York: The Overlook Press, 2000, pp. 72–73.

[87] Dewar, M., *The Art of Deception in Warfare*, Devon, U.K.: David & Charles Publishers, 1989, p. 69.

[88] Masterman, J. C., *The Double-Cross System: The Incredible True Story of How Nazi Spies Were Turned into Double Agents,* New York: The Lyons Press, 2000, p. 20.

[89] Fischoff, B., P. Slovic, and S. Lichtenstein, "Fault Trees: Sensitivity of Estimated Failure Probabilities to Problem Representation," *Journal of Experimental Psychology: Human Perception and Performance,* Vol. 4, 1978, pp. 330–334.

[90] Hohenemser, K. H., "The Failsafe Risk," *Environment,* Vol. 17, No. 1, 1975, pp. 6–10.

[91] Hesketh, R., *Fortitude: The D-Day Deception Campaign,* New York: The Overlook Press, 2000, p. 186.

[92] "The Big Lie—Tell a Big Enough Lie Often Enough and Some People, Often Many People, Will Believe It," http://en.wikipedia.org/wiki/Big_Lie.

[93] Gilovich, T., *How We Know What Isn't So: The Fallibility of Human Reason in Everyday Life,* New York: The Free Press, 1991, p. 111.

[94] Heuer, R. J., "Cognitive Factors in Deception and Counterdeception," in Daniel, D., and K. Herbig, (eds.), *Strategic Military Deception,* New York: Pergamon Press, 1982, p. 33.

[95] Gilovich, T., and D. Griffin, "Introduction—Heuristics and Biases: Then and Now," in Gilovich, T., D. Griffin, and D. Kahneman, (eds.), *Heuristics and Biases: The Psychology of Intuitive Judgment,* Cambridge, U.K.: Cambridge University Press, 2002, pp. 7–15.

[96] Ross, L., and C. A. Anderson, "Shortcomings in the Attribution Process: On The Origins and Maintenance of Erroneous Social Assessments," in Kahneman, D., P. Slovic, and A. Tversky, (eds.), *Judgment Under Uncertainty: Heuristics and Biases,* Cambridge, U.K.: Cambridge University Press, 1982, p. 151.

CHAPTER 4

Technical Methods of Deception

We have shown that operational deception is based on fundamental principles and operations (Chapter 2) that are carefully implemented by methods that ultimately deceive the human mind (Chapter 3). This chapter introduces the categories of *technical methods* (activities, equipment, or tools) that are employed by the methodologies in the last chapter to carry out deception. Technical methods—the resources, techniques, and tools that are used to convey deception-related information to a deception target—are often divided into three categories: physical, technical, and administrative means [1]. In this chapter we distinguish the categories of methods in terms of the *channels* that are used to convey the deception: via physical phenomena, via information system channels, and via human communications, especially the role of agent operations of intelligence services in strategic deception.

To the magician, technical methods are most often crafted as physical apparatus and props that hide back doors, mark playing cards, disguise mirrors, and conceal padlock releases from credulous audiences, but the magician's physical means are supported by performance methods that misdirect the cognitive attention and perception of the audience. Similarly, those who seek to deceive intelligence analysts, military officers, and career diplomats employ carefully crafted technical tools that exploit subtle weaknesses in the channels of human senses, technical sensors, and computer processors as well as human perception, trust, and reasoning.

4.1 Taxonomy of Technical Methods

This chapter surveys the variety of technical tools that implement the deceptive methods introduced in earlier chapters. The chapter is organized to first describe the tools used to directly influence physical sensing channels, either by the human senses directly, or through remote sensors employed to extend the human senses. Next, the methods that employed to deceive signal and computer processors are described, before introducing the deceptive methods that are employed in the human intelligence (HUMINT) trade to exploit the information channels of intelligence agents and their case officers. Finally, this chapter illustrates how these three channels are often integrated to achieve a desired deception effect—in a sensor, an information system, or the mind of a human target.

The organization of this chapter follows the taxonomy of deception channels that distinguishes the three fundamental domains (introduced earlier in Chapter 1) in which the methods operate. Table 4.1 summarizes the distinctions in the domains of these deceptions, the manipulated channels and representative methods in each quadrant of the deception matrix format introduced earlier in Chapter 2.

Table 4.1 Categories of Deception Channels and Methods

Section	*Channels manipulated*		*Examples in the Deception matrix*	
			Reveal	*Conceal*
4.2 Sensory Channels CC&D	Channels: Physical sensors (technical and human sense) Governing principles: Physics—Manipulate physical phenomena, electromagnetic spectra	True	Reveal limited real units and activities to show strength, influence enemy sensor coverage, sensitivities Reveal true commerical capability of dual-use facilities, provides a true "cover" to misdirect from noncommercial weapons use	Camouflage paint and nets Radar nets Thermal, audio, radar signature suppression Activities in facilities that are underground (to avoid surveillance) or hidden in dual-use facilities (e.g., industrial complexes)
		False	Thermal, radar , audio signature simulation Physical vehicle and facility decoys	Maintain OPSEC (operational security) on existence of methods and extent of CC&D capabilities (equipment, nets, decoys, support).
4.3 Signals Channels D&D	Channels: Abstract symbolic representations of information Governing principles: Logic/game theory; manipulate information and timing of information	True	Reveal limited alluring information on honeypots (deceptive network servers) to lure attackers and conduct network sting operations.	Cryptographic and steganographic hiding of messages Polymorphic (dynamic disguise) of worm code
		False	Communication traffic simulation Reveal false "feed" information on honeypots. Decoy software agents and traffic	Maintain OPSEC on known opponent vulnerabilities, penetration capabilities.
4.4 Human and Media Channels	Channels: Human interpersonal interaction; individual and public Govering principles: Psychology; manipulate human trust, perception, cognition, emotion, and volition	True	Reveal valid sources of classified (but nondamaging) information to provide credibility to double agent channels.	Agent channel cover stories conceal existence of agent operations. Covert (black) propaganda organizations and media channels hide true source and funding of operation.
		False	False reports False feed materials (papers, plans, codes, and so forth) False agent channels (to distract counterintelligence)	Maintain OPSEC on agent operations; monitor assets to validate productivity, reliability, and accuracy.

Section 4.2 describes the methods that focus on deception in the physical domain of mass and energy by influencing target signatures and backgrounds. In contrast, Section 4.3 describes deception methods that occur in the symbolic or logical domain of automated processing systems. Section 4.4 introduces the classical use of the channels of media, public and private diplomacy to convey deception, and the use of clandestine agents as special channels to convey deception.

4.2 Technical Sensor Camouflage, Concealment, and Deception

The first category of technical methods seeks to manipulate physical phenomena to deceive human senses and remote sensor systems. Deception in this domain involves the control of the signatures and backgrounds of physical objects in relationship to local context to avoid detection and targeting; the deception channel includes electronic sensors, human observers, and the human interpreters of the sensed information.

4.2.1 Tactical and Operational Sensory Deception

Technical camouflage, concealment, and deception (CC&D) has a long history in warfare, hiding military personnel and equipment from long-range human observation [2] within the visible spectrum and more recently from a wide variety of electro-optical, infrared, and radar sensors that span the electromagnetic spectrum [3]. The military purpose of CC&D is, first, to prevent detection by surveillance sensors, then to deny targeting by weapons systems, and ultimately to disrupt weapons (e.g., the seekers of precision guided munitions) from successful attack. The focus of CC&D is the use of physical laws to suppress physical phenomena and observable signatures that enable remote detection of a target by discrimination of the target's signature from a natural background. The distinctive roles of CC&D on the battlefield include:

- *Camouflage:* The use of natural or artificial material on personnel, objects, or tactical positions with the aim of confusing, misleading, or evading the enemy.
- *Concealment:* The protection from observation or surveillance. Concealment can include *blending*, where the parts of a scene or target are combined so as to render the parts indistinguishable, and *cover* the measures necessary to give protection to a person, plan, operation, formation, or installation from the enemy intelligence effort and leakage of information.
- *Deception:* performs the function of misdirection, modifying signatures to prevent recognition of the true identity or character of an asset or activity, and providing decoy signatures to attract the attention of sensors away from real assets or activities.

Camouflage reduces the physical phenomena used by an observer to discriminate a target from its background context. The primary physical phenomena that must be suppressed to camouflage physical objects include:

1. *Spectral signature*, which distinguishes a target by its contrast from background spectra; this includes direct and secondary effects on the surrounding environment (e.g., shadows);
2. *Spatial signature*, which distinguishes the spatial extent, shape and texture of the object from natural background objects;

3. *Spatial location*, which is relative to background context and often identifies a target (e.g., a railcar on a railroad track or vehicles relative to a military garrison);
4. *Movement*, which distinguishes an object from the natural background and allows detection by moving target indicator (MTI) sensors that discriminate the phase shift of reflected radar or laser energy.

Typical doctrine for the CC&D of physical objects on the battlefield requires attention to suppression of unique signatures across the entire electromagnetic spectrum and control of the physical context of the object. The standard considerations include the following [4].

1. *Siting* is the most basic method of concealment by careful selection of the location of military vehicles, equipment and people within the natural concealment provided by local terrain features.
2. *Pattern painting* reduces the threshold of visibility (and therefore reduces the detection range), and reduces the uniquely discriminating properties of shape, shadow, and color.
3. *Screening by visual-radar nets* further reduces visibility of stationary objects by reducing optical visibility and by scattering radar energy to minimize return due to the radar cross section of the camouflaged object.
4. *Smoke* provides an active countermeasure to optical and near infrared detection; it provides a temporary screen to prevent targeting of vehicles during critical activities.

Table 4.2 organizes the major CC&D methods in the four categories of activities defined by the deception matrix. The concealment methods suppress the signatures of ground targets and blend their signatures into background clutter. The reveal or disruption methods attempt to confuse or disrupt the attention of humans or the focus and detection sensitivity of automated sensors ("dazzling the sensor").

While the emphasis here has introduced battlefield CC&D, sensor deception measures encompass all aspects of tactical warfare including deception of the sensors employed in air (e.g., radar, electro-optical sensors) and sea (e.g., sonar) operations. In each area there is a D&D measures and countermeasures cycle in which target detection measures are developed (sensors and associated analysis) and deception countermeasures are employed; the measure countermeasure cycle is repeated (Table 4.3) in sensor deception—counterdeception cycles that increase the spectrum, resolution and revisit rate of sensors and counterdeceptive measures. (Sensor countermeasures are described further in Chapter 7.)

4.2.2 Strategic Sensory Deception

Sensor deception is employed at the strategic level to protect large-scale, long-term, high-value national assets (e.g., weapons of mass destruction programs, advanced research and production facilities, related construction and testing activities, proliferation activities, and so forth) and large-scale military activities. Such deception activities are orchestrated to deny and deceive national technical means, including

Table 4.2 Ground Target CC&D Methods

Deception Matrix Quadrant	*Spectral Region Sensors* / *CCD methods*	*Optical*: Human vision, telescopic-aided, and optical TV	*Thermal*: Thermal IR sensors	*Radar*: Ground target radar; imaging radar, MTI radar
Conceal facts (dissimulation)	Hiding, suppression of signature	Earth cover, embankment Heavy vegetation Smoke	Earth cover; embankment Heavy vegetation Smoke	Chaff, radar absorbent materials and nets Earth cover, embankments
	Blending with natural background	Paint, foam Lights Vegetation Textured mats	Thermal paint, foam Air conditioning/heating Use of vegetation	Locating equipment near objects that provide radar clutter to confuse target return
	Disguise as target of different type	Reshaping, paint, and camouflage nets	Reshaping and paint	Corner reflectors
Reveal fiction (simulation)	Disruption of signature	Smoke screens	Flares and smoke generation	Jamming, chaff, corner reflectors
	Misdirection by decoys	Decoy target (static or dynamic) Lights, smoke	Decoy target enhanced by air conditioning/ heating; flares and smoke	Decoy targets enhanced by corner reflectors and signal generators
Conceal fiction	Withhold deception	Protect wartime signatures and methods until operational use to achieve surprise and maintain OPSEC to protect technical characteristics of CC&D methods (above).		
Reveal facts	Surveillance conditioning	Display equipment to reveal standard signatures and to expose and attract intelligence, surveillance and reconnaissance assets.		

Adapted from: [5].

Table 4.3 Representative Sensor Measure and Deception Countermeasure Cycles

Area	*Detection Measures*	*First Generation CC&D Response*	*Detection Response*	*Second Generation CC&D Response*
Tactical ground forces	Airborne and electro-optical sensors	Paint Camouflage nets	MTI radar, Foliage Penetration (FOPEN) radar	Multispectral decoys, radar nets
Tactical air forces	Ground and airborne radar	Jamming, electronic deception and UAV decoys	Networked radars, broadband discrimination	Radar-absorbent materials (RAM), low RCS designs
Antisubmarine warfare	Acoustic arrays (towed, dipped, ocean floor)	Acoustic signature suppression, acoustic decoys	Expanded spectral sensing processing;	Wideband signature suppression, ops changes, decoys

space reconnaissance and surveillance, global fixed sensor detection networks, and clandestine sensors. The means employed to prevent intelligence discovery and analysis include:

- *Program cover:* The finances, resources, and activities of programs are covered by carefully compartmented OPSEC or dual-use configurations (commercial-military) to enable covert military use or rapid conversion.

- *Resource concealment:* Underground facilities are employed to hide leadership, command and control, research, and production capabilities from overhead surveillance and the use of encryption and fiber optic channels to deny intercept and cryptologic analysis of communications [6]. Dispersal and mobility may also be employed to distribute and dynamically move capabilities across a wide search area.
- *Surveillance defeat and misdirection:* Diversionary activities may be employed to distract or overwhelm limited surveillance capabilities during critical periods of activity and the specific exploitation of vulnerabilities (e.g., resolution, timing, revisit, and so forth) based on knowledge of technical capabilities and vulnerabilities. The Indian nuclear test conducted in May 1998 was undetected by U.S. overhead reconnaissance partly because of a deception operation based on what the Indian government had learned from prior *demarches* by the United States in 1995 and 1996. On those occasions the United States provided evidence of the U.S. knowledge of India's test preparations that revealed national technical surveillance capabilities and limitations [7]. In addition, the United States acknowledged limitations in supporting HUMINT capabilities to provide complementary cueing and sourcing [8].

The widespread availability of global strategic reconnaissance, enabled by national and commercial high-resolution spacecraft, has increased the development and deployment of large-scale strategic D&D methods to deny and deceive strategic intelligence collection. Gupta has described the implications of openly available commercial high-resolution satellite imagery and the rise of passive deception methods to protect strategic assets [9]:

> States are likely to increase their reliance on passive measures because such measures are immediately available and are not inherently provocative. They could intensify the application of camouflage, concealment, and deception to obstruct the overhead viewing of their military forces and other strategic assets. Garages, warehouses, tunnels, foliage, and natural cloud cover could be used to hide supplies and hardware. Deception tactics could be devised to cover up the true purpose of strategic facilities. Decoys could lure observers away from key sites and satiate their appetite for information. If certain activity could not be concealed or masked (e.g., military redeployments, ship loading, etc.), it could be scheduled to take place at times when commercial satellites were not within view.

Indeed, the methods of CC&D to counter strategic surveillance have been widely deployed by weapons proliferators, treaty violators, and illegal traffickers. Preston and Baker have projected a competition between increasing capabilities of commercial imaging spacecraft (broader spectral coverage by electro-optical, synthetic aperture radar, and hyperspectral imaging and increased revisit rates) and increasing sophistication in deceptive countermeasures [10].

Case Study 4A: Strategic D&D at the Rabta Libya Pharma 150 Facility Libya began construction of a large pharmaceutical plant, "Pharma 150," in the area of Qabilat az Zaribah (Rabta) over 50 miles southwest of Tripoli in the early 1980s to develop an indigenous chemical weapons capability. U.S. and European intelligence services became aware of the activity and began observing the large construction project, overseen by a financially stressed West German chemical contractor, Imhause-Chemie AG. Suspicious characteristics of the project indicated that the Libyans were employing strategic D&D methods to protect the construction process as well as the ultimate capability of the facility. These methods, typical of covert, dual-use strategic D&D activities to cover Weapons of Mass Destruction (WMD) programs, included:

1. *Program cover:* The project was openly described as a pharmaceutical facility, with all the outward indications of commercial pharmaceutical use.
2. *Clandestine dual-use capability:* The capability to produce chemical agents and then transfer the agent materials to munitions was hidden within the larger chemical producing capability and capacity of the facility.
   a. The facility was unusually large by commercial standards, enclosing the entire operation in a warehouselike structure to conceal the component parts from overhead surveillance, and provide sufficient room for munitions and agent storage.
   b. The chemical precursors used in production had dual-use applications to produce mustard and nerve agent.
   c. An adjacent metal fabrication facility, unnecessary for a standard pharmaceutical facility, would provide the necessary capability to produce bombs and artillery rounds.
3. *Operational security:* A high level of OPSEC was employed to deny access to details of the entire program, its resources, processes or capabilities of the facility.
   a. The direct contractor, Ishan Barbouti International (IBI), acted as middleman to separate Libya from Imhause-Chemie AG and lesser contractors.
   b. Over 30 front companies were employed to transfer design plans and ship materials and equipment to Libya. Material and equipment were transshipped through ports in the Far East, rather than normal direct shipping routes.
   c. Contract payments were routed through Swiss banks rather than by direct payments.
   d. Workers were imported from Thailand and Pakistan to perform the construction under unusually tight operational security for a standard commercial project.
   e. Physical security for the facility included high fences and 40-foot sand revetments—unusual for a commercial operation.
4. *Special deception actions:* On March 14, 1990, the Libyans openly claimed that a fire had destroyed the Rabta plant. It was widely believed that the fire (causing minor damage, but clearly observable by U.S. and French space reconnaissance) was a deception operation conducted to confuse intelligence services of the status of the facility, and reduce the Libyans' perceived threat of a U.S. attack on the site.

The indicators of strategic denial (OPSEC in all phases of construction and operation and deception (the pharmaceutical chemical cover to hide the dual-use capability of the facility) were present, to raise suspicion, yet provided significant barriers to understanding the intentions, capabilities, and production yields of the facility.

These activities are organized in the deception matrix (Figure 4.1) to illustrate the Libyan strategic deception approach to protect the existence of the CW capability and, even if suspected, to protect the capabilities (e.g., production types and yields and storage capacity) and status of the operation (e.g., readiness and schedules of activities). In Chapter 7, we will distinguish the concept of legitimate signals (reveal the true) and spurious signals ("sprignals") caused by the deception activities that provide cues to the existence of deception; in the Rabta case, the unusually large warehouse and the complexity and makeup of the supplier network were significant sprignals that cued intelligence to the suspicious nature of the construction activity.

Sources: Unclassified Report to Congress on the Acquisition of Technology Relating to Weapons of Mass Destruction and Advanced Conventional Munitions for the Period 1 July Through 30 December 2003, Central Intelligence Agency, Nonproliferation Center, Director of Central Intelligence, November 2004; Sinai, J., "Libya's Pursuit of Weapons of Mass Destruction," *The Nonproliferation Review*, Monterey Institute of International Studies, Spring-Summer 1997, pp. 92–100; Office of Technology Assessment, U.S. Congress, "How Libya's Secret CW Plant Was Detected," *Technologies Underlying Weapons of Mass Destruction*, Washington, D.C.: U.S. Government Printing Office, December 1993, pp. 42–44; Waller, R., *Chemical and Biological Weapons and Deterrence Case Study 2: Libya*, Alexandria, VA: Chemical and Biological Arms Control Institute, 1998, p. 5.

4.3 Signal and Information Systems Denial and Deception

The second category of technical methods seeks to deceive the information channel provided by electronic systems. These methods issue deceptive signals and processes that influence automated electronic systems rather than sensors of physical

	Reveal	Conceal
True	• Reveal legitimate front companies. • Reveal actual Pharma 150 limited commercial potential capability. • Reveal construction design of pharmaceutical nature.	• Pharmaceutical cover story conceals real dual-use CW production intentions • Large warehouse building conceals physical plant internal construction and components
False	• Reveal simulated destruction of the facility by simulated fire damage.	• Employ front companies and construction middleman to compartment knowledge of capability. • Employ indirect payments and transship materials to hide participants in construction and equipment suppliers. • Employ physical and operational security to prevent access.

Figure 4.1 Rabta strategic deception matrix.

processes. Deception in this domain involves the manipulation of signals and symbols (rather than physical phenomena) to deceive symbolic (logical) processing as well as human interpreters of the processed information. This form of deception was most prominently introduced in World War II in the domain of radar and communications deception where the deception targets included early signal processing systems that provided radio navigation, detected targets or relayed messages. Known as the "wizard war," competitions between electronic systems introduced methods of denial and disruption (e.g., jamming), deception (e.g., false target insertion), and exploitation (e.g., traffic analysis, intercept, and decryption of internal messages) [11].

Deception capabilities matured throughout the Cold War, developing sophisticated deception techniques applied within electronic warfare and intelligence; more recently, deception techniques have become an important component of information operations.

4.3.1 Electronic Warfare

The discipline of electronic warfare (EW) includes electronic support (ES) to monitor the RF environment, electronic protection (EP) to guard friendly systems from hostile attack, and electronic attack (EA) to deny, disrupt, deceive, exploit, and destroy adversary electronic systems. The information channels of EW include radar and data link systems, satellite links, navigation systems, and electro-optical (EO) systems (e.g., laser radar and EO missile seekers). EA methods include a range of jamming techniques that degrade the detection and discrimination performance of signal processing systems and complementary deception techniques. Within EA, *electromagnetic deception* [12] is "the deliberate radiation, re-radiation, alteration, suppression, absorption, denial, enhancement, or reflection of electromagnetic energy in a manner intended to convey misleading information to an enemy or to enemy electromagnetic-dependent weapons, thereby degrading or neutralizing the enemy's combat capability." These deceptive actions can include the direct exploitation of processing vulnerabilities (e.g., overloading a simple detection algorithm by inserting too many target signatures for the detection buffer) or by an actual deception of the signal processing logic (e.g., spoofing a discrimination algorithm to label a fighter aircraft as a commercial airliner). Table 4.4 provides the standard taxonomy of representative electromagnetic deception techniques within the format of the deception matrix [13].

4.3.2 Signals Intelligence

Deception techniques are also employed with the signals intelligence (SIGINT) community that gathers intelligence from a wide range of critical signal sources. SIGINT often employs deceptive methods to enable the intercept, collection, and analysis of both external traffic, and the communications intelligence (COMINT) branch of SIGINT uses deception to decrypt and analyze internal content. Cryptanalytic methods often employ a variety of deceptive methods to gain keying information or to disrupt encrypted channels, for example [14]:

Table 4.4 Representative Electronic Warfare Deception Methods

Deception Matrix Quadrant	*Electromagnetic Deception Categories*	*Representative EW Deception Techniques*
Conceal facts (dissimulation)	*Type 1 manipulative EM deception:* eliminate revealing, EM telltale indicators that may be used by hostile forces.	*Radar cross section (RCS) suppression* by low observable methods: radar absorption materials or radar energy redirection to reduce effective RCS Conceal signals within wideband spread spectrum signals (e.g., direct sequence, frequency hopping). *Radar chaff* and *cover jamming* to reduce signal quality and mask a target's signature
Reveal fiction (simulation)	*Imitative EM deception:* introduces EM energy into enemy systems that imitates enemy emissions	*Radar signature, IFF spoofing:* store-and-repeat or imitate signals (RCS, reflected power signature, or IFF codes) to appear as an enemy system.
	Type 2 manipulative EM deception: convey misleading EM telltale indicators that may be used by hostile forces.	*Deceptive jamming* to induce error signals within receiver-processor logic (e.g., induce range estimation errors)—methods include range deception, angle deception, range and velocity gate pull-off, gain deception, and cross-polarization jamming *Navigation beaconing:* intercept and rebroadcast of beacon signals on the same frequency to cause inaccurate bearings and erroneous navigation solutions.
	Simulative EM deception: simulate friendly, notional or actual capabilities to mislead hostile forces.	*Saturation decoys:* Misdirection and overloading by *decoy* signal generators on decoy platforms *Seduction decoys:* Misdirect and draw attention away from intended targets; cause fire control to break lock on intended targets.
Conceal fiction	Withhold deception capabilities until wartime to achieve surprise.	Protect wartime electronic deception emissions and modes; limit use of decoy and spoofing signatures until appropriate operational events to reveal them to achieve surprise.
Reveal facts	Surveillance conditioning	Display peacetime signatures and modes; present electronic order of battle of selected capabilities to emphasize strengths, desensitize radar surveillance.

- *Cyphertext replay:* Valid but unencrypted cyphertext may be recorded, modified, and replayed within a valid key interval to disrupt or reduce trust in a targeted system (even when the deceiver is unable to decrypt internals).
- *Key spoofing:* Impersonate a key distributor and issue a key to a target; then decrypt traffic issued under the spoofed key.
- *Man-in-middle:* Secure a position between two secure parties (A and B) and issue spoofed keys to each; become a secure intermediary between the parties, able to intercept transactions while both parties are "secure."

These and other deceptive methods may be used to intercept or disrupt adversary communications by inserting misleading transmissions to deceive or reduce trust in communication channels.

4.3.3 Information Operation (IO)

In the 1990s the proliferation of networked computer systems introduced a significant new channel for deception—and enabled operational deception to include the methods and tools to attack all aspects of the network channel: network modulation, transfer protocols, and application layers of computer systems in the domain of information warfare [15]. Deception in IO has expanded to include application in:

- *Communications electronic warfare:* This discipline is dedicated to protecting and attacking military communication networks. Signal deception is employed to intercept, capture, and then manipulate with signal envelopes and the internal contents of free space communication systems [16].
- *Computer network exploitation (CNE):* Intelligence collection operations that obtain information resident in files of threat automated information systems (AIS) and gain information about potential vulnerabilities, or access critical information resident within foreign AIS that could be used to the benefit of friendly operations [17]. CNE operations often employ deceit to survey, penetrate, and access targeted networks and systems.
- *Computer network attack (CNA):* Operations conducted using information systems to disrupt, deny, degrade, or destroy information resident in computers and computer networks, or the computers and networks themselves [18]. These operations follow CNE operations that gain targeting information, and often employ deception to gain entry, defeat security processes, and hide malicious code. (It is worthy to note that computer network defense may also employ deceptive methods to lure, discover, disrupt, and defeat attackers.)

In each of these domains, deception is applied either to: (1) *exploit a vulnerability* (e.g., spoof an IP address by directly exploiting the protocol's lack of authentication, or exploit a buffer overflow vulnerability to insert code enable subsequent access); (2) *induce a vulnerability* in a system (e.g., cause a network firewall misconfiguration to enable brief access); or (3) *escalate a vulnerability* to a greater degree (e.g., move from unauthorized user access to root access). CNA attackers employing deceptive acts in each of these cases may exploit one of two targets:

1. *Human targets.* The targets of many attacks are naïve users or administrators who, wittingly or unwittingly expose access to a system host, a service, or channels by being induced to reveal security-relevant information or taking actions that expose a system (even if only briefly). The methods used to exploit the targets, called *social engineering* by hackers, generally exploit the vulnerability of human trust; attackers pose as trusted (but needy) individuals in person, over the phone or via e-mail to secure information. Former hacker Kevin Mitnick has noted [19]: "Savvy technologists have painstakingly developed information-security solutions to minimize the risks connected with the use of computers, yet left unaddressed the most significant vulnerability, the human factor."
2. *Computer targets.* A computer agent (a computer host, a service, or any other autonomously acting computer agency in hardware or software) can also be the target of deception when trust is exploited to gain unauthorized access, or when a vulnerability is exploited to operate an unauthorized process.

In both targets, the deceptive attacker seeks to exploit trust—by the human or by the computer agent. The fundamental methods of CNA deception are, or course, similar to the methods described earlier in physical sensory deception and in electronic warfare. The computer network operations (CNO) deception matrix (Table 4.5) summarizes the methods and terminology adopted in the IO community, using general descriptions of the actions on hosts or services A, B, and C. We present the general characteristics of deceptive mechanisms These mechanism are unique to the vulnerabilities of operating systems, protocols and applications. For a

Table 4.5 Representative CNO Deception Operations

Deception Matrix Quadrant	*Deceptive Mechanism*	*Description and Representative Examples*
Conceal facts (dissimulation)	Cryptography	Openly hide A by encryption process protected by public or private key.
	Steganography	Secretly hide A within open material protected by a secret hiding process and private key.
	Trojan or backdoor access concealment	Hide C within A: conceal malicious code within a valid process; dynamically encrypt code (polymorphic) or wrap code while not running in memory to avoid static signature detection while in storage; hide process when running and reduce trace log evidence.
Reveal fiction (simulation)	Masquerade (decoy)	Present C as B to A: spoof IP address by inserting a false source address; spoof access by repeating captured authentication information.
	Buffer overflow	Present C as B to A: spoof a service, A, to execute code C when appearing to request B by exploiting a vulnerability in the service that does not recognize that more data is put into a buffer than the buffer can handle. Usually, this includes overwriting a function's return address on the stack to point to another location that executes a function desired by the attacker.
	Session hijack Session co-opt	Capture session information from B, then Present A as B: intercept and replay security-relevant information to gain control of a channel or process; co-opt a browser when user accesses.
	Man-in-middle	Present C to B as A then present C to A as B and establish trusted link between A and B: establish a logical position between two processes, and establish the role of exchanging security information.
	Honeypot, Honeynet [21]	Present C as a valid service; track and trace user A: a network, system, or service that is established to lure, monitor, and track naïve user targets (used offensively) or unauthorized attackers (used defensively); value of the honeypot is in its unauthorized use.
	Denial of service	Request excessive services from A: issue false requests from distributed hosts to overpower a targeted process to disrupt its ability to provide valid service; may be used for misdirection (analogous to a seduction or saturation decoy).
	Reroute	Route traffic intended for A to B: control routing of information to intercept, disrupt, or deny traffic services.
Conceal fiction	Withhold deception operational capabilities	Maintain OPSEC, INFOSEC, and TRANSEC to protect CNA and CND operational capabilities.
Reveal facts	Selective conditioning of network surveillance	Publish limited network capabilities and accesses to selectively attract attention and reduce attacker sensitivity.

comprehensive enumeration of specific mechanisms, see texts such as *Malware: Fighting Malicious Code* [20].

These deception mechanisms may occur at each of the hierarchical levels of network processes represented by the International Standards Organization (ISO) reference model that identifies layers of abstraction of system functions, often called the protocol stack [22]. Attacking the stack refers to applying methods at appropriate protocol layers to defeat the lower-level hardware layers or higher-level software layers. Methods range from deception of basic signals (e.g., modulated waveforms at radio frequency, on wired or fiber optic nets, and so forth) to deception of high-level software applications by exploiting software vulnerabilities. Computer security policies may be implemented at each layer, and Figure 4.2 illustrates how the deception mechanisms introduced earlier may likewise be implemented at each ISO reference model layer to target the typical security protocols.

In addition to applying the methods across layers, the attacker may coordinate deception on human and computer targets to escalate access to the system. For example, the attacker may first deceive a user to gain low-level access to a system, and then exploit a system vulnerability to become installed as a legitimate user. As a valid user, the attacker then escalates access by emailing the administrator to deceptively gain increased access to a service with a buffer overflow vulnerability, to further escalate access toward a level of access where a sniffer can installed to capture administrator passwords that will ultimately allow root access.

Case Study 4B: The Role of Deception in Network Worms Computer network attacks may support larger-scale strategic deception operations, by introducing

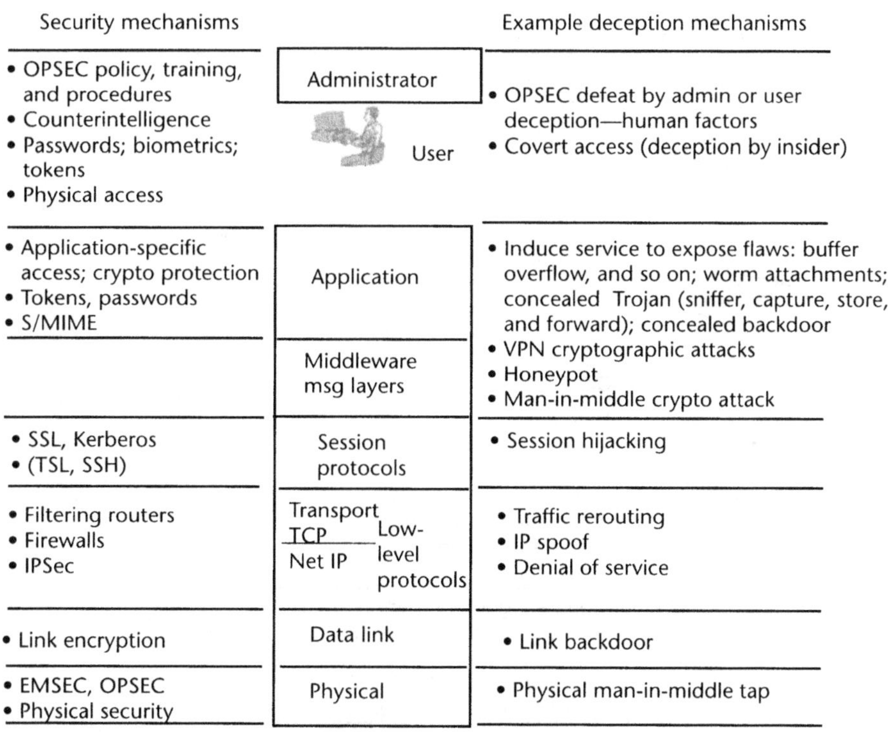

Figure 4.2 D&D mechanisms applied at different ISO layers.

malicious processes into targeted systems to introduce disruptions (misdirection or denial), distortions or erroneous information (deceit). These attacks are often enabled by deception methods that exploit system or human vulnerabilities—or both to breech system security. Internet worms provide an excellent case study in the methods used by autonomous agents (worms) to detect vulnerabilities, penetrate hosts, replicate and grow using the deceptive mechanisms described earlier. The general phases of the worm (Figure 4.3) require the self-replicating worm to (1) scan net address space to find a vulnerable target hosts for access, (2) exploit discovered vulnerable machines, and (3) pass the worm payload to the new host, and then (1) initiate scans from the new worm code. Upon a predetermined condition, an attack function (4) may be initiated by the distributed network of worm-infected hosts.

Worm propagation that exploits both system and human cognitive vulnerabilities can be illustrated by a simple example, the Bagle.A "mass mailing" e-mail worm that was released on the Internet in January 2004. The worm code is contained inside an executable file attachment to e-mail message; the message appeared harmless and contained a short subject, "Hi," and the simple deceptive message that indicated it was a harmless test from a known source: "Test =) [random characters] — Test, yep." Bagle.A operated in the following sequence as shown in Figure 4.3:

1. *Scan for access.* Once the worm was installed on a host, it harvested a hit list of e-mail addresses from the host computer to generate addresses, and then broadcast the standard "Hi" message with the worm attached.
2. *Exploit entry.* Once a user receives the message from a known address (because the addressee was on the parent's address book), it is "spoofed" into opening the attachment under the guise of a test.

Propagation process	Propagation events	Role of deception
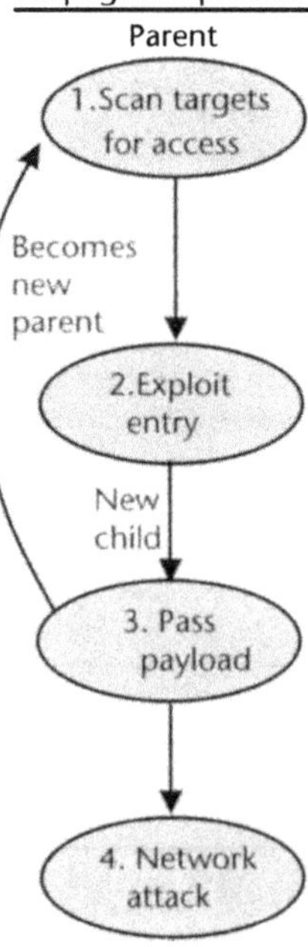	1. Worm scans for potential victim hosts in network space guided by a target list, or hit list of previously identified vulnerable nodes.	• Worm adapts the scan process to fall below the threshold of scan detection of firewalls and intrusion detection systems. • Worm conceals scan within legitimate service requests; scans from co-opted hosts.
	2. Worm scans to a host address and verifies a host that is vulnerable to access (a "hit"). 3. Worm adds the new address to an establish network of worm addresses.	
	4. Worm sends the worm scan code from a single or distributed (parent) source to the newly discovered vulnerable (child) to continue to expand the scan and propagation 5. Propagation establishes parent-child network communication topology.	• Payload is concealed within child's host system by disguised labeling and code signature hiding. • External traffic connection to parent attempts to evade firewall by disguising activity.
	6. Upon a triggering event (e.g., date, event, or command from parent to children), the worm net executes the attack operations (e.g., a distributed denial-of-service attack).	• Attack external connections are disguised or co-opt other network services.

Figure 4.3 Deceptive mechanisms in worm propagation process.

3. *Pass payload.* The payload is effectively passed when the attachment is inadvertently opened by the user, infecting (installing within the Windows operating system) the worm on the new child system. The attachment contains a valid attachment function (a calculator), but the worm code is hidden. The new child begins harvesting new addresses for further propagation (return back to step 1). Bagle.A specifically excluded Hotmail and MSN domains—to mitigate early detection by the large Internet service providers. The worm installed a file named "bbeagle.exe" in the Windows system folder (i.e., the worm did not attempt to hide and its signature was easily detectable and removed).
4. *Network attack.* Bagle.A included a Trojan backdoor program that was installed within Windows, which listened on TCP port 6777, allowing subsequent access by the creator.

Sources: Nazario, J., *Defense and Detection Strategies Against Internet Worms,* Norwood MA: Artech House, 2003; *Symantec Internet Security Threat Report,* Vol. V, March 2004; Security Advisory CERT-IST/AV-2004.015 "Bagle" worm on Microsoft Windows systems Version 1.3, 22/01/2004.

4.4 Human Deception Channels

There exist a wide range of channels by which a government and individuals deceive other governments and individuals. The broadest channels by which deceptive information (to achieve deceit or misdirection) include five strategic influence channels (Table 4.6) that access broad target audiences, with different means of implementation and objectives [23]. These methods employ human interactions and communications across a variety of human channels: the open public media (broadcast, Internet, newsprint, and so forth), private communications (letters, e-mails, instant messages), and direct personal exchanges at formal and informal meetings.

Propaganda or psychological operations (PSYOP) target a general population using several approaches. *White propaganda* openly acknowledging the source of the information; gray propaganda uses undeclared sources. *Black propaganda* purports to originate from a source other its actual sponsor, protecting the true source (e.g., clandestine radio and Internet broadcast, independent organizations, agents of influence [24], and so forth). Coordinated white, gray, and black propaganda efforts were strategically conducted by the Soviet Union throughout the Cold War as "active measures" of disinformation that supported strategic deception goals [25]:

> .... for the Soviet Union, active measures constitute a dynamic and integrated array of overt and covert techniques for influencing events and behavior in, and the actions of, foreign countries. These measures are employed to influence the policies of other governments, undermine confidence in the leaders and institutions of these states, disrupt the relations between various nations, and discredit and weaken major opponents. This frequently involves attempts to deceive the target, and to distort the target's perception of reality.

Table 4.6 Categories of Strategic Deception Operations

Influence method	*Propaganda (Psyop)*			*Deception*	
Type	*White*	*Gray*	*Black*	*Leadership Deception*	*Intelligence Deception*
Objective	Influence a general belief to an audience with a general interest.			Induce a specific belief to an audience with focused interest on a given topic (or target).	
Target audience	Population at large			National or military leadership	Intelligence collectors or analysts
Deception methods and objectives	Use declared sources and organizations to influence target audiences to accept general beliefs.	Use undeclared sources and organizations to influence target audiences to accept general beliefs.	Use false sources and organizations to influence target audiences to accept general beliefs.	Use diplomatic channels, sympathetic influences to induce beliefs. Use open news sources and channels to induce beliefs.	Deceive and defeat human and technical collectors.

It is important to note that U.S. doctrine specifically prohibits the intentional deception of domestic or foreign audiences by the public dissemination of misinformation by strategic communications, public diplomacy, public affairs, or military PSYOP. U.S. PSYOP is constrained to the projection of truth [26]: "The planned use of psychological actions and propaganda influences the attitudes, opinions, and behaviors of opposing or neutral groups in a manner favorable to US objectives. PSYOP techniques are used to plan and execute truth projection activities intended to inform foreign groups and populations persuasively." U.S. PSYOP activities are therefore doctrinally distinct from military deception operations, which do not target broad foreign audiences, but specific military and leadership targets. The global information environment poses severe challenges to making these distinctions. The U.S. creation and immediate closure of a Pentagon-based Office of Strategic Influence in early 2002 was a result of the concern over the blurring of lines between legitimate deception and legitimate public influence. Brig. Gen. Mark Kimmitt, the U.S. military's senior spokesman in Iraq in the spring of 2003, remarked [27] that Public Affairs "... is tough business. Are we trying to inform? Yes. Do we offer perspective? Yes. Do we offer military judgment? Yes. Must we tell the truth to stay credible? Yes. Is there a battlefield value in deceiving the enemy? Yes. Do we intentionally deceive the American people? No.... There is a gray area. Tactical and operational deception [operations] are proper and legal on the battlefield.... In a worldwide media environment, how do you prevent that deception from spilling out from the battlefield and inadvertently deceiving the American people?" The global information environment blurs the distinction between legitimate and illegitimate channels for deception.

Leadership deception targets leadership or intelligence consumers, attempting to bypass the intelligence process by appealing directly to the intelligence consumer via other channels. Commercial news channels, untrustworthy diplomatic channels, suborned media, and personal relationships can be exploited to deliver deception messages to leadership (before intelligence can offer D&D cautions) in an effort to establish mindsets in decision-makers. D&D methods may be used in concert to distract or disrupt media and intelligence analysts, introducing distortions in the collection channels, ambiguity in the analytic and reporting processes, errors in the resulting intelligence product, and misjudgment in decisions based on the product—ultimately leading to a distrust of the intelligence product by leadership consumers. The literature examining the examples and principles of military leadership that D&D employed through history and particularly during World War II is extensive [28]. The effects of leadership deception in international politics by means of diplomatic, rhetorical and unofficial channels have been described by Jervis [29].

Intelligence deception specifically targets intelligence collectors and subsequently analysts by combining the denial of information, misdirection and introduction of false data to disrupt, distract or deceive the collection or analysis processes, or both. The previous sections have introduced the channels and methods for deception of sensors and information systems that lead to intelligence analysis to target leaders. In Section 4.41, we introduce the additional channel of clandestine (covert) human intelligence (HUMINT) that may be used to carry out deception operations to influence analysis and ultimately leaders and policymakers.

4.4.1 The Use of HUMINT Channels for Deception

The foundation of human collection operations is the clandestine recruitment, development and maintenance of human *agents* or *assets* operating as an information channel [30]. While there is a rich and interesting body of literature on the conduct of historical HUMINT operations, we focus here only on the role of these channels in deception operations [31].

We consider two fundamental cases in which the HUMINT channel is exploited to support a larger deception operation (Figure 4.4). In the first case, the agent provides a feedback channel for intelligence service A to monitor the effect of its deception operation (conveyed over channels 1, 2, and 3) against service B. In this

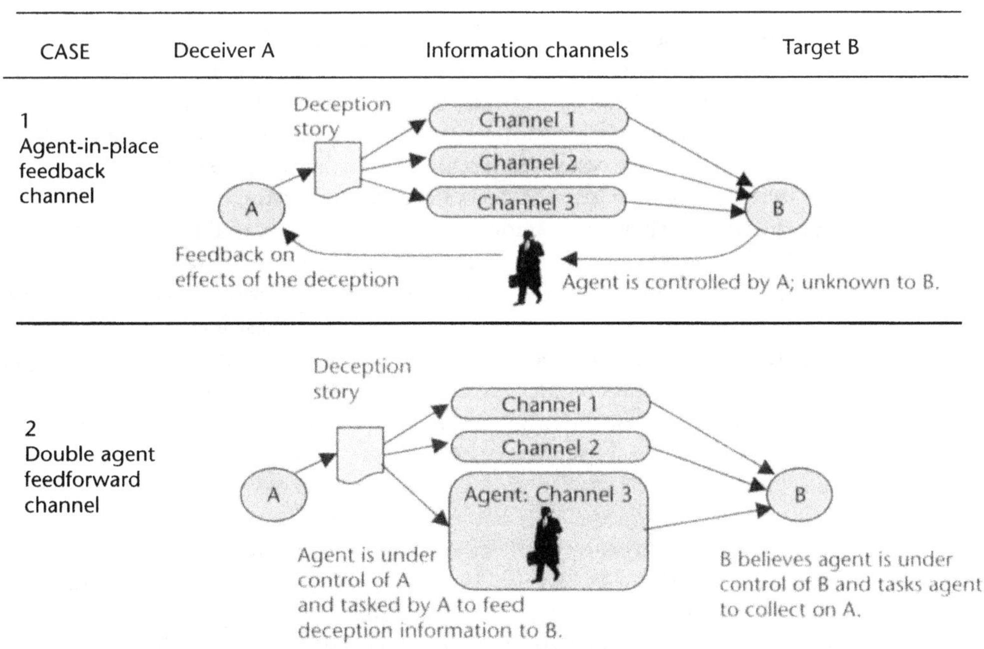

Figure 4.4 Two roles of HUMINT channels in deception operations.

straightforward case, a recruited or defecting *agent in place* collects information from B and reports the effects of the deception to intelligence service A via an intermediary case officer. Penetrating the target's military, intelligence, and leadership with a well-placed agent or asset can provide reporting to service A about the target's reactions to the deception—though the agent may have no direct role (*or even knowledge of*) the deception. (Note that in the competing direction, such assets if held by service B would also have a role in the counterdeception activities of service B if they were in a position to discover the deception plan and/or service A's actual intentions and capabilities.)

The second case considers the case in which an agent believed to be under control of service B is actually under the control of service A. Such an agent, who is cooperating with one intelligence service on behalf of and under the control of another intelligence service, and is manipulated by one to the detriment of another, is referred to as a *double agent* [32].

The double agent provides an excellent direct (or feedforward) channel to "feed" deception information to service B [33]. The agent is expected by service B to supply useful intelligence, and service A forward truthful (but undamaging) intelligence to establish the reliability of the agent, as well as critical deception content. When controlled by A, the agent can also provide valuable intelligence on the agent operations employed by intelligence service B (e.g., information on the processes, organization, and interests of B). For this reason the double agent has often been the channel of choice for effective deception operations, demonstrated by the significant use of double agents by the British in World War II to mislead German intelligence [34].

In a declassified CIA article on double agent operations, F. M. Begoum has described the operational role of the agent in deception and the skill required to control the channel [35]:

> The double agent serves also as a controlled channel through which information can be passed to the other service, either to build up the agent in its estimation or for purposes of deception. Often operational build-up material is passed first to establish a better reception for the deception material: obviously the greater the stature of the agent in the eyes of the other service, the better the reception of the reports he provides. In the complex matter of deception we may distinguish here between operational deception, that concerning the service's own capabilities, intentions, and control of the agent, and national deception, that concerning the intentions of the controlling government or other components of it. National deception operations are usually very delicate, frequently involving the highest levels of the government, and therefore require prior coordination and approval at the national headquarters level. The double agent channel can be used by the controlling service to insert data into the mechanisms of the other service with a number of possible objectives, for example, to detect its activities in some field. The inserted material is designed to induce certain actions on the part of the other service, which are then observed through another operation or group of operations. The material has to be designed very skillfully if it is to deceive the other service and produce the desired reactions. A sophisticated operation of this type is most likely to be used when the stakes are high or the case complicated. Such a situation might arise if a case officer handling several operations wanted to set up still another and needed to find out in advance what the pertinent operational pattern was. The passing of data through the double agent

channel for the consumption of the other service for whatever purpose requires a great deal of knowledge about the other service.

Case Study 4C Cassidy Double Agent Deception Operation Perhaps the longest running U.S. counterintelligence case of the Cold War involved a two-decade-long double agent deception operation against the former Soviet Union. Through the 1960s and 1970s, the United States and the Soviets conducted substantial and competing chemical and biological weapons (CBW) research and development, programs. U.S. Army Master Sergeant Joseph Cassidy acted as a double agent channel to supply deceptive information to mislead, disrupt and reduce the effectiveness of the Soviet chemical weapons program. Operation SHOCKER's purpose, deception plan, and results are summarized below, according to the unofficial sources listed at the end of the case study.

Purpose: The purpose of the operation was fourfold: (1) to conduct a strategic deception of the Soviet chemical weapons program, reducing its effectiveness by wasting resources on unfruitful research, (2) to identify agents of the Soviet military intelligence (GRU) in the U.S., (3) to learn the Soviet recruitment and agent operation process in the United States, and (4) to infer gaps in Soviet military intelligence from queries tasked to Cassidy.

Plan: The deception plan moved from double agent initiation and confidence-building to the deception operations.

1. *Initiation:* Cassidy was selected by an extensive interview process, based on his personal profile and ability, to perform the double agent role. He was trained for the role and then "dangled" before known Soviet agents in 1959. He was placed (in uniform, regularly playing volleyball) at a Washington, D.C., YMCA gymnasium near the Soviet embassy where GRU agents operating under diplomatic cover frequented. The Soviets initiated contact and recruited Cassidy, ultimately training and trusting him as he incrementally produced viable classified materials.
2. *Double agent activity:* The Soviets provided the tools and tradecraft to allow Cassidy to photograph classified materials, then produce microdot products and deliver the materials to dead drops, where Cassidy received money in exchange. The Soviets also provided an encoded messaging systems to exchange instructions and reports. Cassidy was handled by FBI personnel, who managed the creation of material fed by Cassidy back to his Soviet handlers.
3. *Deception operation:* The chemical weapon deception operation was conducted in the period 1966–1969, in which Cassidy supplied over 4,500 pages of classified materials—some undamaging material to support Cassidy's credibility and other feed material to influence the Soviets to research and attempt to develop a nerve agent known as GJ. The deceptive material provided incentive to develop GJ, but did not reveal that the United States had determined that the experimental agent was unstable and not practical to produce or weaponize.
4. *Supporting operation:* A separate and follow-on double agent operation began in 1967 employing Colonel Dmitri Polyakov (a Soviet military

intelligence agent in the United States who was doubled in 1961) to initiate a sequel to the deception story that the United States was continuing a clandestine biological weapons program, in spite of the U.S. agreement to the Biological Weapons Convention in April 1972. The purpose was to negatively influence the Soviet Biopreparat programs.

Results: The operation ran without detection over a span of 21 years. Cassidy passed over 4,500 pages of carefully selected classified documents and spurred the Soviets to waste research the nonweaponizable GJ gas. It remains controversial if the operation may have also had unintended consequences, spurring the Soviets on to expanded CW research that resulted in the successful gas, Novichok, because of their belief (based on deception) that the United States enjoyed a significant advantage. SHOCKER also exposed 10 Soviet spy handlers and 3 "illegal" agents not operating under official covers.

Sources: Wise, D., *Cassidy's Run: The Secret Spy War over Nerve Gas,* New York: Random House, 2000. See also Garthoff, R. L. ,"Polyakov's Run," *Bulletin of Atomic Scientists*, Vol. 56, No. 5, September/October 2000, pp. 37–40; and Alibek, K., *Biohazard:. The Chilling True Story of the Largest Covert Biological Weapons Program in the World*, New York: Random House, 1999.

4.5 Coordinated Technical Deception Methods

Sir Walter Scott's famous aphorism "Oh what a tangled web we weave, When first we practise to deceive!" emphasizes the pitfalls of the liar, but also hints to the complexity of coordination required to weave a successful deception operation [36]. Increasingly sophisticated coordination of deception operations is required as an increasing number of channels and methods for D&D are available to both deception planners and those who perform counterdeception by cross-checking multiple sources [37].

The deception planner must coordinate technical methods to achieve the desired effect in the intended target; this should be captured in a *deception plan* that coordinates methods should include the following elements [38]:

- *Deception objective:* The deception objective describes the intended target ultimate effect of the operation; the context in which the operation is conducted and critical assumptions must be clearly stated.
- *Target vulnerabilities exploited:* Define the target vulnerabilities exploited and assumptions about channel access and availability of methods,
- *Deception story:* A narrative description (a scenario or use case) should describe how the operation is expected to unfold, what indicators of success or failure will provide feedback, and what branches and sequels are possible as the operation proceeds.
- *Coordination plan:* The plan must include the methods, channels, and intended effects of each method. While the deception matrix, introduced in Chapter 2, is a static organization of the technical methods employed in a plan, the timing must be described (e.g., in the form of synchronization matrix

to sequence multiple concurrent or overlapping events, or in the form of a decision flow to describe the interdependency of events) and the gaming strategy that considers moves and countermoves by the target (e.g., discovery of one method, denial of one channel, and so forth)

The planning process must consider the relative timing and synchronization of coordinated methods across various channels, as well as the strategy for conducting deception against the wary target. In the following sections we introduce quantitative methods from classical probability and game theory that may be applied to assess deception value in support of the strategic planning of coordinated deception.

4.5.1 Coordinating Stratagem

We distinguish three levels of formality of the process of coordinating *stratagem*, the elaborate strategic plan to deceive a target by coordinating multiple means and channels of deception.

At the first level are the individual *tactical methods of deception*, described in the previous sections of this chapter, coordinated to achieve a specific tactical effect on sensors, systems, or humans. Quantitative methods such as utility and game theory may be applied to assess the relative utility of alternate methods and timing to achieve desired effects (e.g., surprise, critical decision error, or delay). In many cases, a single deceptive act can achieve the desired effect—a single decisive error by the target.

Perception management, the next level of deception coordination, considers all elements of the deception matrix to influence a decision-maker's perception of reality. Beyond a rational-player game theoretic analysis that deals with strategy alone, this level introduces psychological analysis to influence the perceptions and attitudes of selected individuals or groups and, over time, to manage their behavior. It targets foreign audiences (i.e., populations) as well as intelligence systems and individual leaders using actions that combine all elements of the deception matrix, including truth projection, OPSEC, simulation, and dissemination [39]. Quantitative methods for conducting and monitoring perception management have gained increasing interest in the information operations community, who seek to influence the perception and ultimately the will of policymakers, military commanders, and forces, applying a wide variety of information channels [40].

Reflexive control seeks to provide the most refined level of influence on human targets, modeling the opponent's cognitive-emotive process in an effort to convey specially prepared information to the target to produce mental states that will cause the target to voluntarily make decisions in favor of the deceiver. Based on the mathematical approach to psychology of Russian researcher V. A. Lefebreve in the 1960s, the process of *reflexion* attempts to construct a mental representation, first of the self, then of a target's thoughts and feelings (their "image" of reality) with multiple representations. *Reflexive control* is the formal method to quantify the influence on a target's perception, decisions and goals, based on an understanding of the target's awareness of reality, and a mathematical procedure to guide that perception by "transferring" an image to the target that may have several effects:

- Transfer an incorrect image of the situation (e.g., weakness where there is strength, incomplete presented as complete, and so forth) to induce specific decision errors.
- Transfer an image of the situation that guides the target to select goals that can be exploited.
- Transfer an image of the deceiver that leads the target to incorrectly infer the deceiver's goals, situation, and doctrine.

Reflexive control, organized in typical control system configuration (Figure 4.5), manipulates the target using all four methods of the deception matrix and tracks the resulting behavior to refine the target model and update control actions [41]. The model is an effects-based approach to operations that follows four steps in a competition between two parties A and B:

1. A defines the desired goals and the effects (perceptions, attitudes, decisions, behaviors) within the target, B, that will support those goals.
2. Party A develops multiple-representation reflexion models of itself, of B, and of B's perception of A's self-model. Using these models, A conducts assessments of alternative control actions to influence B to make decisions favorable to A.
3. Once a deception plan is accepted and information is presented to B, the effects are observed and compared to the expected responses by the reflexion model of B.
4. Differences in anticipated and actual responses may be used to: (a) refine the deception plan in a typical feedback control manner, and (b) refine (or choose among alternative) reflexion models of B.

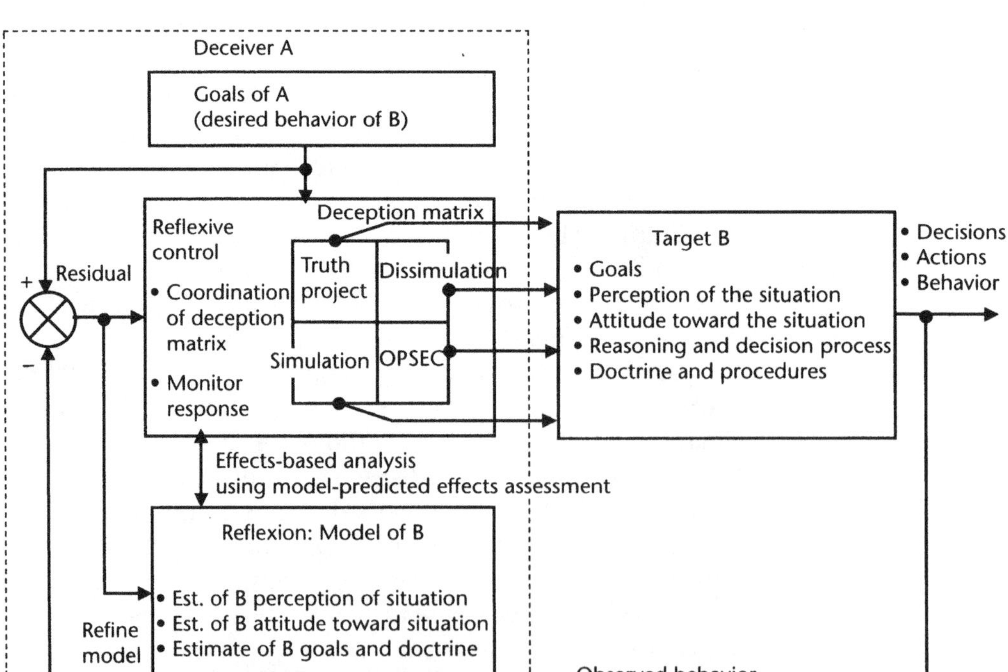

Figure 4.5 Deception elements of a reflexive control loop.

Thomas has summarized practical applications of reflexive control in anecdotal applications by the Russians and alternative analytic methods develop by Russian leaders in the field [42]. Most important to the reflexive control concept is the recognition that the target (individual or group decision-making) is regarded as a complex and adaptive system that is characterized by the behavioral issues of stability and unpredictable emergence.

4.5.2 Deception Timing and Surprise

Axelrod has illustrated a procedure to quantify the relative utility of holding back a capability (by deception) for a future surprise effect, versus the risk of the capability being revealed prematurely (by discovery) due to holding the capability too long [43]. His quantitative model to account for the variation in stakes over time, the costs of maintaining secrecy to protect the capability, the risk of exposure each time a capability is used, and the value of the capability (and resulting surprise) that is discounted over time.

Axelrod's model is formulated as an expected value (EV) problem, computing the expected value of V at any point in a "game"; V is the value of continuing to withhold the capability over a sequence of rounds of the game. In each round, the value of the resource being protected by deception is discounted by D and the probability of surviving detection is Q. The EV of continuing to withhold the capability is then a function of the weighted averages of the payoff for continuing to withhold and the payoff of proceeding to use the capability [44]:

$$V = \text{Prob. of Use } (EV \text{ of use}) + \text{Prob. of Withold } (EV \text{ of Withold}) \tag{4.1}$$

$$V = P[E\,S_{gtr} + Q(1 - D)\,V] + (1 - P)\,[-S_{less} + (1 - D)\,V] \tag{4.2}$$

where the variables are:

P = probability of using the resource at a given interval in the game

S_{gtr}, S_{les} = average stakes if the if the stakes are greater than, or less than the computed threshold, respectively (stakes are the value of the resource at risk if used)

E = enhancement factor, a constant that is multiplied by the stakes to provide the value of surprise (the use of the resource)

Q = probability of survival of a resource each time it is used and exposed to the adversary

D = discount rate, the rate at which a resource is discounted each interval of the game

Using the above expected value expression, Axelrod solved for the value of V:

$$V = \frac{E\,P\,S_{gtr,}\ (1-P)\ S_{les}}{D+\ (1-D)\ (1-Q)P} \tag{4.3}$$

The formulation allows the deception planner to compute the expected value of a surprise resource, by computing V and applying a threshold decision rule to test when to apply the resource (i.e., spring the surprise) whenever the stakes meet or exceed the threshold. The value of such a model is the understanding that it provides into the structure of the problem and the quantitative trades involved. Axelrod acknowledges the difficulty in assigning values to E, P, D, and Q, but points out the importance of relating the value of deception relative to the stakes involved. As the stakes of a military situation increase, the value of surprise increases and the relative value of deception resources can be evaluated using models like the one illustrated in this example.

4.5.3 Deception Strategy

Deception planning must also consider the target as a dynamic, reactive agent rather than a static entity. Game theory has been applied to analyze the effects of deception in policy and intelligence "competitions" where one player introduces incorrect information to an opponent to induce a belief that the game is in a state other than the truth. By misleading the opponent to the state of the game or "bluffing" about the deceiver's capability, position, or will, the opponent may induce strategy errors to the benefit of the deceiver.

To introduce the application of game theory to deception analysis, we consider how a simple game is formulated and deception is modeled. Classic game theory defines the number of players (N), each of whom has a finite set of strategies (policies or actions) and the combined result of each player applying their strategy results in a score or payoff, a. for each set of The option space for a two-player game (N = 2, players A and B) is formed by the game matrix [Figure 4.6(a)] that computes the resulting payoff, a_{ij}, for each player over all possible strategies. Player A may execute strategies $\{i|i = 3\}$ and player B may execute strategies $\{j|j = 2\}$. The utility for each player a_{ij} and b_{ij} are organized in the cells of the matrix. Once enumerated, the relative utility of the opposing strategies may be compared to develop strategies that allow all players to find an equilibrium state in the strategy space. The *Nash equilibrium* strategy for a player is the strategy where any change from the strategy will yield lower expected value given that all other players maintain their own respective

Player A \ Player B	Option j=1	Option j=2
Option i=1	$(a_{11}\ b_{11})$	$(a_{12}\ b_{12})$
Option i=2	$(a_{21}\ b_{21})$	$(a_{21}\ b_{21})$
Option i=3	$(a_{31}\ b_{31})$	$(a_{32}\ b_{32})$

(a)

Player A \ Player B	Honeypot	Exploit Vul 1	Exploit Vul 2
Honeypot	(0, 0)	(–1, 1)	(1,–1)
Exploit Vul 1	(1, –1)	(0, 0)	(–1, 1)
Exploit Vul 2	(–1, 1)	(1,–1)	(0, 0)

(b)

Figure 4.6 Deception strategies formulated in a game matrix: (a) a 2 × 4 game matrix and (b) an example of a 3 × 3 CNA game.

Nash equilibrium strategies; at equilibrium all players are satisfied by playing their own equilibrium strategies.

We briefly illustrate such a game structure in a very simple symmetric two-player CNA competition; consider three strategies that two computer attackers, A and B, may consider, in which each player has *complete information* on the state of the game (options and rules) and the outcome of each iteration:

- Employ a honeypot trap that reveals (defeats) an attacker that attempts to exploit vulnerability type 1.
- Exploit vulnerability type 1 that disables (defeats) vulnerability type 2.
- Exploit vulnerability type 2 that deposits a Trojan horse to enable the honeypot to be evaded.

If both competitors employ the same strategy, the result is a tie. The game matrix [Figure 4.6(b)] for this situation illustrates the utility for each player over all available strategies—it is a zero sum game in which the sum of all players' payoffs is 0 for all outcomes. (The sum of any cell is zero; this example is, of course, recognized as the form of the classic rock-paper-scissors game.)

In this example, *equilibrium* can be achieved over many iterations of the game when mixed strategies are applied, where the player chooses each strategy randomly with equal (0.3) probability, resulting in an expected payoff of zero for both players. The game model, so far, is competition based on choosing a strategy that takes the game to a winning state, and accumulating payoff over many iterations of the game.

So far, the complete information game had no opportunity to induce strategic deception beyond the inherent deception of the computer exploits—both players had complete information and there was no learning of the opponent's game-play behavior. Deception is introduced into this game when the game has *partial information* (where at least one of the players has incomplete knowledge of the state of the game) and one player attempts to provide information to induce an opponent into believing the game is in a different state than it actually is—to force a move to the advantage of the deceiver.

Hespanhaz, Ateskan, and Kizilocak have quantified the benefits of deception in noncooperative stochastic games with partial information, where one player can manipulate the information available to others. Their result, however, also demonstrates that as the degree of manipulation increases (e.g., number of methods and channels available to the deceiver) and the wary opponent learns over game iterations, the potential for deception diminishes as the target ignores the information and judges it useless [45]. Brams has similarly applied game theory to the analysis of deception in national security strategy and policy [46]. Brams illustrated the relative value of misdirecting opponents in multiplayer negotiations and voting (games with incomplete information), showing that the utility of deception is function of the degree to which a deception is revealed (by voting differently than a previously declared preference to mislead a target) and disagreement between other nondeceiving targets [47]. Bennett and Vane have applied hypergame theory to deception planning and counterdeception, using the unique hypergame formulation that allows each of the players to have perceptions and beliefs about important aspects of the game and even of the very nature of the game being played.

Above all, the planner must be sensitive to the context and be knowledgeable about the perceptual ability of the target to draw the desired (deceptive) inferences from the information provided [48]; while a plan may include all of the sophistication of the methods just described, it must have a high likelihood of being accepted by the target. Handel illustrates the specific concern about overly complex plans [49]:

> Deception should not be a mere exercise in intellectual gratification. A stratagem that is too sophisticated may be intellectually satisfying to those who devise it, but may not be picked up by the intended victim. Israel, for instance, often found that very polished and seemingly simple deception plans were not picked up Arab intelligence organizations because they were not able to identify the bait offered. There is an obvious danger the message developed by the deception planners is *understood by them* in the context of the endless meetings in which the alternatives were weighed and details worked out. They are so familiar with their own thinking that they risk overlooking the degree to which the message is clear to them only because *they know what to look for* [emphasis added].

4.6 Summary

Deception planning requires careful application of multiple methods across channels to limit the target's ability to compare multiple sources for conflicts, ambiguities, or uncertainties, minimizing cues to simulated or hidden information. As the number of channels and methods increase, the challenge to deception planners is to develop strategies to coordinate multiple methods, validate multiple deception channels, and track the effectiveness of the operation by monitoring integrated effects. Likewise, as we will see in later chapters, counterdeception analysts track the validity of multiple channels, monitor for the presence of multiple methods, and hypothesize the effects that a deceiver may be attempting to achieve.

Endnotes

[1] The DoD definitions of these terms were provided in Chapter 1. In this chapter, we introduce a refinement to these distinctions.

[2] We focus on the visual human spectrum, but the shorter-range auditory, smell (olfaction), touch (Somatosensation; tactile, pressure, and temperature), and taste (gustation) senses may also be the targets of deception.

[3] Hartcup, G., *Camouflage: A History of Concealment and Deception in War*, Newton Abbot, Devon, U.K.: David and Charles Military Books, 1979.

[4] *Counter Surveillance and Camouflage*, TRADOC Bulletin 6, U.S. Army Training and Doctrine Command, January 30, 1976.

[5] *FM 20-3 Camouflage, Concealment and Decoys*, Headquarters Department of the Army Washington, D.C., August 30, 1999, Section II, Table 3-1.

[6] "Military Threats and Security Challenges Through 2015," Statement for the Record by Vice Admiral Thomas R. Wilson, Director, Defense Intelligence Agency before Senate Select Committee on Intelligence, February 2, 2000, p. 12.

[7] Magnan, S., "Safeguarding Information Operations," *Studies in Intelligence*, Unclassified Edition, No. 9, Summer 2000.

[8] Adm. Jeremiah, News Conference on Recommendations from a Study of U.S. Intelligence Community Performance in Detecting Indian Nuclear Testing, June 2, 1998, released CIA Public Affairs Staff on June 4, 1998.

[9] Gupta, V., "New Satellite Images for Sale," *International Security*, Vol. 20, No. 1, Summer 1995, p. 118. See also U.S. Congress, Office of Technology Assessment, *The Future of Remote Sensing From Space: Civilian Satellite Systems and Applications, OTA-ISC-558*, Washington, D.C.: U.S. Government Printing Office, July 1993.

[10] Preston, B., and J. Baker, "Through a Glass Darkly: Deception in the Era of Commercial Imaging Satellites and Global Transparency," *Proc. Military Operations and Deception in the Age of Transparency of the International Studies Association Conference*, February 22, 2001, http://www.isanet.org/archive/darkly.html.

[11] Jones, R. V., *The Wizard War: British Scientific Intelligence, 1939–1945*, New York: Coward, McCann & Geoghegan, 1978; see also Jones, R. V., *Most Secret War*, Conshohocken, PA: Combined Publishing, 1998.

[12] Joint Doctrine for Electronic Warfare, Joint Pub 3-51, April 7, 2000, p. I-6. See also *Intelligence and Electronic Warfare Operations* U.S. Army FM 34-1, 27 September 1994, and *Communications Techniques: Electronic Counter-Countermeasures* U.S. Army FM 24-33, July 17, 1990.

[13] For an overview of the basic techniques, see Adamy, D., *EW 101: A First Course in Electronic Warfare*, and *EW 102: A Second Course in Electronic Warfare*, Norwood MA: Artech House, 2001 and 2004, respectively. See also Vakin, S., L. Shustov, and R. H. Dunwell, *Fundamentals of Electronic Warfare*, Norwood, MA: Artech House, 2001; Schleher, D. C., *Introduction to Electronic Warfare*, Norwood, MA: Artech House, 1986, "Deception Electronic Countermeasures (DECM)," pp. 138–143.

[14] For more on cryptographic attack methods, see Sections 1.2 and 3.6 of Stinson, D. R., *Cryptography: Theory and Practice*, Boca Raton, FL: CRC Press, 1995. See Section 2.1 on attacks in Purser, M., *Secure Data Networking*, Norwood, MA: Artech House, 1993.

[15] See Waltz, E., *Information Warfare Principles and Operations*, Norwood, MA: Artech House, 1998; *Joint Doctrine for Information Operations*, Joint Pub 3-13, Joint Chiefs of Staff, October 9, 1998.

[16] Poisel, R., *Introduction to Communication Electronic Warfare Systems*, Norwood, MA: Artech House, 2002; Frater, M., and M. Ryan, *Electronic Warfare for the Digitized Battlefield*, Norwood, MA: Artech House, 2001.

[17] Definition of CNE per CJCSI 3210.01A, reference f.

[18] Definition per Air Force Doctrine Document AFDD 2-5, Information Operations, January 4, 2002.

[19] Mitnick, K., *The Art of Deception: Controlling the Human Element of Security*, New York: John Wiley & Sons, 2002, p. 8. This book enumerates the variety deceptive human factor attack methods used by the hacking community.

[20] See Skoudis, E., *Malware: Fighting Malicious Code*, Upper Saddle River, NJ: Prentice-Hall, 2004; Cohen, F., "Simulating Cyber Attacks, Defenses, and Consequences," IFIP TC-11, *Computers and Security*, 1999; Cohen, F., "A Note on the Role of Deception in Information Protection," *Computers and Security*, 1999, and Cohen, F., "A Mathematical Structure of Simple Defensive Network Deceptions," 1999, http://all.net (InfoSec Baseline Studies).

[21] See Honeynet Project; Rowe, N. C., et al., "Research on Deception in Defense of Information Systems," *Proc. DoD Command and Control Research Program Conference*, San Diego, CA, June 2004.

[22] The Open Systems Interconnection OSI 7 layer Reference Model is officially known as ISO Standard 7498, 1984, 7498-1:1994. and CCITT standard X.200.

[23] The discussion of strategic influence operations is based on Waltz, E., *Knowledge Management in the Intelligence Enterprise*, Norwood, MA: Artech House, 2003, Chapter 6, Section 6.8, "Countering Denial and Deception."

[24] Agent-of-influence operations carry out the subornation (knowing or unwitting) of a person who will use their position, influence, power, or credibility to promote the objectives of a foreign power.

[25] Schultz, R. H., and R. Goodson, *Dezinformatsia: Active Measures in Soviet Strategy*, Washington, D.C.: Pergamon-Brasseys, 1984, p. 16. See also Bittman, L., *The KGB and Soviet Disinformation*, Washington, D.C.: Pergamon-Brasseys, 1985.

[26] Doctrine for Joint Psychological Operations, Joint Pub 3-53, July 10, 1996, pp. I-5 and III-1.

[27] Shanker, T., and E. Schmidtt, "Pentagon Weighs Use of Deception in a Broad Arena," *New York Times*, December 13, 2004.

[28] See Herbig, D., and K. Herbig, *Strategic Military Deception*, New York: Pergamon Press, 1982; Wohlstetter, R., *Pearl Harbor: Warning and Decision*, Palo Alto, CA: Stanford University Press, 1962; and Hesketh, R., (with foreword by Nigel West), *Fortitude: The D-Day Deception Campaign*, London, U.K.: St. Ermin's Press, 1999.

[29] Jervis, R., *Perception and Misperception in International Politics*, Princeton, NJ: Princeton University Press, 1976.

[30] Intelligence services distinguish between *agents* who are under control and the more general term *asset.* An *agent* is: (1) a person who engages in clandestine intelligence activity under the direction of an intelligence organization but who is not an office, employee, or co-opted worker of that organization; (2) an individual who acts under the direction of an intelligence agency or security service to obtain, or assist in obtaining, information for intelligence or counterintelligence purposes; or (3) one who is authorized or instructed to obtain or to assist in obtaining information for intelligence or counterintelligence purposes. An *asset* is: (1) any resource—a person, group, relationship, instrument installation, supply—at the disposition of an intelligence agency for use in an operational or support role; or (2) a person who contributes to a clandestine mission but is not a fully controlled agent. (*Source:* Glossary, Report of the Joint Inquiry into the Terrorist Attacks of September 11, 2001, House Permanent Select Committee on Intelligence and the Senate Select Committee on Intelligence, December 2002, p. 444.)

[31] For a historical summary of HUMINT double agent operations, see Rafalko, F. J., (ed.), *An American CounterIntelligence Reader: American Revolution into the New Millennium*, (4 vols.), Office of the National Counterintelligence Executive, 2004. For a Soviet perspective of agent channels to convey deception, see Cherkahin, V., with F. Feifer, *Spy Handler: Memoir of a KGB Officer*, New York: Basic Books, 2005.

[32] The agent dangle is equivalent to the computer network honeypot—these counterintelligence deceptions attempt to attract the adversary's interest, to detect and expose their clandestine activities—and to open a new channel to insert the deception.

[33] The double agent relationship begins in one of three primary means: (1) the *walk-in* where the agent of service B establishes contact with intelligence service A (in person, via mail, phone, the Internet, or an intermediary) to offer to turn against service B; (2) *the detected and doubled agent* where the agent of service B is discovered by service A and is offered a double agent role, under the duress of adverse alternatives [the loyalties of such agents who switch under duress are unusually questioned; they may "redouble" and switch again (the "triple agent"), or degenerate into "mailmen," who change loyalties as they move from country to country]; and (3) the *provocation agent* where the agent of service A is presented ("dangled") to lure service B to recruit him/her to switch loyalties. This *active provocateur* maintains a covert channel with service A (for genuine control of the operation) while actively supplying controlled information to service B over a separate channel. See Begoum, F. M., "Observations on the Double Agent," *Studies in Intelligence,* Vol. 6, No. 5, Declassified and Approved for Release CIA Historical Review, September 18, 1995, p. 59.

[34] The spectacular British use of doubled German agents in World War II is recounted in the comprehensive text, Hold, T., *The Deceivers: Allied Military Deception in the Second*

World War, New York: Scribner, 2004. For the role of coordinated deception in supporting the Operation Fortitude landing on D-Day, see also Hesketh, R., *FORTITUDE: The D-Day Deception Campaign*, Woodstock, NY: The Overlook Press/Peter Mayer Publishers, 2000.

[35] Ibid., pp. 62–63.

[36] Sir Walter Scott (1771–1832), Scottish novelist and poet; quotation from *Marmion. Canto vi. Stanza 17.*

[37] For a discussion of new D&D challenges, see Wirtz, J. J., and R. Godson, *Strategic Denial and Deception: The Twenty-First Century Challenge*, New Brunswick, NJ: Transaction Publishers, 2002.

[38] For the general military deception planning process, see: *Joint Doctrine for Military Deception,* Joint Publication 3-58, Chapter IV "Military Deception Planning Process" Washington, D.C.: Joint Chiefs of Staff, May 31, 1996. For an example of a military battlefield deception planning process, see FM 90-2 Battlefield Deception, HQ Dept. of Army, October 3, 1988, including the deception planning worksheet in Appendix B.

[39] The U.S. DoD definition of perception management: Actions to convey and/or deny selected information and indicators to foreign audiences to influence their emotions, motives, and objective reasoning as well as to intelligence systems and leaders at all levels to influence official estimates, ultimately resulting in foreign behaviors and official actions favorable to the originator's objectives. In various ways, perception management combines truth projection, operations security, cover and deception, and psychological operations (Joint Publication JP 1-02). See also O'Neill, R. P. (CDR, USN), *Toward a Methodology for Perception Management,* Newport, RI: Naval War College Center for Advanced Research, June 1989.

[40] Szafranski, R., "Neocortical Warfare? The Acme of Skill," *Military Review*, U.S. Army Command and General Staff College, November 1994, pp. 41–55; this is also Chapter 17 in Arquilla, J., and D.Ronfeldt, (eds.), *In Athena's Camp: Preparing for Conflict in the Information Age*, Santa Monica, CA: RAND, MR 880, 1997.

[41] See the overview: Lefebvre, Vladimir A. "Sketch of Reflexive Game Theory," *Proc. Workshop on Multi-Reflexive Models of Agent Behavior*, 1998, pp. 1–42; original concepts were published in Lefebvre, V. A., "Basic Ideas of the Logic of Reflexive Games," in *Problemy Issledovania Sistemi Struktur*, Moscow, Russia: Academy of Sciences of the USSR Press, 1965;

[42] Thomas, T. L., "Reflexive Control in Russia: Theory and Military Applications," *International Interdisciplinary Scientific and Practical Journal, Issue on Reflexive Process and Control*, Vol. 1, No. 2, July–December 2002, pp. 60–76. See also Thomas, T. L., "Dialectical Versus Empirical Thinking: Ten Key Elements of the Russian Understanding of Information Operations," *CALL Publication #98-21*, Fort Leavenworth, KS: U.S. Army Foreign Military Studies Office, 1998 and Thomas, T. L., "Russian Information-Psychological Actions: Implications for U.S. PSYOP," Special Warfare, Vol. 10, No. 1, Winter 1997, pp 12–19. For a description of reflexive control principles, see Reid, C., "Reflexive Control in Soviet Military Planning," in Dailey, B., and P. Patker, (eds.), *Soviet Strategic Deception*, Stanford, CA: The Hoover Institution Press, 1987, pp. 293–312.

[43] Axelrod, R., "The Rational Timing of Surprise," *World Politics*, Vol. 31, No. 2, January 1979; New Jersey: Princeton University Press, 1979, pp. 228–246.

[44] The reader is referred to the original article for a thorough description of the formulation, and derivation; the summary here is intended to illustrate principles, key variables and application.

[45] Hespanhaz, J. P., Y. S. Ateskan, and H. H. Kizilocak, "Deception in Non-Cooperative Games with Partial Information," *Proc. of the 2nd DARPA-JFACC Symposium on Advances in Enterprise Control*, July 2000. For a similar assessment of the gaming of information in military engagements, see Darilek, R., et al., *Measures of Effectiveness for the Information-Age Army*, RAND MR 1155, 2001, Ch. 3, "Gaming Information."

[46] See Brams, S. J., and D. M. Kilgour, *Game Theory and National Security*, Oxford, U.K.: Basil Blackwell, 1988, for an introduction; specific analyses are includes in the following: Brahms, S. J., and F. C. Zagare, "Double Deception: Two against One in Three-Person Games," *Theory and Decision*, Vol. 13, March 1981, pp. 81–90; Brahms, S. J., "Deception in 2 × 2 Games," *Journal of Peace Science*, Vol. 2, Spring 1977, pp. 171–203.

[47] Brams, S. J., and F. C. Zagare, "Deception in Simple Voting Games," *Social Science Research* 6 September 1977, pp. 257–272; see an application in Zagare, F. C., "The Geneva Conference of 1954: A Case of Tacit Deception," *International Studies Quarterly*, Vol. 23, No. 3, September 1979, pp. 390–411.

[48] Bennett, M., and R. R. Vane III, "Using Hypergames for Deception Planning and Counterdeception Analysis," *Defense Intelligence Journal*, Fall 2006.

[49] Handel, M., *War, Strategy, and Intelligence,* London, U.K.: Frank Cass & Co., Ltd., p. 329.

CHAPTER 5

Principles of Counterdeception

Chapters 1 through 4 provided a general introduction to deception by describing its increasing role in the global security environment, the various models and theories that have been developed in order to describe and understand it, the various biases that contribute to its seemingly almost certain success, and the variety of technical and nontechnical methods that support the conduct of deception operations. We also proposed that there are four fundamental principles that form the foundation for the different models and methods of strategic deception. Now, we turn our attention to the topic of counterdeception and attempt to answer several questions. What is counterdeception? What guidance can be found in the literature for countering deception? Is there a corresponding set of fundamental principles of counterdeception that can guide analysts and decision-makers? What can be done to overcome the various biases that we saw contribute to deception's success? What technical and nontechnical means can be employed to counter strategic and tactical deception operations? And, perhaps the most intriguing question of all: Is Barton Whaley right? Is deception almost always successful as the historical evidence implies? This chapter addresses the first three of these questions. After defining what we mean by counterdeception, we will examine the variety of models, concepts, and approaches found in the literature related to counterdeception in the national security context. We will then examine the common themes that emerge from this work, and derive a set of basic principles of counterdeception.

5.1 What Is Counterdeception?

The U.S. Department of Defense [1] defines counterdeception as: "Efforts to negate, neutralize, diminish the effects of, or gain advantage from a foreign deception operation. Counterdeception does not include the intelligence function of identifying foreign deception operations." This is an operationally oriented definition that emphasizes mitigating deception's effects (like surprise) and exploiting knowledge of the adversary's deception. Our focus will be primarily on the intelligence function part of that definition, but the concept of counterdeception goes beyond just "identifying foreign deception operations." We believe that the purpose of counterdeception is to find the answers to two fundamental and highly interdependent questions. First, counterdeception must make it possible for analysts and decision-makers to penetrate through the deception to discern the adversary's real capabilities and intentions, in other words, to answer the question: What is real? Simultaneously, analysts and decision-makers must determine what the adversary is trying to make them believe in order to consider the second question: What does the adversary want you to do? The answers to these two questions are absolutely essential to the success of one's own strategies, policies, and operations.

The intelligence aspects of counterdeception are aimed at detecting, characterizing, and penetrating foreign deception operations. It is important to keep in mind that there is no sharp demarcation line between normal intelligence activities and counterdeception intelligence activities. This is because no such line exists between the adversary's normal security activities and his calculated deception operations. Although large, sophisticated deception operations (like Plan FORTITUDE in World War II) are rare, as we saw in Chapter 2 deception itself is a phenomenon that everyone experiences in one form or another on a daily basis. This presents intelligence analysts and decision-makers with a paradox: *Deception is simultaneously both common and rare*. As a result, analysts face a continuum of deception ranging from basic security activities aimed at the deliberate concealment of facts, to sources who engage in deceit and misrepresentation for personal reasons (e.g., a human asset who fabricates information in order to remain on an intelligence organization's payroll), to deliberate ad hoc official deceit, and finally, to deliberate well-planned, well-coordinated deception operations. This is why counterdeception in the national security context is more than just detecting deception. Just what kind of deception are we trying to detect? How do we distinguish between deliberate deception and the types of misperceptions that Jervis describes? As Rossa points out [2]: "Faced with an array of information on a subject, the analyst who is to put the pieces of the puzzle together must first determine which pieces to use and which to discard or reshape on the basis of whether it was obtained despite foreign denial operations, as a result of foreign deception operations, or in the absence of either." This leads us to conclude that counterdeception is characterized by three dimensions of action: *awareness*, *detection and exposure*, and *discovery and penetration*.

Awareness primes the observer to register cues in the environment that signify either a threat or an opportunity. Anyone who has ever taken a personal security training course knows that awareness is considered the first line of defense; being aware what is happening around you often allows you avoid trouble before it even happens. Awareness is also analogous to the activation step in the Johnson et al. fraud detection model. The auditor is aware of certain cues that, if detected, lead to further questioning of the financial statement. A simple example of awareness in the intelligence context is when an analyst recognizes that a situation presents the adversary both the opportunity and motive to employ deception.

The *detection and exposure* dimension involves intelligence collection and analysis activities that are aimed at determining what the adversary is trying to make you believe and, as a result, what he wants you to do [3]. In essence, the objective is to accurately reconstruct the deceiver's deception story from the data and information available. The *discovery and penetration* dimension, on the other hand, focuses on revealing what is real. In this case intelligence collection and analysis assets are used to sort out the relevant from the irrelevant and the real from the false in order to determine what are the adversary's real capabilities and intent [4]. These two dimensions are not independent. They are highly coupled and interdependent and both employ similar processes and methods to reveal that which is concealed, separate deliberate distortions from unintentional misperceptions, and disentangle the real from the false in order to determine what really to believe.

5.2 The Search for Ways to Counter Deception

In Chapter 2 we saw that much of the literature related to military and strategic deception concentrates on the historical description and analysis of deception operations and their associated methods. The 1970s saw the beginnings of a theoretical phase of deception analysis where several authors used basic principles from psychology, systems engineering, communications theory, and other fields to begin the development of conceptual models of the process of deception itself. In this literature, the subject of counterdeception is, if addressed at all, treated almost as an afterthought. An author might devote a few paragraphs or perhaps a section of a chapter or paper to the topic. As Harris [5] observed in 1973, "There is hardly an adequate theory of deception, much less a theory of counterdeception." Events in the late 1990s (e.g., the 1998 Indian nuclear test and especially Iraq's efforts to hide its WMD program) generated significantly more interest in counterdeception; however, the literature on topic is still relatively sparse. This section mirrors the approach taken in Chapter 2 and summarizes the various counterdeception conceptual models, theories, and approaches that can be found in the literature. Like Chapter 2, they are presented in rough chronological order so that the reader can see how the thinking about counterdeception has changed over the years.

5.2.1 Early Pioneers [6]: "Is there, then, no way by which the target of stratagem can untangle the web of deceit?"

In 1942, R. V. Jones wrote [7]: "No imitation can be perfect without being the real thing [7]." The implication of this observation is that imitations should differ from the real thing in one or more ways, that is, observations made of the imitation should be inconsistent with those of the real object or event, thus leading to Jones to the conclusion that [8], "If there is inconsistency between the impressions derived from the several channels, the potential deceivee would do well to suspect a deception." Jones goes on to offer advice on what the target can do in this situation. First, he recommends [8] a "critical reappraisal of the intelligence picture" that "should include examining afresh the evidence coming in through each channel in turn, and particularly those channels giving conflicting evidence." In addition, there are other actions that analysts can take based on two principles that Jones offers for unmasking deception [9], "(1) in any channel of intelligence through which you may be deceive, arrange to work down to a greater level of sophistication than your opponent expected you to adopt, and (2) bring all other possible channels of intelligence to bear on the problem, to see whether the evidence that they can provide is consistent with the evidence in the channel through which you suspect you are being deceived." The first principle involves going beyond the obvious conclusions offered by an observation and subjecting the data to further scrutiny in search of clues that might reveal inconsistencies. Examining the Doppler characteristics of radio navigation signal is an example of this "deepening" examination of an information channel. If the source of the deceptive signal is ahead of an aircraft while the source of the authentic signal is behind it, the frequency of the real signal should be slightly lower than that of the deceptive one, thus, in principle, unmasking the deception [10]. An example of the second principle might be to double-check the observations of the radio navigation signal with other channels of information such as inertial guidance systems or dead reckoning methods using magnetic compass and clock. Once again, the detection of inconsistencies is cause for suspecting deception.

Jones also offers two maxims that are also quite relevant to counterdeception. The first [11] is "Crow's Law: Do not believe what you want to believe until you know what you ought to know." As we saw earlier, knowing what you ought to know will undoubtedly involve reappraising any evidence that is inconsistent with what you want to believe. The second is Occam's Razor: Hypotheses are not to be multiplied without necessity. Given missing, ambiguous, and contradictory information, analysts should seek the simplest hypotheses that will account for the information on hand. Jones points out that this will not necessarily produce the correct explanation, but that it provides the best basis to start from. Only rarely, he says, has Occam's Razor failed him. This is sound advice in the face of our human ability to make too much out of too little, as Jones [12] subsequently points out with "Crabtree's Bludgeon: No set of mutually inconsistent observations can exist for which some human intellect cannot conceive a coherent explanation, however complicated."

Barton Whaley briefly addressed the question of counterdeception in his famous 1969 book. In the chapter where he describes his theory of stratagem, he also proposes a decision-making model analogous to the one he describes for stratagem itself (see Section 2.2.2). Whereas a stratagem decision-making model is used to create a set of signals that the target observes and fits to a plausible alternative, a counterdeception decision-making model should be designed [13] "to analyze the signals of stratagem rather than the one designed to synthesize their false signals." Whaley offers two examples only one of which we will discuss here. While intelligence analysts consistently strive to expose an adversary's attempts at camouflage, Whaley observes that he could find no example of where the deceiver's attempts at camouflage were reported [13] "for their own sake." Whaley concludes that [13], "having done their work to identify camouflage, the analyst uses his findings only to correct the regular situation reports, order-of-battle maps, or traffic analysis studies. He does not use these findings to analyze the patterns of camouflage or 'noise' to see if they could imply a positive deception plan or campaign." In other words, the existence of camouflage becomes a signal of deception and such signals can be analyzed in order to detect patterns that might suggest the alternative objective of the adversary.

Harris, who, according to Whaley, coined the term *counterdeception* in 1968 [14], proposes that countering deception involves three related concepts [5]:

- The *detection* of an adversary's deceptions;
- The adoption of *countermeasures* that reduce the likelihood and adverse consequences of those deceptions;
- The *coordination* of both of these into a counterdeception system.

Harris concentrates primarily on the first two concepts and leaves it to the reader to "read between the lines" in order to identify the organizational implications of creating a system to coordinate the two activities. Therefore, we will concentrate on the three techniques that Harris describes for detecting the existence of deception operations and for uncovering the facts. These are: *reconstructive inference*, *incongruity testing*, and *vulnerability assessment* (see Figure 5.1). The first, reconstructive inference, involves attending to the patterns of misleading and deceptive signals that are transmitted by the deceiver. These spurious signals, or *sprignals*, appear to be directly analogous to the "signals of stratagem" that Whaley suggested looking for and therefore reconstructive inference—analyzing patterns of sprignals and their relationships—should make it possible to identify the "stratagemic plans" of an adversary. The analysis of sprignals also makes it possible to identify those channels that that are most likely to be used to disseminate disinformation at critical times. It may also be possible to correlate masses of sprignals with different deception styles. Of course, separating sprignals from real signals and noise is no easier than separating signals for noise and Harris suggests concentrating on separating sprignals from signals while recognizing the fact that some noise will wind up contaminating both categories. Sprignals are also likely to be sensitive to both time and context. Making things even more difficult, patterns of sprignals may provide clues that are only relevant to past encounters but not necessarily future ones. In addition, even if sprignals analysis yields insights into an adversary's initial plan, that analysis might not be relevant in a fluid situation (e.g., situations where a commander changes his plans and the deception plan winds up becoming the real plan).

The second technique is incongruity testing, which Harris defines as the matching and testing of alternative patterns for internal and interpattern consistency. He does not offer much detail regarding the methods for such testing, but simply states that [15]: "at least theoretically" incongruities could be discovered "given sufficient data and hypothesis testing." Reading through Harris's section, one comes to the

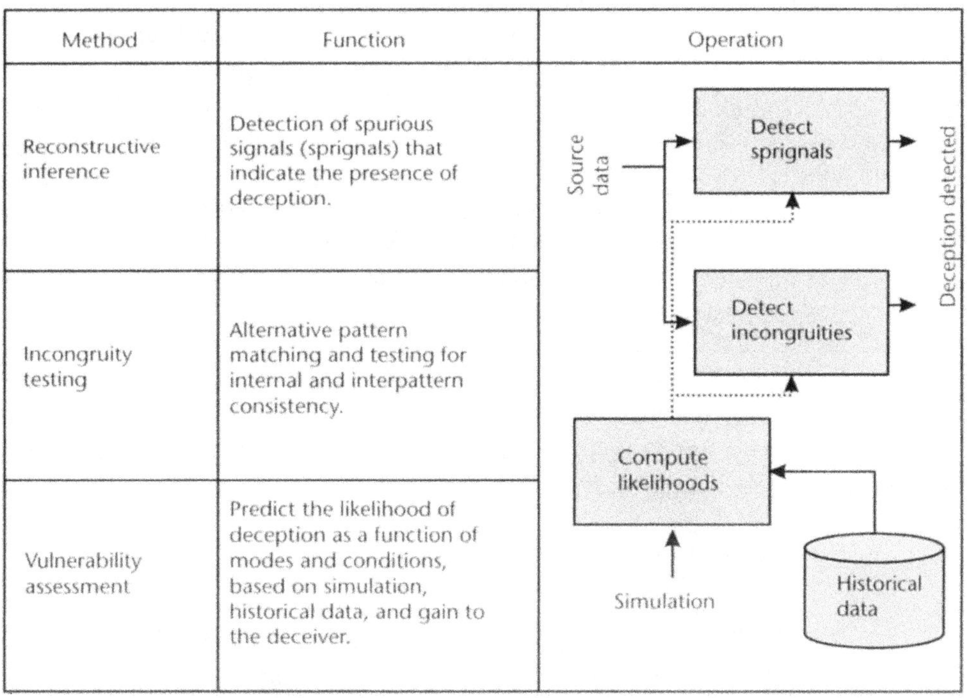

Figure 5.1 Harris's deception detection techniques.

conclusion that it involves the generation of alternative hypotheses that represent "alternative perceptual patterns" of the signal and sprignal data.

Harris notes that incongruity testing faces two main limitations: *disjointed incongruities* and *false incongruities*. Disjointed incongruities [16] "involve inconsistencies that have become, in the perceptions of the viewer if not in fact, separated or mismatched." The incongruities are not recognized because the different sets of inconsistent patterns are never paired. Jokes, hoaxes, and deceptions all rely on disjointed incongruities. Jokes are funny because the question sets up an incongruity and the punch line reveals the hidden resolution to the incongruity—a surprising alternate interpretation [17]. Deceptions work if the incongruities between the real and false situations are not resolved. Harris calls these *clandestinely* disjointed incongruities. The challenge to incongruity testers is that deception planners do their best to prevent their target from detecting the incongruities. Another form of disjointed incongruity that has counterdeception implications are *mutually* disjointed incongruities. In this case, observer A perceives situation A and observer B perceives situation B. It may be the case that situations A and B are representations of the same situation, but unfortunately this situation is not the true situation, C.

The other limitation to incongruity testing is the need to deal with false incongruities. Harris defines false incongruities as [16]: "The pairing of two or more apparently inconsistent patterns that represent a consistent underlying reality." These complicate the task of incongruity testing by adding clutter to the process. They can result from different perspectives of the underlying pattern or as the result of our ability to detect order in random patterns.

Some of these apparent but unreal incongruities are a matter of different perspectives; some are a consequence of the random distribution of noise in perceptual systems. In either case, they must be identified.

The third technique, vulnerability assessment, uses statistical approaches to predict future vulnerabilities to deception. Bayes' theorem, multivariate statistical analysis, game theory, and other modeling and simulation methods can all be used to explore the likelihood of encountering deception in different situations and under various conditions. Likewise, these methods can be used to assess the risks and costs of making Type I (failure to detect the deception) or Type II (false positive) errors. In addition, Harris suggest that rigorous studies of the deception styles and practices of prospective adversaries can help assess both one's own potential vulnerabilities as well as provide potential indicators of deception through the reconstruction of sprignal patterns.

In 1976, Robert Jervis concluded his book, *Perception and Misperception in International Politics*, with a chapter on minimizing misperception [18]. Although his focus was on misperception, not deception, his suggestions for minimizing misperception are equally applicable to situations where deliberate deception is involved. Jervis suggests four broad themes for compensating for perceptual errors:

- Making assumptions and predictions explicit;
- The use of devil's advocates;
- Making sure that identities and missions do not become linked with specific theories and images;
- Awareness of common misperceptions.

When considering deception, the first theme might be restated as making assumptions, preconceptions, and beliefs explicit. Jervis writes [19]:

> The failure to examine the plausibility of crucial beliefs, especially those relating to ends and means, is evident when the environment changes in a way that should, but does not, lead to changes in beliefs and policies. For example, one reason why the United States was taken by surprise at Pearl Harbor was that the initial analysis of Japan's alternatives had led to the reasonable conclusion that Japan would not attack American territory. But as the situation changed, American decision makers realized that Japan might strike at the Philippines. Since such an attack meant war with the United States, Americans should have noted that one of the major reasons why the Japanese would not attack Pearl Harbor was now removed and should have looked at the dangers again.

Jervis states that making beliefs and assumptions explicit requires not only understanding the elements that make up those beliefs and assumptions but also an examination of what evidence would confirm or disconfirm them. He suggests that [20], "If they are aware of what they expect, or rather what their images and beliefs should lead them to expect, actors will be more apt to heed unsettling incidents." Such awareness also extends to thinking about what events are excluded by the actor's assumptions and beliefs with the hope that he would be more likely to notice and react to those events if they occur as well as heighten his sensitivity to discrepant information.

Jervis [21] uses the concept of devil's advocates to emphasize the need for encouraging the "formulation and application of alternative images" noting that it is often politically and psychologically difficult for any one person to consider multiple alternatives. Jervis also has an interesting perspective on cognitive bias in this regard [22]: "Rather than seeking 'unbiased' treatments of the data, decision-makers should seek to structure conflicting cognitive biases into the decision making process to help themselves maintain their intellectual freedom." In other words, instead of trying to eliminate cognitive biases altogether, decision-makers should take advantage of them in order to produce differing perspectives of a given situation. In that same vein, Jervis continues [22], "To make it more likely that they will consider alternative explanations of specific bits of data and think more carefully about the beliefs and images that underlie their policies, they should employ devil's—or rather devils'—advocates." Jervis admits that a devil's advocate is unlikely to produce the correct image; however, incorporating devil's advocacy into the process has two major benefits. First, it exposes decision-makers to alternative explanations of events, thereby forcing them to exercise judgment as opposed to seeing one view as the only possible alternative. Second, devil's advocacy helps to expose the assumptions and beliefs discussed earlier.

Jervis offers less detail regarding the last two themes. The third theme addresses the potential dangers that arise when the mission and identity of individuals and organizations becomes too closely tied to specific theories and images of other actors. He cites as an example the U.S. Air Force's post–World War II resistance to guided missiles [23]: "The members of the organization had come to see its distinctive mission not as carrying out strategic bombardment, but as carrying out strategic bombardment by means of manned bombers." The deception implications should be obvious. If mission and identity are too closely tied to specific beliefs, a deceiver can manipulate those beliefs knowing that it is likely that information about other alternatives will be made to fit those beliefs or will not even be considered. Finally, Jervis [24] concludes his chapter on minimizing misperception with a general call "for decision makers to take account of the ways in which the processes of perception lead to common errors." The hope is that if decision-makers are aware of these biases and errors, they will be more likely to take measures to decrease misperception by avoiding or compensating for common perceptual errors, decrease their overconfidence in prevailing beliefs, become more sensitive to alternative perspectives, and perhaps reduce the amount discrepant information required to make them reconsider those beliefs.

5.2.2 The Theoretical Work of the 1980s

As we saw in Chapter 2, the 1980s saw the publication of a number of journal articles and books marking the start of a more theoretical approach to the study of deception. In 1980, the CIA's Mathtech Deception Research Program published a report, *Deception Maxims: Fact and Folklore*, which described the 10 deception maxims summarized previously in Figure 2.7. That report also addressed the counterdeception implications for three of those maxims in a single paragraph at the end of their report. Maxim 1 states that it is easier for the target to maintain preexisting beliefs even in the face of evidence that contradicts those beliefs implying that it is important to examine one's own beliefs for exploitable weaknesses in order to be less susceptible to deception. Maxim 4, Jones' Lemma, suggests that the deceiver should try to control as many of the channels available to the target as possible. The counterdeception implication is that the target should not rely on only one or two channels of information but should employ redundant sensors to increase the likelihood that incongruities can be detected. Finally, Maxim 6 counsels the deceiver that there are situations where deception assets should be husbanded until they can be put to more fruitful use. The implication of this maxim then is for the target to consider the stakes involved in any situation when evaluating the adversary's options: higher stakes may warrant the adversary using those husbanded deception assets.

Shortly thereafter, Richards Heuer published his landmark article, "Strategic Deception and Counterdeception: A Cognitive Process Approach." Although his article dealt primarily with the cognitive biases relevant to the problem of deception, Heuer also addresses the subject of counterdeception by reviewing three "commonly advocated approaches" and suggesting two more approaches of his own. The first three approaches are:

- Improved intelligence collection;
- Increased alertness to deception;
- Weighting of tactical indicators.

With regard to improved intelligence collection, Heuer notes [25] that advances in technical collection systems have improved the intelligence community's overall capabilities but that such systems "have contributed little toward improving estimates of intentions, strategy, or political dynamics." While improvements in intelligence collection are desirable, Heuer offers his belief [25] that such improvements are unlikely to significantly reduce one's vulnerability to deception and goes on to state, "Any systematic counterdeception program must focus primarily on problems of analysis, only secondarily on collection." Ideally, increased alertness to deception would stimulate a more thorough review of the information available and Heuer concedes that this is possibly the case if the possibility of deception has not already been considered. In such a case, Heuer [26] notes that "simply focusing on this possibility may be sufficient to identify overlooked information or prompt a change in analytical perspective." Nevertheless, he is generally pessimistic about the ability of alertness alone to detect deception and makes the case that such alertness is more likely to detect deception where it does not exist, lead analysts to be overly skeptical of all the information on hand, and when deception is present, cause analysts to dismiss the wrong evidence. The weighting of tactical indicators approach is based on Abraham Ben-Zvi's [27] study of surprise military attacks. Ben-Zvi found that tactical indicators of an impending attack were often discounted because they did not agree with the preconceptions and strategic assumptions held by analysts and commanders. Although Heuer agrees that analysts and decision-makers should be more open to changing their minds in the fact of discrepant information, giving more weight to such indicators will increase the false alarm rate and it is often difficult or impossible to know whether in any given situation it is better to heed the indicators or hold on to the established view.

Heuer's own suggestions fall into two categories: cognitive aids to analysis and organizational measures. The first category consists of alternative hypotheses and breaking mental sets. What has become to be known as Alternative Competing Hypotheses (ACH) is in response to the fact that research shows that people do a poor job of generating a sufficiently full set of hypotheses when analyzing a situation. As Heuer notes [28], "If the correct hypothesis is not even formulated for consideration, there is clearly little chance of making an accurate judgment." This failure to generate sufficient hypotheses is aggravated by other biases such as confirmation bias. Evidence tends to be evaluated in terms of how well it supports a hypothesis and the fact that such evidence may be consistent with other alternative hypotheses is often overlooked. For Heuer [28], "The systematic identification, examination, and testing of alternative hypotheses is one of the keys to the successful uncovering of deception." We will examine ACH in more detail in later chapters. Heuer [29] also proposes that "methods for breaking mental sets are particularly relevant for counterdeception analysis." He suggests methods such as the devil's advocate, interdisciplinary brainstorming, and "other techniques that facilitate the identification and systematic analysis of alternative perspective" [29]. The organizational measures that Heuer proposes focus primarily on the creation of a counterdeception staff as a form of "deception insurance." Heuer bases this suggestion on research showing that one of the most difficult cognitive tasks that a person can be called upon to perform is to reorganize information that they are already familiar with in order to view it from a totally different perspective. The more complex the information and the longer that one has held certain beliefs about what the information means, the more difficult this task becomes. Heuer suggests that a dedicated counterdeception staff is necessary to address complex questions concerning deception that cannot be handled by an individual analyst using cognitive aids.

In 1982 two books were published that addressed deception and surprise: *Strategic Military Deception,* edited by Daniel and Herbig, and *Military Deception and Strategic Surprise,* edited by Gooch and Perlmutter. In *Strategic Military Deception,* Daniel and Herbig [30] describe two groups of factors that influence the likelihood of deception. The first group is related to the different situations that confront a would-be deceiver, while the second group reflects certain characteristics of the deceiver. Although Daniel and Herbig do not mention that these factors could be used for counterdeception, we suggest that these factors represent potentially useful cues for analysts and decision-makers to be aware of. The situational factors include:

- *High-stakes situations.* Such situations encourage an adversary to use every capability at his disposal to ensure success or avoid defeat.
- *Lack of confidence in a situation's outcome due to military weakness.* Deception is a useful way of compensating for an adversary's superior strength.
- *Lower the costs of even an optimistic situation.* In addition to using deception in order to avoid human and material losses, an adversary may employ deception in order to avoid the political and economic costs of being viewed as an aggressor.
- *Uncertain situations.* A deceiver may use deception in order to keep his options open and to test his adversary's reactions to different actions.

The second group consists of factors related to the deceiver's previous conditioning or personal predilection and includes:

- *Cultural norms.* Cultural factor may affect when and how deception is used.
- *Political leaders that play a strong, central role in military decisions.* Deception may be more common in situations where this is the case, particularly in dictatorships and authoritarian regimes.
- *Bureaucratic and psychological pressure.* This factor is based on two traits common to many bureaucracies. The first trait is that organizations trained for particular tasks will seek to perform them. The second trait is related to the availability heuristic—people tend to think in terms of what is available to them. The first trait implies that an adversary that maintains the capability to plan, organize, and execute deception operations is more likely to use deception than one that is not. The second trait suggests that, even if not incorporated formally as doctrine, an adversary that has some familiarity with deception is more likely to use it than one that is not.
- *Personal predilection.* Leaders and commanders who appreciate deception and have relied on in the past are likely to do so again.

Paul Moose's chapter in *Strategic Military Deception* [31] presents an elementary systems model that envisions a dynamic relationship between two adversaries (Green and Purple) and their environment. This produces an "event stream" that is the result of each side's actions in response to the other as well as the environment. Moose's concept of counterdeception [31] involves a plan where the target (Purple) "hypothesizes two measurably different near-term event streams, depending on whether a deception is present or not" and initiates activities that precipitate some action on the deceiver's (Green) part in one of these streams which may reveal the deceiver's real intentions. The target then uses his own feedback channels to observe how the deceiver reacts to the target's reaction. Of course, the risks of waiting while the counterdeception plan unfolds versus acting on one of the hypothesized event streams must be considered. Moose also provides some general prescriptions regarding counterdeception. He states that [31], "The most effective way to prevent deception is to be continually aware of one's vulnerabilities as a target." He also notes that one should be skeptical about signals that encourage procrastination or inactivity and that the "leaky" nature of the adversary's internal communications (i.e., unintentional signals that might reveal the adversary's true intentions) should be exploited.

Also in *Strategic Military Deception* is a chapter by Theodore Sarbin, a narrative psychologist [32]. He proposes a theory of counterdeception that assumes that [33] "human beings think, perceive, and imagine according to a narrative structure." As we saw in Section 3.2.2.2, he suggests that the authors of strategy emplot narratives and observes that [33], "The task of the counterdeception analyst of strategy is like the task of the literary critic or the dramatic critic—to fathom the intentions of the author, to 'understand,' to decipher the meaning of the creative work." Given that deception typically represents a unique case where the context is a critical determinant of the actors' behavior, the target of deception cannot rely on statistical approaches or case studies (*sagacity*) to predict the deceiver's real intentions due to the lack of meaningful base rates. Therefore, the counterdeception analyst must rely on *acumen*—the empathic skill to take on the role of another. This ability is related to the person's ability to *decenter*—the ability to switch from one's own egocentric perspective and see things from another's perspective—and Sarbin suggests that [34], "From literary and autobiographical sources, one can infer that the person who is successful in taking the role of another is able to construct a scenario, a story, and place himself in relation to the other features of the story, physical features such as geography and climate, social features, such as role relationships with multiple role players." Such abilities help the person gifted with acumen succeed in consistently predicting the actions of others and are "the stock in trade of someone who can penetrate the masks or expose the lie of the adversary" [34].

Acumen is therefore an important skill for intelligence and counterdeception analysts to possess and Sarbin offers the hypothesis that analysts possessing the skill of acumen are more likely to identify the form of the narrative contained in the strategic plans of an adversary. He also poses two interesting questions in this regard. Are certain kinds of plots related to kinds of ethnic origins or national heritages? Can acumen be taught and learned? Sarbin asserts that literary historians are able to successfully identify the different forms of emplotment they encounter but admits that they have the benefit of hindsight. On the other hand, analysts face the problem of having to construct a plot from antecedent events and try to predict the outcome making their task tremendously more difficult. The difference is that [35], "Unlike the historian who emplots a narrative about events that have occurred in the past, the analyst of strategy must emplot concurrent events, events that are not frozen but fluid." With regard to teaching and learning acumen, Sarbin suggests that there may be ways to recognize "optimal cognitive strategies" for identifying the events associated with a specific plot structure [36], that is, "When is an 'event' an event?"

In the mid-1980s three closely related books by British authors (see the Haswell, Dewar, and Latimer portion of Section 2.2.3) appeared, but only one specifically addressed the topic of counterdeception. In *The Art of Deception in Warfare,* Dewar devotes a chapter to counterdeception [37], in which he summarizes Whaley's concepts of deception and uses them to make a number of points. These can be categorized into two broad areas:

- Macroscopic knowledge of the adversary;
- Microscopic analysis aimed at discovering inconsistencies.

Dewar notes [38], "A detailed knowledge of the enemy is as important in countering deception as it is in achieving it." This knowledge must extend to [39] "a macroscopic appreciation of the enemy's fears, aims, prejudices, and habits" and analysts "must also be able to see things from the enemy's point of view, think as the enemy thinks, list the options open to him and decide what is most probable" [40]. At one point Dewar goes as far as stating [41], "Thus the main, almost the only, weapon of the deception analyst is to put himself in the mind of the deceiver." This knowledge includes recognizing that the adversary's deception plans are themselves seldom flawless thus creating the opportunity for the "microscopic" search for the flaws in the pattern of the deceiver's deception plan. Here Dewar seems to be advocating a kind of analytical preparedness [42], "Defence against deception therefore requires a sustained questioning of evidence, a search for its corroboration and a review of previous deductions as fresh evidence is produced. In particular, it is helpful to look for small and obscure clues which are missing and which would prove or disprove the authenticity of the existing evidence." For Dewar, the golden rule of counterdeception is to avoid jumping to conclusions. He warns that deceivers thrive on the pressure that analysts labor under to provide timely assessments and predictions and urges analysts to resist the temptation to jump to conclusions whenever possible.

Dewar acknowledges the difficulty of looking at a situation from different perspectives noting that "increased alertness" to the potential for deception is largely ineffective, but suggests that a devil's advocate is one way that the data can be subjected to competitive analysis. Dewar summarizes his approach to counterdeception by reminding analysts that "first impressions are difficult to change and different starting points lead to different conclusions" and concludes [43]: "That is why competitive analysis should be undertaken whenever possible. Or to put it more simply, two heads are better than one."

The end of the 1980s saw the publication of Michael Handel's *War, Strategy, and Intelligence.* This book includes work that appeared as journal articles or as chapters in other books (e.g., Gooch and Perlmutter) and several of these address the topic of counterdeception both directly and indirectly. Handel is strongly pessimistic with regard to the possibility of preventing or forestalling surprise attack and this pessimism is reflected in his general skepticism regarding counterdeception. Nevertheless, he offers six possible deception countermeasures, noting that [44], "Some can be suggested, although their effectiveness cannot be guaranteed." The first suggestion, *avoid overreliance on one source of information*, emphasizes that potentially valuable information collected in one channel should be independently verified by sources in other channels. As we saw in Chapter 3, German over reliance on one channel of information (their network of agents in Britain—all controlled by the Allies) was a major factor in the success of Allied deception efforts. The next four suggestions address what can perhaps be the most important channel of information available to the deceiver—the double agent. His suggestions reflect several lessons that can be drawn from Germany's experience as the target of the Allies' Double Cross operations in support of the Fortitude deception. These include:

- *Never rely exclusively on nonmaterial evidence.* Handel quotes Clausewitz's remark that [44], "Words being cheap, are the most common means of creating false impressions." In other words, written or verbal information that an agent provides about physical entities must be checked and verified by other sources (e.g., an agent report about the location of a missile battery should be verified by imagery or signals intelligence). This suggestion also applies to information obtained through communications intercepts.
- *Never rely on agents who have not been seen or directly interviewed.* Much of the success of the FORTITIDE SOUTH deception is credited to the double agent GARBO and much of GARBO's success as a double agent was due to his ability to convince the Germans that he controlled a network of subagents. Unfortunately for the Abwehr and the German high command, this entire network was fictitious. All of GARBO's subagents, including his deputy, were notional. Handel [44] notes that this suggestion carries even more weight if the information that is received from possibly notional agents "dovetails nicely with one's own preferences or needs, or when it fits without contradictions into the reports of other possibly notional agents."
- *Check and double-check discrepancies in agent reporting.* Handel suggests that there are two situations where extra caution should be exercised when relying on agent reporting. First, there is the situation in which an agent's reports initially appear to be correct but then turn out to be wrong on an important issue and yet somehow the agent always seems have a good explanation for each discrepancy. The second situation calls for even more caution. Here Handel even suggests a special investigation of any agent who supplies high quality information of the greatest importance [44, 45], but "*only when it is too late to be of any use*—even if it arrives before the action it warns against has taken place."
- *Controllers of agents should also be encouraged to heed more closely the opinions of lower-level intelligence analysts.* Since the target of most strategic deception operations are top-level decision-makers, commanders, and intelligence managers, Handel suggests that deception has a better chance of being detected by lower level (not necessarily lower expertise or experience) analysts since they are less likely to be biased by any specific strategy, wishful thinking, or political interests. Handel cites examples from World War I, World War II,

> and the 1973 Yom Kippur War noting that many of the "negative or unpleasant conclusions" reached by lower level analyst were often ignored [46].

Handel's sixth suggestion makes it clear that it is necessary to know the adversary's limitations as well as his capabilities. This suggestion has its roots in mirror imaging and ethnocentric biases. The failure to analyze information about an adversary's capabilities and intentions must be done in accordance with the *adversary's* political and military needs—not one's own. Projecting one's own preferences, fears, and doctrine onto the adversary only increases the likelihood that one will be deceived or surprised.

Handel provides other direct references to the problems associated with counterdeception using a puzzle metaphor. For example [47], "Under certain circumstances, the more perfectly an intelligence puzzle fits together, the greater the danger of a possible deception ploy. This is particularly true when information—the solution to an important and complex intelligence puzzle—is received in the absence of much noise or contradictory evidence, and when the resulting conclusions conform neatly to one's hopes and expectations." Other "precautions" for avoiding deception are related to anticipating surprise attack and include asking [48]: "what are the most likely directions from which an adversary might attack, even if the available evidence contradicts these contingencies."

Handel's writings on strategic surprise and intelligence also indirectly address important counterdeception issues. For example, Handel discusses the roles that preconceptions, ethnocentrism, and misperception play in the problem of strategic surprise, and he attributes perceptual errors [49] to "projecting one's own culture, ideological beliefs, military doctrine, and expectations on the adversary (i.e., seeing him as a mirror image of oneself) or of wishful thinking...." To counter these ethnocentric biases, Handel makes the general suggestion of "know thine enemy," that is, develop a thorough and in-depth knowledge of an adversary's language, culture, politics, and values, as well as devoting more time and resources to knowing "thyself."

In addition, Handel discusses two mechanisms that are related to the subject of improving the objectivity and variety of input into the intelligence process. These mechanisms are also relevant to the challenge of countering deception. The first is *multiple advocacy*. The idea behind this concept is that multiple, independent intelligence agencies do a better job of providing decision-makers with a wider spectrum of views than does a single, centralized intelligence organization. The pros and cons of multiple advocacy are beyond the scope of this chapter; however, the contribution that it makes to counterdeception is to counteract a number of factors that tend to make the deceiver's job easier (e.g., the tendency to jump to conclusions and groupthink). The second mechanism is the *devil's advocate*. The purpose of a devil's advocate is to help ensure that dissenting, possibly unpopular, opinions are heard and evaluated. Again, the pros and cons of devil's advocacy are outside the scope of this chapter, but it is interesting to imagine what the results might have been in May 1940 if the French had an effective devil's advocate to warn them of the possibility of a German offensive through the Ardennes.

The end of the 1980s also saw the end of the Cold War, and as we noted in Chapter 2, deception research entered a hiatus period that was to last until the revelations of Operation Desert Storm and other events like the Indian nuclear test in 1998 made it clear that the need for understanding deception and improving ways to counter it had not disappeared. Interest in deception surfaced once again and has resulted in new practical and theoretical work by both some familiar early researchers and some new faces.

5.2.3 Current Directions

On the practical side, there is the 1997 CIA release of a set of analytic tradecraft notes that are a standard counterdeception reference for analysts both inside and outside of the CIA [50, 51]. *Note 10, Tradecraft and Counterintelligence* begins with an admonition to analysts "to show increased respect for the deceiver's ability to manipulate perception and judgments" and then describes two sets of warning signs that signal the possible existence of a deception operation. The first set goes by the acronym MOM, which stands for *means*, *opportunity*, and *motive,* and addresses the likelihood that a potential adversary is deliberately trying to distort the analyst's perceptions. *Means* addresses the adversary's experience and capabilities with regard to planning and executing sophisticated deception operations, while *opportunity* is related to the sources (channels) of intelligence available to the analyst. If the adversary is known to have knowledge of a source (e.g., a technical collection system), then he may likely have the opportunity to conceal information from that source or to deliberately distort the information the source collects. Finally, does the adversary have a *motive* to use deception? If all three warning signs are present, the analyst is wise to suspect that an adversary may resort to deception in order to achieve his goals.

The second set of warning signs focus on anomalies that analysts should be on the look out for regarding what they know, how they know it, and what they don't know. These warning signs include *suspicious gaps* in collection, *contradictions* to carefully researched patterns, and *suspicious confirmations*. Gaps in collection can be considered suspicious when information received through one channel is not supported by other channels especially when such confirmation would be considered normal. If new information contradicts well-supported trends and patterns, analysts need to critically examine such new information if it signals "inexplicable change" in the adversary's priorities, behaviors, and practices. Information received from one or more sources that seem to conveniently reinforce the rationale for or against one's own strategy or policy might also be considered suspicious. In such cases, the fact that multiple sources seem to corroborate one another may not necessarily mean the information is authentic.

Finally, Note 10 offers analytical tradecraft tips for dealing with the risk of deception when making intelligence assessments on complex issues. In the case of "regular" issues (those where there is no specific reason to suspect deception), the analyst is advised to employ a two-step process as insurance against the risk of deception. The first step is to organize information important to his conclusions and then critically examine it using the six warning signs mentioned previously. The second step calls for the analyst to play the role of devil's advocate and develop a hypothetical argument that deception is in fact taking place. In the case of "suspect and sensitive" issues, the note recommends undertaking an even more in-depth evaluation of the information at hand and annotating any resulting reports with a text box or annex that conveys to the reader that the possibility of deception has been considered seriously, appropriate analytic testing to determine the likelihood of deception has been done, and any reasonable doubts about the resulting analysis are noted.

The scientific community's interest in deception, which had been primarily focused on lying and deceit, also began to attract attention in national security circles in the 1990s. For example, Johnson et al. [52] have investigated the processes used by accounting auditors to detect the fraudulent manipulation of information in financial statements. They use Whaley's model of deception (i.e., masking, repackaging, dazzling, mimicking, inventing, and decoying) as the basis for the tactics that a deceiver can use to manipulate the target's processes of searching, processing, and interpreting information. They then propose a process for detecting deception that consists of three components:

- First the deception target identifies inconsistencies between his observations and his expectations for the observations.
- The target then determines that those inconsistencies are functional to the goals of the deceiver.
- Finally, the deception target identifies the potential actions of the deceiver that can be associated with one or more deception tactics and assesses the deceiver's ability to create the observed inconsistencies.

They then develop a *competence model* based on this process for detecting financial statement fraud. This model (see Figure 5.2) consists of four steps:

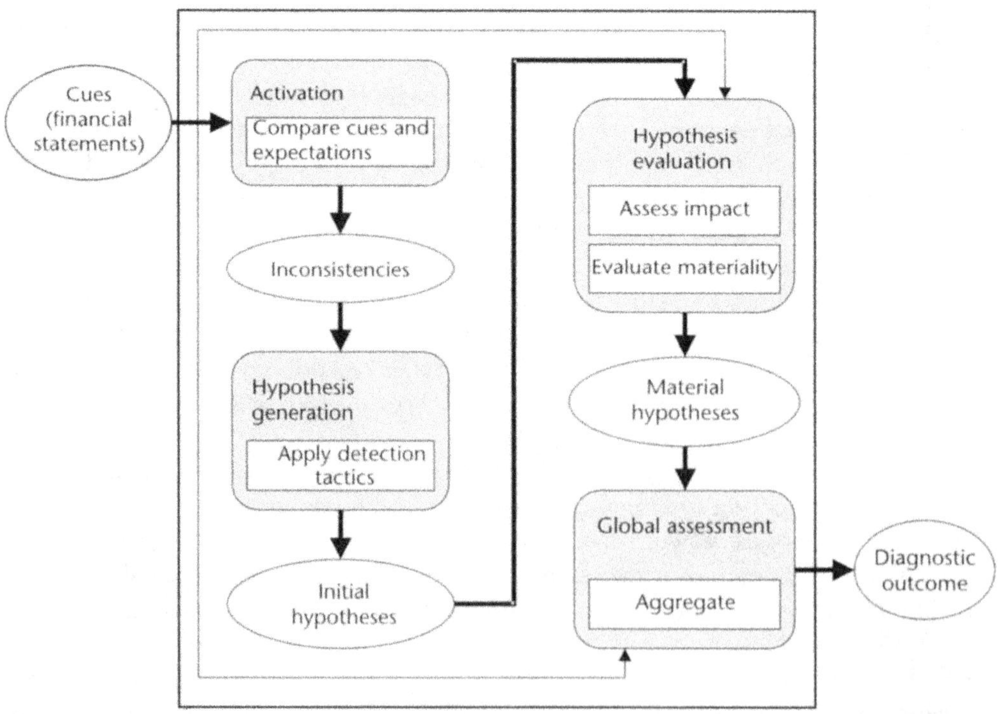

Figure 5.2 Fraud detection method. (*From:* [52]. © 2001 Cognitive Science Society. Reprinted with permission.)

activation, hypothesis generation, *hypothesis evaluation*, and *global assessment*. The activation step produces the expectations for the values of the various cues that might be found when an auditor examines a financial statement (e.g., an inventory balance value). These expectations are then compared to the actual observed values. Observed values that exceed expectations by some amount are then labeled as inconsistencies. The next step is to generate a set of hypotheses that explain the inconsistencies. In the auditing process examined by Johnson and his team, there are three possible hypotheses: accounting errors, insufficient disclosure, and, of course, deception. In this model, the deception hypothesis is generated when the inconsistencies satisfy the additional conditions of the detection process described earlier (i.e., functionality and feasibility).

In step three, the hypotheses are evaluated on the basis of their *materiality*. Materiality is an accounting term that is defined as [53] "...the magnitude of an omission or misstatement of accounting information that, in the light of surrounding circumstances, makes it probable that the judgment of a reasonable person relying on the information would have been changed or influenced by the omission or misstatement." The error and disclosure hypotheses are evaluated primarily on the magnitude of the difference between the expected and observed values of the financial statement cue. The basis for evaluating materiality for the deception hypothesis though depends on the deception tactic that is suspected to have been used (e.g., if the repackaging deception tactic is suspected, then the items that have been deliberately miscategorized should be recategorized using a worst-case scenario assumption). The global assessment step "aggregates and evaluates confirmed hypotheses" to produce the final rating of the company's financial statement—*unqualified* (the statement is "clean"), *unqualified+* (the auditor adds a paragraph noting a lack of consistency or some other concerns or uncertainty), or *misleading*. Finally, the model was implemented as a computer program that uses various data from financial statements to produce the final rating. The program successfully issued the correct global assessment rating for each of six cases it was given.

Even while counterdeception was attracting the interest of new researchers like Johnson and his associates, some familiar names were still active in field. It should probably not be a surprise that, over 30 years later, Barton Whaley was still active, contributing two chapters (one with magician Jeff Busby) to a book, *Strategic Denial and Deception: The Twenty-First Century Challenge* [54]. In the chapter coauthored with Busby, Whaley focuses entirely on counterdeception. Whereas many authors in the field of strategic deception are quite pessimistic about the prospects of successful counterdeception, Whaley (the principal author) offers a surprisingly optimistic perspective on the topic [55]: "I am optimistic that deceptions can be detected regardless of the field in which they occur. In theory, deception can always be detected, and in practice often detected, sometimes even easily." He proposes a general theory of counterdeception based on a wide range of sources, including results from case studies of different types of professionals who regularly deal with deception (e.g., intelligence analysts, police detectives, forensic scientists, art experts, and magicians). Whaley found that all the professionals who were highly successful at detecting deception used a common set of methods and that those same methods were never or only infrequently used by those who did poorly. In addition, he found these methods to be largely intellectual rather than technological in nature. Technology in the form of sensors that extend our natural senses and information technology that extends our ability to recall and manipulate information is important; however, deception detection remains a subtle, human intellectual process, as we will see when we examine the different elements of his theory.

This theory of counterdeception starts with two general components (see Figure 5.3): a taxonomy of "detectables" and the *Plus-Minus Rule*. Five of the nine categories of detectables (intention, time, place, strength, and style) have their origins as modes of surprise in Whaley's original work on stratagem [56]. The remaining four (pattern, players, payoff, and channel) make their appearance in Bell and Whaley's *Cheating and Deception* [57] in 1991. Together they represent the set of things that the deceiver will either conceal or reveal and they provide the counterdeception analyst with a checklist for the kinds of questions that must be considered when trying to determine the existence and form of a deception operation. The Plus-Minus Rule, on the other hand, is the cornerstone of their theory. This rule is based on the fact (noted by R. V. Jones in 1942) that [58], "No imitation can be perfect without being the real thing." Therefore, even though the imitation may share many of the characteristics of the original, it *must* lack at least one characteristic marking the original and it will often have at least one characteristic that the original does not possess. According to Whaley [59], "If either a plus (added) or a minus (missing) characteristic is detected, the imitation stands revealed. Note that a most important corollary of this rule is that the detective need not discover all the discrepancies or incongruities, a single false characteristic, whether plus (added) or (minus) is quite enough to prove the fakery."

Whaley is quick to note, however, that the Plus-Minus Rule demands total certainty about the added or missing characteristic and that while this is always possible, it is seldom likely in the real world. With this in mind, the next components of their counterdeception theory can be thought of as applied theory suitable to decision making under uncertainty. The first element, the *Congruity-Incongruity Rule,* flows from the Plus-Minus Rule and appears to be based on the results of Whaley's case studies of deception detection professionals. He found that these professionals clustered into two groups: *congruity testers* (e.g., scientists, internists, and historians) and *incongruity testers* (e.g., police detectives, interrogators, trial lawyers, and forensic pathologists). In the Congruity-Incongruity Rule, the emphasis is obviously all on incongruities [60]: "Every deception operation necessarily leaves at least two clues: incongruities about what is hidden; and incongruities about what is displayed in its stead" and "because neither simulation nor dissimulation can ever be done flawlessly, however, their detection also is always possible. In other words, discrepancies (incongruent clues) inevitably suggest alternative patterns (hypotheses) that themselves are incongruent (discrepant, anomalous, paradoxical) at some point with reality." In other words, detecting incongruities is the key to detecting deception.

The next several elements of the Busby and Whaley theory represent a portfolio of methods applicable to detecting deception:

- *Locard's Exchange Principle*. Although normally associated with *physical* evidence, Whaley suggests it can also be applied to deception by adding "psychological perceptions" to the principle. Unfortunately, he does not offer any insights into how these perceptions are to be added.

		Description
Genearl theory	Categories of detectables	Pattern, players, intention, payoff, place, time, strength, style, and channel
Genearl theory	The plus-minus rule	A single false characteristic—either one the real entity does not possess (a plus) or one it lacks (a minus)—is sufficient to prove the entity is fake.
Decision making under uncertainty	The congruity-incongruity rule	Real entities are completely congruent with all of their characteristics; therefore, every false entity will display at least one incongruity.
Decision making under uncertainty	Locard's exchange principle	A perpetrator always leaves some physical evidence at the crime scene and always takes some away.
Decision making under uncertainty	Verification	It is always possible to find a way to verify a hypothesis.
Decision making under uncertainty	The law of multiple sensors	Multiple sensors will almost always prove more effective than a single one, even when each is less precise.
Decision making under uncertainty	Passive and active detection	Deception may be detected by analysis (passive) supported by active intervention aimed at collecting missing key facts. This intervention takes the form of defining new collection requirements or by running controlled experiments, including the use of traps and tripwires, to trick the adversary into betraying himself.
Decision making under uncertainty	Predetection	Predicting an adversary's deception plans by analysis of his deceptive style, capabilities, and goals.
Decision making under uncertainty	Penetration and counterespionage	The adversary's deception plans can be discovered through the use of *espionage*, penetrating the adversary's organization with human agents or technical collection devices, and *counterespionage*, discovering the deceiver's double agents within one's own organizations.
Decision making under uncertainty	The prepared mind and intuition	The ability to not only discover the meaning of chance events but to also make effective use of that knowledge depends wholly on systematic mental preparation. Such mental preparation also makes intuition possible.
Decision making under uncertainty	Indirect thinking and the third option	The goal of indirect thinking is to come up with an indirect answer—the third option that the adversary was not expecting.
	Busby's ombudsman	"The essence of the Ombudsman Method is to force one to confront straight on that nagging, almost subliminal, sense of unease about a situation or person that somehow does not seem quite right, that does not quite fit as it should those little incongruities that signal a deception in progress" [66, p. 217].

Figure 5.3 The Busby-Whaley theory of counterdeception.

- *Verification.* Once the Congruity-Incongruity Rule, Locard's Exchange Principle, or some other method provides evidence of deception, Whaley suggests that it is "always" possible to find a means of verifying the deception hypothesis. Of course, the costs of doing so may be prohibitively high, but it could be done.
- *The Law of Multiple Sensors.* This law is based on the insights of R. V. Jones who noted that [60], "The ease of detecting counterfeits is much greater when different channels of examination are used simultaneously." Whaley notes that multiple sensors are almost always more effective than a single one and are also less vulnerable to countermeasures.
- *Passive and active detection.* To Whaley [61], passive detection is synonymous with the "straightforward analysis" of evidence and "always leads to inconclusive results unless all the key facts are available." Therefore, active detection must be used to collect the missing facts. Active detection involves levying new collection requirements on the various INTs (e.g., HUMINT, IMINT, and SIGINT) or by running "controlled experiments" to provoke the adversary into creating new evidence that might reveal the deception.
- *Predetection.* J. C. Masterman of World War II Double Cross fame was also the author of two detective novels. In the second of these, *The Case of the Four Friends: A Diversion in Pre-Detection*, the detective in the story, Ernest Brendel, is persuaded [62], "...to tell the tale of how he 'pre-constructed' a crime, rather than reconstructing it in the detective's normal fashion. As he says, 'To work out the crime before it is committed, to foresee how it will be arranged, and then to prevent it! That's a triumph indeed, and is worth more than all the convictions in the world.'" Whaley makes the connection that predetection is a method whereby an adversary's deception plans can be discerned and defeated by analysis of the adversary's deception style, capabilities, and goals.
- *Penetration and counterespionage.* Espionage is a powerful form of active detection that can be used to penetrate the adversary's intelligence, military, and command organizations. A well-placed asset in the right place is all that may be needed to reveal the adversary's deception plans. Counterintelligence (CI) and counterespionage (CE), on the other hand, seek to identify and neutralize the adversary's intelligence collection efforts, especially agents who have penetrated one's own organizations. CI and CE activities can cut off important paths through which the adversary obtains information about the target's preconceptions and beliefs as well as the feedback needed to know how his deception operations are doing. In addition, CI and CE operations can reveal the existence of double agents being used as a channel for feeding the adversary's disinformation to the target.
- *The prepared mind and intuition.* The prepared mind refers to a famous quotation by Louis Pasteur: "Dans les champs de l'observation le hasard ne favorise que les esprits prepares." Pasteur made this comment at a lecture given at the University of Lille in December 1854. Translated into English, it means "In the fields of observation, chance favors only the prepared mind," or more succinctly, "chance favors the prepared mind." The essence of Pasteur's

remark is that the ability to recognize the significance of chance events and make effective use of that knowledge depends wholly on systematic mental preparation. On the other hand, intuition is [63] "our capacity for direct knowledge, for immediate insight without observation or reason." It is the police detective's hunch, Irwin Rommel's *fingerspitzengefühl*, or the scientist's sudden awareness of the solution to a difficult problem while taking a shower. It is not unreasonable to think that accurate intuition is also a result of the same systematic mental preparation associated with the prepared mind.

- *Indirect thinking and the third option.* Whaley uses the term *indirect thinking* in honor of B. H. Liddell Hart's theory of the *indirect approach* to strategy [64]. The essence of this theory is to avoid direct confrontations with the enemy but instead upset his equilibrium—keeping him uncertain about the situation and your intentions—and confront him with what he does not expect and is therefore not prepared for. Such an approach often yields a third option—one that the adversary was not expecting. The German advance through the Ardennes in 1940 is an excellent example of the indirect approach and the third option. The French expected a German attack against either the Maginot Line or through Belgium. Instead, the Germans came up with a third option—the attack through the Ardennes and the Battle of France was over in just 44 days. Whaley is suggesting that the purpose of indirect thinking is to come up with an "indirect answer"—that third option—and that this ability to envision options available to an adversary that would be otherwise hidden or ignored is an essential method of counterdeception.

The final component of Whaley's overall theory of counterdeception is a specific method—the Jeff Busby *Ombudsman Method*. This method was developed by Busby in 1978 as a means of teaching casino employees to detect cheating without teaching them how to cheat at the games themselves. Whaley does not describe any of the details of the Busby Method; however, it is apparent that it is based on looking for discrepancies, irrelevancies, and misdirection [65] as well as some indirect thinking. He does state that [66], "The essence of the Ombudsman Method is to force one to confront straight on that nagging, almost subliminal, sense of unease about a situation or person that somehow does not seem quite right, that does not quite fit as it should those little incongruities that can signal a deception in progress." Whaley suggests that the method "seems the most promising of several suggested approaches" for use in training analysts about deception as well as in the analysis of both current and historical cases of deception.

In another chapter of Godson and Wirtz's book, Paul Rossa identifies several key issues germane to counterdeception [67]. The first of these affirms the second principle of deception we proposed in Chapter 2: *denial.* Rossa notes that [68], "Uncovering secrets also is key to exposing deceptions. Consequently, counteracting foreign denial efforts is critical to countering foreign denial and deception." Even identifying the deceiver's denial operations helps the counterdeception effort by helping to task collection resources where they are most likely to do the most good. An adversary's efforts to conceal information about a subject can also suggest the possibility that deception operations associated with the subject may also exist, thereby by affecting how all information on that subject is interpreted.

Other issues are related to recognizing the existence of a deception operation. Rossa points out that determining what information the analyst decides to use, discard, or "reshape" is hard enough, but it is even more difficult when deception is involved. Rossa makes the point that recognizing the existence of a deception operation depends heavily on the metadata (data about data) that is available. Examples of metadata include the way in which the data was acquired and the circumstances surrounding the acquisition. The metadata, along with the content of the information, may provide some hints regarding the presence or absence of a deception operation. Unfortunately, these hints are all too often ambiguous or contradictory.

Another important part of recognizing deception is paying close attention to information about a potential or suspected deceiver. What are his motives? Would the use of deception increase the likelihood of achieving his objectives? Has the adversary demonstrated a strong predisposition to the use of deception in the past? Does he possess the knowledge and capabilities to mount an effective deception operation?

Finally, Rossa addresses the issues of reducing one's own "susceptibilities" to deception. One of the most important factors affecting the deception target's susceptibility to deception is the extent of the adversary's knowledge about the target's strategies and methods of collecting intelligence, his analytic methodologies, and how the resulting intelligence is used to form judgments and make decisions. Such knowledge can come from a variety of sources, including the adversary's espionage operations or the unauthorized disclosure of secret information [69]. Reducing that susceptibility depends on counterintelligence and counterespionage operations as well as the development of information gathering and processing methods that are unknown to potential deceivers or that are difficult to manipulate. Nevertheless, such efforts do not entirely eliminate the risk of deception. Deception can still succeed even when the deceiver's information about the target is incomplete and secret intelligence collection and analysis methods may still be affected by deception operations. Better analytic methods and tools can also contribute to reducing susceptibility to deception. Rossa suggests that [70]: "The intelligence community would profit by development of conceptual frameworks, indicators, and analytic techniques that hold promise for recognizing and countering foreign D&D as it occurs." He calls for qualitative and quantitative analysis of historical cases of deception and the need for D&D analysis to continue to evolve in order to keep pace with the issues and technologies associated with the post–Cold War world.

Scott Gerwehr and Russell Glenn represent a new generation of national security analysts whose focus is on strategic deception. In their report *Unweaving the Web*, Gerwehr and Glenn also address counterdeception and hypothesize that [71], "the most effective approaches to penetrating deception entail (1) combining more than one category of counterdeception and (2) applying the right category of counterdeception." They then identify five categories of counterdeception, three of which focus on defeating deception by emphasizing the collection and processing of data. The first three categories are:

- The type or amount of data collected (e.g., using radar or hyperspectral sensors to defeat camouflage paints and netting).

- The methods for collecting data (i.e., the methods by which the sensors are employed). For example, changes to collection plans or search plans may disrupt an adversary's attempts to conceal his movements.
- The analysis of the data collected (for example, can alternative scenarios be developed using the same data?)

The fourth category focuses on unmasking deception through the use of one's own deceptions. For example, a feint or demonstration might force concealed units to maneuver or engage. The final category consists of strategies for rendering the adversary's deceptions moot. This is often the U.S. military's approach to counterdeception. For example, if an adversary has deployed numerous decoys among its real units (e.g., tanks or surface-to-air missile), the U.S. ability to employ overwhelming firepower makes it possible to target all potential targets without bothering to tell them apart.

Effective counterdeception therefore depends not only on applying the right category of counterdeception methods but also on applying methods from more than one category. Gerwehr and Glenn suggest that much more research needs to be done to resolve the issues raised by questions such as:

- What counterdeception methods should be matched to particular types of deception?
- Which of those methods are the most effective against individual deception techniques or are effective against the broadest range of deception techniques?
- What are the situational factors that affect their use?
- Which methods require the most time or manpower to use effectively?
- Which methods complement or interfere with each other?
- Do any of the methods work against one type of deception technique but in turn increase the vulnerability to another?

Even more recent work has been done by Stech and Elsässer who extend Johnson et al.'s model to develop a counterdeception "business process" [72]. The process links previous work done by Whaley, Jones, and Heuer to the Johnson model (see Figure 5.4) and Stech and Elsässer then use this process to in an effort to improve the effectiveness of Heuer's alternative competing hypothesis (ACH) method as a counterdeception tool. The first step of the process addresses the detection of anomalies using techniques based on Whaley's congruity-incongruity rule. One challenge for analysts though is that the detection of anomalies (incongruities) is not necessarily evidence of detection of deliberate deception. They may result from sensor malfunctions, unintentional distortion or corruption of data or information during transmission, or analytical error. In fact, deception is often successful because the deception target explains away such anomalies and failing to correctly attribute them to deception. That is where the next step in the process comes in. There must be some way of linking anomalies to deception, and Stech and Elsässer propose that R. V. Jones's concepts of deception masking provides such means—analyzing the anomalies through multiple information channels. The third and fourth steps use ACH to assess the likelihood that the observed anomalies are

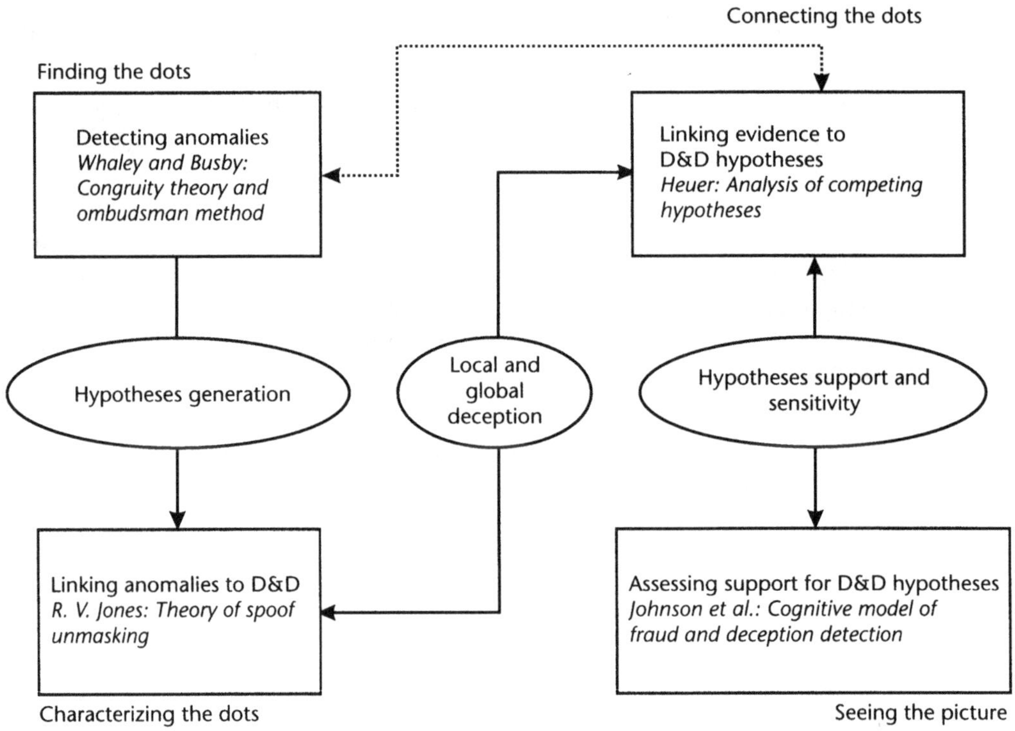

Figure 5.4 The Stech-Elässer counterdeception business process. (*Source:* [72].)

associated with a probable deceptive course of action (COA) and to evaluate the level of support for each identified hypothesis.

Stech and Elsässer have also developed what they call *alternative competing hypotheses for counterdeception* (ACH-CD). Their most significant adaptations to Heuer's original eight-step outline for the analysis of competing hypotheses are [73]:

- Adding the "other" or "unknown" hypothesis to step 1 (i.e., "Identify the possible hypotheses to be considered"). This modification supports further Bayesian analysis of the alternative hypotheses.
- Making sure that step 2, "Make a list of significant evidence and arguments for and against each hypothesis," considers not only the case where evidence supports a hypothesis, $p(E|H_i)$, but also the likelihood that observing that same evidence if the hypothesis is not true, $p(E|\neg H_i)$.
- Specifically considering deception-related COAs in steps 4 ("Refine the matrix") and 5 ("Draw tentative conclusions about the relative likelihood of each hypothesis").
- Adding the concept of conducting operational "experiments" to step 8 ("Identify milestones for future observation that may indicate events are taking a different course than expected") in order to provide additional intelligence that would reveal evidence of deliberate deception.

The first two adaptations support Stech and Elsässer's work on developing Bayesian belief networks to model the alternative COAs, perform sensitivity analysis in order to analyze the diagnosticity of the evidence (part of Step 3 in ACH), and to suggest possible key indicators to look for that would reveal the adversary's intentions.

5.3 Searching for Common Themes

In Chapter 2 we saw that there was considerable agreement on a range of topics in the deception research community, which we then organized into six general themes (Figure 2.15). We then examined these themes in the context of a generalized deception cycle (Figure 2.13) and Waltz's three-level hierarchy of information. In this chapter, we propose to take a similar approach and organize the various counterdeception concepts, approaches, models, and methods presented in the previous sections into general themes using a framework based on the counterdeception definitions presented in Section 5.1. These counterdeception themes are then compared to the deception themes of Chapter 2 and used to synthesize a set of fundamental principles of counterdeception.

5.3.1 A Holistic Approach to Counterdeception

In Section 5.1, we saw that counterdeception consists of both intelligence and operational functions. These can be broken down as follows:

- *Intelligence functions.* Awareness of deception cues, detection and exposure of deception operations, and discovery and penetration the adversary's real capabilities and intentions;
- *Operational functions.* Negate or mitigate deception's effect and exploit the adversary's own deception plan.

These five functional dimensions form a simple, yet useful framework for thinking about counterdeception; however, keep in mind that these dimensions are not mutually exclusive. They are, in fact, highly interdependent and form more of a continuum of functions than a set of independent activities. This suggests that counterdeception requires a more holistic approach than is suggested by the traditional intelligence cycle. As we will see, the themes that emerge from the counterdeception literature reinforce this idea.

Our examination of the research suggests that there are nine themes representing processes and methods that would ideally work together synergistically to identify and defeat the adversary's attempts at deception. Figure 5.5 shows these themes arranged within the framework of the five intelligence and operations functions. Like the functional dimensions of our counterdeception framework, these themes are themselves interdependent and reflect a holistic approach to counterdeception.

The first theme, *human reasoning capabilities*, is probably the most important since it binds the other themes together. All of the authors we have reviewed, whether in Chapter 2 or this chapter, have either explicitly or implicitly recognized

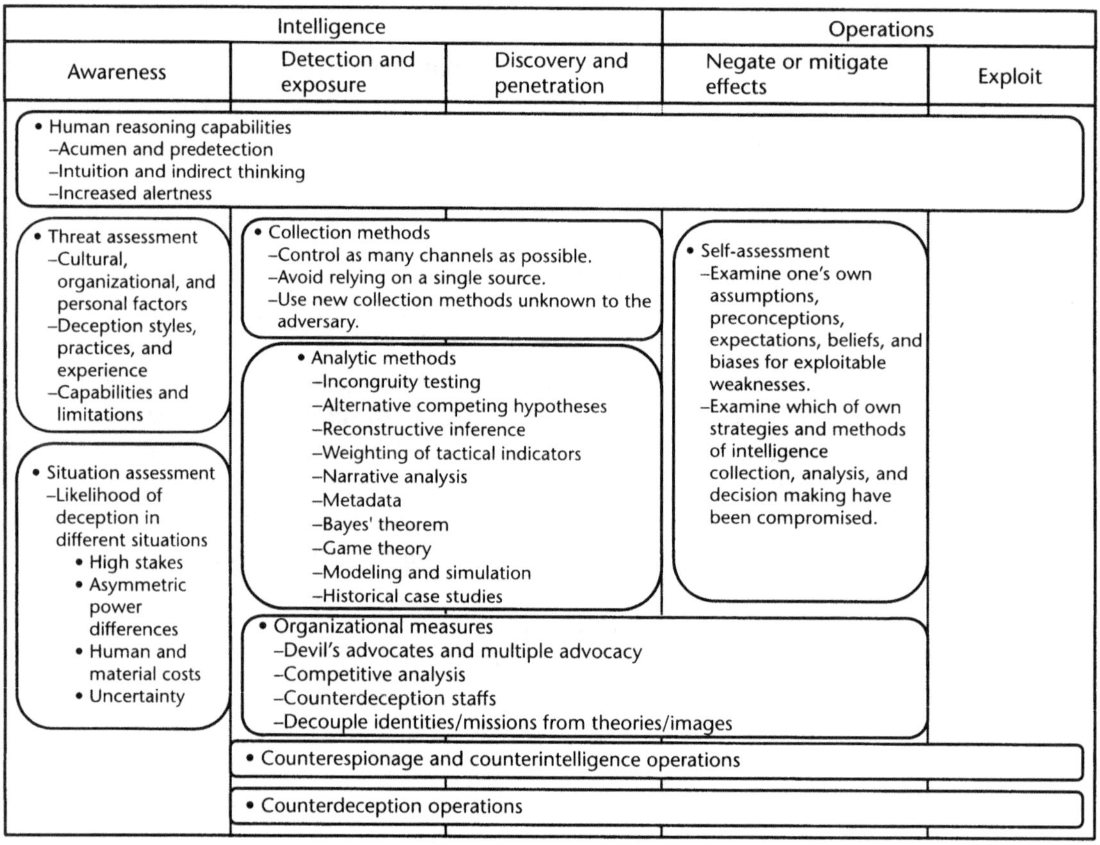

Figure 5.5 Counterdeception themes in the deception literature.

that the success or failure of deception occurs in the minds of the analysts, commanders, and decision-makers who are its targets. Heuer is often quoted in this regard [74]: "Deception is, above all, a cognitive phenomenon; it occurs in our minds." Likewise, it is clear that many of these same researchers believe counterdeception is primarily a cognitive phenomenon as well. As Whaley concludes after examining 47 categories of real-life professionals who deal with deception [75], "Successful detection procedures were found to be largely or entirely intellectual rather than technological in nature." All of the counterdeception concepts dealing with human reasoning emphasize the role that broad, subtle powers of awareness, discernment, and discovery play in distinguishing between what is real and what is deceptively constructed by the adversary. This is why this theme covers all five dimensions of our framework in Figure 5.5.

This emphasis on concepts such as acumen and intuition has interesting implications for how one goes about implementing these ideas in real organizations. For example, Johnson et al. found that none of the 24 auditors in their study successfully identified the presence of fraud in all of the four cases they were given and, in fact, 20 auditors failed to detect fraud in at least three out of the four cases. In addition, two auditors failed to detect any fraud in any of the four cases and seven auditors failed to give an unqualified opinion on the clean cases they were presented. Obviously, not only is detecting deception difficult, but auditors also differ significantly in their fraud detection capabilities. In addition, if there is considerable variation in the counterdeception performance of highly skilled auditors examining relatively well-structured data in the form of financial statements, what must the situation be like for the analysts in the intelligence and military community who have to deal with information that is far more unstructured and ambiguous? How then can concepts like acumen and intuition be operationalized in those settings and applied to the problem of counterdeception? We will look into what approaches might provide some answers to this difficult question in the next chapter.

The next three themes working together also have the potential to make human reasoning capabilities more effective when it comes to counterdeception. These themes are themselves characterized by yet another theme (i.e., the concept of an assessment process). These three themes, *self-assessment*, *threat assessment*, and *situation assessment*, focus on what Handel referred to as "knowing thine enemy" and "knowing thyself." Of course, Handel was not the first to draw this conclusion. The ever-quotable Sun Tzu observed [76], "Therefore I say: 'Know your enemy and know yourself; in a hundred battles you will never be in peril. When you are ignorant of the enemy but know yourself, your chances of winning or losing are equal. If ignorant of the enemy and of yourself, you are certain in every battle to be in peril.'" What was true over 2,000 years ago is amazingly still true today. Perhaps that was why the FORTITIDE deception was successful; Hitler was ignorant of both his enemy *and* himself.

The need for *self-assessment*, to know thyself, is a response to the empirical evidence that deception is almost always successful especially when the deception operation exploits the target's own preconceptions and expectations (M-1 type deceptions). Given this obvious vulnerability, several authors advocate conducting such assessments as an important means of negating or mitigating deception's effects and their work suggest that this should be a two-pronged process. First and foremost is the need to make both analysts and decision-makers aware of their own assumptions, preconceptions, beliefs, and biases. This type of awareness is not quite the same kind of vigilance implied in the awareness dimension of our framework, which involves an awareness of the presence or absence of external environmental cues. Rather it is inwardly focused and stresses consciousness of one's own self. As Jervis notes [77]:

> People often not only have a limited understanding of the workings of other's arguments, they also do not know the structure of their own belief systems—what values are most important, how some beliefs are derived from others, and what evidence would contradict their views. Particularly dangerous is the tendency to take the most important questions for granted. Analysis of policies that failed indicates that many crucial errors occur not because decision-makers arrive at the wrong answers, but because they ask the wrong questions. This often involves taking too many things for granted and failing to scrutinize basic assumptions.

Such knowledge is essential to mitigating and negating the adversary's attempts at deception since deception relies so heavily on just such ignorance. The hope is that the self-assessment process will make analysts and decision-makers more alert to information and situations that appear to be too good to be true as well as making them less likely to casually dismiss information that conflicts with their expectations or beliefs. As Handel points out [78], "Under certain circumstances, *the more perfectly an intelligence puzzle fits together, the greater the danger of a possible deception ploy*. This is particularly true when information—the solution to an important and complex intelligence puzzle—is received in the absence of much noise and contradictory evidence, and when the resulting conclusions conform neatly to one's hopes and expectations."

The second prong of the self-assessment theme stresses the need to know which of your own strategies and methods of intelligence collection, analysis, and decision-making have been compromised. The importance of this vulnerability cannot be stressed enough since deception is in one sense a battle for control of information channels. Deception practitioners and researchers urge both the deceiver and target to try to control as many channels as possible. The deceiver seeks to compromise channels that the target considers to be credible and reliable without the target's knowledge. In a similar manner, the target seeks to develop channels unknown to the deceiver. The knowledge that the existence of a secret channel has been compromised or that an adversary has discovered a channel considered to be particularly valuable by the target is absolutely critical to the detection and discovery dimensions of counterdeception.

Since knowing thyself is likely to only produce a 50–50 chance of success according to the venerable Sun Tzu, if you want to be victorious in the next 100 battles, you need to know your enemy as well. The *threat assessment* and *situation assessment* themes focus on the various factors that influence an adversary's decision to use deception. In a counterdeception context, the factors suggested by Daniel and Herbig provide an excellent starting point for any threat assessment and should be supplemented with information about the adversary's capabilities and experience with running deception operations For example, is deception part of the adversary's doctrine? Does he typically rely on specific styles of deception? Have previous attempts at deception resulted in success or failure? The *situation assessment* theme recognizes that the use of deception is likely to be highly situation dependent. Normal situations will most likely only call for normal deception measures (i.e., denial in the form of security measures). For example, sophisticated deception operations are not normally associated with conventional weapons development programs such as routine improvements to armored vehicles. On the other hand, other situations (high stakes or asymmetric differences in power or capability between the adversary and the target) may make it more likely that an adversary will employ more sophisticated deception measures. One needs only to watch the evening news to see any number of stories (nuclear proliferation for instance) that are examples of potential high-stakes situations where deception is likely to play a role. These two assessment processes fit naturally under the awareness dimension of our framework since the resulting knowledge helps to prime analysts to recognize and register both the obvious and subtle cues (e.g., the MOM warning signs in the CIA tradecraft note) that help them to detect deception operations.

Our next two themes, *collection methods* and *analytic methods*, form the methodological foundation for both detecting and exposing deception and discovering and penetrating the real story behind the deception. Collection methods drive what the target observes and subsequently perceives. From the days of R. V. Jones to the present, the number-one prescription for countering deception has been to try to control as many channels (sources) of information as possible with the corollary to this rule being that one should avoid relying on a single source of information wherever possible. This is especially true when the stakes are high. Since human sources and technical collection systems provide the data and information needed to both detect and penetrate a deception, it is also highly advisable to exploit channels that are unknown to the adversary, either by using new methods unknown to him or known methods that have been compromised without his knowledge (e.g., the Allies' ability to exploit the German Enigma code).

Human history includes thousands of years of trying to understand the events and phenomena we observe in the world around us. As a result, philosophers and scientists have developed methods of thinking (from the Socratic method of natural philosophy to the scientific method of the scientific revolution) as well as innumerable specific techniques (logic, mathematics, algorithms, and other tools) that have transformed our world. It is no surprise therefore that *analytic methods* should be a major theme that emerges from the counterdeception literature. Counterdeception relies on intelligence analysis and intelligence analysis relies first and foremost on the capabilities of human analysts. They in turn rely on analytic methods and techniques to help them make sense of the data and information pouring in from multiple sources. Two methods stand out in the literature when it comes to counterdeception. First, incongruity testing is a fundamental method that supports the detection and exposure function within our framework. Likewise, Heuer [76] emphasizes the importance of generating and evaluating alternative hypotheses (essentially an adaptation of the scientific method) "as a tool to aid judgment on important issues requiring careful weighing of alternative explanations or conclusions." Here the emphasis is less on detecting deception and more on selecting the adversary's actual course of action from other potential COAs where deception is likely a factor. The results of incongruity testing and hypotheses evaluation will more than likely raise further questions. The answers will require additional information to resolve real from false incongruities, eliminate information gaps (missing evidence), and find information that can disprove hypotheses. These information needs can be satisfied by tasking collectors and integrating their inputs with information from counterintelligence and counterdeception operations. Other methods and analytic techniques support not only the detection and discovery dimensions but also the processes associated with other themes (e.g., the use of the Bayes' theorem, game theory, and other modeling and simulation methods to support situation assessment activities). Finally, the information uncovered about the adversary's deception operations drives the planning and execution of counterdeception operations aimed at exploiting the adversary's own plans. Given the importance of these themes, we will delve further into the details of counterdeception analytic and collection methods in Chapter 7.

Although deception occurs in the human mind, we have also seen that there are organizational processes and biases that can make the deceiver's job either easier or harder. Factors such as the size of the target's decision-making groups, their goals and mindset, resources and resource allocations, the size and numbers of intelligence and military organizations, and the nature of their bureaucratic political processes all affect how information is acquired, filtered, shared, and interpreted. For example, as we saw in Chapter 3, Hitler's leadership style and the nature of the

German command structure made the Allies' job of deception notably easier than it might have been under other circumstances. The *organizational measures* theme gathers together a set of ideas that counterdeception researchers believe, theoretically anyway, should make the deceiver's job harder. The primary focus of the subjects within this theme is on ways that an organization can overcome organizational mindsets and remain open to the possibility of what Whaley called the "third way." Devil's advocacy and multiple advocacy are both simply means of putting alternative interpretations of a situation in front of decision-makers. None of these interpretations may actually reflect the true situation, but such processes help to ensure that the situation is at least seen from different perspectives and any questions about assumptions and evidence are properly raised and addressed. Jervis probably does the best job of making this point when he writes [22]:

> Of course the correct image will not necessarily emerge from this adversary process. But—and this is important enough—the decision-maker can be given a wider range of choice in two related ways. First, because he is exposed to conflicting interpretations of events and shown how alternative images make the world appear differently, he will have to exercise explicit judgment to select his explanations and images rather than immediately seeing one view as the only possible one. Second, debates will help bring out the implicit assumptions discussed above. An individual rarely has the ability or the incentive to expose the structure of his beliefs, and interaction with someone who holds a different position is usually the best, if not the only, way for those he is advising, and indeed for the person himself, to see where his arguments are most vulnerable. It is unlikely that any participant will be converted. But those who listen to the arguments are in a good position to learn what perspectives they are rejecting, what evidence they should examine more closely, and what assumptions need further thought. As a result, fewer important questions will be overlooked because everyone agrees on the answer.

Our two final themes represent proactive means of counterdeception that play important roles across both the intelligence and operational dimensions of our framework. The potential target of deception does not have to be, and in fact should not be, a passive participant in the process. Instead of simply accepting the data and information (both real and false) received through his information channels, the target can conduct his own espionage and technical collection operations aimed at gathering intelligence about the adversary—his plans, capabilities, and real intentions. Counterespionage and counterintelligence operations focus on denying the adversary the information he needs to plan and execute his deception operations and, most importantly, uncovering his double agents in order to negate their value or even turn them against the deceiver. In cases where deception is suspected, counterdeception operations can be used to probe the environment in order to provoke the adversary to some action that will confirm the deception or, better yet, reveal his true plans. Likewise, if intelligence confirms the existence of a deception operation, the target can conduct his own counterdeception operations to deceive the adversary that his deception working while simultaneously undertaking operations to exploit the adversary's plans.

5.3.2 Counterdeception Themes and the Deception Cycle

In Chapter 2 we proposed that a model of a general deception cycle could be used to understand the basic workings of deception. Figure 5.6 shows the impact the nine counterdeception themes can have on the different steps in the cycle. At the far right-hand side of the figure we see that, as always, *human reasoning capabilities* play a decisive role in how observations of the environment are transformed into knowledge and how that knowledge is transformed into decisions and actions. Human acumen, sagacity, and intuition determine the most likely explanation (the reconstructed story) that accounts for the observed data as well as what to make of it and what to do about it. Also on the right-hand side of Figure 5.7 are three of the themes that help leverage those human capabilities. The main impact of the analytical methodologies theme is on helping analysts to reconstruct the deception story and, more importantly, recognize that it is a deception. The self-assessment theme influences the target's perceptions of the story. It enables analysts and decision-makers to ask questions like: Does the reconstructed story fit a little too well with expectations? Finally, the impact of the organizational measures theme is on the target's understanding (and timeliness) of the situation as well as on the resulting decisions and actions that need to be made.

On the left-hand side of Figure 5.7 are the threat and situation assessment themes—the "know thine enemy" themes. The impact of these themes is to try to get one step ahead of a potential adversary by identifying his possible motives for deception as well as the situations where those motives are likely come into play.

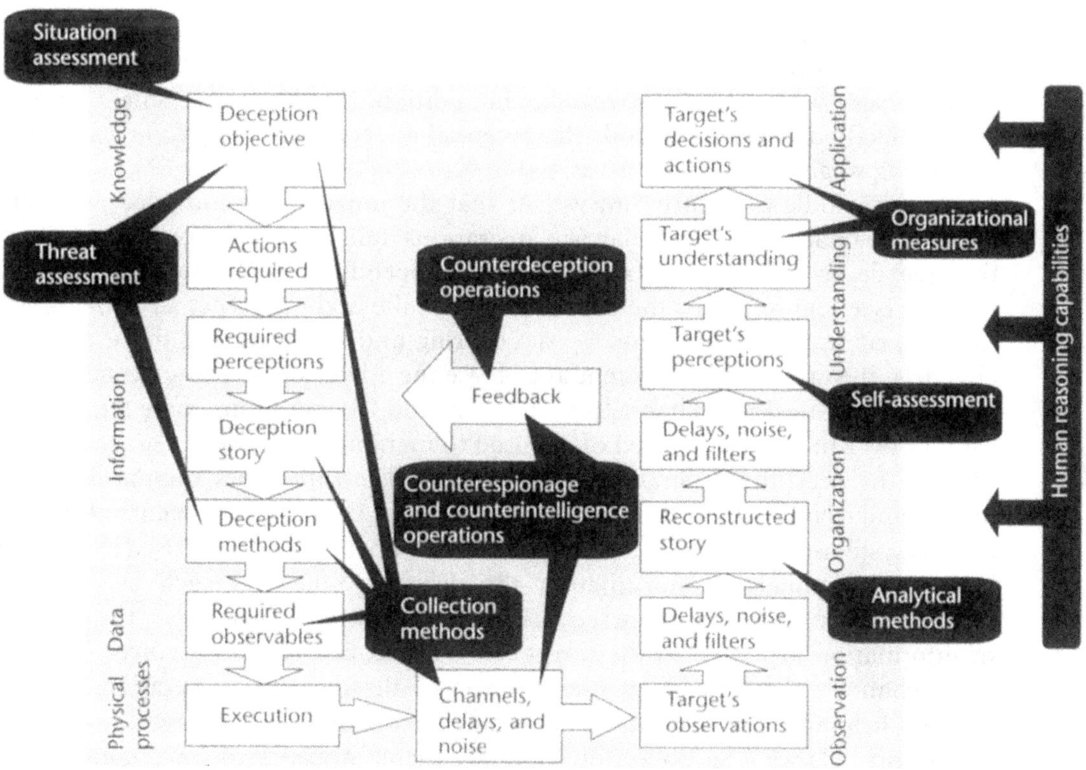

Figure 5.6 Counterdeception themes in the general deception cycle context.

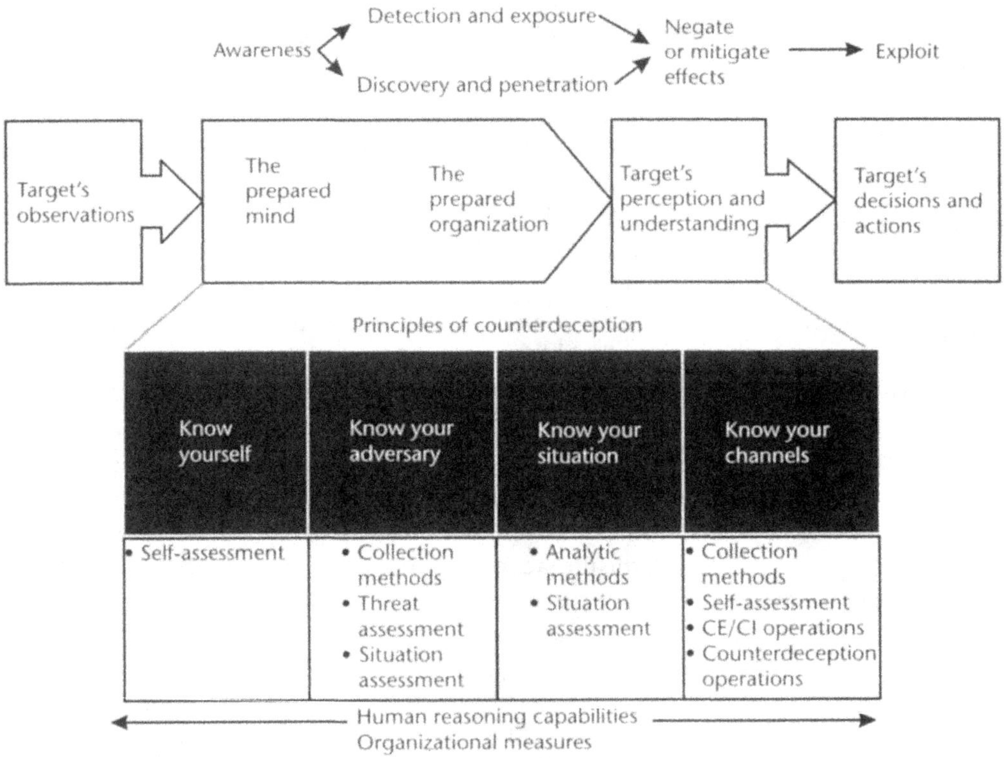

Figure 5.7 Principles of counterdeception within the context of the counterdeception framework.

These motives drive the adversary's deception objectives and the subsequent actions the adversary wants the target to take. In addition, the threat assessment helps to identify likely deception methods the potential adversary is likely to be capable of employing to achieve his objectives.

In the middle of Figure 5.6, we see that the impact of counterdeception and counterespionage/counterintelligence operations falls primarily on the feedback that the deceiver receives from the target. Depending on the feedback that he receives (see Figure 2.10), the deceiver must make a choice whether to maintain, escalate, or stop the deception. By discovering and manipulating those feedback channels, the target has the potential to force the adversary to show his hand. Discovering those feedback channels is where CE and CI operations come into the picture. Leaks can either be closed off or used to manipulate the deceiver's perception of how the deception operation is proceeding. The same goes for the deceiver's human and technical collection sources (spies, bugs, compromised secure communications systems, and so forth). Counterdeception operations can be used to manipulate other channels of information the deceiver relies on such as overhead reconnaissance or diplomatic assets. CE and CI operations also impact the channels of information available to the target. As we said before, this involves exposing those channels that are being used as part of the deception operation but also involves helping to protect the channels that the deceiver is unaware of.

At first glance, the collection methods theme appears to have considerable potential for counterdeception. As we have seen, controlling as many channels of information as possible is a key counterdeception maxim. Not only is this necessary from an analytical sense, but controlling as many channels as possible may also restrict range of deception methods available to the deceiver and drive his cost of deception up by increasing the number of observables that are required to produce a realistic deception scenario. A broad range of robust collection methods across all the INTs increases the likelihood that the target may be able to penetrate the deceiver's security measures and discover the existence of the deception operation (say, through a human asset or a COMINT intercept), the details of the plan (the deception story), and the deceiver's objectives themselves. Nevertheless, it is important to recall one more time Heuer's cautionary words [79]: "The kinds of additional information one might realistically expect to obtain through enhanced collection capabilities, however, are unlikely to reduce vulnerability to deception significantly. Any systematic counterdeception program must focus primarily on problems of analysis, only secondarily on collection."

Before moving on it is important to once again stress that our interpretation of the counterdeception literature leads us to the conclusion that it represents a holistic process. Harris [5] decries "seat-of-the-pants counterdeception efforts" as "uncoordinated, perhaps sporadic efforts to detect and outwit foreign deception operations and calls for "the coordination of *detection* and *countermeasures* programs in a *counterdeception system*." Systems are holistic; their properties cannot be explained simply by examining the properties of their components. Nothing in the counterdeception literature contradicts Harris's recognition that counterdeception has this same characteristic. Although our nine themes do not yet constitute a formal counterdeception system, it should be clear that they can only be effective when used in a highly coordinated, mutually supportive manner. With that in mind, let's move on and introduce our proposed principles of counterdeception.

5.4 Proposed Principles of Counterdeception

Centuries of conflict have seen strategic and tactical deception [80] transformed from "an idiosyncratic fad of exceptionally imaginative leaders" to a fairly well understood component of strategic and tactical doctrine. Our review of the literature leads us to conclude that no similar process or doctrine of counterdeception has as yet evolved. The adversary's deception planners, armed with a wide array of deception methods honed by hundreds of years of practical experience, do not face a corresponding counterdeception organization armed with a similarly wide range of practical counterdeception tools. Instead, we see that the contest between deceiver and target pits deception methods against basic human reasoning capabilities and the formal and informal processes, procedures, policies, and structures of the organizational they operate in. In essence, all that really stands in the way of the deceiver is what Pasteur called "the prepared mind" and, extending that concept, the prepared organization.

The concepts of the prepared mind and the prepared organization correspond well with the intelligence functions within the counterdeception framework introduced in Section 5.3. Pasteur's original comments were made to emphasize that only the prepared mind is receptive to the significance of anomalies or surprising results when making scientific observations. The prepared mind and "chance" combine to produce serendipitous scientific discoveries and insights. In a counterdeception context, the prepared mind is receptive to both positive and negative cues (i.e., something is different, surprising, or missing) and is then able to bring to bear a number of counterdeception methods—collection, analytical, or operational—on the problems of simultaneously detecting and penetrating the deception. The prepared organization is able to collect and organize insights and discoveries generated by individuals and teams and integrate it into the target's (political leaders and military commanders) common perception and understanding of the environment and situation in a way that negates or mitigates the effects of the intended deception. It is the prepared mind and organization, supported by a range of collection methods, analytical methods and techniques, and operational capabilities that makes the target less susceptible to deception. This basic idea is summarized in Figure 5.7, which shows how four basic counterdeception principles support the prepared mind and organization to make the target's perceptions and understanding less susceptible to the effects of deception. With that as our context, let's look at our four proposed principles.

5.4.1 Know Yourself

Sun Tzu makes it clear that, at a minimum, you must know yourself if you wish to have any reasonable hope of success in battle. The same is true in the battle of mirrors, masks, lies, and secrets [81] that characterizes the contest between deceiver and target. In Chapter 2 we saw that deception is particularly successful when it exploits the target's expectations and preconceptions, or paraphrasing Whaley, the best stratagem is one where the course of action suggested by the deception is more plausible in terms of the target's prior experience and knowledge then other COAs. Later in Chapter 3 we saw this phenomenon summed up by the simple phrase *seeing what we expect to see*. Such observations are the basis for the self-assessment theme that emerges from the counterdeception literature and lead us to our first fundamental principle of counterdeception: *know yourself*. Putting it another way, if you know you are going to see what you expect to see, you better know what those expectations are and how they came about.

Although it was made in a different context, U.S. Secretary of Defense Donald Rumsfeld's comment about known knowns, known unknowns, and unknown unknowns [82] represents an important feature of the know yourself principle. Counterdeception requires that you not only evaluate what you know and don't know (recall Crowe's Law), but that you must also consciously consider how that knowledge came about. Is what you think you know (or believe) based on fact, or is it really just an assumption or a preconception? Is what you think you know biased by expectations or ethnocentric biases? And although Rumsfeld was accused of gobbledygook [83] in many circles for the "But there are also unknown unknowns—the ones we don't know we don't know" comment [83], the consideration of the unknown unknowns critically depends on the know yourself principle because this is where expectations and biases are most likely to blind the target to potential courses of action available to the deceiver (the third option).

If Sun Tzu was right, then knowing yourself gives you at least a fighting chance at detecting deception. It also helps to bear in mind that Whaley also said [84]: "If the victim does not suspect the possibility that deception is operating, he will inevitably be gulled." Knowing yourself plays a critical role in awareness, that sense of vigilance that triggers some suspicion that something is quite not right or conversely that things are going just a bit too perfectly. Such self-awareness and self-reflection is the first step towards avoiding being "gulled."

5.4.2 Know Your Adversary

"Know your enemy." Once again our ancient Chinese stratagemist Sun Tzu points the way to another fundamental principle of counterdeception. The second principle of deception is *know your adversary*. We use the term adversary here in order to make the point that the threat of deception is not limited strictly to military enemies. The potential for deception exists in any situation—military, diplomatic, or economic—where one side can gain competitive advantage through its use. The know your adversary principle is the foundation of the two Ms in CIA Tradecraft Note No. 10—means and motive. Handel's deception typology (see Figure 2.5) provides a good framework for understanding the importance of this principle. According to Handel, all deception is directed at manipulating two categories of information: *capabilities* and *intentions*. Using the military context as an example, an adversary attempts to:

- Conceal his real capabilities in order to cause the target to underestimate the deceiver's real strength.
- Exaggerate his real capabilities in order to appear stronger than he really is.
- Conceal his plans and readiness for some action (e.g., an attack).
- Exaggerate his readiness (e.g., to deter attack).

From the counterdeception perspective, the know your adversary principle reminds analysts and decision-makers to consider the *means* the adversary has at his disposal (doctrine, training, personnel, experience, and technology) for concealing or exaggerating his capabilities if it is in his best interests to do so. Likewise, the principle focuses attention on the adversary's *motives* for concealing or exaggerating his capabilities and/or intent. These motives could range from achieving surprise, bluffing, deterrence, seeking prestige or influence, blackmail, or seeking concessions from the target. Daniel and Herbig's second set of factors related to the likelihood of deception are pertinent here. In addition, motives may change depending on the situation, so there is also a dynamic component to this principle. A country that is considerably stronger than a neighbor does not need to resort to deception in order to threaten or otherwise influence its victim. On the other hand, that same country when put into another situation involving a considerably stronger nation than itself might resort to deception in order to deter or bluff the stronger adversary.

We have taken Sun Tzu's "know your enemy" principle and interpreted it in a broader counterdeception context we label "know your adversary." Nevertheless, we have to take care not to fall into a potentially dangerous mindset involving the use of the words *enemy* and *adversary* by remembering that although large sophisticated deception operations are rare, deception itself is common. Everyone is a potential deceiver as Handel points out in one of his paradoxes discussed in Chapter 2 [85]: "*The more one has a reputation for honesty—the easier it is to lie convincingly.*" Even more concisely: *Honest people/states can deceive the best.*" This is why the concept of the prepared mind and the use of a holistic approach to counterdeception is so important; whether dealing with enemies (in a military sense), potential enemies, real and potential adversaries, or "honest people/states," the prepared mind and organization must be able to draw on a wide and deep pool of information about the other party. More importantly, in-depth knowledge of the adversary makes it possible to begin breaking down ethnocentric biases and come to see things from the adversary's perspective. As Dewar noted, being able to put yourself into the mind of the adversary may be the counterdeception analyst's main, perhaps only, effective weapon.

5.4.3 Know Your Situation

Our third principle, *know your situation*, focuses on the necessity for continually evaluating the environment for the cues indicating deception will have to be a considered as a major factor when formulating strategies, considering options, making decisions, or taking action. Earlier in this chapter we suggested that analysts are confronted by a continuum of deceptive activity, and most of it, like the normal security activities of an adversary (denial), can be considered normal and likely to occur no matter what the situation is. In addition, as numerous authors have pointed out, the use of large-scale, sophisticated deception operations is usually rare. This can be attributed to the fact that, with the exception of totalitarian regimes that usually have few scruples about the use of deception, most adversaries are unlikely to go to the effort to plan and execute extensive deception operations on a regular basis. As Handel points out [86], "To begin with, those who frequently make use of stratagem rapidly lose their credibility; what they may get away with one, two, or three times in succession they cannot hope to succeed with indefinitely." In addition, Maxim 6 in Figure 2.7 states [87]: "There are circumstances where deception assets should be husbanded despite the costs of maintenance and risk of waste, awaiting a more fruitful use." This maxim implies that each situation forces the adversary to perform a cost benefit tradeoff—should high value deception assets be used to take advantage of an opportunity even though their use will compromise them and render them valueless, or should they be saved in expectation of higher gains in some future situation?

The idea that the likelihood of deception is related to situational factors seems intuitively obvious. CIA Tradecraft Note 10 makes the distinction between "regular" and "suspect and sensitive" issues and it would be surprising if the distinction between the two did not include some sort of situational context aspect. There are also the obvious situational factors that we enumerated earlier such as high stakes situations and those involving asymmetric power relationships between the participants. Another important situational factor is change. Although some situational factors can be considered to be static (e.g., it is unlikely that the United States will be in the position of a second rank state caught between two large power blocs as some countries were during the Cold War), change is a constant factor in the calculus of international relations [88]. Changes in leadership, motives, political goals, military doctrine, or technological capabilities could all conceivably have an impact on the likelihood of deception. An absolutely essential aspect of knowing your situation is to recognize when such changes affect your assumptions, expectations, preconceptions, and beliefs in a fundamental way as we saw in Chapter 2, the United States' failure to recognize that Japanese naval doctrine had changed helped set the stage for the success of Japanese deception operations leading to the attack on Pearl Harbor.

Another situational factor that is important to consider is risk. In any situation, but especially those involving high stakes, it is important to remember that the high-risk, high-gain strategy is always an option available to the adversary [89]. Assessing the risks of a situation brings all three of the principles introduced so far into the picture. It relies heavily on the know your adversary principle, since estimating risk requires detailed knowledge of the adversary's culture, the frame of mind of the leadership, and what the adversary believes he knows about the target [89]. It also depends on the know yourself principle in order to mitigate the ethnocentric biases that produce mirror imaging—high-risk options are regarding as having a low likelihood of occurring because "that's what we would do in that situation." When it comes to risk, knowing your situation means memorizing Handel's second paradox [90]: "The greater the risk, the less likely it seems, and the less risky it actually becomes. Thus, the greater the risk, the smaller it becomes."

There is one final situational factor to mention. In matters of national security, the international environment is capable of distorting the perception and understanding of a situation. The signals produced by the international environment affect the target in two ways. First, events in the international environment, especially those associated with conflict, occupy the target's attention and serve as form of misdirection—focusing the target's attention away from the situation he faces with the adversary. In Chapter 2 we gave the example of how events in Europe tended to divert American attention away from Japanese intentions in the Pacific. On the other hand, a generally quiet and peaceful international environment produces another form of misdirection by reducing the target's attention and suspicions regarding important situational cues. Handel points out that this was the case at the outbreak of the Yom Kippur War [91].

The knowing your situation principle stresses the importance of human reasoning capabilities when confronted with situations that potentially involve deception. Sarbin's concept of acumen is at its core, requiring the potential target of deception to be able to switch back and forth between his perspective of the situation as well as the adversary's. It also highlights the importance of indirect thinking. Counterdeception analysts must develop the ability to break loose of potentially blinding mindsets in order to see the situation in a completely different light. Nevertheless, as powerful as these skills are, especially when combined with our first two principles, there is one more important principle that all three rely on for their effectiveness.

5.4.4 Know Your Channels

Over 2,000 years after Sun Tzu, another pioneer of deception and counterdeception, R. V. Jones, reiterated repeatedly the importance of controlling multiple channels in unmasking deception. If a playing field or game board exists for deception and counterdeception, it must surely be the channels of information over which each party vies for control. Thus, R. V. Jones's wisdom forms the basis for our last principle: *know your channels.*

This principle recognizes that data and information are the raw material from which knowledge is formed and decisions made. Our first three principles all rely on data and information in one way or another. Data and information about the success or failure of his decisions and actions influences the target's preconceptions, expectations, and beliefs. Data and information collected about an adversary contributes to the target's knowledge of the adversary's military capabilities, leadership, politics, organizations, economics, and culture. Data and information are essential to the adversary and target's understanding of situations in which they find themselves involved. All this data and information is obtained from a variety of sources, human and technical, commonly referred to as channels. The data and information flowing from these channels in turn possesses characteristics of its own; it can be relevant or irrelevant, tangible or testimonial, direct or ancillary, solicited or unsolicited, fact or fiction, clear or ambiguous, confirming or contradictory, and most importantly, credible or noncredible. Since most of these channels represent second-hand, third-hand, or even greater sources of information (see the believing what we are told category of biases in Chapter 3), the likelihood that the data and information will be distorted increases even when deception is not a factor.

Gilovich reminds us that the old maxim to *consider the source* is one of the most important ways of avoiding erroneous beliefs in everyday life but he points out that this is something that everyone recognizes in theory but is often overlooked in practice [92]. Our fourth principle is, essentially, the conscientious application of this everyday maxim to the channels of information used by intelligence analysts and political leaders. If it is only recognized in theory but overlooked in practice, the outcomes are likely to be much worse than believing what appears in the *Weekly World Review.*

5.5 Summary

The purpose of this chapter has been to derive a set of fundamental principles of counterdeception that can be used as a framework for exploring both technical and nontechnical approaches to countering deception. As in Chapter 2, our strategy for achieving this purpose has been to provide the reader with an overview of the counterdeception literature as it relates to strategic deception and then identify any common themes that emerge from that review. We then examined the impact that the resulting themes have on the general deception cycle. The resulting nine themes were then further consolidated into four fundamental principles that emphasize a holistic analytical approach to counterdeception relying on the concepts of the prepared mind and the prepared organization. In the next two chapters we will use these principles to organize our examination of ways to make human beings and organizations less susceptible to deception. Chapter 6 examines the concepts of the prepared mind and organization in greater detail and takes a high-level look at non-technical methods and approaches for mitigating deception's effects. Chapter 7 delves even deeper into the subject of counterdeception methodology, examining technical methods of deception detection and discovery and their implementation. We will then be in a better position to decide whether or not Barton Whaley's optimism regarding the detection of deception is warranted.

Endnotes

[1] Department of Defense Dictionary of Military and Associated Terms, Joint Publication 1-02, 12 April 2001 as Amended Through 9 May 2005, p. 126, http://www.dtic.mil/doctrine/jel/new_pubs/jp1_02.pdf.

[2] Rossa, P., "The Denial and Deception Challenge to Intelligence," in Godson, R., and J. Wirtz, (eds.), *Strategic Denial and Deception: The Twenty-First Century Challenge,* New Brunswick, NJ: Transaction Publishers, 2002, p. 225.

[3] In this chapter, we are using the general dictionary definition of the word *detection*, that is, to discover something is to determine its existence or presence. Later in Chapter 7, a more precise, technical definition will be used when discussing technical methods for counterdeception.

[4] In this chapter, we are using the general dictionary definition of the word *discovery*, that is, discovery requires exploration or investigation in an effort to find out the facts or the truth about something. Later in Chapter 7, a more precise, technical definition will be used when discussing technical methods for counterdeception.

[5] Harris, W. R., *On Countering Strategic Deception*, R-1230-ARPA, November 1973, p. 33.

[6] Whaley, B., *Stratagem: Deception and Surprise in War*, Cambridge, MA: Center for International Studies, Massachusetts Institute of Technology, 1969, p. 146.

[7] Jones, R. V., *Reflections on Intelligence*, London, U.K.: Mandarin Paperbacks, 1990, p. 131.

[8] Ibid., p. 144.

[9] Ibid., p. 132.

[10] Ibid., p. 129.

[11] Ibid., p. 134.

[12] Ibid., p. 88.

[13] Whaley, B., *Stratagem: Deception and Surprise in War,* Cambridge, MA: Center for International Studies, Massachusetts Institute of Technology, 1969, p. 147.

[14] Whaley, B., and J. Busby, "Detecting Deception: Practice, Practitioners, and Theory," in Godson, R., and J. Wirtz, (eds.), *Strategic Denial and Deception: The Twenty-First Century Challenge,* New Brunswick, NJ: Transaction Publishers, 2002, p. 189.

[15] Harris, W. R., *On Countering Strategic Deception*, R-1230-ARPA, November 1973, p. 40.

[16] Ibid., p. 42.

[17] Ritchie, G., "Developing the Incongruity-Resolution Theory," *Proc. of AISB Symposium on Creative Language: Stories and Humour*, Edinburgh, U.K., 1999, pp. 78–85, http://citeseer.ist.psu.edu/ritchie99developing.html.

[18] Jervis, R., *Perception and Misperception in International Politics,* Princeton, NJ: Princeton University Press, 1976, pp. 409–424.

[19] Ibid., p. 412.

[20] Ibid., p. 413.

[21] Ibid., p. 415.

[22] Ibid., p. 416.

[23] Ibid., p. 422.

[24] Ibid., p. 423.

[25] Heuer, R. J., "Strategic Deception and Counterdeception: A Cognitive Process Approach," *International Studies Quarterly*, Vol. 25, No. 2, 1981, p. 318.

[26] Ibid., p. 320.

[27] Ben-Zvi, A., "Hindsight and Foresight: A Conceptual Framework for the Analysis of Surprise Attacks," *World Politics,* Vol. 28, No. 3, 1976, pp. 381–395.

[28] Heuer, R. J., "Strategic Deception and Counterdeception: A Cognitive Process Approach," *International Studies Quarterly*, Vol. 25, No. 2, 1981, p. 322.

[29] Ibid., p. 323.

[30] Daniel, D., and K. Herbig, "Propositions on Military Deception," in Daniel, D., and K. Herbig, (eds.), *Strategic Military Deception*, New York: Pergamon Press, 1981, pp. 12–14.

[31] Moose, P., "A Systems View of Deception," in Daniel, D., and K. Herbig, (eds.), *Strategic Military Deception*, New York: Pergamon Press, 1981, pp. 136–150.

[32] Narrativepsych.com describes narrative psychology as "a viewpoint or a stance within psychology which is interested in the 'storied nature of human conduct' (Sarbin, 1986)—how human beings deal with experience by constructing stories and listening to the stories of others. Psychologists studying narrative are challenged by the notion that human activity and experience are filled with 'meaning' and that stories, rather than logical arguments or lawful formulations, are the vehicle by which that meaning is communicated." See http://web.lemoyne.edu/~hevern/nr-basic.html.

[33] Sarbin, T., "Prolegomenon to a Theory of Counterdeception," in Daniel, D., and K. Herbig, (eds.), *Strategic Military Deception*, New York: Pergamon Press, 1981, p. 157.

[34] Ibid., p. 162.

[35] Ibid., p. 170.

[36] Ibid., p. 168.

[37] Dewar, M. *The Art of Deception in Warfare*, Devon, U.K.: David & Charles Publishers, 1989, pp. 194–203.

[38] Ibid., p. 194.

[39] Ibid., p. 200.

[40] Ibid., p. 195.

[41] Ibid., p. 198.

[42] Ibid., pp. 195–196.

[43] Ibid., p. 202.

[44] Handel, M., *War, Strategy, and Intelligence,* London, U.K.: Frank Cass & Co., Ltd., 1989, p. 396.

[45] Holt provides an excellent example from World War II where a double agent provided high quality, high importance information too late to be of use. While describing GARBO's role in the TORCH deception operation that protected the Allied landings in North Africa, Holt provides this anecdote: "Under date of October 29, GARBO reported that a convoy had sailed from the Clyde (this was true), and that 'an operation of great importance is imminent and I think I fulfill my duty by advising you of this danger.' Under date of November 1, he wrote that he had learned at the Ministry of Information that the Allies were about to land in French North Africa. Alas, through some unaccountable mishap in the post office these vital messages were delayed and only reached the Germans on November 7, just before the landings. Though the information was now useless, the Abwehr was overwhelmed by the skill of their star agent. 'Your last reports are all magnificent,' GARBO was told on November 26 'but we are sorry they arrived late.'" Holt, T., *The Deceivers: Allied Military Deception in the Second World War*, New York: Scribner, 2004, p. 271.

[46] Handel, M., *War, Strategy, and Intelligence,* London, U.K.: Frank Cass & Co., Ltd., 1989, p. 397.

[47] Ibid., p. 341.

[48] Ibid., p. 333.

[49] Ibid., p. 250.

[50] "CIA Opens Door on the Craft of Analysis," *Center for the Study of Intelligence Newsletter*, Winter–Spring 1997, No. 7, http://www.cia.gov/csi/bulletin/csi7.htm#toc9.

[51] "Note 10 Tradecraft and Counterintelligence," 1995, http://www.au.af.mil/au/awc/awcgate/cia/tradecraft_notes/note_10.htm.

[52] Johnson, P., et al., "Detecting Deception: Adversarial Problem Solving in a Low Base-Rate World," *Cognitive Science*, Vol. 25, 2001, pp. 355–392.

[53] Reyhl, D., "Peer Review Guide—Materiality," 2001, http://www.reyhl.com/peer_review/materiality.html#definition.

[54] Godson, R., and J. Wirtz, (eds.), *Strategic Denial and Deception: The Twenty-First Century Challenge,* New Brunswick, NJ: Transaction Publishers, 2002, Chs. 3 and 7.

[55] Whaley, B., and J. Busby, "Detecting Deception: Practice, Practitioners, and Theory," in Godson, R., and J. Wirtz, (eds.), *Strategic Denial and Deception: The Twenty-First Century Challenge,* New Brunswick, NJ: Transaction Publishers, 2002, p. 182.

[56] Whaley, B., *Stratagem: Deception and Surprise in War,* Cambridge, MA: Center for International Studies, Massachusetts Institute of Technology, 1969, pp. 210–212.

[57] Bell, J. B., and B. Whaley, *Cheating and Deception*, New Brunswick, NJ: Transaction Publishers, 1991, pp. 328–331.

[58] Whaley, B., and J. Busby, "Detecting Deception: Practice, Practitioners, and Theory," in Godson, R., and J. Wirtz, (eds.), *Strategic Denial and Deception: The Twenty-First Century Challenge,* New Brunswick, NJ: Transaction Publishers, 2002, p. 197.

[59] Ibid., p. 192.

[60] Ibid., p. 191.

[61] Ibid., p. 200.

[62] Edwards, M., "J. C. Masterman," 1998, http://www.twbooks.co.uk/crimescene/jcmastermanme.html.

[63] Myers, D. G., *Intuition: Its Powers and Peril,* New Haven, CT: Yale University Press, 2002, p. 1.

[64] Whaley, B., and J. Busby, "Detecting Deception: Practice, Practitioners, and Theory," in Godson, R., and J. Wirtz, (eds.), *Strategic Denial and Deception: The Twenty-First Century Challenge,* New Brunswick, NJ: Transaction Publishers, 2002, p. 209.

[65] Ibid., pp. 213–214.

[66] Ibid., p. 217.

[67] Rossa, P., "The Denial and Deception Challenge to Intelligence," in Godson, R., and J. Wirtz, (eds.), *Strategic Denial and Deception: The Twenty-First Century Challenge,* New Brunswick, NJ: Transaction Publishers, 2002, pp. 223–228.

[68] Ibid., p. 224.

[69] See Jim Bruce's chapter, "The Impact on Foreign Denial and Deception" in *Strategic Denial and Deception: The Twenty-First Century Challenge* for a more detailed treatment of the impact of unauthorized disclosures on U.S. intelligence capabilities as it elated to deception.

[70] Rossa, P., "The Denial and Deception Challenge to Intelligence," in Godson, R., and J. Wirtz, (eds.), *Strategic Denial and Deception: The Twenty-First Century Challenge,* New Brunswick, NJ: Transaction Publishers, 2002, p. 227.

[71] Gerwehr, S., and R. Glenn, *Unweaving the Web: Deception and Adaptation in Future Urban Operations*, Santa Monica, CA: RAND, 2002, p. xiv.

[72] Stech, F., and C. Elsässer, "Midway Revisited: Detecting Deception by Analysis of Competing Hypothesis," 2004, p. 3, http://www.mitre.org/work/tech_papers/tech_papers_04/stech_deception/, to appear in *Military Operations Research* in early 2007.

[73] Heuer, R. J., "Chapter 8, Analysis of Competing Hypotheses," *Psychology of Intelligence*, 1999, http://www.cia.gov/csi/books/19104/art11.html.

[74] Heuer, R. J., "Strategic Deception and Counterdeception: A Cognitive Process Approach," *International Studies Quarterly*, Vol. 25, No. 2, 1981, p. 321.

[75] Whaley, B., and J. Busby, "Detecting Deception: Practice, Practitioners, and Theory," in Godson, R., and J. Wirtz, (eds.), *Strategic Denial and Deception: The Twenty-First Century Challenge,* New Brunswick, NJ: Transaction Publishers, 2002, p. 187.

[76] Sun Tzu, *The Art of War*, trans. S. B. Griffith, New York: Oxford University Press, 1963, p. 84.

[77] Jervis, R., *Perception and Misperception in International Politics,* Princeton, NJ: Princeton University Press, 1976, pp. 410–411.

[78] Handel, M. I., *War, Strategy, and Intelligence,* London, U.K.: Frank Cass & Co., Ltd., 1989, p. 341.

[79] Heuer, R. J., "Strategic Deception and Counterdeception: A Cognitive Process Approach," *International Studies Quarterly*, Vol. 25, No. 2, 1981, p. 318.

[80] Whaley, B., *Stratagem: Deception and Surprise in War,* Cambridge, MA: Center for International Studies, Massachusetts Institute of Technology, 1969. p. 4.

[81] Sarbin, T., "Prolegomenon to a Theory of Counterdeception," in Daniel, D., and K. Herbig (eds.), *Strategic Military Deception*, New York: Pergamon Press, 1981, p. 163.

[82] United States Department of Defense News Transcript, February 12, 2002, 11:31 a.m. EST, http://www.defenselink.mil/transcripts/2002/t02122002_t212sdv2.html.

[83] Plain English Campaign, "The Foot in Mouth Award," 2005, http://www.plainenglish.co.uk/footinmouth.html.

[84] Whaley, B., *Stratagem: Deception and Surprise in War,* Cambridge, MA: Center for International Studies, Massachusetts Institute of Technology, 1969, p. 142.

[85] Handel, M. I., *War, Strategy, and Intelligence,* London: Frank Cass & Co., Ltd., 1989, p. 335.

[86] Ibid., p.334.

[87] Everest Consulting Associates and Mathtech, Inc., *Deception Maxims: Fact and Folklore,* Princeton, NJ, 1980, pp. 26–27.

[88] Jervis, R., *Perception and Misperception in International Politics,* Princeton, NJ: Princeton University Press, 1976, p. 19.

[89] Handel, M. I., *War, Strategy, and Intelligence,* London, U.K.: Frank Cass & Co. Ltd., 1989, p. 243.

[90] Handel, M., *Perception, Deception, and Surprise: The Case of the Yom Kippur War.* Jerusalem: The Hebrew University, 1976, p. 16.

[91] Ibid., pp. 16–17.

[92] Gilovich, T., *How We Know What Isn't So: The Fallibility of Human Reason in Everyday Life,* New York: The Free Press, 1991, p. 109.

CHAPTER 6

Nontechnical Approaches to Counterdeception

In Chapter 5 we considered three of the six questions having to do with counterdeception. In answer to the first question of what counterdeception is, we suggested that counterdeception goes well beyond just detecting deception. Instead, counterdeception activities are characterized by three dimensions of action: *awareness*, *detection and exposure*, and *discovery and penetration*. Awareness and detection focus on detecting the existence of deception. Exposure emphasizes revealing the purpose of the deception (i.e., what does the adversary want you to do?), while discovery and penetration attempt to reveal the adversary's actual intended course of action and capabilities. The second question asked what could be learned from the literature regarding counterdeception concepts and approaches. Our review of the literature uncovered a wide variety of counterdeception concepts and approaches that we have organized into nine themes. We used those themes to address the third question regarding the existence of counterdeception principles and proposed four fundamental principles of counterdeception: know yourself, know your adversary, know your situation, and know your channels. These principles, combined with the idea of "the prepared mind" (and by extension the prepared organization), are critical to negating and mitigating the effects of deception. Now, in Chapters 6 and 7, we will address the remaining questions related to what can be done to counter deception. In this chapter we will integrate our counterdeception principles and the concepts of the prepared mind and prepared organization into high-level, nontechnical approaches for building deception-resistant humans and organizations. Chapter 7 will then expand on these approaches to examine how technology can be brought to bear on the problem of countering deception.

6.1 The Vulnerable Mind and the Vulnerable Organization

As we saw in Chapter 2, successful deception planners exploit the target's expectations, preconceptions, beliefs, fears, and biases to design a deception story that provokes a particular action (or inaction) from the target. The deception story is presented to the target through various channels some or all of which are known to be monitored by the target. If the deception is successful, the target will be able to reconstruct the basic elements of the deception story and since the story is consistent with the target's beliefs, it will be accepted and acted upon in the manner that the deceiver intended. Chapter 3 showed that deception is a cognitive phenomenon—it occurs in the mind of the intended target—and that cultural and organizational factors can also significantly affect the target's perceptions. Therefore, before we consider approaches for making human beings and organizations more resistant to deception, it may be helpful to review the characteristics of the vulnerable mind and organization. The resulting profiles of the vulnerable mind and organization can then be used as baselines against which to evaluate the characteristics of the prepared mind and the approaches by which we can achieve a deception-resistant system of prepared minds and organizations.

6.1.1 The Vulnerable Mind

History makes it clear that humans and human organizations are vulnerable to deception. Time and time again, highly intelligent, well-meaning, and well-informed analysts and decision-makers have been the victim of deception and often wind up being accused of incompetence as well by those blessed with 20–20 hindsight. However, as Gilovich points out, people do not hold questionable beliefs simply because they are stupid or gullible [1]: "Quite the contrary. Evolution has given us powerful intellectual tools for processing vast amounts of information with accuracy and dispatch, and our questionable beliefs derive primarily form the misapplication or overutilization of generally valid and effective strategies of knowing." The label *vulnerable*, therefore, is not meant to be pejorative but is intended to be a way of helping us to distinguish the important ways in which humans and organizations are open to attack or damage by deception. Such information can aid us in constructing the desired profiles of the mind and organization that will be less vulnerable to deception as well as a guide to what actions might be taken to reduce that vulnerability.

In Chapter 3 we used Gilovich's determinants of questionable beliefs as a framework for understanding how cognitive biases affected the target's acceptance of the deceiver's deception story (see Figure 3.6). We also examined the impact that personal experiences as well as cultural and organizational biases had on that acceptance. Distilling these factors still further, we can produce a profile of the vulnerable mind consisting of four major characteristics (see Figure 6.1). This profile of the vulnerable mind shows that it:

- Sees reality according to its own preconceptions and expectations;
- Is unduly influenced by a good story;
- Tends to be overconfident;
- Lacks accurate, in-depth knowledge of its adversary.

The first two characteristics are driven primarily by three of the six determinants of belief we looked at in Chapter 3: too much from too little, seeing what we expect to see, and believing what we are told. These are the determinants of belief that are most closely intertwined with the individual's expectations and preconceptions. Figure 6.1 also shows that cultural biases and personal experiences are important drivers in the formation of those preconceptions, expectations, and beliefs. In addition, when presented with ambiguous, inconsistent, or contradictory information, the vulnerable mind's use of normally reliable heuristics produces behaviors that are the

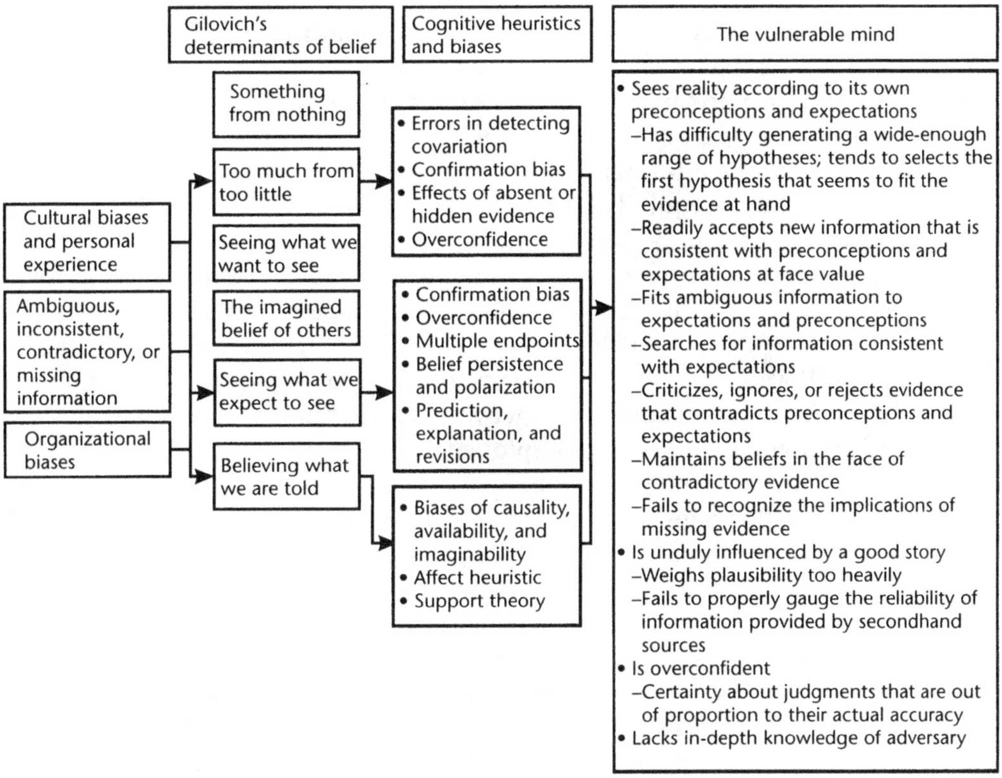

Figure 6.1 Characteristics of the vulnerable mind.

key contributor to deception's success namely seeing reality according to its own preconceptions and expectations.

History repeatedly shows that the vulnerability created by the first characteristic, the target's own expectations and preconceptions, is the critical gap in the target's defenses that makes deception so successful. Bounded rationality (satisficing) produces the vulnerable mind's tendency to pick the first hypothesis that seems to fit the evidence immediately at hand (i.e., jump to conclusions). This tendency is further aggravated by confirmation bias—the tendency to readily accept new information that is consistent with preconceptions, expectations, and beliefs at its face value; fit ambiguous information to the favored hypothesis; criticize, ignore, or reject evidence that contradicts preconceptions, expectations, and beliefs; and continue to actively seek evidence that supports the favored hypothesis. The deceiver is further aided by the vulnerable mind's stubbornness in the face of contradictory evidence. If its expectations are strong enough, the vulnerable mind is capable of maintaining its beliefs in spite of seemingly irrefutable evidence [2].

The second characteristic represents another case where powerful human abilities have not only useful benefits but also carry potential costs. Stories are powerful ways for exchanging information and for learning. This benefit is offset by the vulnerability that arises when analytical judgment is unduly influenced by a compelling story or a particularly plausible scenario. As Tversky and Kahneman note [3], "A good story is often less probable than a less satisfactory one." The prospect of Allied landings in the Pas de Calais area made for a plausible and compelling scenario but one that turned out to be actually less probable than a less plausible and less compelling one like Normandy. The vulnerability resulting from the undue influence of a good story is aggravated still further when the target fails to properly gauge the credibility of the information provided by his sources.

The vulnerable mind also tends to be an overconfident mind. This third characteristic is significant because confidence ultimately controls action. The more confidence you have that your judgment about a situation is correct, the more likely you are to take whatever action the judgment suggests. Take, for example, France's defeat in 1940 [4]: "Whatever doubts may have obtained earlier, French leaders in 1939–40 were sure of French power, indeed arrogantly so." Of course, the deceiver's goal is to make the target very certain but very wrong therefore overconfidence is a vulnerability to be exploited.

The fourth characteristic, the lack of accurate, in-depth knowledge of the adversary, is a well-recognized factor in deception's success. Inadequate knowledge of the adversary contributes to a host of misperceptions—the meaning of the messages and signals the adversary sends; his preconceptions, expectations, and beliefs; his attitudes towards risk; and his policies and military doctrines. Such misperceptions can arise when the target and the adversary are from essentially the same culture. Major cultural differences produce even more profound misperceptions. This is not a new problem but many analysts, policymakers, and decision-makers often fail to realize that they are often up against an adversary with a completely different way of organizing life, of thinking, and of conceiving the underlying assumptions about the family and the state, the economic system, and even of mankind [5].

The misperceptions that flow from inadequate knowledge about the adversary form the basis for a wide range of flawed judgments and decisions. Grabo writes [6]: "Fantastic errors in judgment, and the most calamitous misassessments of what the adversary was up to have been attributable to such a lack of perception or understanding." This was the case with Pearl Harbor where the United States failed to realize that Japan's plans for the conquest of Asia went beyond ambition and the desire for territorial expansion. To the Japanese it was a question of survival, a matter of prestige, and a matter of life and death [7]. A more recent example was the U.S. intelligence community's failure to predict India's 1998 nuclear test. Much of the blame can be laid on inadequate knowledge of Indian politics and motivations; a fact Admiral David Jeremiah addressed in his 1998 press conference after the release of his commission's report on the Indian tests [8]: "I suppose my bottom line is that both the intelligence and the policy communities had an underlying mindset going into these tests that the BJP would behave as we behave." The lack of adequate knowledge about Indian politics when combined with common American ethnocentric biases and further exasperated by India's denial and deception activities created a classic example of mirror imaging and produced what was commonly interpreted as another failure of intelligence.

In summary, the profile of the vulnerable mind that we have constructed is meant to represent the deception planner's ideal target. It can be the profile of an analyst or a decision-maker. Analysts and decision-makers, however, rarely act alone, and so we not turn our attention to the profile of the vulnerable organization.

6.1.2 The Vulnerable Organization

Over the last 100 years large private and public sector organizations have transformed our world socially and economically. Yet the very features that make these organizations effective and efficient (hierarchical control structures, standard policies and procedures, planning, and the division of labor) also produce unwanted side effects (bureaucracy, rivalry, and politics) that increase their vulnerability to deception. These unwanted features and side effects affect information flows within and between organizations as well as the group dynamics of the organization's members. This makes large intelligence organizations vulnerable to deception in five ways (see Figure 6.2):

- An overemphasis on consensus, consistency, and being decisive;
- Inadequate collaboration processes;
- An emphasis on security over effectiveness;
- Inadequate learning processes;
- An overemphasis on current intelligence.

The first vulnerability is related to an organizational bias we described in Chapter 3—the coordination process among analysts in differing intelligence organizations. For example, even though the U.S. intelligence community believes in the concept of competitive analysis [9], it is also highly consensual in nature [10], that is, there is a strong expectation that analysts from the different intelligence organizations will come to a common consensus on major issues. Ideally, the coordination

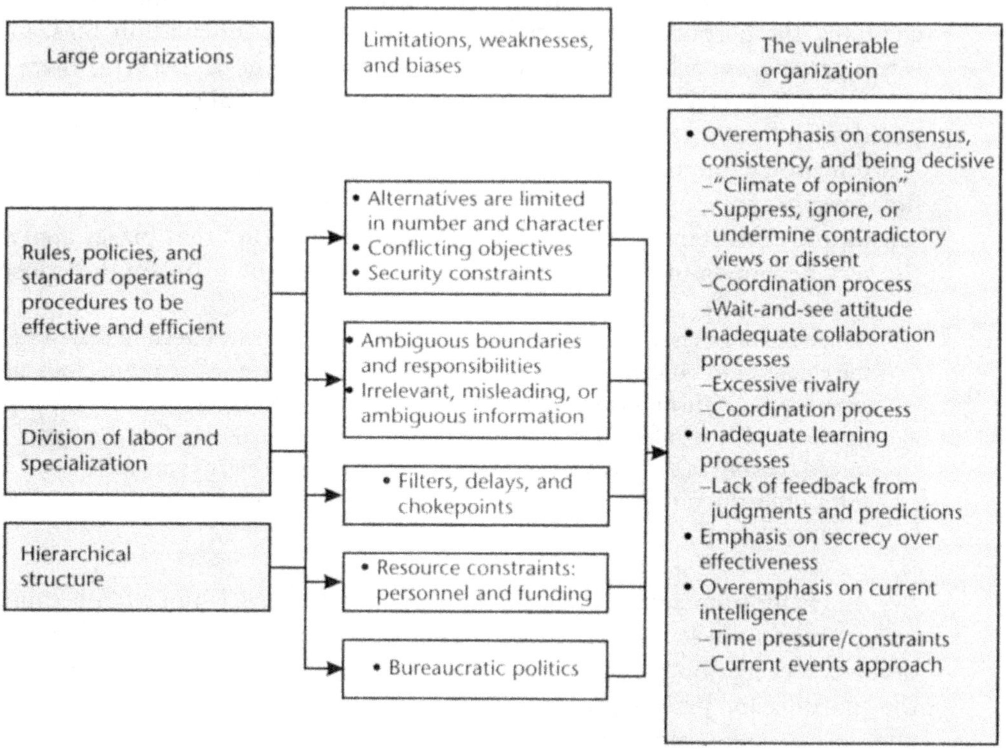

Figure 6.2 Characteristics of the vulnerable organization.

process is supposed to uncover new information, take into account differing views, and ensure the most effective presentation of an intelligence issue to decision makers [11]. The coordination process is absolutely essential to getting high quality strategic intelligence to decision-makers; however, it can also contribute to the organization's vulnerability to deception if the coordination process acts to reinforce preconceptions, expectations, and beliefs that can be exploited by the deceiver. One effect that contributes to this particular vulnerability is when the coordination process suppresses dissenting views that run counter to the majority's beliefs. This is a critical vulnerability since experience has shown that the minority is often right; a point Grabo makes when she writes [12]:

> Lamentable as it may be, the fact is that the most nearly correct judgments in crisis situations over a period of years often have been reached by a minority of individuals. This does not mean that one agency is right and others are wrong—it is not that political analysts will come to right conclusions and military analysts to wrong conclusions, or vice versa. What usually happens is that a majority in all agencies will likely be wrong. Thus the situation is not taken care of by the usual device of a dissenting agency footnote, since it will be a minority in each agency (not a majority in one) which will be in dissent.

A second effect is that once a consensus is obtained and delivered to decision-makers, the maintenance of that official opinion, like individual beliefs, is highly resistant to change. In his ethnographic study of the U.S. intelligence community, Johnston points out that this form of belief persistence is so strong that it is equivalent to a cultural taboo [13]: "The maintenance of a corporate judgment is a pervasive and often-unstated norm in the Intelligence Community, and the taboo against changing the corporate product line contributes to confirmation bias. Once any intelligence agency has given its official opinion to policymakers, there exists a taboo about reversing or significantly changing the official or corporate position to avoid the loss of status, trust, or respect."

Johnston's statement also contains a reference to the third impact that emphasis on consensus and consistency has, namely, confirmation bias. The emphasis on consensus and consistency can create a "climate of opinion" that biases analysis from the very beginning in most cases. Johnston describes the problem this causes [14]:

> ... instead of generating new hypotheses based solely on raw data and then weighing the evidence to confirm or refute those hypotheses, the analyst begins looking for evidence to confirm the existing hypothesis, which came from previous intelligence products or was inferred during interactions with colleagues. The process is reinforced socially as the analyst discusses a new finding with group members and superiors, often the very people who collaborated in producing the previous intelligence products.

As Heuer points out [15], "If the correct hypothesis is not even formulated for consideration, there is clearly little chance of making an accurate judgment." If the deceiver's deception story is in line with the general climate of opinion generated by the coordination process, there is little chance that the target will seriously consider alternative explanations for the evidence.

The second and third characteristics are related to the way information flows and changes within and between organizations. Inadequate collaboration processes are the second characteristic of the vulnerable organization and represent the dark side of hierarchical control structures and the division of labor in large organizations. In large intelligence organizations the functions of intelligence collection and analysis are often broken down into various specialties and geographic regions. For example, most collection is typically referred to by the "INTs": HUMINT, SIGINT, IMINT, OSINT, and MASINT [16]. Analytical specialties may be also organized along INT lines (e.g., imagery analysts) but may also be further categorized by discipline (e.g., economics, politics, leadership, or military) and geographic region (Latin America, China, Europe, Africa, and so forth). There are also *all-source* analysts whose job it is to integrate the intermediate intelligence produced by first and second phase analysts [17]. This division of labor and specialization, although necessary for the efficient collection and production of intelligence, filters and changes the raw intelligence data in numerous ways. Kam points out that [18], "Different estimates from different units produce ambiguity and ambivalence, while estimates that agree may conceal deviating opinions and tend to obscure issues." The result is likely to be overconfidence and confirmation bias as policy and decision-makers fit the information to their own expectations.

A hierarchical management structure can compound collaboration problems further by blocking, filtering, or distorting upward communications and it allows high-level officials to effectively ignore low-level personnel—especially if they don't agree with their views [18]. Combine hierarchical structure, specialization, inter- and intra-organizational rivalry, and bureaucratic politics with inadequate collaboration processes and you have the potential to severely distort the analytic process itself. Kam summarizes all the different things that can go wrong [19]:

> Subordinates, who have to decide what information to pass on to their superiors, may withhold a disproportionate amount of discrepant information. Subunits tend to exaggerate the importance of some events and minimize that of others. The content of data may be changed in transmission. Ambiguity about responsibilities and standard operating procedures pertaining to the handling of information may lead to ignorance and neglect of critical evidence. Different units within the organization may hold conflicting assumptions regarding the significance of incoming information and consequent warning. Interpersonal difficulties may result in inadequate or distorted transmission of information. Scarcity of time and resources prevents proper handling of information and may lead to the selective and incomplete dissemination of information to its consumers.

The third characteristic of the vulnerable organization represents another paradox. The organization that emphasizes security, particularly with regard to the protection of sources and methods, over effectiveness must face the fact that such emphasis is also likely to increase its vulnerability to deception. The problems are very similar to those created by inadequate collaboration processes. The unequal distribution of highly classified or compartmented information means that analysts and decision-makers in one organization may not be privy to information held by another. The consequences can include the failure to act in a timely manner, duplication of efforts, the inadvertent interference in the operations of one organization and that of another, a less effective coordination process or perhaps no coordination at all, and the general failure to use valuable information to its fullest possible extent [20]. Other effects create confusion that further degrades analytical and decision-making effectiveness. The unequal distribution of information creates the situation where no one really knows who has access to what; actors with access may assume that others are equally informed while those without access but are still aware of its existence have mistaken assumptions about its content and accuracy [21]. Kam summarizes the resulting trap [22]: "In general the result of selective distribution of information is the prevalence of a feeling in the intelligence community that somebody else probably knows what is going on and will take care of the situation." In addition, since lower-level subject matter experts may not have access to the information, decision-makers are put into the position of doing their own analysis even though they lack the very depth and breadth of knowledge possessed by the analysts that are supposed to be supporting them.

The fourth characteristic of the vulnerable organization is inadequate organizational learning processes. Learning and deception are closely related. The *cry wolf* phenomenon is a good example. If analysts repeatedly warn of an event (like a surprise attack) and it does not occur, they are said to be crying wolf. After repeated warnings, decision-makers learn to ignore them. An adversary can take advantage of this phenomenon in order to prevent the target from acting effectively when the actual attack occurs. The problem facing the organization is that there is no accurate feedback regarding *why* the previous events did not occur—there is usually no way determine if the warning was correct or not. For example, a warning might be correct but the adversary decides to change his mind at the last minute or the warning might have been correct and the adversary, realizing that the target is now forewarned, decides to postpone his plans. The lack of accurate feedback means there is little opportunity to correct the errors that produced a false warning. Heuer reinforces this point with the observation that [23]:

> Learning to make better judgments through experience assumes systematic feedback on the accuracy of previous judgments and an ability to link the accuracy of a judgment with the particular configuration of variables that prompted an analyst to make that judgment. In practice, intelligence analysts get little systematic feedback, and even when they learn that an event they had foreseen has actually occurred or failed to occur, they typically do not know for certain whether this happened for the reasons they had foreseen.

The nature of deception itself contributes to inadequate organizational learning. Strategic deception is primarily associated with high stakes situations and such situations are usually produced by complex combinations of factors that tend to occur in nonrepetitive contexts. Such situations make learning difficult because of their rarity. After all, there was only one world war in the twentieth century that produced a strategic deception operation like FORTITUDE. Even FORTITUDE's creators recognized that the lessons they learned might not apply in the future.

The last characteristic, an overemphasis on current intelligence, is not related to any organizational obstacles created by bureaucratic structure and politics but is an important organizational bias just the same. Over the years there has been increasing emphasis on providing information regarding current issues that are of immediate importance to policymakers and decision-makers. They want answers to today's problems and as Lowenthal notes, they have little time to give attention to in-depth analytical reports, not out of lack of interest but because of the pressures of current events [24]. Thus, another paradox is created since being successful at delivering current intelligence produces corresponding vulnerabilities that can be exploited by the deceiver. The first is time pressure. Time is the deceiver's enemy. The longer the target has to evaluate the data and information received through various channels, the more opportunity there is to detect the deception. The pressure produced by the emphasis to produce timely current intelligence products means that analysts are less likely to examine the information at hand with any degree of thoroughness. In fact, as we saw in Chapter 3, they are likely to fall back on automatic, System 1 processes prone to bias. Time pressure makes the mind more vulnerable to deception.

The second vulnerability is that the emphasis on current events is likely to reduce the organization's ability to see the situation as a whole. Grabo's comments on current intelligence with regard to warning are pertinent [25]: "The effects of this type of preoccupation with the currency of information is twofold: long-term, basic intelligence and in-depth analysis tend to suffer both in the allocation of personnel and prestige; and the cumulative analysis of indications tends to be forgotten in favor of portraying the latest information on charts or display boards in situation rooms." Deception operations, like other preparations for war, reflect the whole pattern of what an adversary is doing over weeks and months, perhaps even years. Thus, to paraphrase Grabo, deception is cumulative, not merely current.

A vulnerable organization made up of vulnerable minds sees what it expects to see. It is likely to be a sitting duck for deception. It should also be clear that reducing the mind's vulnerability alone is insufficient since the vulnerable organization can easily suppress or ignore views that differ from the acceptable climate of opinion. As a result, a deceiver who is only roughly aware of what the climate of opinion is can exploit the vulnerable organization. Both must be addressed.

6.2 Deception-Resistant Humans and Organizations: The Prepared Mind and the Prepared Organization

The vulnerable mind and organization is an easy target for the deceiver's manipulations. The litany of deception's successes far outweighs the number of examples where it has failed [26] leading many to the pessimistic conclusion that counterdeception has no real chance of success. Handel was clearly pessimistic [27] and even Grabo [28] notes that the study of deception "will only reinforce a conclusion that the most brilliant analysis may founder in the face of deception and the most expert and experienced among us on occasion may be as vulnerable as the novice." Nevertheless, the historical record also shows that in many of the cases of successful deception there were individuals and organizations who were not fooled. Kam cites the example of an Israeli lieutenant who correctly assessed that Egyptian deployments and military exercises were a prelude to war—his reports were not distributed or included in his command's intelligence report [29]. This suggests that although it may not be possible to build deception-proof humans and organizations, it may be possible to make humans and organizations more resistant to deception's manipulations. At the end of Chapter 5, we suggested that there is something about the idea of the prepared mind that might act as a foundation on which to base efforts to mitigate deception's effects. In this section we will look at ways of transforming vulnerable minds and organizations into prepared, deception-hardened ones.

6.2.1 Building and Maintaining the Prepared Mind

Just what are the characteristics of the prepared mind? Whaley posed a similar question and provided his own answer when he wrote [30]: "What kind of person combines the four qualities necessary for first-rate deception and its detection—a prepared mind, a Machiavellian personality, empathy, and the ability to think indirectly?" The "prepared mind" to which he refers is that described by Pasteur—a mind that is receptive to the significance of anomalies or surprising results when making observations. This is not surprising given that incongruity testing lies at the core of Whaley's counterdeception theories. His reference to the Machiavellian personality is based on the work of Christie and Geis [31], who studied this personality type and developed a questionnaire (the Mach IV Scale) which assesses an individual's degree of cynical, suspicious, and skeptical attitudes to human relationships [32]. Whaley seems to be suggesting that high scorers on the Mach IV Scale may be less inclined to be gullible or easily misled. There seems to be, however, little empirical research to support this, though. The quality of empathy is important to accurately discerning the adversary's motives and intentions. Finally, the ability to think "indirectly" addresses the need for imaginative generation of alternative explanations for what is observed. Whaley's "qualities" are thought-provoking and broad in scope, but what is needed is a set of specific strategies and methods for getting from here to there—ways of creating minds with characteristics that are likely to throw a wrench in the deceiver's plans. The rest of this section covers how we can combine the counterdeception principles we proposed in Chapter 5 with insights from different academic, management, and national security disciplines in order to do just that.

6.2.1.1 Strategies and Substrategies

Our starting point for the process of building the prepared mind is shown by the simple model in Figure 6.3. In this model, the vulnerable mind must process ambiguous, inconsistent, and contradictory information (some of which has been deliberately manipulated by the deceiver) in order to develop perceptions about the world. It is

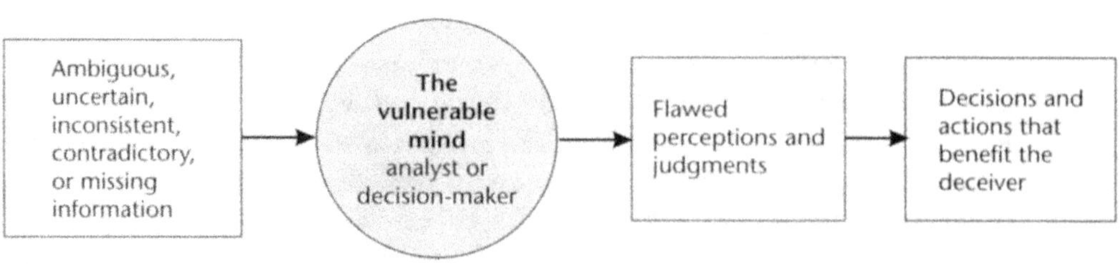

Figure 6.3 The vulnerable mind produces flawed judgments that benefit the deceiver.

also important to remember that some information is missing either due to the deceiver's deliberate denial activities or because of the target's failure or inability to collect the information. When such information is evaluated by the vulnerable mind, the result is likely to be flawed perceptions and judgments which themselves produce decisions and actions that benefit the deceiver. Our desired goal of reducing the mind's vulnerability to deception implies that the objective of the prepared mind is to deliver better, more accurate judgments, judgments that will enable making decisions and taking actions that will negate or mitigate deception's effects. This simple model suggests that there are two possible strategies for achieving this goal: (1) improve the data and information available and (2) improve the functioning, the basic reasoning, of the vulnerable mind.

Improve the Data and Information Available

Our review of the counterdeception literature suggests that there are two substrategies for improving the data information available to analysts and decision-makers (see Figure 6.4). One is more relevant to technical methods of counterdeception and will only be briefly covered here while the other concerns the characteristics of the information itself and affects how the information is perceived and used. Such perceptions about the evidence at hand play an important role in determining whether the preconceptions, expectations, and beliefs that the deceiver is trying to exploit can be overcome and thus are an important part of building the prepared mind.

Better Collection

The first substrategy is related to the collection methods theme we presented in Chapter 5. The basic counterdeception tenets of that theme were for the target to

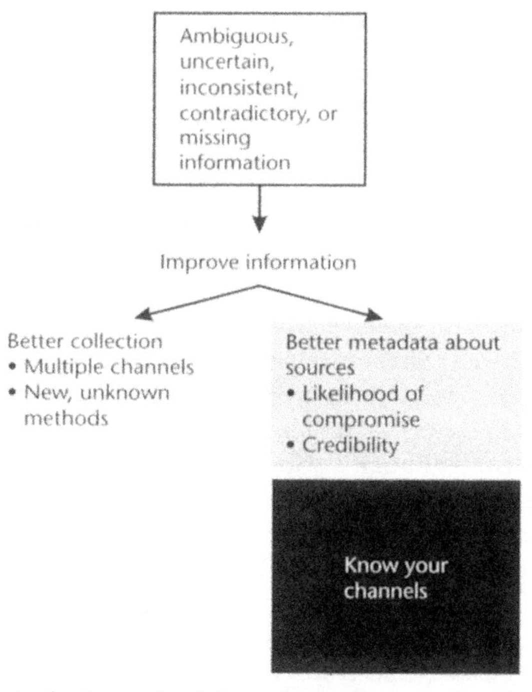

Figure 6.4 Basic strategies for improving information available to the vulnerable mind.

control as many collection channels as possible and to try to use collection methods unknown to the adversary. The ability to collect data and information through multiple channels makes the deceiver's task more difficult and increases the likelihood that the target may detect incongruities and flaws in the deception story. The imaginative use of improved collection, both human and technical, remains an important counterdeception approach; however, collection is unlikely to be a silver bullet that can significantly reduce one's vulnerability to deception. Deception occurs in the mind and that is where the battle must really be fought.

Better Metadata

The second substrategy is based on the know your channels principle and stresses the importance to counterdeception of information *about* information. Gilovich observed that [33]: "A person's conclusions can only be as solid as the information on which they are based." He was referring to the biasing effects that secondhand sources of information have on beliefs. Even where deception is not a factor, secondhand sources of information produce distortions in the stories we hear and use to try to make sense of our world. These distortions include simple errors of fact, sharpening and leveling effects, and attempts to make the story more immediate, more entertaining, or more plausible. Gilovich offers five guidelines [34] for helping people think about the secondhand information they receive about everyday life; however, we are going to focus on only one in the context of strategic deception: *consider the source*.

The injunction to "consider the source" is a call to evaluate not only the *content* of the evidence that a source provides, but also information about the source itself in order to determine the *credibility* of that evidence. They are often considered separately; however, they are closely linked with one affecting the other [35]. It is obvious that where deception is involved, evidence is not always what it appears to be. The history of deception is filled with stories of false documents, feints and demonstrations, camouflage and decoys, and false testimony. However, what is not so obvious is that metadata can be at least as important to analysis as the evidence itself [36]. This leads to the question: What kind of metadata should the prepared mind consider in order to reduce its vulnerability to deception? The counterdeception literature suggests that, at a minimum, two kinds of metadata are required.

The first kind of metadata takes into consideration the knowledge that the deceiver will always try to identify, compromise, and exploit information channels that the target believes to be credible. In peacetime, intelligence sources can be compromised in a variety of ways including espionage, unauthorized disclosures (leaks), intelligence shared with other nations, intelligence used to support a diplomatic demarche, and even routine declassification activities [37]. In wartime, captured equipment (e.g., the German Enigma code machine), documents, or prisoners can be added to the list. Although a wide variety of sources can be used for deception, the target's secret intelligence sources are the deceiver's primary target because the target's intelligence service is the "transmission belt" for getting the deception story in front of the target's decision-makers [38]. If the deception target collects and uses evidence from several channels while remaining ignorant of its potential compromise, he plays into the deceiver's hands and makes the deceiver's job that much easier. Common sense therefore dictates that metadata regarding compromised intelligence sources (either known to be compromised or are likely to have been compromised) should be collected and made available to analysts. Such metadata would, at a minimum, identify the source that was compromised, how and when the compromise occurred, and the extent to which the source was compromised (e.g., its existence was revealed, technical details and operational characteristics, or information about the collection target).

Not all compromises are cause to stop using a source. There have been numerous cases of the unauthorized release of information about U.S. technical collection systems but that does not always negate their usefulness. Even human assets that have been known to have been discovered and turned (double agents) often continue to provide useful information. Nevertheless, any use of compromised sources forces analysts to continually assess the possibility that the information collected from such systems might have been arranged for their benefit. In addition, if information from a compromised source is used in an intelligence report or estimate, the fact that the information comes from a compromised source must be made known to the policymaker, military commander, or leader who receives it.

Even if there is no reason to believe a source has been compromised, the source's credibility still remains an issue that must be addressed. The credibility of a source or the lack thereof has played a significant role in many cases of deception. On some occasions, sources of questionable credibility provided extremely accurate information that revealed the deceiver's true purpose [39, 40] and were duly ignored while in other situations, sources that were considered to be highly reliable provided disinformation that was readily accepted without question and were critical to the success of the deception. Source credibility therefore is our second type of metadata.

Intelligence analysts receive data and information from a wide variety of sources. For the purposes of our discussion here, we will assume that technical collection sources like imagery and signal intelligence satellites that are under the direct control of the analyst's government can be considered to be credible (e.g., a picture of a ship in port taken by a satellite can be taken to be authentic and not a forgery). Whether it is actually a ship and not something that only looks like a ship is, of course, another matter and answering that question depends on the extent to which information about the satellite system has been compromised. Our focus here is on the credibility of human sources of information. Spies are often the first human source that people think of when they think of intelligence but analysts rely on information that is produced and transmitted by a wide range of human activities. Human sources include not only spies but also diplomats, defense attachés, and other government officials, who, of course, usually get their information from yet other human sources, like foreign government officials, with whom they come into contact. In addition, there is the entire field of open source information (OSINT) consisting of the media, public data, and professional and academic sources [41]. OSINT as well is produced and transmitted by human sources. It should be clear that the data and information provided by such sources will almost always be secondhand information, probably even third- or fourth-hand, creating the potential for the distortions that Gilovich discusses.

Given that we need to consider the credibility of a source, how is it done? The answer depends on what kind of evidence it is. Schum describes two basic types of evidence. *Tangible evidence* is evidence that you can examine in some way in order to determine what it reveals [42]. Examples of tangible evidence include objects, documents, sensor images (e.g., that satellite image), and the output of measuring devices (e.g., a thermometer). Tangible evidence also includes demonstrative evidence—maps, charts, diagrams, or demonstrations—that we can examine ourselves. The other basic type of evidence is *testimonial evidence*. Testimonial evidence comes from another person in the form of an assertion that some event did or did not happen [43]. Such evidence can result from *direct observation* where the source was in a position to observe whether or not an event occurred. The difference between testimonial and tangible evidence is that although the person's testimony (speech or written statement) is certainly tangible, the evidence itself is not available for you to directly examine. Testimonial evidence where the source did not directly observe the event but heard about it from someone who did is called *secondhand evidence* or *hearsay*. *Rumor* or *gossip* is a form of secondhand testimonial evidence in which the primary source cannot be identified. Finally, there is a form of testimonial evidence where no one directly observed the event. A source can report information about an event by *inference*—person A observes events C and D and infers that E also occurred [44].

Determining the credibility of tangible evidence involves an evaluation of two variables: *authenticity* and *accuracy* [45]. Authenticity focuses on whether or not the evidence is genuine. Is the document authentic or counterfeit? Is an object genuine or is it an imitation? Has a photograph been doctored? Questions of authenticity also concern how the evidence was acquired and who had access to it before you were able to observe it—the *chain of custody* [46]. Accuracy is an issue with regard to evidence produced by sensing devices. Physical measuring instruments have natural limits related to their design and often require periodic recalibration. In addition, sensors can be manipulated either directly through tampering or indirectly such as jamming. An excellent example of the manipulation of the target's sensors is the escape of the German battle cruisers *Scharnhorst*, *Gneisenau*, and *Prinz Eugen* from Brest through the English Channel right under the noses of the British. German radar jamming was slowly and subtly increased in intensity over a period of time so that British radar operators would become acclimatized to it [47]. Eventually the jamming was so intense the British radars become useless allowing the warships to escape [48]. Determining authenticity and accuracy is a job for experts and we can only assume that large intelligence organizations have the means to determine the authenticity of tangible evidence when required and that the technical collection systems they employ are accurate.

The credibility of sources providing testimonial evidence is an issue that affects all aspects of human activity but becomes absolutely crucial when deception is involved.

Evaluating the credibility of a source providing testimonial evidence involves three variables: observational *sensitivity*, *objectivity*, and *veracity* [49]. Sensitivity takes into account that our five senses are not infallible (our apologies to those readers with psychic or super powers). Like the physical sensors that are associated with tangible evidence, humans have natural limits; we don't see very well in the dark, our vision and hearing are not often perfect, or the conditions at the time interfere with our senses (e.g., fog or street noise). Sensitivity poses the question: Can the source discriminate between the occurrence and nonoccurrence of some event?

The objectivity of a source is related to a characteristic of human beings with which we are already well familiar: seeing what we expect to see. Schum [50] defines an objective observer to be "one who attends to the evidence of her senses and who does not let her motivations or expectancies determine what she will believe." Thus, objectivity poses the question: Is the source's belief about the occurrence or nonoccurrence of an event consistent with the evidence he obtained from his senses?

Veracity, of course, involves the truthfulness of the evidence a source provides. If a source believes that some event has occurred and reports that the event did not occur, then the source is telling a lie. Note however that if a person who reports the occurrence of an event, and the event did not actually occur, that person is not necessarily telling a lie. If the person's observation is inaccurate or not objective, he might believe the event occurred and would be truthful in reporting that they believed it occurred. Questions of veracity are questions of a source's *beliefs* about what has or has not occurred.

There is one more variable that is important when heeding the advice to "consider the source." The *competence* of a source is often an important variable when considering the source's evidence. A competent source is not only one who is in a position to make an observation, but is also able to understand what he has observed [51]. Credibility and competence are not the same [51]: "Not all credible persons are competent, and not all competent persons are credible."

It is also important to recognize that an individual's veracity, objectivity, and sensitivity are context dependent. A source may be more truthful about some matters than others. Objectivity and sensitivity are likely to depend on circumstances as well. For example, psychological factors undoubtedly play a role in objectivity while sensitivity is affected by physical conditions. Time is also a factor that must always be kept in mind. People change over time. A source that has been truthful in the past may not necessarily remain so in the future. A source's objectivity may change in one direction or another depending on the circumstances. Sensitivity changes with time as well; a person's physical capabilities such as vision or hearing may not be what they used to be. The effects of completely normal changes alone make source credibility an important factor to be considered in intelligence analysis even when deception is not a factor. Source credibility must be regularly evaluated and the more sensitive an issue becomes, the more vital it is to accurately assess the credibility of the sources being used.

When deception is a factor the importance of evaluating a source's credibility becomes even more critical. There are two main concerns that must be addressed from a counterdeception perspective. First and foremost is the possibility that a human source has been discovered and turned by a hostile intelligence service. This is critical since there is no doubt that the double agent is one of the most powerful information weapons in the deceiver's arsenal. The second concern involves the circumstances (context) under which the source obtained the information. Even in cases where it is extremely unlikely that a source is not a double agent, analysts must still consider whether or not the source is being manipulated. Perhaps a well-placed source has been discovered but the hostile service has decided not to arrest the individual. Doing so gives them two main options. They may decide to observe the source in order to learn information about the target's intelligence operations, or they may decide to manipulate the source in preparation of his use as a deception channel in the future. Another excellent example is the use of unwitting sources of unquestionable veracity to feed the target disinformation. The Germans routinely used this technique during their clandestine rearmament activities between World War I and World War II [52]. The observers' were completely honest about what they had seen and heard; however, the circumstances under which the information was obtained were clearly suspect.

In summary, the credibility of human sources must *never* be taken for granted. New sources must be evaluated in excruciating detail and existing sources, no matter how credible they are believed to be, must be critically reevaluated on a regular basis. If deception is considered to be a factor, such reevaluations must be given even higher priority (see Handel's suggestions related to agent reporting in Chapter 5).

Improve Human Reasoning

The second strategy for building the prepared mind is based on the counterdeception theme discussed in Chapter 5 that addresses the critical importance of human reasoning to counterdeception. The literature regarding human reasoning is large and diverse and trying to summarize all the possible approaches to improving reasoning would fill several books in itself. In this section we are going to narrowly limit our discussion to approaches that have the potential to make the mind less vulnerable to deception. The know yourself, know your adversary, and know your situation principles suggest the four interdependent substrategies shown in Figure 6.5: mitigate

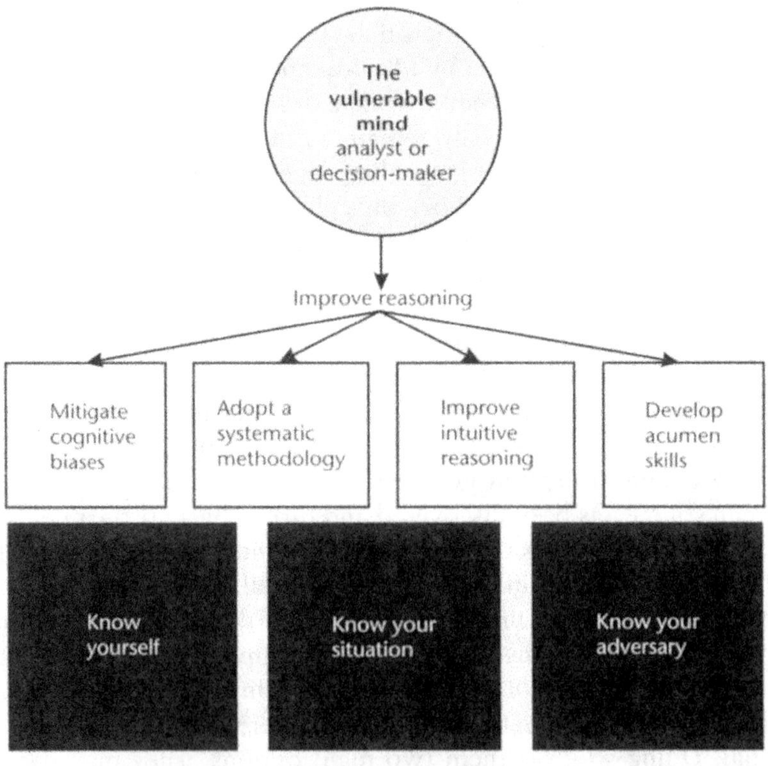

Figure 6.5 Substrategies for improving the vulnerable mind's reasoning and its relationship to counterdeception principles.

cognitive biases, adopt a systematic methodology, improve intuitive reasoning, and develop acumen skills.

Mitigating Bias

The know yourself principle emphasizes continuous awareness of the vulnerable mind's most exploitable weakness—its own preconceptions, expectations, and beliefs. From a counterdeception perspective, overcoming the behaviors associated with the too much from too little and seeing what we expect to see determinants of belief is a critical goal of any strategy for improving reasoning. In Chapter 3, Figure 3.6 showed that certain cognitive biases played a role in "selling" the vulnerable mind on the deceiver's deception story. The too much from too little determinant is related to errors in detecting covariation, confirmation bias, the effects of missing evidence, and overconfidence. Likewise, the seeing what we expect to see determinant is related to confirmation bias, overconfidence, the effect of multiple endpoints, belief persistence and polarization effects, and errors in prediction and explanation. Hardening the vulnerable mind requires mitigating the effects of those biases.

Fischhoff was one of the first heuristics and biases researchers to review the debiasing literature and propose a general framework of debiasing strategies [53]. His review addressed hindsight bias and overconfidence and focused primarily on debiasing during psychological experiments in the laboratory. In Fischhoff's framework, biases are attributed to one of four categories: faulty tasks, faulty judges, a mismatch between judges and tasks, and education. Each category is associated with a set of debiasing strategies that have appeared in the literature to address each category (see Figure 6.6). Arkes also provides a taxonomy of judgment and decision-making errors [55] that he groups into three categories: strategy-based errors, association-based errors, psychophysically-based errors, and training. Like Fischhoff, he also describes possible debiasing strategies (see Figure 6.6). Note that Fischhoff's framework and Arkes' taxonomy overlap. Fischhoff's "restructuring" debiasing strategy is clearly comparable to the strategies that address Arkes' association-based errors and both frameworks include education and training as a strategy. These frameworks and the nature of the cognitive biases associated with too much from too little and seeing what we expect to see suggest that the two most important debiasing strategies relevant to counterdeception are:

- Raising the cost of using suboptimal strategies;
- Restructuring the psychological nature of the task.

One of the most important strategy-based errors that contribute to the success of deception is the failure to generate adequate hypotheses [15]. This failure can be attributed to the suboptimal strategy of jumping to conclusions (choosing the first hypothesis that seems to be the closest fit to the evidence). Jumping to conclusions is also an example of an error in detecting covariation—people tend to focus exclusively on the present-present cell of the 2 × 2 covariation matrix. Although such quick and dirty strategies are easy to execute and may be effective under a wide range of circumstances, they are clearly suboptimal when deception is involved. Figure 6.6 shows that an effective debiasing strategy for these errors is to raise the cost

<table>
<tr><td>Fischhoff
Debiasing hindsight and overconfidence</td><td colspan="2">Arkes</td></tr>
<tr><td>Category
Subcategory
–Strategies for debiasing</td><td>Category</td><td>Strategy</td></tr>
<tr><td rowspan="4">Faulty tasks
Unfair tasks
–Raise stakes
–Clarify instructions/stimuli
–Discourage second guessing
–Use better response models
–Ask fewer questions
Misunderstood tasks
–Demonstrate alternative goal
–Demonstrate semantic disagreement
–Demonstrate impossibility of task
–Demonstrate overlooked distinction
Faulty judges
Perfectible individuals
–Warn of problem
–Describe problem
–Provide personalized feedback
–Train extensively
Incorrigible individuals
–Replace them
–Recalibrate their responses
–Plan on error
Mismatch between judges and task
Restructuring
–Make knowledge explicit
–Search for discrepant information
–Decompose problem
–Consider alternative solutions
–Offer alternative formulations
Education
–Rely on substantive experts
–Educate from childhood</td><td>Strategy-based errors
–For example, satisficing and covariation detection</td><td>• Raise cost of using suboptimal strategies.</td></tr>
<tr><td>Association-based errors
–Explanation bias
–Hindsight bias
–Ignoring P(D|¬H)
–Confirmation bias
–Pseudodiagnosticity
–Overconfidence
–Representativeness</td><td>• Instructions to perform a debiasing behavior
• Cueing a debiasing behavior</td></tr>
<tr><td>Psychophysically-based errors
–Errors related to prospect theory such as the sunk cost effect and the psychophysics of spending
–Errors related to framing effects like the reflection effect
–Anchoring</td><td>• Add new gains or losses to those currently under consideration.
• Change the concatenation of related items.
• Change one's reference point.
• Reframe losses as gains or gains as losses.</td></tr>
<tr><td colspan="2">Training</td></tr>
</table>

Figure 6.6 Summary of debiasing approaches.

of using the suboptimal strategy. Two such approaches typically appear in the literature in this regard. The first concerns the use of *incentives*, either rewards for accurate judgments or penalties for inaccurate ones. The second approach concerns ways of manipulating an individual's perception of *accountability* for his judgments and opinions.

Research shows that the use of incentives for reducing strategy-based errors produces mixed results. Camerer and Hogarth conducted an informal review of 74 studies involving the use of incentives and found that the effectiveness of financial incentives varies with the nature of the task [55]. Judgment tasks that respond to financial incentives include those that can be independently measured (e.g., response times) and where increased effort improves performance. Examples include memory or recall tasks, probability matching and muliticue probability learning tasks, and clerical tasks [55]. Incentives appear to have little or no effect on difficult tasks where sufficient intrinsic motivation already exists, additional effort is seen not to matter, or where the incentive schedule is flat. Finally, incentives can actually have a negative effect on task performance when they cause people to overlearn a problem-solving heuristic, overreact to feedback, or exert effort out of proportion the task required, when arousal caused by incentives raises self-consciousness.

Are incentives likely to be an effective means for generating more hypotheses rather than jumping to a conclusion? The studies that Camerer and Hogarth reviewed were organized into two main categories: *judgments and decisions* and *games and markets*. The task of generating hypotheses falls into the judgments and decision category as a *problem-solving* task. Four of the studies that Camerer and Hogarth reviewed involved problem solving and they found that incentives improved the mean performance in two of the experiments but failed to improve the subjects' performance in the other two experiments. In one study involving easy problem solving, incentives produced faster solutions, more solutions, and faster word recognition. On the other hand, another study involving a difficult problem requiring insight (the Duncker candle problem) and the recognition of familiar and unfamiliar words produced the exact opposite effect (i.e., slower discovery of solutions, fewer solutions, and slower word recognition). These results suggest that incentives may not be the most effective means of deterring the use of suboptimal strategies when generating additional hypotheses. Additional research examining the use of incentives in realistic intelligence analysis situations would be of tremendous value from both a theoretical and practical perspective.

The other approach that can be used to raise the cost of using suboptimal strategies is *accountability*. Accountability is a fact of life. In our informal interactions with other people we routinely consider how others will react to what we say and do. We also talk of accountability in more formal situations when we hold business leaders and politicians accountable for their actions or statements. Socially, it acts as a mechanism for enforcing societal norms and the failure to act appropriately can result in varying degrees of censure [56]. Tetlock's social contingency model (SCM) predicts that accountability to audiences with unknown views triggers preemptive self-criticism in which the individual tries to anticipate any possible objections the audience might raise to the judgment or decision being under consideration [57]. Under SCM this is an adaptive strategy to protect both the individual's self-image and social image.

In order to be effective, the individual should perceive an evaluative audience with unknown views to be well informed (making it unlikely that they can be duped) as well as powerful (approval is good and might lead to reward; disapproval is bad and might lead to censure). In addition, the individual should not feel constrained by prior commitments that would be embarrassing to reverse; otherwise, the preemptive self-criticism turns instead into self-justifying defensive bolstering. Such *predecisional* accountability has been found to increase the complexity of argumentation [58, 59], improve the accuracy of probabilistic predictions (calibration) [60], reduce biases due to anchoring [61], and to reduce illusory correlations and improve the accuracy of covariation assessments [62]. Accountability has also been found to be effective at mitigating biases of primacy (the tendency to remember the pieces of evidence a person is first exposed to more than evidence that is received later), overattribution (fundamental attribution error), and overconfidence when individuals learn of being accountable *prior to* their exposure to the evidence on which they are to base their judgments [60, 63, 64]. In this situation accountability promotes a more self-critical approach that makes people more cautious about drawing conclusions from incomplete or fragmentary evidence, more willing to revise preliminary conclusions in response to unexpected feedback, and less likely to be swayed by the last most memorable items of evidence presented [65].

On the minus side, the self-criticism triggered by accountability can also amplify bias. These biases [66] result "from trying too hard to integrate irrelevant considerations into one's mental representation of the problem." *Trying too hard* can produce a variety of results including ambiguity aversion and effects related to compromise (choosing the middle option), attraction (the tendency to choose a dominant option because it might be less vulnerable to criticism), dilution (the tendency for nondiagnostic evidence to dilute the power of diagnostic evidence), and the status quo (the status quo option holds a privileged position forcing other options to be held to a higher standard of proof).

Research results that show predecisional accountability can mitigate important cognitive biases linked to deception is encouraging. Accountability makes social expectations clear and signals the person that evidence should be processed in more self-critical and thoughtful ways such as considering a wider array of evidence or arguments, paying closer attention to the evidence used, anticipating possible counterarguments, and impartially evaluating one's own analytical strengths. Accountability obviously already plays a role in intelligence analysis, policymaking, and decision-making in the form of review and coordination processes; however, the research also suggests that, like incentives, its effects are mixed and in many situations can aggravate error and biases in judgment. Nevertheless, this seems to be an extremely promising area for further research with real potential towards further development of the prepared mind.

If the failure to generate adequate hypotheses is the most important strategy-based error, than confirmation bias and overconfidence are probably the most important association-based errors contributing to the target's vulnerability. The second debiasing strategy, *restructuring the task*, is aimed at upsetting the mindsets that make confirmation bias so pernicious. Several methods of restructuring the analytical task can be found in the literature. *Counterfactual primes* have been found to make it significantly more likely that a small group will make a correct decision and that they would also be more likely to seek disconfirming information [67]. Asking individuals to list reasons why their answers to questions might be wrong has been found to reduce overconfidence [68]. Several researchers have shown that instructions to *consider the opposite* are a useful debiasing technique that works for a variety of biases such as overconfidence, hindsight bias, and confirmation bias [69].

Hirt, Kards, and Markman found that encouraging individuals to *generate multiple alternatives*, or even being asked to explain a single plausible alternative, tended to debias judgments if the generation of alternatives was experienced as easy [70]. Their experiments also produced another interesting finding that showed that this debiasing could be generalized to other knowledge domains depending on the individuals need for structure (NFS). They found that [71]: "Low NFS individuals indeed adopt a simulation mind-set, showing evidence of generalized tendency to spontaneously consider alternative possibilities in a variety of domains. Conversely, high NFS individuals showed no evidence of considering additional alternatives in the same domain much less the ability to transfer those effects to other domains, suggesting that these procedures fail to evoke a simulation mind-set in these individuals." This finding suggests that low NFS individuals might be better at counterdeception than their high NFS counterparts.

In a related article, Hirt and Markman found that giving individuals a *counterexplanation* task was also an effective debiasing method [72]. Asking individuals to consider the opposite is one form of counterexplanation task, but what Hirt and Markman discovered was that asking individuals to engage in *any* second explanation task (e.g., explaining a different version of the same outcome) is sufficient to debias their judgments. They also discovered that the greater the perceived plausibility of an alternative, the greater the debiasing effect. This result suggests that asking individuals to explain highly implausible alternatives would be less effective as a debiasing technique.

Finally, Klein [73] lists some additional practical techniques for breaking mindsets that fall into the restructuring category of strategies for mitigating bias. These include:

- *Test for fixation:* This involves considering what evidence would be required to convince yourself that your interpretation is wrong, change your mind, or to give up your opinion.
- *Assess how far you have bent the map:* In many situations there will be a considerable amount of evidence that is inconsistent with what is believed to be true. Confirmation bias often involves explaining such evidence away (i.e., "bending the map" to fit the evidence). Monitoring the inconsistencies and discrepancies you have explained away provides an indication that you are ignoring other possibilities.
- *Tripwires:* These are events that should not be occurring or levels that should not be exceeded if your hypothesis is correct. If too many tripwires are tripped, it could be an indication that your hypothesis is wrong.

Methodology

A methodology is nothing more than the methods, rules, and postulates that a discipline such as science, medicine, or engineering use in order to accomplish something. The term usually implies that the methodology is employed systematically and consistently by all members of the discipline. Science is the discipline that is probably recognized the most for its use of a systematic methodology, the well-known scientific method [74]. The use of a methodology as a substrategy for improving the reasoning of the vulnerable mind is driven by two of our counterdeception principles. First, the know yourself principle emphasizes recognizing the assumptions, preconceptions, and expectations that influence beliefs and using a methodology is a way to capture and test them. Second, the know your situation principle focuses on continually evaluating the environment for the cues that indicate deception is likely to be a factor in any given situation under consideration. A sound methodology helps to reduce the likelihood that important cues are not ignored or overlooked.

In science, the scientific method is used to construct an accurate, consistent, and nonarbitrary representation of not only our world but the universe as a whole [75]. The engineering disciplines apply scientific and mathematical principles using systematic and consistent principles, methods, and practices to create things. In medicine, doctors employ diagnostic methods that are generally both systematic and consistent as well. So it may come as a surprise to those not intimately familiar with the subject of intelligence that intelligence analysts do not employ any specific formal analytical methodology. In fact, in his ethnography of the U.S. intelligence community, Johnston observes that [76]: "The idea that intelligence analysis is a collection of scientific methods encounters some resistance in the Intelligence Community. The interview data analyzed in this study highlight many subtle—and not so subtle—prejudices that analysis is not a science. That is, it is an art or craft in which one can attain skill but not a formal discipline with tested and validated methodology." Instead, the U.S. intelligence community uses the term "tradecraft" to refer to its methods of analysis, a term [77] that "implies a mysterious process learned only by the initiated and acquired only through the elaborate rituals of professional indoctrination." In fact, the U.S. intelligence community has been criticized for its failure to employ a rigorous method of analysis [78, 79]. Just what methodology is appropriate to the discipline of intelligence analysis is an important issue that the intelligence community will have to address; however, our purpose here is to identify those methodological issues that play an important role in reducing one's vulnerability to deception.

In Chapter 3 we examined how a wide range of biases—cultural, personal, organization, and cognitive—contributed to our vulnerability to deception. Earlier in this chapter we examined possible approaches to mitigating cognitive biases. The use of a systematic and consistent analytical methodology provides another strategy for minimizing the influence of biases on the analyst when making judgments. It is another way of psychologically restructuring problems so that assumptions, preconceptions, and mental models are not taken for granted but are made explicit so that they can be examined and tested. Gilovich asserts that this is what distinguishes formal science from informal everyday life [80]: "The biggest difference between the world of science and everyday life in protecting against erroneous beliefs is that scientists utilize a set of formal procedures to guard against the sources of bias and error discussed in this book—a set of procedures of which the average person is insufficiently aware, and has not adequately adopted in daily life."

There is presently widespread attention in the U.S. intelligence community on Richards Heuer's alternative competing hypotheses (ACH) technique (described briefly in Chapter 5) which addresses the failure to generate adequate hypotheses that might account for the evidence. As we saw earlier this is a strategy-based error that results from the adaptational success of various cognitive heuristics. Quite simply, the success of these heuristics has resulted in the reinforcement of mental bad habits. Formal methods of analysis are powerful strategies for instilling better habits of thinking. As Gilovich writes [81]: "Perhaps the most general and most important mental habit to instill is an appreciation of the folly of trying to draw conclusions from incomplete and unrepresentative evidence." It is perfectly natural to jump to conclusions; however, it takes real effort to go further and generate additional hypotheses and evaluate the weight, strength, and discriminability of the evidence on hand against those hypotheses. ACH is representative of many useful analytical methods and techniques that can make this process easier. And if it is easier, it is more likely to be done.

It takes even more effort to overcome another bad mental habit that affects the mind's vulnerability to deception—persistence of belief. In their discussion on biased searching, recollection, and assimilation, Ross and Anderson write [82]: "The critical assumption here is that people do not constantly update or revaluate the evidence relevant to their beliefs. They do not commonly decide 'now that my prior hypothesis has been undermined somewhat I must go back and reassess all the evidence that I ever considered in the light of that hypothesis.'" The mental habits formed by the use of formal analytical methods help make going back and reassessing all that evidence easier. As we pointed out earlier, if it is easier it is more likely to become a habit. Mental habits like these just might be the factor that determines whether or not the deceiver's deception succeeds or fails.

Howver, the value of a sound methodology goes further than just instilling good analytical habits. One of the strengths of the scientific method is that it requires that the possible outcomes of a hypothesis be made explicit. There are numerous examples of this in theoretical physics (e.g., the discovery of gravitational lenses as predicted by Einstein's general theory of relativity). Explicitly specifying the expected outcomes of a hypothesis makes it more difficult to interpret ambiguous results as supportive of the most popular hypotheses or to discard discrepant evidence. Unfortunately, as Gilovich points out, this is a mental habit that is not often used outside of science [80]: "This kind of precise specification of what constitutes 'success' and 'failure' is something we rarely do in everyday life, and consequently our preconceptions often lead us to interpret the meaning of various outcomes in ways that favor our initial expectations."

Finally, a systematic methodology like the scientific method offers the prospect that a discovery or conclusion can be verified through *replicability*. In science, replicability means that other researchers can perform the same experiment in order to determine if they get the same results and it is the key to the validity and credibility of research results. We suggest that, in the context of intelligence analysis and counterdeception, replicability has a similar meaning. In other words, the assumptions, evidence, and methodology used by one analyst to expose or penetrate an adversary's deception could be examined by any other qualified analyst and that person would either likely come to the same conclusion or would be in a position to find some flaw in the assumptions, evidence, or methodology that might suggest an alternative interpretation.

Improving Intuition

Rule-based (System 2) forms of reasoning that employ critical thinking skills and formal analytical methods play an important role in building the prepared mind; however, we cannot ignore the important role that associative (System 1) cognitive processes play as well. Cognitive functions like fantasy, creativity, imagination, visual recognition, associative memory, and intuition are all representative of the operation of System 1 processes [83]. The two systems both overlap and interact therefore we must consider that *both* will be used when assessing a situation (know your situation) or an adversary (know your adversary).

Intuition is the power or faculty of attaining to direct knowledge or cognition without evident rational thought and inference [84]. This is characteristic of System 1 processes since we are only aware of the result and not the process by which we obtained the result, (e.g., the "Aha!" experience). Since both processes simultaneously try to solve a problem, there are times when intuition out performs the more deliberative and analytical System 2 and times when it does not. The history of scientific discovery is replete with examples of the former. Henri Poincaré recognized the role that both systems played in mathematical research when he wrote [85], "C'est par la logique que nous prouvons, c'est par l'intuition que nous inventons." This is usually translated as: "It is by logic that we prove, but by intuition that we discover." However, since intuition is also wrong at times, a fact that is also well known among scientists, the fact that both systems must work together in order to produce sound judgments needs to be reinforced as well. Hogarth calls this making the scientific method intuitive, that is, educating people's intuitive learning processes so that they are more closely aligned with the scientific method [86].

Intuition plays much the same role in counterdeception as it does in science. It helps the prepared mind to see the significance of anomalies, discern patterns and relationships, and discover previously unidentified options (the "third way"). It is an integral part of the *awareness* and *detection and exposure* dimensions of counterdeception introduced in Chapter 5 and it is an important factor in mitigating the natural tendency to accept a good story (leading to errors in believing what we are told). Maybe something about the story is too good to be true; information seems to fall too neatly into a pattern that excludes other possible courses of action. This possibility is captured in one of Handel's paradoxes [87]: "Under certain circumstances, *the more perfectly an intelligence puzzle fits together, the greater the danger of a possible deception play.*" Grabo also weighs in on the topic with [88]: "Too many facts or indications may even be suspect—why should it be so obvious? There must be something more (or less) than meets the eye." Finally, perhaps collecting the evidence has been a bit too easy (e.g., the Meinertzhagen "Haversack Ruse"); the evidence is surprisingly unambiguous and little contradictory evidence is to be found. In such cases, it is likely to be intuition that sets off alarms in an analyst's mind in response to cues from the environment.

The role intuition plays in the detection and exposure dimension is related to its power to discern patterns, connections and relationships, and new ways of seeing the situation. Schum provides a good example of this power with his description of the role that *trifles* play in discovery. Trifles are data; at the moment they are observed there is no way of knowing yet whether or not they will become evidence (i.e., data relevant to a hypothesis) [89]. Trifles are also the underpinning for the success of the greatest intuitive detective of all time, Sherlock Holmes, who explains to Watson [90]: "You know my method. It is founded upon the observance of trifles." Intuition is the process by which trifles are recognized for their significance and by which hypotheses are formed, new relationships revealed, and new patterns recognized. In the context of counterdeception, the ability to put the trifles together intuitively is vital to recognizing that deception should be considered a possibility in a situation. Grabo captured the importance of trifles when she wrote [91]: "Events which appeared to have no relationship at the time they were reported may suddenly assume a meaningful pattern," and again with [92]: "In these circumstances, many seemingly unrelated things really do have relevance to the situation—if not directly, then indirectly. They are part of an atmosphere; they contribute to the sense of unease that things are not right or normal, and that something big is brewing." Until science and technology can deliver systems that can effectively recognize environmental cues and make meaningful connections between trifles, human intuition will be continue to be called on to discover them.

However, since intuition is not infallible, this leads to the question of how it can be improved. Hogarth [93] proposes seven guidelines for education intuition:

- *Select and/or create your environments.* Effective intuitive learning requires a learning environment that features immediate and unambiguous feedback. Educating intuition involves actively seeking to create an appropriate learning environment whenever possible.
- *Seek feedback.* If the environment is not conducive to effective intuitive learning then it is important to actively and systematically search for feedback in order to test the connections, ideas, and hypotheses that are generated by automatic, System 1 processes.
- *Impose circuit breakers.* "Circuit breakers" are Hogarth's term for the deliberate effort to interrupt automatic, tacit cognitive processes (e.g., stopping to think twice before deciding).
- *Acknowledge emotions.* Emotions are a natural part of human behavior and affect decision-making and judgment. Listening to one's emotions (i.e., treating them as data) provides information that must be taken into account when relying on intuition.
- *Explore connections.* As we saw in Chapter 3, the tacit cognitive system is particularly sensitive to the use of narrative stories. Instead of simply accepting the terms in which a problem is explicitly stated, this guideline emphasizes leveraging that sensitivity and the give imagination free rein in order to discover new connections.
- *Accept conflict in choice.* Conflict avoidance is often a characteristic of problem solving. The effortless use of tacit, System 1 processes means that decisions requiring the assessment of trade-offs may not receive the deliberative attention needed to make a sound judgment. The use of a circuit breaker question like "What are the trade-offs?" can ensure that conflict is accepted, not avoided.
- *Make scientific method intuitive.* As mentioned earlier, Hogarth advocates training and practice in the scientific method as a means of making those methods more habitual and automatic.

Building the prepared mind requires integrating both associative (System 1) and rule-based (System 2) reasoning processes as well as making them more effective. Making intuition more effective is primarily a process of building expertise through disciplined experiential learning. Such an approach means hard work for both the individual and the organization. Psychologist Gary Klein describes it as [94]: "... continually challenging yourself to make tough judgments, honestly appraising those judgments to learn from the consequences, actively building up an experience base, and learning to blend intuitions with analyses."

Improving Acumen

Over 20 years ago, narrative psychologist Theodore Sarbin summarized the central issue facing the counterdeception analyst [95]: "The basic problem for the strategist and for the analyst of strategy, including deception analysts, centers on the ability to predict the actions of an adversary." As we saw in the previous chapter, Sarbin argued that, given that strategic deception represents a series of unique cases, analysts cannot rely on *sagacity* (making predictions based on knowledge of the characteristics of a class) alone to predict the actions of a deceiver. Instead, he suggested that predicting the actions of an adversary in unique situations required *acumen*—the emphatic skill that gives one the ability to see the situation from the other person's perspective.

The dictionary definition of acumen describes it as [96] "keenness and depth of perception, discernment, or discrimination especially in practical matters." Sarbin on the other hand clearly identifies it with concepts such as empathy, Einfuhling, and social intelligence. Taking the two together (i.e., *empathic* keenness and depth of perception, discernment, or discrimination) is what makes acumen so relevant to the know your adversary principle. Our proposition is that the development of acumen is an essential step towards mitigating the vulnerabilities to deception that arise from ethnocentric biases—biases that have played a role in so many cases of strategic surprise and deception. How then can acumen be acquired and how do you assess one's competence?

Developing acumen goes well beyond classroom cultural awareness training. Cultural awareness, or cross-cultural training, is big business and multinational companies spend millions of dollars a year in order to be more competitive in global markets. Much of this training focuses mostly on basic dos and don'ts and provides only the minimal level of cultural competence (see Stage 1 in Figure 6.7) that employees might need when going on business trips overseas. More sophisticated programs focus on employees assigned to jobs requiring them to live overseas for extended periods of time. Training programs alone, even when they include language instruction, are insufficient to develop acumen to the level needed for dealing with counterdeception. As Hall points out [97], "Since culture is learned, it also seemed clear that one should be able to teach it. Yet in the past there had been singularly little success in this regard with the important exception of language, one of the dominant threads in all cultures. The answer to this question is rooted in understanding the difference between acquisition and learning. Most of culture is acquired and therefore cannot be taught." What is needed for that level of acumen is *acculturation*, not training, in order to build cultural competence up to the highest levels (see Stage 4 in Figure 6.7).

When it comes to acculturation, most theorists and educators dealing with cross-cultural issues would likely agree that long-term immersion in a foreign culture is essential. For example, Hall writes [98], "Understanding the reality of covert culture and accepting it on a gut level comes neither quickly nor easily, and it must be lived rather than read or reasoned." As Johnston points out, travel consisting of short trips is not enough [99]: "Living in a foreign region, speaking the language,

	Empathy	Ability to observe and analyze a culture	Communication in cultural context
Stage 1	• Is curious about similarities and differences between the home and the target culture • Shows willingness to understand the differences encountered	• Can give examples of the relationship between language and culture • Can identify a few characteristics of the target cultural as cultural patterns • Can identify a few common cultural differences between home and target cultures • **Can identify some commonly held images of the target culture as stereotypes**	• Knows what verbal behavior is appropriate in different greeting and leave-taking routines • Knows that there are familiar and polite forms of address • Recognizes some easily interpreted gestures • Is aware of differences in demeanor in formal and informal social settings
Stage 2	• Is tolerant of differences between the home and target culture • Is open and accepting of different peoples • Recognizes the depth and complexity of cultural differences • Shows an active interest in the search for understanding of the target culture	• **Can demonstrate understanding that cultural values, patterns, and institutions cannot be used to predict the behavior of all individuals** • **Can give examples of one observer's own cultural biases interfering with understanding of the target culture** • Can give an example of how cultures change over time • Can discuss ways in which cultural norms and values are transmitted	• Uses appropriate titles of address and formula in survival-level situations • Can use familiar and polite forms of address appropriately • Demonstrates knowledge of some common formulas used in communications • Is aware of the difference in conversational distance in the home and target cultures
Stage 3	• Is aware of the problem of accepting the norms of another culture while maintaining one's own values and identity • Shows fairmindedness and tolerance in trying to solve an embarrassing situation or a cross-cultural conflict • Can adjust behavior and conversation according to the situational context and to the expectations of participants	• Can give examples of social behaviors that express the target culture's underlying value system • **Can describe and explain important elements of major institutions in the target culture** • **Can interpret social phenomena within the context of the target culture** • **Can describe several instances of major change within the target culture** • **Can describe some major forces that influence culture and cultural change**	• Can express attitudes towards people, taking into account social context • Has some knowledge of regional variations in the target language • Can interpret some common target culture gestures not used in the home culture • Can establish and maintain appropriate distance in conversations with individuals of the target culture
Stage 4	• **Recognizes the importance of understanding manifestations of the target culture in terms of its own context** • **Is aware of his/her own cultural perspective and of how this perspective influences one's perceptions of phenomena** • Can act and react in a culturally appropriate way while being aware of his/her "otherness"	• **Recognizes that a culture is not uniform and can identify the principal subcultures of the target culture** • **Can critique phenomena of the target culture with a minimum of bias** • **Can interpret social phenomena at several layers of generalization** • **Can describe the multifaceted character of sociocultural phenomena**	• Is able to function in a wide range of social and professional contexts • **Can understand and explain humor or irony in a cultural context** • Can use target culture typical gestures and sounds • Understands some current physical gestures that accompany or evoke colloquialisms

Figure 6.7 Indicators of cultural competence.

interacting with the people, developing community ties, and establishing an identity with that community are all part of the acculturation process and allow one to alter the cognitive filters through which one interprets the world. Time spent on a US military base, in a US embassy, or in a Western hotel overseas does not lead to acculturation." Obviously, long-term immersion is costly and difficult to implement for a large population of intelligence analysts, policy makers, and decision makers. Nevertheless, if intelligence analysts are expected to develop the acumen skills expected of them (see the bold items in Figure 6.7 for examples), serious consideration must be given to investing the time and resources necessary to begin the process. Potentially good news is found in at least one practical "experiment" showing that a well-designed two-month immersion program, including both preimmersion and postimmersion activities, has been found to increase cross-cultural sensitivity [100].

Learning the target culture's language, both speaking and writing, is vital to acculturation since culture and language are inseparable. In addition, it is hard to picture how a cultural immersion program could be successful if the participants were not sufficiently proficient in the language (the students in the experiment mentioned above all had *intermediate high* or *superior* language skills). Moore et al. recognize the importance of foreign language proficiency in the context of intelligence analysis and make it one of the eight skill types that they believe are necessary for intelligence analysts to possess. They write [101]: "Foreign language proficiency yields unique cultural and societal insights that reveal intentions of individuals and the groups in which they act. These are not available to the non-linguist, for they are often implied with language used for other purposes. Lacking a tangible for, they reveal themselves through 'hunches' the linguist may have in concert with other analyzed evidence." Like cultural immersion programs, language programs are also expensive and time consuming; but, once again, serious consideration must be given to making those investments if analytical acumen is to be improved.

Finally, the acculturation process starts with a concerted effort to learn about the target culture. Such learning is an important part of pre-immersion preparation in order to provide a sense of history and context and to help minimize culture shock. Classroom instruction plays an important role in such learning and can provide a setting for important activities such as group discussions and role-playing. Nevertheless, much of the learning effort requires continuous self-study. Such study involves a lot of reading—books, magazines, newspapers, and the Internet—supplemented with multimedia materials like movies and computer-based training where available. In-depth knowledge of the target culture is also linked to literacy for some languages (e.g., Chinese) [102]. Likewise, developing in-depth knowledge of a culture requires literacy and fluency in order to read and listen to materials in the original language. Once again, significant effort is required to develop the acumen skills of the prepared mind but such skills cannot be ignored if the know your adversary principle is to be followed.

When taken as a whole, a program for putting these strategies and substrategies into effect requires a tremendous commitment of both individual and organizational resources. In addition, it is clear that significant cultural change will be required as well. At the individual level, a program for developing a mind that is less vulnerable to deception's effects will require:

- Extensive education in a wide variety of areas—critical thinking, history and culture, doctrine, personalities, and even statistical techniques;
- Exhaustive research using systematic methodologies and techniques;
- Constant practice and feedback to improve intuition;
- Accountability for the quality of one's analytical processes whether deliberative or intuitive.

The ultimate goal of such a program is to transform the vulnerable mind into the prepared mind (see Figure 6.8). Where the vulnerable mind overconfidently sees reality according to its own preconceptions and expectations, the prepared mind continually tests and retests its judgments, updates and evaluates all the evidence at hand, and is alert to cues and anomalies in the environment that something is not right, has changed, or is missing. Where the vulnerable mind is unduly influenced by a good story, the prepared mind diligently updates and evaluates the credibility of information sources and does not ignore its intuition when it signals that something doesn't quite feel right about the situation and the story. Where the vulnerable mind lacks in-depth knowledge of the adversary, the prepared mind makes a conscientious effort to see the problem or situation from the adversary's point of view. The four substrategies we have discussed are aimed at putting the analyst in a proper state of mind, literally preparing him, to better deal with the deceiver's efforts to manipulate his perceptions.

At the beginning of this chapter we described the characteristics of the vulnerable mind. The strategies and substrategies that we have presented are no guarantee that deception can be reliably detected and countered. Grabo acknowledges this fact with respect to the warning problem when she writes [103]: "Nothing is going to remove the uncertainties of the warning problem. There is no way, short of being able to read the adversary's mind, that we can be confident that our warning judgments, or even many of our 'facts,' are going to be correct. Even the finest collection

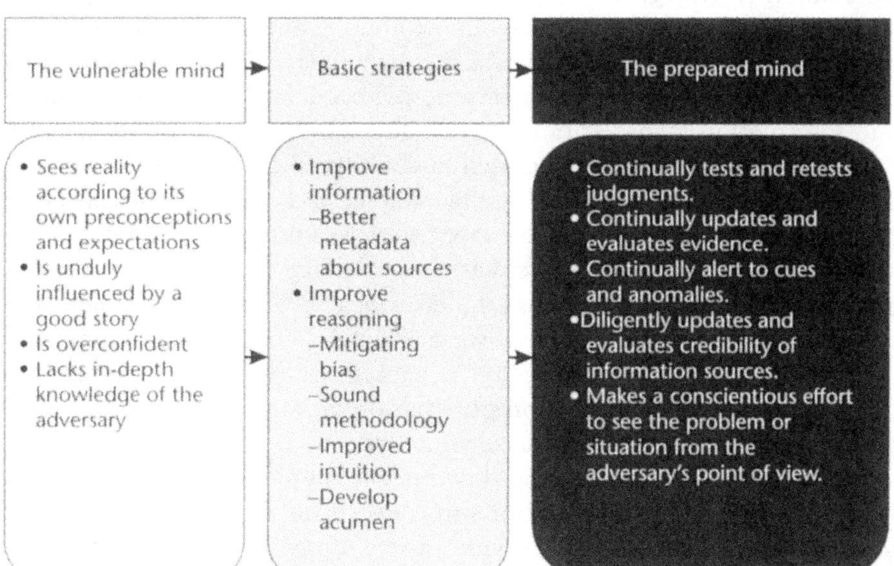

Figure 6.8 Characteristics of the prepared mind.

and analysis cannot insure that we will have accurate insight into the enemy's intentions....As we have been surprised in the past, we shall be surprised again in the future." We could easily substitute "deception" for "warning" in this quote—we have been deceived in the past and shall be deceived again in the future. Nevertheless, the strategies for building the prepared mind are analogous to those of preventive medicine. Prevention can reduce the likelihood of infection and can often reduce the severity of the diseases effects. Likewise, ensuring that the mind is prepared as it can be makes deception less certain for the adversary and can go a long way to containing the effects of deception when it is a factor.

6.2.2 Building the Prepared Organization

We introduce this section by acknowledging that other authors with greater experience in the matters of intelligence and policy than ourselves have written extensively on the topic of intelligence reform. Much of their work is highly relevant to the challenge of counterdeception and they offer a variety of specific recommendations for change. Our intent in this section is not to go over that same ground but instead to focus on key organizational cultural and process issues that are relevant to the success or failure of any systematic counterdeception effort. Also, since it is the people in the organizations, not the organizations themselves that do the analysis, form the judgments, make the decisions, and take action, we want to emphasize what it is that organizations can do to enable those people—those prepared minds—that are so essential to making the organization itself less vulnerable to deception.

6.2.2.1 Fostering a Culture of Mindfulness: A Strategy for Building the Prepared Organization

We start as we did in Section 6.2.1.1 with a simple model (see Figure 6.9) that corresponds roughly to the target side of our model of deception shown in Figure 2.13. In the context of strategic deception, the large triangle in Figure 6.9 represents a nation state made up of its various civilian, military, and intelligence departments and agencies (the small gray triangles). Like the vulnerable mind, the vulnerable organization ingests ambiguous, inconsistent, contradictory, and possibly deceptive data and information from various sources through its collection organizations. These data and information are processed and analyzed by various organizations and in the process can undergo considerable change. For example, it can be delayed, its content filtered, its importance exaggerated or minimized, and it can be shared or withheld. Once it reaches the country's leadership at the peak of the triangle, it is compared with information that the decision makers obtain on their own. And, as we saw in Chapter 2, if the deceiver has done a good job designing the deception story, the organizational biases that characterize the vulnerable organization will reinforce the effect the deception story has on the target and thereby help to produce the decisions and actions the deceiver desires.

It is easy to become bogged down in the myriad details associated with transforming a vulnerable organization into a deception-resistant one. Decades of intelligence reform literature reveal a wide variety of recommendations that focus mainly on redrawing Figure 6.9 [104]. There are recommendations for adding, combining,

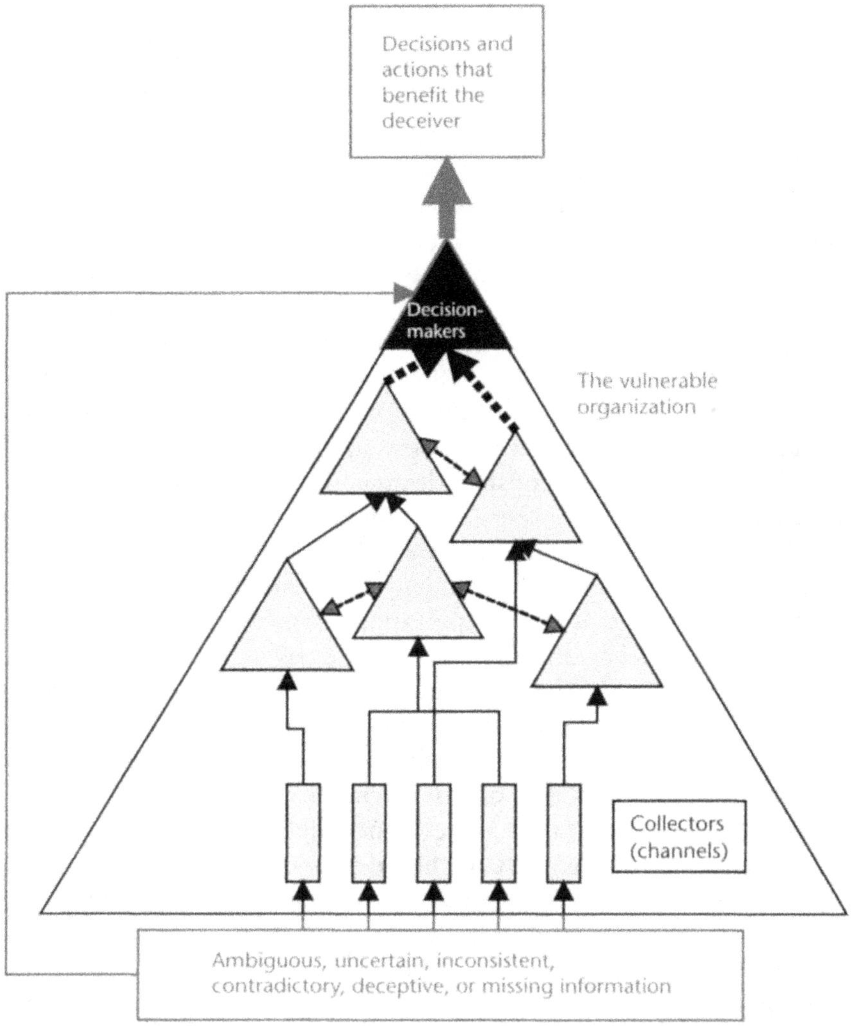

Figure 6.9 Vulnerable organizations produce decisions and take actions that benefit the deceiver.

or reorganizing the small triangles, changing how they interact (the gray dotted lines), reorganizing how data and information are collected (the rectangles), and how information should flow to and from the top of the triangle. There are also recommendations for changing the processes within the triangles themselves (e.g., workforce training, the information technology infrastructure, and the use of analytical tools). Instead of attempting to wade through all the various ideas looking for those that are applicable to counterdeception, what we would like to propose instead is an overarching strategy to guide the development of the prepared organization—a strategy within which those charged with reform could evaluate the various ideas for change in the context of the counterdeception dimensions discussed in Chapter 5. If the goal is to transform the vulnerable organization into the prepared organization, then we propose that the overall strategy for doing this is to *create a culture of mindfulness* at all levels across the organization.

The concept of mindfulness is the work of Dr. Ellen Langer at Harvard University and consists of three key qualities: the creation of new categories, openness to new information, and an awareness of more than one perspective [105]. Weick and Sutcliffe have built upon this concept in their studies of how people organize to achieve high performance in settings with high potential for error and catastrophic results such as nuclear aircraft carrier operations, air traffic control systems, nuclear power generation, and firefighting organizations. What they found was that the best of these high reliability organizations (HROs) rarely failed even though they are responsible for the operation of highly complex systems, which tend to encounter an excess of unexpected events in their operational environments. They attribute the success of these organizations [106] to "their determined efforts to act *mindfully.*" The concept of acting mindfully is very relevant to counterdeception since the problems posed by deception are very similar to those faced by HROs.

Weick and Sutcliffe consider dealing with the unexpected to be one of the greatest challenges any business organization must face [107]. Such unexpected events do not have to take the form of a major crisis. Instead, the problems caused by unexpected events tend to unfold gradually over time with the result that people take too long to recognize that their expectations about a situation are being violated and that a problem is becoming worse [108]. Early signals of the unexpected, little surprises are uncomfortable and are ignored or explained away. By the time that people belatedly discover that the unexpected is unfolding, it is too late and the situation quickly spins out of control. This should sound very familiar. As we saw in Chapter 2, a good deception story is closely aligned with the target's expectations. The story gradually unfolds over time and evidence that disconfirms the deception story—the unexpected—tends to be fit to the target's expectations, explained away, or just ignored. By the time analysts or decision-makers recognize they have been deceived, it is too late to take any effective action. The consequences are usually severe.

What does it mean to act mindfully? In the context of HROs, it involves: (1) organizing in a way that allows the organization to quickly recognize the "unexpected in the making and halt its development"; (2) if the development of the unexpected cannot be stopped, the focus switches to containing it; and (3) if containment fails, the focus emphasizes resilience and the rapid restoration of system functioning [106]. The first step obviously offers the greatest leverage for dealing with the unexpected since a strong response to the weak signals given off early in the process is more likely to prevent the problem from going out of control. Likewise, acting mindfully means much the same for the prepared organization dealing with deception. Since successful deceptions depend heavily on the target's expectations, the prepared organization must quickly recognize the unexpected (recall Whaley's incongruities we described in Chapter 5) and respond to it rather than ignore it or explain it away. In a similar manner, the prepared organization takes immediate action to mitigate or negate (contain) the deception plan's impact. This can be done in a variety of ways including tasking additional collection assets, reviewing counterespionage and counterintelligence files in order to revalidate the credibility of key sources, or even launching counterdeception operations. The earlier this is started, the more effective the deception countermeasures are likely to be.

Finally, there is the issue of resilience. HROs know that no system is perfect and actively develop capabilities that allow them to "bounce back" when the inevitable occurs [109]. Although resilience goes beyond the scope of a book on counterdeception, it is an idea that does not seem to receive much attention in intelligence reform circles. In fact, perhaps the most effective counterdeception strategy does not depend on detecting the adversary's deception, but instead ensures that if the deceiver succeeds, his plan achieves only a tactical success, not a strategic one. Grabo addressed this point in her book *Anticipating Surprise* [110]: "Finally—more for policymakers and commanders—the best defense of all against the enemy's deception plan may be the alerting and preparedness of one's own forces. If these are ready for the possibility of attack, no matter how unlikely that may seem, the enemy's efforts may be largely foiled even though his operations itself is really not anticipated. In other words, it is possible to be politically or psychologically surprised, and at the same time be militarily prepared."

The Weick and Sutcliffe description of mindfulness in high reliability organizations is a rich and complex one but at its core is a focus on expectations. In fact, Weick and Sutcliffe introduce their section on the "idea of mindfulness" with a summary of the importance of expectations [111]: "Expectations act like an invisible hand that guides you toward soothing perceptions that confirm your hunches, and away from more troublesome ones that don't. But it is these very same troublesome perceptions that foreshadow surprises, the unexpected and tougher problems. If you depend too much on a simple set of expectations, unusual events can develop to more serious levels before you even notice them." Mindfulness involves the continuous updating of expectations in order to create a more complete and nuanced interpretation of what the situation is and the problems that define it [106]. This concept of mindfulness neatly captures the spirit of our know yourself and know your situation counterdeception principles. The know yourself principle emphasizes awareness of one's own expectations, while the know your situation principle focuses on the necessity for continually evaluating the environment for the cues that those expectations may have changed.

Creating a state of mindfulness in the prepared organization depends on fostering cultural change but such change is difficult and dangerous. As Robbins points out [112], "A reorg can be done on paper in an afternoon. But changing just one person is hard, even when he or she understands the need for change...." We are not advocating that intelligence managers and military commanders immediately implement mindfulness programs in their organizations. Instead, we think it is important to recognize the potential that the concept of mindfulness has for reducing the organization's vulnerability to deception. Although there is no empirical evidence that we can point to, it seems reasonable to hypothesize that fostering the cultural attributes of mindfulness in intelligence and military organizations can make them more effective in all three dimensions of counterdeception.

Turning to the characteristics of the vulnerable organization shown in Figure 6.2, we find that three out of the five characteristics are clearly cultural in nature. These are:

- Overemphasis on consensus, consistency, and being decisive;
- Emphasis on secrecy over effectiveness;
- Overemphasis on current intelligence.

The first characteristic—the vulnerable organization's overemphasis on consensus, consistency, and being decisive—is the one that stands out most clearly in contrast to the cultural attributes of the HROs that Weick and Sutcliffe describe. Looking at Figure 6.10, we can see that such a culture is almost the complete antithesis to a culture characterized by mindfulness. The vulnerable culture reinforces expectations—the "climate of opinion"—while the mindful culture continually updates its expectations. The vulnerable culture tends to suppress, ignore, or undermine (explain away) contradictory or alternative views in the interest of consensus. The mindful culture does almost the exact opposite. It defers to expertise, even if that expertise resides in the most junior members of the organization and it is willing to invent new expectations that take into account the unexpected in order to create a more complete and nuanced appreciation of the situation.

The vulnerable culture also strongly resists reversing or significantly changing an official judgment or opinion out of fear of being considered incompetent [13]. This is a serious issue when strategic surprise is an issue. For example, Grabo calls the fear of being wrong the "primary *reason*" for the reluctance to provide unambiguous warning [113. This fear creates pressure to try to appear to be "right" by using ambiguous language that makes it unlikely that the analyst can be proven to be "wrong." Mindful cultures, on the other hand, are not only far more tolerant of making mistakes and being wrong, but they also concentrate on making it safe to speak up when mistakes do occur. Weick and Sutcliffe cite the example of a seaman on board the nuclear aircraft carrier USS *Carl Vinson* who reported the loss of a tool on the flight deck [114]. Even though all the aircraft aloft at the time were redirected to land bases until the tool was found, the seaman was *commended* the next day in a formal ceremony for recognizing the potential danger and reporting it. This does not mean that grave errors are not taken seriously—they are; but punishing minor mistakes means that they will go unreported, and eventually such small mistakes invariably lead to a major catastrophe. Like HROs, the prepared organization should treat small analytical errors as signals about the actual condition of the organization

Vulnerable organization	Mindfulness culture
• Overemphasis on consensus, consistency, and being decisive –"Climate of opinion" –Suppress, ignore, or undermine contradictory views or dissent –Taboo against reversing or significantly changing a judgment –Wait-and-see attitude	• Continuous updating –Ongoing scrutiny of existing expectations –Continuous refinement and differentiation of expectations based on new experience –Willingness and capability to invent new expectations that make sense of unprecedented events –Create more complete, nuanced appreciation of context • OK to be wrong • Freedom to speak up • Act while thinking instead of think before acting • Deference to expertise

Figure 6.10 Cultural characteristics of the vulnerable organization versus cultural attributes of mindfulness.

as a whole. Commending those analysts who have reported that they made an error allows learning to occur with the expectation that the likelihood of larger analytical errors in the future will be reduced.

Finally, there is the tendency of vulnerable organizations to take a wait-and-see attitude when faced with high stakes situations. Fred Feer, a former intelligence analyst, addressed this characteristic in an informal talk at the National Defense University in 1989 [38]: "There's also this terrible tendency of intelligence to delay, to cue, to confirm. That's all wasting time in a situation when there may be very little time to waste." The vulnerable organization thinks that waiting will eventually produce the data or information that will eliminate the uncertainty of a situation and indicate the "right" or "optimum" course of action to be taken. In contrast, mindful cultures are characterized by commitment to resilience that drives them to begin taking action to address anomalies even before they have a complete diagnosis of the situation [115]. As we saw earlier, this can range from more aggressive collection efforts all the way to precautionary military preparations.

The second cultural characteristic of the vulnerable organization, the emphasis on security over effectiveness, poses a unique challenge even to mindful cultures. The HROs' characteristic "sensitivity to operations" involves maintaining accurate situational awareness—the big picture—and this requires providing everyone in the organization with detailed, real time information about what is happening [116]. Secrecy and compartmentation clearly are at odds with his aspect of mindfulness. The protection of vital intelligence sources and methods is essential to national security—some sources, once compromised, are gone forever; they cannot be reconstituted or replaced by other sources. Nevertheless, the investment in developing, maintaining, and keeping such sources secure is wasted if the information they provide fails to reach the right person at the right time.

One approach is to emulate the HROs characteristic deference to expertise and treat analysis like HROs treat operations. In HROs, operations drive the system and authority moves towards expertise [117]. Small interruptions in operations get management's undivided and widespread attention. Authority and resources are concentrated on the problem in order to contain it. If analysis were in the same manner, the discovery of something unexpected, especially in high stakes situations, would receive immediate and widespread attention. Also, like the HROs, authority and resources, including compartmented information, would move to the analytical expertise in order to address the issue. This is likely to make a lot of people uncomfortable, but since only the analysts dealing with the issue can accurately assess the value of the compartmented information, the risks and benefits of such an approach need to be considered.

Finally, there is the vulnerable organization's overemphasis on current intelligence. As we discussed earlier, the pressure produced by this emphasis is likely to cause analysts to fall back on automatic, System 1 processes. The danger is that these automatic, habitual thought processes are associated with the concept of *mindlessness*, the complete opposite of mindfulness [118]. In addition, we saw that an emphasis on current intelligence also interferes with the organization's ability to see the situation as a whole—the big picture. How then are we to resolve the paradox—provide decision-makers with timely, current intelligence *and* the big picture at the same time? Nuclear aircraft carrier crews seem to be able remain mindful under considerable time pressure. Somehow they are able to overcome the negative effects of grinding time pressure and continuous operations. The captain of a nuclear aircraft carrier does not run his ship by collecting a steady stream of status reports. The combat information center keeps track of the threat environment, the air boss and his staff keeps air operations running, and the officer of the deck and the bridge crew navigate the ship itself. All three are tightly knit by continuous communications and all three and the captain share that big picture of the situation—the bubble. This suggests that the prepared organization will likely need to have an information structure that is similar to that of the aircraft carrier. Current intelligence will still be produced continuously; however, that information will have to be integrated and synthesized at some point in order to build up the required situational awareness. That situational awareness is shared throughout the organization so that those producing the current intelligence will recognize something unexpected when it occurs. The production of current intelligence can then become a mindful process as opposed to an automatic, *mindless* one.

Our goal in this section was to show how the concept of mindfulness captures the essence of the know yourself and know your situation counterdeception principles. Fostering a culture of mindfulness is a way of institutionalizing the surfacing and reflecting upon expectations and mental models. Perhaps most importantly from a counterdeception perspective, a culture of mindfulness encourages sharing the alternative and dissenting views that help to continually update those expectations and models, as well as making sure that little surprises—those unexpected events no matter how inconsequential they are—don't become big surprises. Finally, mindfulness relies on a constant dialogue that involves all levels of the organization in order to develop *and continually update* its situational awareness. Now, in the next section, we will look at two processes that are absolutely essential to high reliability organizations and will likewise be critical to the organization that is well prepared to deal with deception.

6.2.2.2 Implementing Processes for Enabling Mindfulness

In the previous section we looked at how fostering a culture of mindfulness can play an important role in the development of the prepared organization. Referring to Figure 6.2 once again, we can see that the two remaining characteristics of the vulnerable organization are related to organizational processes. These are:

- Inadequate collaboration processes;
- Inadequate learning processes.

In this section we will look at the collaboration and learning processes of high reliability organizations as well as how those processes can be employed to reduce the organization's vulnerability to deception.

Horizontal and Vertical Collaboration

As we saw earlier, most collaboration problems in the vulnerable organization are the result of the "normal" functioning of large bureaucracies. Hierarchical organizational structures and the division of labor affect the flow of information in the organization. Information is filtered, blocked, distorted, withheld, or exaggerated producing an end result where different parts of the organization (both within and between the gray triangles in Figure 6.9) may have completely different views of what is known about a situation or problem. Without an accurate and up-to-date picture of the situation at hand, decision-makers are more likely than not to rely on their own sources of information and intuition when making decisions. High reliability organizations, on the other hand, depend heavily on collaboration both horizontally across the organization but also vertically to continually monitor and react to the big picture that unfolds.

One of the characteristics of high reliability organizations is the reluctance to accept simplification. They know that the world is complex, unstable, unknowable, and unpredictable, and they take deliberate steps to develop as complete a picture of a situation as possible [119]. Horizontal collaboration, collaboration across the organization, is the primary process that makes this possible. As Weick and Sutcliffe point out [120], "It is not just interaction by itself that decreases simplification and increases mindfulness. It is the fact that the interaction is among people who have diverse expectations. This diversity enables people to see different things when they view the 'same' event." When it comes to expectations and seeing things differently, the deception literature makes it clear that there is almost always someone in the organization who looked at the situation and saw through the deception. For example, German Admiral Theodor Krancke, in charge of German Naval Command Group West, consistently argued that Normandy was the Allies' real invasion target [121]. In vulnerable organizations, such views tend to be suppressed or ignored; in mindful organizations they are taken seriously and acted upon.

The reluctance to accept simplification by emphasizing collaboration might also account for another observation that is found in the intelligence literature, namely, the significant contribution that "amateurs" and other outsiders can make to intelligence analysis [122]. Weick and Sutcliffe [123] write that: "They [HROs] encourage boundary spanners who have diverse experience, skepticism toward received wisdom, and negotiating tactics that reconcile differences of opinion without destroying the nuances that diverse people detect." Intelligence amateurs possessing domain expertise clearly can play such a "boundary spanner" role and can often provide insights about a problem that has gone unnoticed by those working on it.

Examples of horizontal collaboration in HROs tend to take three basic forms: interdepartmental meetings, oversight committees, and operations control teams. This is typical of the operations oriented organizations that Weick and Sutcliffe studied, but note that all three forms involve a great deal of *face-to-face* interaction. Continuous face-to-face interaction helps to nurture credibility and trust among the members of the different departments in the organization [124], and it is such trust and credibility combined with interpersonal skills that are absolutely necessary for effective collaboration.

The implication for the prepared organization dealing with deception is that significantly more face-to-face collaboration, both within an organization and between organizations, is something to be strongly encouraged. The potential benefits of surfacing diverse expectations, using them to form a more complex picture of a situation, and then ensuring that those expectations are continuously examined and updated, are an essential element of the know yourself and know your situation counterdeception principles. We recognize that this poses a considerable challenge to a large and geographically distributed analytical community like that found in the United States. Face-to-face meetings and informal interaction are daily events on an aircraft carrier so finding ways to encourage similar behavior in something like the U.S. intelligence community poses quite a challenge. Nevertheless, it seems obvious that the importance of face-to-face collaboration should not be overlooked and, in fact, should receive just as much as attention as that paid to expanding the use of collaboration technologies (e.g., e-mail, instant messaging, videoconferencing, and Web meetings) in the intelligence community.

The high reliability organization's "sensitivity to operations" depends heavily on vertical communications within the organization. According to Weick and Sutcliffe [117], "The key to effective performance lies in maintaining situational awareness, the big picture of current operations, or, in the language of aircraft carriers, having the bubble." Once again, face-to-face interactions are the norm not the exception, and decision-makers in HROs pay constant attention to real-time information about their operations. If the analysis process is equivalent to the operations in HROs, then notice that this emphasis on real-time information about analysis is *not* the same as emphasizing current intelligence. Nor does it involve micromanaging the analytical process. The emphasis is on making sure that the unexpected gets noticed and that the operations people (or analysts) get the support they need in order to do something about it. This is also where the HROs' characteristic "deference to expertise" comes in. Being sensitive to operations means that authority moves towards expertise when needed. We might also propose that the same is true for compartmented information—decision-makers must make sure such that information flows to where it is needed in order to ensure accurate situational awareness.

Once again, the implication for counterdeception is that more, not less, face-to-face vertical collaboration is something to be strongly encouraged in the prepared organization. The unexpected, little surprises (Whaley's incongruities yet again) that line analysts discover offer a brief moment in which to improve the organization's situational awareness. The prepared organization will ensure that they are not fit to expectations (the "prevailing climate of opinion") but are communicated, shared, and acted upon. Managers in the prepared organization must work to ensure that authority and information flows to whoever needs it in order to resolve the anomalies and update the big picture, and that updated big picture has to be communicated to decision-makers continuously as well. Grabo has written that one of the most difficult things to do in intelligence is to "come to judgments which the policymaker does not want to hear," but also that doing so in time for the policymaker to take appropriate action is also the greatest service that intelligence can perform on behalf of the nation [125]. This means that cultural change and the associated enabling process will have to occur at all levels of the organization and especially at that critical interface between decision-makers and analysts.

The goal of the prepared organization must be continuous, vertical collaboration that will ensure that changes in the situation are brought to the decision-maker's attention early enough to take action that will negate or mitigate the effects of the deceiver's deception plan. Implementing such processes like these will vary from organization to organization; however, the message from the study of high reliability organizations is that more, not less, fact-to-face collaboration is vital to hardening the prepared organization against deception.

Processes for Facilitating Learning

In Section 6.1.2 we attributed the vulnerable organization's inadequate learning processes to two factors: (1) the lack of normal feedback from the analytical judgments that are made, and (2) the rarity of major events that involve deception. In this section we will see that there are also lessons to be learned from high reliability organizations that address these issues.

Let's start off by examining the second factor first. The rarity of events involving strategic surprise or deception is often cited as a reason for why organizations continually fail to avoid surprise or anticipate deception. This view is based on the belief that learning from unique historical events is difficult since each event is a unique data point that occurs within its own context. March [126] observes that although "history is not generous with experience," the view that little can be learned from unique historical events "overlooks the wealth of experience that is represented in each historical event." In fact, learning from unique events *is* possible and is done all the time. For example, the whole purpose of after action reports and postmortems is to explore a broader range of experience about an event than simply considering its outcome. This is why HROs put so much emphasis on the reporting of mistakes and errors. Since the cost of failure is high, and the occurrences of failure are relatively rare, mistakes and errors provide HROs with ways to maximize what they can learn from the incidents that do occur [127].

Numerous authors in the intelligence field have recognized the importance of postmortems and the role they play in organizational learning. As usual, Heuer provides a ready summary of the issue [23]:

> To facilitate institutional memory and learning, thorough postmortem analyses should be conducted on all significant intelligence failures. Analytical (as distinct from collection) successes should also be studied. These analyses should be collated and maintained in a central location, available for review to identify the common characteristics of analytical failure and success. A meta-analysis of the causes and consequences of analytical success and failure should be widely distributed and used in training programs to heighten awareness of analytical problems.

In a similar manner, Johnston recommends that a formal after action review (AAR) process (similar to that used by the U.S. Army) be implemented at the end of each analytical "production cycle" [128]. Likewise, Recommendation 16 in the final report of The Commission on the Intelligence Capabilities of the United States Regarding Weapons of Mass Destruction [129] calls for "routine and ongoing" examinations of finished intelligence and "the lessons learned from the 'post mortems' should be incorporated into the intelligence education and training program."

Obviously, it is a given that the prepared organization should have an active program to capture and share analytical lessons learned. There are, however, three issues that affect or have the ability to affect not only the organization's ability to learn from unique events but also the success or failure of any postmortem program.

The first issue is time. Time is of the essence since people tend to be candid about an incident for only a short period of time [130]. If given time to get their stories straight, in an effort to justify their actions and to protect their reputations, learning essentially stops. Therefore, for maximum learning effect, postmortems or after action reviews must be performed as soon as possible or they lose much of their value. The second issue is also related to time—it is critical that organizations make time for such activities if there is to be any hope of learning from them. Calls for analytical postmortems and after action reports are useless if the time pressure of day-to-day operations (i.e., providing current intelligence) makes actually performing those activities impossible. As Stever Robbins notes, the danger is twofold [131]: "Organizations rarely build in time to do thoughtful learning, and when they do, that time is the first to go when emergencies beckon." Vulnerable organizations are to be easily distracted by day-to-day events. On the other hand, the prepared organization, like its high-performance relatives, makes the extra effort to devote time to learning from the unexpected events, knowing that if it fails to do so, it will be overtaken by those events.

Finally, there is the issue regarding the politicization of the information obtained in the postmortems or after action reviews. A number of successful postmortem efforts in the U.S. intelligence community produced tangible organizational and procedural improvements in the 1970s; however, most of these efforts were discontinued [132] when they were "seized upon as a political football." Clearly, if such programs are to be successful, the senior leadership of the prepared organization will have to foster a culture that gives very high priority to organizational learning efforts. Postmortems or after action reviews will have to explicitly be made part of everyone's job and appropriate rewards and incentives will have to put in place. Finally, the entire organization must be willing to take the heat when attempts are made to politicize what has been learned. Otherwise, such programs will disappear like they did in the 1970s.

Although capturing the lessons learned from "significant" intelligence failures or successes is valuable and necessary, inadequate learning processes are the real challenge that faces the vulnerable organization. Intelligence analysts work in an environment that is generally unfavorable to learning from experience, what Hogarth refers to as a "wicked" learning structure [133]. In wicked learning structures the quality of feedback is noisy, delayed, or characterized by uncertainty, and there are serious consequences associated with errors of judgment. Warning intelligence, counterdeception, and in fact, nearly all of intelligence analysis have these characteristics. The problem is well recognized in the intelligence community and, once again, we turn to Heuer for an effective summary of the problem [23]:

> Obtaining systematic feedback on the accuracy of past judgments is frequently difficult or impossible, especially in the political intelligence field. Political judgments are normally couched in imprecise terms and are generally conditional upon other developments. Even in retrospect, there are no objective criteria for evaluating the accuracy of most political intelligence judgments as they are presently written. In the economic and military fields, however, where estimates are frequently concerned with numerical quantities, systematic feedback on analytical performance is feasible.

Despite this pessimism, the prepared organization needs to make a committed effort to learn from each and every judgment it makes. When ground truth is "difficult or impossible" to obtain, the prepared organization needs to employ imaginative ways to make up for the lack of feedback. The challenge is to find ways to both improve the quality of learning in the existing environment and to create new, "kind" learning structures where analysts can develop expertise in areas relevant to counterdeception.

Such a goal will require a major paradigm shift regarding organization learning in most intelligence organizations. For example, the U.S. intelligence community places tremendous emphasis on training, and when there is an intelligence failure, training is a quick and easy solution to recommend and implement. The failure to find weapons of mass destruction in Iraq led the Commission on the Intelligence Capabilities of the United States Regarding Weapons of Mass Destruction to call for even more training in the form of a "Community program for training analysts" and stated that [134] "both analysts and managers must prioritize this career-long training." The emphasis is all on training; yet the real issue is *learning*, which requires *feedback* and *practice*. Without practice, and the feedback it provides, what is learned in the classroom is soon forgotten. Given that intelligence analysts work in a wicked learning environment, can regular practice and quality feedback somehow be incorporated into the prepared organization? We believe that there are three possible strategies to consider, all of which aim to make a proactive effort to change the analytical learning environment from one that is not conducive to organizational learning into one that is.

The first strategy is quite simple in concept but poses a considerable challenge at both the individual and organizational level. It involves nothing more than keeping track of the day-to-day thoughts and judgments that analysts make—a process similar to the laboratory notebooks that scientists and engineers maintain. Before the howling begins, it is worthwhile to consider the following comments that Nobel Prize winner Daniel Kahneman made in an interview in 2003 [135]: "The thing that astonishes me when I talk to business people in the context of decision analysis is that you have an organization that's making lots of decisions and they're not keeping track. They're not trying to learn from their own mistakes; they're not investing the smallest amount in trying to actually figure out what they've done wrong. And that's not an accident. They don't want to know." Substitute "judgments" for "decisions," and Kahneman could be talking about the vulnerable organization. Keeping track of judgments allows the organization as well as the individual analysts themselves to ask questions like: How many times has this kind of judgment been made in the past? Do we really know what our track record is? As Hogarth points out, unless we keep track of our judgments and develop some feel for their accuracy, simply making judgments repeatedly (the *mere-exposure effect*) can make people unjustifiably overconfident in their performance [136]. In addition, even if ground truth is immediately unavailable, there is simply no reason to make matters worse by making it impossible to match judgments to ground truth if and when it does appear at some point. If nothing else, keeping track of judgments would likely improve any postmortem process that the organization puts into place. Let the howling begin!

How to implement such a strategy is best left up to individual organizations, but suggestions for how to do so does exist in the intelligence literature. Although she was writing specifically on the topic of indications and warning, Grabo [92] describes one method, the *indications chronology*, which could be applied to keeping track of judgments. The indications chronology is used to briefly document "all known facts, alleged actions or plans, rumors, or anything else which might be an indication of impending aggressive action or other abnormal activity." This information is recorded in the order it occurs (not when it was reported) and should include significant actions by "our side" or by allies that might be relevant to the situation. This sounds suspiciously like the kind of material an analyst could record in a daily journal along with any associated judgments that were made regarding a problem or situation. At a minimum, such a chronology could simply keep track of judgments made and why. Of course, Grabo [91] admits that maintaining such records is "a very time-consuming task requiring the most conscientious effort, which is probably the chief reason that so few are prepared." Nevertheless, it should be apparent that mindfulness requires just such a conscientious effort. Without it the organization runs mindlessly on automatic until the unexpected strikes.

Unexpected events bring us to the second strategy for ensuring continuous learning in the prepared organization. As we saw earlier, the high reliability organization's preoccupation with failure drives the continuous reporting of unexpected events, no matter how inconsequential, through the use of incident reports. A similar process is applicable to the problem of counterdeception except that instead of incidents, we can think in terms of anomalies. Anomalies are to intelligence and counterdeception as incidents are to HROs and the reliable operation of complex systems. In each case a fleeting learning opportunity is created. If not immediately noted down and acted upon, it is more than likely that it will be forgotten. Charles Darwin recognized this important fact with regard to his scientific observations [137]: "I had, also, during many years followed a golden rule, namely, that whenever a published fact, new observation or thought, came across me, which was opposed to my general results, to make a memorandum of it without fail at once; for I had found by experience that such facts and thoughts were far more apt to escape from the memory than favourable ones." Heuer too was sensitive to the importance of anomalies [23]: "Analysts should keep a record of unexpected events and think hard about what they might mean, not disregard them or explain them away."

Our second strategy involves emulating the HRO incident reporting process with an analogous *anomaly reporting* process. Not only should analysts keep track of evidence that is "opposed" to their expectations, but anomalies should be treated organizationally in much the same way that incident reports are in HROs. They should be reported and examined for what can be learned about the situation, sources, assumptions, and judgments affected. The goal is the same as that in the HROs, to deal with the small surprises before they become big ones. Many will argue that implementing such a process would too difficult to implement, but, once again, it is worth considering the words of Cynthia Grabo [91]: "*...while not all anomalies lead to crises, all crises are made up of anomalies.*" It may turn out to be impractical to report and respond to each and every piece of anomalous evidence; however, reducing the organization's vulnerability to deception may not be possible with giving serious consideration to such a process.

The first two strategies dealt with ways of obtaining feedback in a *wicked* learning environment. Activities like sports, music lessons, and video games generally have the advantage over intelligence analysis since they are usually pursued in a *kind* learning environment—feedback is obtained quickly and accurately. Even when natural talent is a factor, expertise in those activities is still only achievable through practice, practice, and more practice. Our third strategy focuses on creating a *kinder* learning environment for analysts where they can apply the results of their training on a regular basis—a sort of analytical practice field.

One approach for building such a practice field is a training regime proposed by Klein. It aims to provide meaningful experience through three major activities [138]:

- *Identifying* and understanding the judgment or decision requirements of your job;
- *Practice* making those difficult judgments or decisions in context;
- *Reviewing* those judgment or decision-making experiences.

The identification step is aimed at uncovering the answers to a number of questions in the context of the domain under consideration. For example: What makes the decision or judgment difficult? What kinds of errors are often made? How would an expert make this decision differently from a novice? This final question is useful for uncovering possible cues and strategies that an expert might employ when faced with the same problem. Like the use of any formal method, this activity helps to specify possible outcomes in advance and externalize any assumptions and preconceptions. This regime also helps to guide the preparations and training for any task and makes assessing those outcomes easier to evaluate during the feedback process.

Klein proposes the use of decision-making exercises (DMXs) as an effective way for practicing making difficult decisions or judgments [139]. A DMX is a short (30 minutes or so with another 30 minutes for follow-up discussions), simple, and easy to run scenario or game that provides the simulated experiences that do not always occur in real life. The planning, organizing, and running of such exercises requires organizational commitment and resources. Nevertheless, it is important to recognize that the DMX concept is an effective means of: (1) capturing the essential aspects of making judgments or decisions in challenging situations; (2) providing the means for building expertise through experiential learning; and (3) refining the answers to the questions posed in the previous identification activity. Properly designed DMXs, run on a regular basis, have the potential to let analysts practice making judgments in far more situations involving deception than they are likely to face in reality.

The final step is to review one's judgments or decisions in order to obtain the feedback that is so critical to effective learning. An obvious way to obtain feedback is to ask for it. Talking to more experienced associates can uncover a wide range of tacit knowledge that they likely use in their own intuitive judgments and decision-making [140]. For example, what is it about a situation that they see that the novice does not? What kind of cues are they sensitive to? What other options or implications do they see that the novice misses? A second approach is constructive self-reflection. This form of feedback focuses not on whether or not the judgment or decision was right or wrong, but on the process that was used to reach it. Professor Trisha Greenhalgh provides an excellent summary of the role of critical reflection in clinical intuition [141]: "In particular, critical reflection on past intuitive judgments highlights areas of ambiguity in complex decision-making, sharpens perceptual awareness, exposes the role of emotions in driving 'hunches' (perhaps also demonstrating the fallibility of relying on feelings alone), encourages a holistic view of the patient's predicament, identifies specific educational needs, and may serve to 'kick-start' a more analytical chain of thought on particular problems."

Intelligence analysis represents a particularly wicked learning environment, and the rarity of significant, large-scale deception operations makes it even more so. Turning this wicked environment into a kinder environment is difficult but not entirely impossible. It depends on Hogarth's first two guidelines to educating intuition: finding innovative ways of creating a better learning environment and constantly seeking feedback. DMXs are a way of creating that analytical practice field we mentioned earlier while keeping better track of analytical judgments and anomalies is a way of making sure the organization can glean useful feedback from whatever ground truth becomes available. Such processes require commitment and resources—especially precious time—but, as we have seen, such commitment is essential to achieving the kind of mindfulness that characterizes high performance organizations.

6.3 Summary

Data and information will always be ambiguous, uncertain, inconsistent, contradictory, and where deception is a misleading factor. At times there will be too much information; at other times information will be sparse. A prepared organization based on a foundation of prepared minds offers considerable potential for realizing a deception-resistant system (see Figure 6.11). The prepared organization continuously updates, tests, and retests its assumptions, expectations, hypotheses, beliefs, and judgments. It encourages continuous collaboration and interaction at all levels of the organization, both horizontally and vertically, and is especially attentive to alternative and dissenting views. When such a system is surprised or finds one of its judgments to be wrong, *no matter how inconsequential it may seem*, it works to understand why the surprise or failure occurred. The goal is to arrive at the best possible estimate of what an adversary might want you to believe and do as well as the best possible estimate of what the adversary is really doing.

Even though we have devoted a considerable amount of our discussion to dealing with unexpected events and anomalies, it is worthwhile to consider that incongruities alone are unlikely to solve the counterdeception problem. The unexpected events and anomalous evidence that are cause for surprise provide the cues that signal that the big picture needs to be reexamined. Feer raised this point in his lecture at the National Defense University: "The conceptual basis for analysis has to change from one trying to detect deception by looking for indicators to one of analyzing the operational alternatives available to the enemy and evaluating them given an understanding of the available intelligence with reference to enemy behavior" [142].

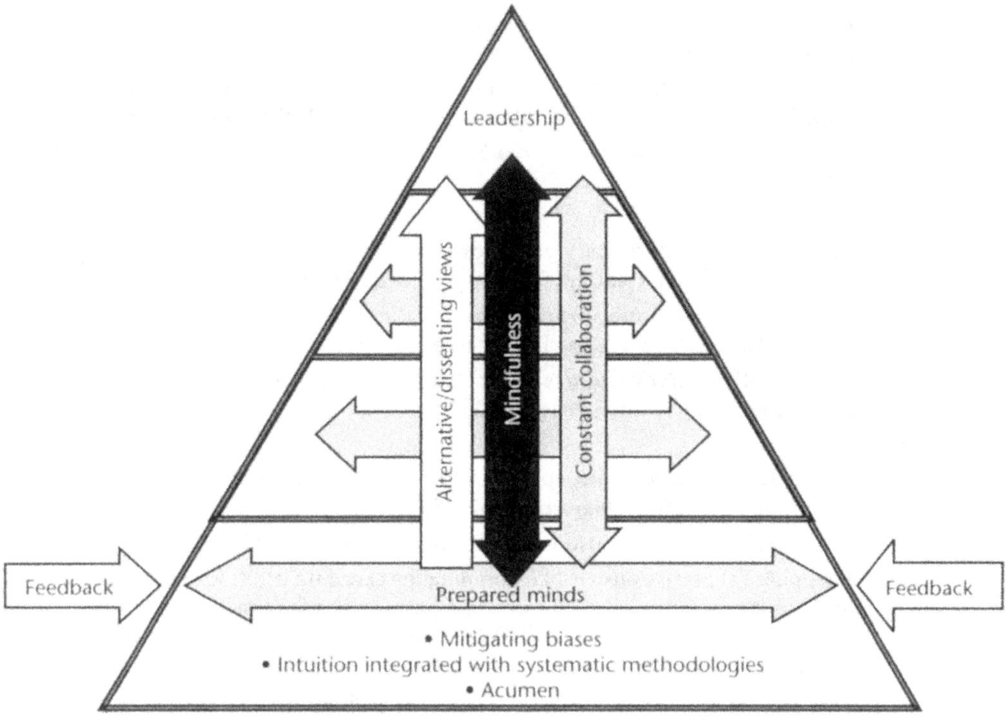

Figure 6.11 The end result: the prepared organization.

Deception is inexpensive and cost effective, while the costs of being deceived are usually high if not catastrophic. Fostering a culture of mindfulness in the prepared organization can help to increase the deception planner's work factor, to make running his deception operation more expensive and more risky, and ultimately, to make its success less certain.

Endnotes

[1] Gilovich, T., *How We Know What Isn't So: The Fallibility of Human Reason in Everyday Life,* New York: The Free Press, 1991, p. 2.

[2] The Normandy landings are a case in point. Eisenhower hoped that the FORTITUDE deception would just keep the German 15th Army out of his hair for the first two days of the invasion and FORTITUDE's planners themselves believed that the Germans could not be fooled for more than 10 days. The Allies were astounded when the Germans continued to believe that the real landings would come at the Pas de Calais for almost 6 weeks after the initial landings.

[3] Tversky, A., and D. Kahneman, "Judgments of and by Representativeness," in Kahneman, D., P. Slovic, and A. Tversky, (eds.), *Judgment Under Uncertainty: Heuristics and Biases,* Cambridge, U.K.: Cambridge University Press, 1982, p. 98.

[4] May, E., *Strange Victory: Hitler's Conquest of France*, New York: Hill and Wang, 2000, p. 8.

[5] Hall, E. T., *The Silent Language*, New York: Anchor Books, 1990, p. 23.

[6] Grabo, C., *Anticipating Surprise: Analysis for Strategic Warning*, Joint Military Intelligence College, Center for Strategic Intelligence Research, 2002, p. 47.

[7] Kam, E., *Surprise Attack: the Victim's Perspective*, Cambridge, MA: Harvard University Press, 1988, p. 71.

[8] "Jeremiah News Conference," CIA Press Release, June 2, 1998–November 20, 2005, http://www.cia.gov/cia/public_affairs/press_release/1998/jeremiah.html, October 9, 2005.

[9] Lowenthal, M., *Intelligence: From Secrets to Policy*, 2nd ed., Washington, D.C.: CQ Press, 2003, p. 103.

[10] Ibid., p. 96.

[11] Cline, R., "Is Intelligence Over-Coordinated?" November 20, 2005, http://www.cia.gov/csi/kent_csi/docs/v01i4a02p_0001.htm, accessed October 9, 2005.

[12] Grabo, C., *Anticipating Surprise: Analysis for Strategic Warning*, Joint Military Intelligence College, Center for Strategic Intelligence Research, 2002, p. 9.

[13] Johnston, R. *Analytic Culture in the U.S. Intelligence Community*, Washington, D.C.: Center for the Study of Intelligence, 2005, p. 23.

[14] Ibid., p. 6.

[15] Heuer, R. J., "Strategic Deception and Counterdeception: A Cognitive Process Approach," *International Studies Quarterly*, Vol. 25, No. 2, 1981, p. 322.

[16] Some intelligence wags also include rumor intelligence (RUMINT).

[17] First phase analysis consists of examining the raw data itself, for example, an ELINT analyst looking at new data collected from an adversary's radar system or an image analyst examining a recently obtained reconnaissance photograph. The results of this phase may or not result in a finished intelligence product that is disseminated to consumers. It often is used to update intelligence databases for use by other analysts. Second phase analysis transforms first phase analysis into finished intelligence reports (e.g., the results of first phase analysis of the radar signal become an intelligence report about a potential new capability that the radar is assessed to have). Third phase analysis—all source analysis—integrates information from across the different INTs in order to produce overall estimates of the adversary's capabilities and intentions.

[18] Kam, E., *Surprise Attack: The Victim's Perspective*, Cambridge: Harvard University Press, 1988, p. 179.

[19] Ibid., p. 180.

[20] Handel, M. I., *War, Strategy, and Intelligence,* London, U.K.: Frank Cass & Co., Ltd., 1989, p. 265.

[21] Kam, E., *Surprise Attack: The Victim's Perspective*, Cambridge, MA: Harvard University Press, 1988, p. 193.

[22] Ibid., p. 194

[23] Heuer, R., *Psychology of Intelligence Analysis*, Washington, D.C.: Center for the Study of Intelligence, 1999, http://www.cia.gov/csi/books/19104/art8.html.

[24] Lowenthal, M., *Intelligence: From Secrets to Policy*, 2nd ed., Washington, D.C.: CQ Press, 2003, p. 89.

[25] Grabo, C., *Anticipating Surprise: Analysis for Strategic Warning*, Joint Military Intelligence College, Center for Strategic Intelligence Research, 2002, p. 164.

[26] The U.S. Army's battlefield deception field manual (FM 90-2) lists only seven deception operations as examples of deception failures. Compare this to Whaley's study of 168 battles from 16 wars that clearly demonstrate the strong association of deception with strategic surprise.

[27] Handel, M. I., *War, Strategy, and Intelligence,* London, U.K.: Frank Cass & Co., Ltd., 1989, p. 396.

[28] Grabo, C., *Anticipating Surprise: Analysis for Strategic Warning*, Joint Military Intelligence College, Center for Strategic Intelligence Research, 2002, p. 119.

[29] Kam, E., *Surprise Attack: The Victim's Perspective*, Cambridge, MA: Harvard University Press, 1988, p. 160.

[30] Whaley, B., and J. Busby, "Detecting Deception: Practice, Practitioners, and Theory," in Godson, R., and J. Wirtz, (eds.), *Strategic Denial and Deception: The Twenty-First Century Challenge,* New Brunswick, NJ: Transaction Publishers, 2002, p. 212.

[31] Christie, R., and F. Geis, *Studies in Machiavellianism,* New York: Academic Press, 1970.

[32] The Mach scale actually captures three components of an individual's behavioral dispositions: the extent to which a subject has a cynical view of human nature and believes that others are not trustworthy; willingness to engage in manipulative behaviors, and the extent of the individual's concern for conventional morality.

[33] Gilovich, T. *How We Know What Isn't So: The Fallibility of Human Reason in Everyday Life,* New York: The Free Press, 1991, p. 111.

[34] The five guidelines are: consider the source, trust facts, distrust projections, be on the lookout for sharpening and leveling, and be wary of testimonials.

[35] Kam, E., *Surprise Attack: The Victim's Perspective*, Cambridge, MA: Harvard University Press, 1988, p. 133.

[36] Schum, D., *The Evidential Foundations of Probabilistic Reasoning*, Evanston, IL: Northwest University Press, 1994, p. 92.

[37] Bruce, J. B., "How Leaks of Classified Intelligence Help U.S. Adversaries: Implications for Laws and Secrecy," in R. Z. George and B. D. Kline (eds.), *Intelligence and the National Security Strategist,* Lankam, MD: Rowman and Littlefield, 2006, pp. 399–414.

[38] Feer, F., *Thinking-Red-in-Wargaming Workshop: Opportunities for Deception and Counterdeception in the Red Planning Process* (P-7510), Santa Monica, CA: RAND, 1989, p. 10.

[39] Kam, E., *Surprise Attack: The Victim's Perspective*, Cambridge, MA: Harvard University Press, 1988, p. 34.

[40] Whaley, B., *Codeword Barbarossa*, Cambridge, MA: The MIT Press, 1974, pp. 100–101.

[41] Lowenthal, M., *Intelligence: From Secrets to Policy*, 2nd ed., Washington, D.C.: CQ Press, 2003, p. 79.

[42] Schum, D., *The Evidential Foundations of Probabilistic Reasoning*, Evanston, IL: Northwest University Press, 1994, p. 93.

[43] Ibid., p. 94.

[44] Ibid., p. 95.

[45] Ibid., pp. 98–99.

[46] Ibid., p. 99.

[47] Jones, R. V., *Most Secret War*, London, U.K.: Wordsworth Editions 1998, pp. 233–235.

[48] In *Most Secret War*, Jones recalls receiving a telephone call from Colonel Wallace on the morning of February 11, 1942. Wallace had recognized that German jamming was getting worse, had reported through the proper channels, but no one took his concerns seriously. Jones promised Wallace to send one of his officers with him to the coastal radar stations the next day, February 12, which turned out to be the very day the *Scharnhorst* and *Gneisenau* sailed.

[49] Schum, D., *The Evidential Foundations of Probabilistic Reasoning*, Evanston, IL: Northwest University Press, 1994, pp. 102–103.

[50] Ibid., p. 102.

[51] Ibid., p. 109.

[52] Whaley, B., "Conditions Making for Success and Failure of Denial and Deception: Authoritarian and Transition Regimes," in Godson, R., and J. Wirtz, (eds.), *Strategic Denial and Deception: The Twenty-First Century Challenge,* New Brunswick, NJ: Transaction Publishers, 2002.

[53] Fischhoff, B., "Debiasing," in Kahneman, D., P. Slovic, and A. Tversky, (eds.), *Judgment Under Uncertainty: Heuristics and Biases,* Cambridge, U.K.: Cambridge University Press, 1982, pp. 422–444.

[54] Arkes, H. R., "Costs and Benefits of Judgment Errors: Implications for Debiasing," *Psychological Bulletin*, Vol. 110, No. 3, 1991, pp. 486–498.

[55] Camerer, C., and R. Hogarth, "The Effects of Financial Incentives in Experiments: A Review and Capital-Labor-Production Framework," *Journal of Risk and Uncertainty*, 1999, pp. 7–42, http://www.hss.caltech.edu/SSPapers/wp1059.pdf.

[56] Tetlock, P. E., "Intuitive Politicians, Theologians, and Prosecutors: Exploring the Empirical Implications of Deviant Functionalist Metaphors," in Gilovich, T., D. Griffin, and D. Kahneman, (eds.), *Heuristics and Biases: The Psychology of Intuitive Judgment*, Cambridge, U.K.: Cambridge University Press, 2002, p. 583.

[57] Ibid., p. 585.

[58] Hagafors, R., and B. Brehmer, "Does Having to Justify One's Judgments Change the Nature of the Judgment Process?" *Organizational Behavior and Human Performance*, Vol. 31, 1983, pp. 223–232.

[59] Tetlock, P. E., L. Skitka, and R. Boettger, "Social and Cognitive Strategies for Coping with Accountability: Conformity, Complexity, and Bolstering," *Journal of Personality and Social Psychology*, Vol. 57, 1989, pp. 632–640.

[60] Tetlock, P. E., and J. Kim, "Accountability and Judgment in a Personality Prediction Task," *Journal of Personality and Social Psychology*, Vol. 52, 1987, pp. 700–709.

[61] Kruglanski, A. W., and T. Freund, "The Freezing and Unfreezing of Lay Inference: Effects on Impressional Primacy, Ethnic Stereotyping, and Numerical Anchoring," *Journal of Experimental Social Psychology*, Vol. 19, 1983, pp. 448–468.

[62] Murphy, R., "The Effects of Task Characteristics on Covariation Assessment: The Impact of Accountability and Judgment Frame," *Organizational Behavior and Human Decision Processes*, Vol. 60, 1994, pp. 139–155.

[63] Tetlock, P. E., "Accountability: A Social Check on the Fundamental Attribution Error," *Social Psychology Quarterly*, Vol. 48, 1985, pp. 227–236.

[64] Tetlock, P. E., "Accountability and Perseverance of First Impressions," *Social Psychology Quarterly*, Vol. 46, 1983, pp. 285–292.

[65] Tetlock, P. E., "Intuitive Politicians, Theologians, and Prosecutors: Exploring the Empirical Implications of Deviant Functionalist Metaphors," in Gilovich, T., D. Griffin, and D. Kahneman, (eds.), *Heuristics and Biases: The Psychology of Intuitive Judgment*, Cambridge, U.K.: Cambridge University Press, 2002, p. 590.

[66] Ibid., p. 592.

[67] Kray, L. J., and A. D. Galinsky, "The Debiasing Effect of Counterfactual Mind-Sets: Increasing the Search for Disconfirmatory Information in Group Decisions," *Organizational Behavior and Human Decision Processes*, Vol. 91, 2003, pp. 69–81.

[68] Koriat, A., S. Lichtenstein, and B. Fischhoff, "Reasons for Confidence," *Journal of Experimental Psychology: Human Learning and Memory*, Vol. 6, 1980, pp. 107–118.

[69] Lord, C. G., M. R. Lepper, and E. Preston, "Considering the Opposite: A Corrective Strategy for Social Judgment," *Journal of Personality and Social Psychology*, Vol. 46, 1984, pp. 1231–1243.

[70] Hirt, E. R., F. R. Kardes, and K. D. Markman, "Activating a Mental Simulation Mind-Set Through Generation of Alternatives: Implications for Debiasing in Related and Unrelated Domains," *Journal of Experimental Social Psychology*, Vol. 40, 2004, pp. 374–383.

[71] Ibid., p. 382.

[72] Hirt, E. R., and K. D. Markman, "Multiple Explanation: A Consider-an-Alternative Strategy for Debiasing Judgments," *Journal of Personality and Social Psychology*, Vol. 69, No. 6, 1995, pp. 1069–1086.

[73] Klein, G., *The Power of Intuition*, New York: Currency Doubleday, 2004, pp. 147–148.

[74] The scientific method has four steps: (1) observation and description of a phenomenon or group of phenomena, (2) formulation of a hypothesis to explain the phenomena, (3) use of the hypothesis to predict the existence of other phenomena, or to predict quantitatively the

results of new observations, and (4) performance of experimental tests of the predictions by several independent experimenters and properly performed experiments.

[75] "Appendix E: Introduction to the Scientific Method," November 8, 2005, http://teacher.nsrl.rochester.edu/phy_labs/AppendixE/AppendixE.html.

[76] Johnston, R., *Analytic Culture in the U.S. Intelligence Community*, Washington D.C.: Center for the Study of Intelligence, 2005, pp. 19–20.

[77] Ibid., p. 18.

[78] The National Commission on Terrorist Attacks upon the United States, *The 9-11 Commission Report*, 2004, http://www.9-11commission.gov/report/index.htm.

[79] The Commission on the Intelligence Capabilities of the United States Regarding Weapons of Mass Destruction, *Report to the President of the United States*, 2005, http://www.wmd.gov/report/index.html.

[80] Gilovich, T., *How We Know What Isn't So: The Fallibility of Human Reason in Everyday Life*, New York: The Free Press, 1991, p. 57.

[81] Ibid., p. 187.

[82] Ross, L., and C. A. Anderson, "Shortcomings in the Attribution Process: On The Origins and Maintenance of Erroneous Social Assessments," in Kahneman, D., P. Slovic, and A. Tversky, (eds.), *Judgment Under Uncertainty: Heuristics and Biases*, Cambridge, U.K.: Cambridge University Press, 1982, p. 150.

[83] Sloman, S. A., "Two Systems of Reasoning," in Gilovich, T., D. Griffin, and D. Kahneman, (eds.), *Heuristics and Biases: The Psychology of Intuitive Judgment*, Cambridge, U.K.: Cambridge University Press, 2002, p. 383.

[84] Merriam-Webster Online, http://www.m-w.com/cgi-bin/dictionary?book=Dictionary&va=intuition.

[85] Poincaré, H., *Définitions mathématiques dans l'éducation*, 1904.

[86] Hogarth, R. M., *Educating Intuition*, Chicago, IL: The University of Chicago Press, 2001, p. 24.

[87] Handel, M. I., *War, Strategy, and Intelligence*, London, U.K.: Frank Cass & Co., Ltd., 1989, p. 341.

[88] Grabo, C., *Anticipating Surprise: Analysis for Strategic Warning*, Joint Military Intelligence College, Center for Strategic Intelligence Research, 2002, p. 8.

[89] Schum, D., *The Evidential Foundations of Probabilistic Reasoning*, Evanston, IL: Northwest University Press, 1994, p. 496.

[90] Doyle, A. C., "The Boscombe Valley Mystery," http://www.citsoft.com/holmes/adventures/boscombe.valley.txt.

[91] Grabo, C., *Anticipating Surprise: Analysis for Strategic Warning*, Joint Military Intelligence College, Center for Strategic Intelligence Research, 2002, p. 31.

[92] Ibid., p. 39.

[93] Hogarth, R. M., *Educating Intuition*, Chicago, IL: The University of Chicago Press, 2001, p. 207.

[94] Klein, G., *The Power of Intuition*, New York: Currency Doubleday, 2004, p. 9.

[95] Sarbin, T., "Prolegomenon to a Theory of Counterdeception," in Daniel, D., and K. Herbig, (eds.), *Strategic Military Deception*, New York: Pergamon Press, 1981, p. 151.

[96] Merriam Webster Online, http://www.m-w.com/cgi-bin/dictionary?book=Dictionary&va=acumen.

[97] Hall, E. T., *The Silent Language*, New York: Anchor Books, 1990, p. 36-37.

[98] Hall, E. T., *Beyond Culture*, New York: Anchor Books, 1989, p. 58.

[99] Johnston, R., *Analytic Culture in the U.S. Intelligence Community*, Washington, D.C.: Center for the Study of Intelligence, 2005, p. 83.

[100] Saint Paul, T., "Developing Cultural Awareness with International Business Students: a Look at Empathy Breakdown," 2000, http://www.mgmt.purdue.edu/centers/ciber/publications/gbl/GBL%20-%202000/2e.Saint%20Paul.doc.

[101] Moore, D. T., L. Krizan, and E. J. Moore, "Evaluating Intelligence: A Competency-Based Model," *International Journal of Intelligence and Counterintelligence*, Vol.18, No. 2, 2005, p. 207.

[102] Hall, E. T., *Beyond Culture*, New York: Anchor Books, 1989, p. 91.

[103] Grabo, C., *Anticipating Surprise: Analysis for Strategic Warning*, Joint Military Intelligence College, Center for Strategic Intelligence Research, 2002, pp. 162–163.

[104] "Each new warning failure, complete or partial, brings forth its rash of postmortem studies and recommendations for changes that will improve our 'warning capabilities.' Rarely, if ever, is there anything new in these recommendations, other than slight variations in the proposal for a revamping of the organizational structure." Grabo, C., *Anticipating Surprise: Analysis for Strategic Warning*, Joint Military Intelligence College, Center for Strategic Intelligence Research, 2002, p. 162.

[105] Langer, E. J., *Mindfulness*, Cambridge, MA: DaCapo Press, 1989, p. 62.

[106] Weick, K. E., and K. M. Sutcliffe, *Managing the Unexpected: Assuring High Performance in an Age of Complexity*, San Francisco, CA: Jossey-Bass, 2001, p. 3.

[107] Ibid., p. 1.

[108] Ibid., p. 2.

[109] Ibid., pp. 14–15.

[110] Grabo, C., *Anticipating Surprise: Analysis for Strategic Warning*, Washington, D.C.: Joint Military Intelligence College, Center for Strategic Intelligence Research, 2002, p. 132.

[111] Weick, K. E., and K. M. Sutcliffe, *Managing the Unexpected: Assuring High Performance in an Age of Complexity*, San Francisco, CA: Jossey-Bass, 2001, p. 41.

[112] Robbins, S., "Organizational Learning Is No Accident," *Working Knowledge for Business Leaders Newsletter*, Harvard Business School, 2005, http://hbswk.hbs.edu/item.jhtml?id=3483&t=srobbins.

[113] Grabo, C., *Anticipating Surprise: Analysis for Strategic Warning*, Joint Military Intelligence College, Center for Strategic Intelligence Research, 2002, p. 168.

[114] Weick, K. E. and K. M. Sutcliffe, *Managing the Unexpected: Assuring High Performance in an Age of Complexity*, San Francisco, CA: Jossey-Bass, 2001, p. 58.

[115] Weick, K. E., and K. M. Sutcliffe, *Managing the Unexpected: Assuring High Performance in an Age of Complexity*, San Francisco, CA: Jossey-Bass, 2001, p. 69.

[116] Ibid., pp. 63–64.

[117] Ibid., p. 63.

[118] Langer, E. J., *Mindfulness*, Cambridge, MA: DaCapo Press, 1989.

[119] Weick, K. E., and K. M. Sutcliffe, *Managing the Unexpected: Assuring High Performance in an Age of Complexity*, San Francisco, CA: Jossey-Bass, 2001, p. 11.

[120] Ibid., p. 60.

[121] Wilt, A. F., *The Atlantic Wall, 1941–1944: Hitler's Defenses for D-Day*, New York: Enigma Books, 2004, p. 123.

[122] Handel, M. I., *War, Strategy, and Intelligence,* London, U.K.: Frank Cass & Co., Ltd., 1989, pp. 336–337.

[123] Weick, K. E., and K. M. Sutcliffe, *Managing the Unexpected: Assuring High Performance in an Age of Complexity*, San Francisco, CA: Jossey-Bass, 2001, pp. 11–12.

[124] Ibid., p. 61.

[125] Grabo, C., *Anticipating Surprise: Analysis for Strategic Warning*, Joint Military Intelligence College, Center for Strategic Intelligence Research, 2002, p. 142.

[126] March, J. G., L. S. Sproull, and M. Tamuz, "Learning from Samples of One or Fewer," *Organization Science*, Vol. 2, 1991, pp. 1–13.

[127] Weick, K. E., and K. M. Sutcliffe, *Managing the Unexpected: Assuring High Performance in an Age of Complexity*, San Francisco, CA: Jossey-Bass, 2001, p. 56.

[128] Johnston, R., *Analytic Culture in the U.S. Intelligence Community*, Washington D.C.: Center for the Study of Intelligence, 2005, p. 85.

[129] The Commission on the Intelligence Capabilities of the United States Regarding Weapons of Mass Destruction, *Report to the President of the United States*, 2005, p. 425, http://www.wmd.gov/report/index.html.

[130] Weick, K. E., and K. M. Sutcliffe, *Managing the Unexpected: Assuring High Performance in an Age of Complexity*, San Francisco, CA: Jossey-Bass, 2001, p. 57.

[131] Robbins, S., "Organizational Learning Is No Accident," *Working Knowledge for Business Leaders Newsletter*, Harvard Business School, 2005, http://hbswk.hbs.edu/item.jhtml?id=3483&t=srobbins.

[132] Hedley, J. H., "Learning from Intelligence Failures," *International Journal of Intelligence and Counterintelligence*, Vol. 18, No. 3, 2005, p. 442.

[133] Hogarth, R. M., *Educating Intuition*, Chicago, IL: The University of Chicago Press, 2001, p. 89.

[134] The Commission on the Intelligence Capabilities of the United States Regarding Weapons of Mass Destruction, *Report to the President of the United States*, 2005, p. 407, http://www.wmd.gov/report/index.html.

[135] Schrage, M., "Daniel Kahneman: The Thought Leader Interview," 2003, http://ebusiness.mit.edu/schrage/Articles/DanielKahnemanInterview.pdf.

[136] Hogarth, R. M., *Educating Intuition*, Chicago, IL: The University of Chicago Press, 2001, p. 219.

[137] Darwin, C., *The Autobiography of Charles Darwin, 1809–1882*, with original omissions, restored edition, Nora Barlow, New York: W. W. Norton & Company, 1958, p. 123.

[138] Klein, G., *The Power of Intuition*, New York: Currency Doubleday, 2004, p. 38.

[139] Ibid., pp. 45–56.

[140] Ibid., p. 57.

[141] Greenhalgh, T., "Uneasy Bedfellows? Reconciling Intuition and Evidence Based Practice," 2002, http://www.youngminds.org.uk/magazine/59/greenhalgh.php.

[142] Feer, F., Thinking-Red-Wargaming Workshop: Opportunities for Deception and Counterdeception in the Red Planning Process (P-1510), Santa Monica, CA, RAND Corp., 1989, p. 10.

CHAPTER 7

Technical Methods of Counterdeception

Joseph Caddell wryly notes [1], in his recent *Primer on Deception*, "A comprehensive methodology for dealing with deception will never be written. It is a nebulous and ever changing field of virtually infinite proportions. Indeed, to believe that such a methodology is possible would be to misunderstand the nature of deception."

With this cautionary note in mind, we proceed to develop in this chapter the basis for a counterdeception methodology built on the principles in the past two chapters, and the direction from Barton Whaley's classic *Stratagem*. Whaley also offered a warning—but with an encouraging hint of a way forward to develop counter deception methodology—in summarizing the results of his exhaustive study of deception in warfare [2]:

> Indeed, this is the general finding of my study—that is, the deceiver is almost always successful regardless of the sophistication of his victim in the same art. On the face of it, this seems an intolerable conclusion, one offending common sense. Yet it is the irrefutable conclusion of historical evidence... Is there, then, no way by which the target of stratagem can untangle the web of deceit? While I recognize the apparent contradiction, I would suggest that it is indeed only apparent. The alert stratagematist should not—need not—be deceived. The contradiction can be resolved, if we recognize that neither sophisticated practice nor reminders of "constant alertness" provide any practical guidance on just how to avoid victimization. Exhortations to avoid being deceived are, I suspect, as uselessly homiletic as those to use it... I suggest that the avoidance of victimization by stratagem requires [a decisional] model, specifically one designed to analyze the signals of stratagem, rather than the one designed to synthesize their false signals.

Here, Whaley refers to a "decisional model" (methodology) to support counterdeception and mitigation of surprise that is analogous to a decision model he presents earlier to support the development of a deception strategy to achieve surprise [3].

A counterdeception methodology translates principles to practical technical methods that can be codified, explained, trained, and applied effectively in a manual sense, or with supporting tools. Indeed, apart from a theory, principles, and methodology, the target of deception is in greater danger of surprise. Of course, any methodology must provide agility, adaptation, and awareness that the envelope of all potential stratagems is beyond prediction. The successful deceit of millennia of magic performances has demonstrated Caddel's basic premise: magic, too, is a nebulous and ever-changing field of virtually infinite proportions of illusion.

We focus here on intelligence counterdeception, where Johnson has noted [4]:

> Intentional deception can occur outside intelligence—in connection with certain law enforcement functions, for example—but most of the professional literature treats this as the exception, rather than the rule. In the case of intelligence analysis, deception is the rule. In intelligence analysis, the validity of the data is always in doubt. Moreover, intelligence analysts are specifically trained to factor in deception as part of the analytic process, to look for anomalies and outliers instead of focusing on the central tendencies of distribution.

This chapter and Chapter 6 focus on the elements of counterdeception that must be a part of that training; Chapter 8 illustrates the implementation of these processes in supporting tools.

Even as in Chapters 2 through 4 we described how deception principles (Chapter 2) to exploit human cognition (Chapter 3) are carefully implemented by technical methods (Chapter 4), we now show how the counterdeception principles (Chapter 5) are implemented by technical means to reduce the vulnerability of the human targets, whether planners, collectors and their processing, or analysts (Chapter 6).

We begin by introducing the principles that underlie the technical detection and discovery of stratagem's signals (Section 7.1), before relating the principles of Chapter 5 to fundamental methods in a counterdeception matrix (Section 7.2). Section 7.3 then relates these methods to practical operations, whose implementations are described in further detail in Section 7.4 (collection), Section 7.5 (processing), and Section 7.6 (analysis).

7.1 The Counterdeception Elements of Detection, Discovery, and Deterrence

Counterdeception is not always an all-or-nothing enterprise (e.g., failure leads to disastrous surprise or success leads to complete knowledge of an adversary's intentions); success at countering an adversary's stratagem may occur in varying degrees. Consider three levels of increasing understanding that the counter deceiver may achieve:

- *Awareness* acknowledges the potential for deception and surprise—apart from any evidence. It is an appreciation that the adversary may have deception motives, opportunities, and means available to carry out deception. Awareness can be cued up by a situation-based (contextual) knowledge apart from any particular evidence (e.g., deception would provide a significant advantage to an adversary in this situation), or it can be cued by the observation of empirical evidence through discovery or detection.
- *Observation* occurs at varying levels of specificity when empirical evidence of deceptive behavior is observed by one of two means: (1) *detection* and recognition of specific evidence that matches a previously known pattern of deception, leading to the identification of the adversary's activities and likely deceptive intentions; or (2) *discovery* of evidence of a pattern not previously identified as deceptive, but suspicious and potentially deceptive. Various levels of observation may occur, ranging from observation of deceptive concealment of activities (without knowing what intention actions may be taken), to

varying degrees of understanding of the adversaries deception plans and capabilities. Active *deterrent* measures may be taken to evoke evidence to support the processes of *detection* and *discovery*.

- *Penetration* of an adversary's deception occurs when the full deception intentions and plans are revealed; often the adversary is kept unaware of this knowledge and the insight may be exploited by a counterdeception operation that mitigates the potential and effects of the adversary's plans.

The degree of understanding achieved is, of course, a function of the sophistication (or effectiveness) of the deception and the effectiveness of the counterdeception analysis and operations that seek to reveal it. This chapter focuses on the technical means to implement two fundamental underlying analytic processes of counterdeception that will be detailed in subsequent sections—detection and discovery.

Deception detection is the analytic process of matching observed empirical evidence to prior, known patterns of deception. These known patterns can be expressed as representative templates that are compared to current observations, and can be based on prior real deceptions, or on conjectured (hypothetical) deception operations developed by the counterdeception analyst. Detection is performed by the reasoning process of *deduction*, the method of inference by which a conclusion is inferred by applying the rules of a logical system to manipulate statements of belief to form new logically consistent statements of belief. The processes of pattern recognition and data fusion generally apply deduction to compare observations with prior (known) patterns or templates to arrive at detection. Matched filters, predicate logic, Bayesian inference, and a variety of other mathematical procedures are applied to implement deductive detection. Many templates for deception are well known; others may be subtle phenomenological or operational cues produced by the unwary deceiver and unique to a particular operation or piece of equipment. Cues provided by the munitions stockpiles of biological weapons (BW) programs, for example, are widely recognized, but are not necessary indicators of a concealed BW program [5]:

> Countries are taking advantage of denial and deception techniques, concealing and protecting BW programs. Concealment is relatively simple with BW because of its overlap with legitimate research and commercial biotechnology. Even supposedly "legitimate" facilities can readily conduct clandestine BW research and can convert rapidly to agent production, providing a mobilization or "breakout" capability. As a result, large stockpiles of BW munitions simply may not be required in today's BW arena.

In this BW example, the detection of extensive biotechnology research and production activities, associated with high security, may be a cue to deduce the *potential* presence of a concealed BW program, but the lack of stockpiles of munitions is not evidence against that potential.

Deception discovery is the second analytic process that occurs when potential deception-related evidence is revealed in the form of empirical data that are recognized as unusual or unexpected or elements of evidence are conflicting or inconsistent. Such data can be recognized as an *incongruity*. This incongruous evidence may reveal to the analyst a new context in which evidence may be viewed that leads to the discovery of a deception pattern not previously known. Consider a geometric analogy to illustrate the discovery process (Figure 7.1). The sequence of evidence is the series of facts (D1, D2...) that may be projected onto one plane (or frame of discernment, A) to reveal a simple curve of the form $y=x^n$. One outlying point, D_x, is an incongruity because it is the only point that does not fit the current (and obvious) hypothesis, $y=x^n$. The analyst must choose to discard the point as an error in observation, or consider alternative (perhaps more difficult and complex) frames of discernment that will allow all observations to fit. In the example in the figure, the probing analyst discovers that if the observations are projected onto an orthogonal plane, B, all of the evidence fits an entirely different explanation: the sinusoid, $y=\sin(x)$. Author Arthur Koestler, in his classic work *The Act of Discovery*, adopted the term "bisociation" to describe the process in many discoveries, where scientists have been able to view multiple explanations (or multiple "associations") of the same data simultaneously [6]. In many intelligence problems, the available data is extremely limited (undersampled) and a new and novel deception explanation may remain hidden if the analyst does not explore more than the common, immediate, or simple interpretation. Hence, the discovery process is necessarily exploratory, requiring the counterdeception analyst to explore alternative frames of discernment and possible realities, especially those that are inspired by incongruities. The deceiver, or course, applies simulation to enhance the visibility of A, dissimulation to hide evidence that would reveal B, and supporting misdirection to keep the analyst's attention away from the discovery of B. Discovery is performed by inductive or abductive reasoning processes, where the conclusions of reasoning can be stronger than the premises (evidence), and the hypothetical inferences also produce fallible knowledge. *Induction* is the method of inference by which a more general or more abstract belief is developed by observing a limited set of observations or instances; it moves from specific beliefs about instances to general beliefs about larger and future populations of instances. *Abduction* is the informal or pragmatic mode of reasoning

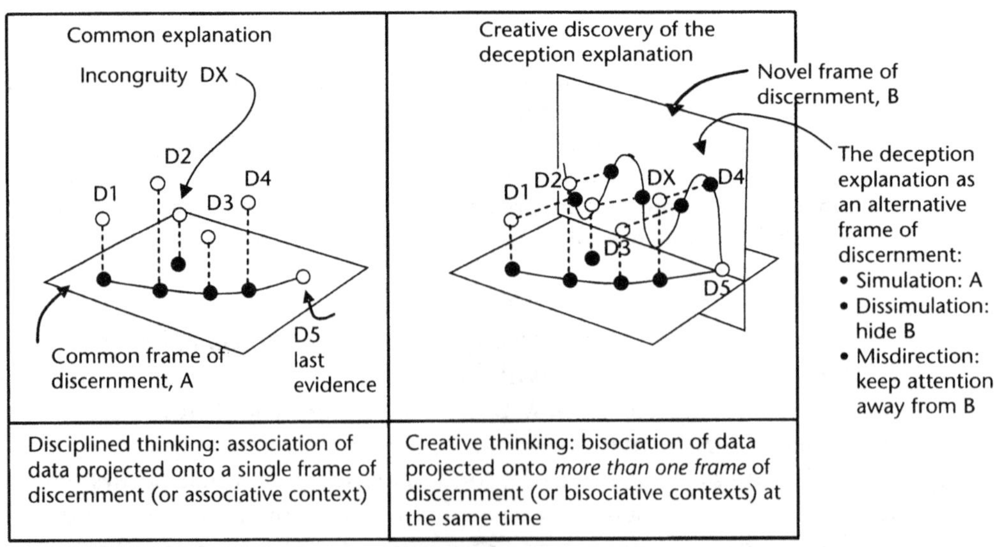

Figure 7.1 Deception discovery as context shifting. (*From:* [8]. © 2003 Artech House, Inc. Reprinted with permission.)

to describe how we "reason to the best explanation"; it is a method to arrive at a solution or explanation by creating and evaluating multiple hypotheses for a given set of data. Abduction incorporates both inductive (hypothesis-creating) and deductive (hypothesis-testing) operations to seek alternative frames of discernment for a given set of observations—and is inherently exploratory in nature [7].

In a RAND study of deception, Gerwehr and Glenn characterized this discovery aspect of the counterdeception process as a *counter adaptation process*, recognizing that deception is a natural adaptation by an adversary to a competitive situation. Even as the United States developed an information superiority in space reconnaissance and a numerical superiority on the symmetric battlefield in the 1990s, adversaries adapted by seeking asymmetries through D&D to thwart surveillance of their activities, the development of WMD to counter conventional warfare superiority, and the use of terrorism to directly attack the will of societies. Counter deception, then seeks to counter the adaptation—learning and innovation—and may include more than improved collection and analysis. Active measures that limit learning (e.g., protection of collection means and deception about counterintelligence measure) retard innovation, and implementation (e.g., constraining access to technology and expertise) should be considered as components of an offensive counterdeception strategy. The RAND study points out [9], "As we consider why combatants innovate, the rate at which such innovation occurs, and with what means innovation is institutionalized, a doctrine for countering adversary adaptation begins to emerge." They further hypothesized that the most effective approaches to countering deception include the selection of appropriate methods for any given situation and the combination of multiple categories of counterdeception methods to detect known deception patterns or to discover new ones.

The distinction between the detection and discovery processes (illustrated in Figure 7.2) is in both the *reasoning direction* and the role of *context*—the interrelated conditions in which an entity or event exists or occurs, that which surrounds and gives meaning to entities or events [10]. *Detection* begins with a hypothesis that sets the context by which all data are evaluated for relevance. Data are filtered (evaluated) by context to determine relevance, and evidence is fitted to known deception model hypotheses (e.g., decoy signatures, typical feint activity patterns, and so forth) In many potentially deceptive situations, the context is known and data are directly matched to deception patterns (e.g., in a submarine tracking situation, the context is narrow and the difference between submarine and decoy sonar signatures are defined statistically). *Discovery*, on the other hand, begins with data, and a correlation-search process (e.g., automated induction using data mining techniques) searches across alternative contexts to identify data sets that meet some criteria that reveals them to be "interesting" (e.g., in the earlier example of a clandestine BW program, a criteria may include associations between security personnel and biological research personnel and *incongruous*, "unusual," or "unexpected" interaction patterns). The discovery of a candidate context—even though existing data may not be complete—allows the creation of a hypothesis that may imply a deceptive activity never before imagined by the analyst. The discovery of a potentially new deception may be modeled to explain the incomplete data. The newly conjectured

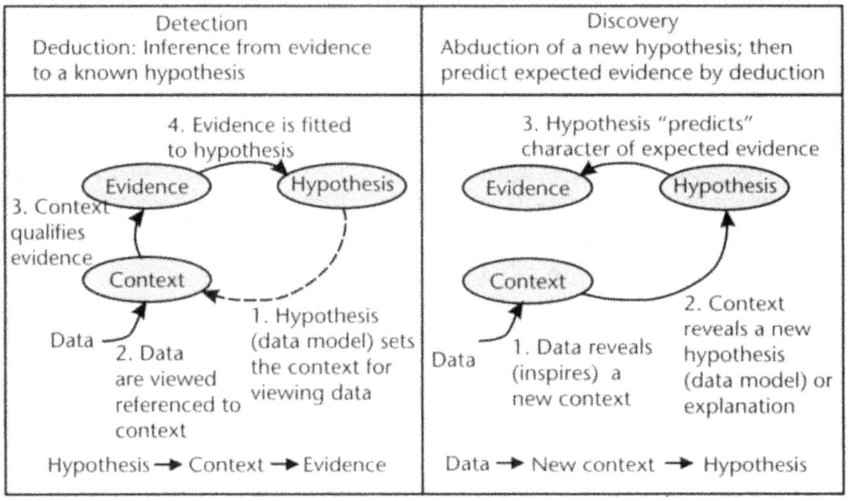

Figure 7.2 The detection and discovery reasoning paths. (*After:* [11].)

deception hypothesis in turn allows the prediction of the complete set of expected evidence that should be present if the hypothesis of deception were true.

The role of context in determining the relevance of data in a particular problem is paramount; it can determine if an incongruity is irrelevant, or the clue that reveals a new frame of discernment and the discovery of a deception. In practical terms, context can be viewed as the collection of relevant conditions and surrounding influences that make a situation unique and comprehensible [12]. While the previous discussions have described the detection and discovery processes in abstract terms, we can now consider the range of practical problem classes that may be distinguished by the degree to which targets and their contexts may be described. Table 7.1 lists three basic classes of situations, organized in terms of increasing problem difficulty. In case 1, the target characteristics and context of the target are well known (e.g., aircraft targets in the context of a defensive counter air mission). Classic statistical automatic target recognition (ATR) and multisource data fusion processes have been developed for these problems; model-based ATR approaches are required

Table 7.1 The Role of Context in Applying Data Fusion and Data Mining to a Problem

Case	*Target Description*	*Target Context*	*Typical Solution Approaches*	*Implementation*
1	Known in detail	Known, static, or multimodal and changing	Template-based automatic target recognition (ATR) or data fusion; model-based ATR; context-sensitive and multiple hypothesis data fusion and tracking	Data fusion-multiple source ATR
2	Only specific cases known; limited general descriptions	Only statistically known, or only specific cases known	Supervised learning (training) using limited known target cases and situations; unsupervised data mining	Data mining to discover new patterns; data fusion for known targets
3	Unknown targets	Unknown context	Exploratory analysis: search for contexts that reveal potential target patterns; simulate target scenarios to create new and novel contexts	Data fusion and data mining, plus simulation to explore contexts

where that target characteristics are dynamic, and multiple hypotheses may be required to be maintained while contexts are clarified to converge on a likely hypothesis.

Case 2 occurs when the target characteristics are known only in a limited sense (e.g., specific cases of terrorist attacks are known, but the only general pattern is too abstract to be a useful discriminator) and knowledge of the context is also limited (e.g., the scope of contexts for attack possibilities seem limitless). In this case, the characteristics that distinguish a target depend upon the context. Supervised and unsupervised data mining processes may be applied to discover the *general* patterns of terrorist attack processes from the cases of *specific* instances of those patterns of targets in various contexts.

Case 3 includes those problems where the target process is a complex adaptive system—both the target descriptions and their context are dynamic and the result of interactions between independent actors (e.g., the adversary continuously adapting concealment techniques and channel deceptions to defeat changing patterns of intelligence collection). *Complexity* is the emergent property of these systems, caused primarily by the *interactions* between independent actors, rather than on the properties of the actors themselves. This behavior cannot be predicted by models of the properties of the individual actors, nor by a linear combination of them. Such irreducible behavior cannot be solved by traditional model-based approaches. The approach to such problems requires an *exploratory analysis* methodology that includes an *analytic*, or top-down, decomposition of raw data that can be later assembled into hypotheses, and a *synthetic*, or bottom-up, creation (or synthesis) of the envelope of possible explanations that encompass, and even exceed, possible explanations from the currently available data. The process explores alternative situations that present new contexts for filtering data. The functional implementation of these processes will be further illustrated in Section 7.4.

In addition to the analytic processes of detection and discovery, the operational process that supports analysis in defeating deception, *operational countermeasures*, must also be considered for the sake of completeness. While the prior two processes are essentially passive in nature, such operations employ active measures to:

- *Probe* the deceiver's activities, in attempts to evoke empirical evidence for detection and discovery ("unmasking");
- *Defeat* potential deceptive activities (e.g., saturation destruction of all targets without distinguishing decoys) if resources are available;
- *Prepare* protective-reactive operations to mitigate the effectiveness (and adverse consequences) of potential stratagems based on any level of awareness by planning for contingencies.

Active probes can be considered special collections and may include a range of actions: outright provocation (e.g., military probing engagements to observe the reactions and behavior of targets to discriminate decoys), searches (e.g., military cordon and search operations), and deceptive actions (e.g., *unmasking* feints designed to evoke responses to produce evidence that will reveal a unit's actual strength). Probes are designed to support collection and analysis to break concealment, reveal decoys, or provide critical evidence with greater diagnostic value to eliminate alternative hypotheses. Whaley and Busby describe this process as the use of "controlled experiments" using probes, traps, and tripwires to develop the necessary evidence to fill critical gaps [13]. The U.S. concept of an intelligence campaign plan is based on the close synchronization of intelligence and operations to "fight for intelligence" by actively probing adversaries (proactive intelligence collection; "if you want actionable intelligence, you must take action first" [14]).

7.2 Fundamental Counterdeception Technical Methods

We can now map the four principles of counterdeception developed in Chapter 5 across the major elements of the intelligence process to move from principle to practice. We adopt the standard stages of the intelligence cycle to represent the major areas in the process—producing a matrix to summarize how each principle is applied throughout the process (Table 7.2) [15]. The table provides an overall summary of the practical methods that are further developed in the next three sections, as referenced in the table.

Notice that the counterdeception process maintains four parallel lines of inquiry that span the entire intelligence cycle and applies the three basic technical methods (or measures) developed in the last section throughout collection, processing and analysis.

- *Plan and direction* manages the intelligence process, beginning with the development of a counterdeception strategy and implementing plans that identify the information needed for decision, the challenges, and the process for acquisition. The plan directs the development of channels required to penetrate concealment and reveal deceptions, the processing and analysis of acquired data, and the assessment of the effectiveness of counterdeception activities. The counterdeception planning effort (like the deception planning effort described earlier in Chapter 4) requires a high-level consideration of the potential perceptions that an adversary might want to achieve, and an objective assessment of one's own policy, operational and analytic factors that pose possible vulnerabilities that expose channels, processing, or analysis to deception. The counterdeception plan also includes a collection plan and supporting the processing and analysis approaches to develop the essential information required by the strategy.
- *Collection* develops the necessary channels of access to target information. The collection plan identifies the multi-INT sources, supporting active probes, coordination of collection timing, and the means of authenticating the reliability and validity of independent and multiple sources. While the collection process focuses on acquiring empirical evidence on specific targets, it also includes the collection of contextual information to support analysis of the situation influencing adversary deception policies, and evidence of motive, opportunity, and capabilities (operational and technical means) of deception.
- *Processing* converts the channel data to a form useable by analysts (this typical includes translation of text, audio, and video data; decryption and other processing of technical data). The front-end processing may include filters set to

Table 7.2 Mapping Principles Across the Intelligence Cycle

Phase of Intelligence Process	*Counterdeception Principles*			
	Know Self	*Know Situation (Context)*	*Know Channels*	*Know Adversary*
Plan and direction (Section 7.3)	Identify policy and operational and analytic factors that pose possible deception vulnerabilities; plan analytic approach to mitigate effects.	Identify situational elements relative to self and adversary; develop collection and analysis approach to collect and analyze essential elements of the situation.	Identify required number and diversity of channels to achieve necessary confidence in assessment; plan coordinated multichannel collection strategies.	Identify essential information required, means of concealment, and potential penetration strategies; plan collection and deception analysis workflow.
Collection (Section 7.3)	Identify collection gaps (time, space, process, and so forth) that render processing or analysis susceptible to deception.	Collect empirical data to support high-level situation tracking.	Collect data across channels, as well as data to evaluate channel performance, reliability, and validity.	Collect empirical data on adversary behaviors; collect contextual data to assess motive, opportunity, means of deception.
Processing (Section 7.4)	Identify processing limitations (e.g., sample aliasing) that open deception vulnerabilities.	Perform front-end detection processes to search for incongruities in raw data (inconsistencies across channels, changes, outlying observations, and suspicious trends); generate automated cues to analysts of relevant evidence.		
Analysis and production (Section 7.5)	Analyze impact of own policy, operations, and analytic factors that may bias analysis; maintain assessments and mitigate impacts.	Perform contextual analysis of deception gains-risks to self and to adversary; detect and discover contextual indicators of deception.	Perform channel performance and cross-channel analysis; detect and discover subtle incongruities; derive channel effectiveness measures.	Detect and discover evidence of deceptive activities; perform inferential and exploratory analysis of adversary data to synthesize alternative explanations (hypotheses).
		Perform analysis of alternative hypotheses; assess counterdeception diagnostic value of evidence and potential for deception across all explanations; apply analytic judgment across all hypotheses, including contextual and empirical evidence; describe all judgments and rationale.		
Dissemination (Section 7.5)	Report own policy positions (desires) and beliefs; identify potential biases relevant to these positions that may produce policy, operational or analytic vulnerabilities.	Report all situational elements that influence the deception analysis; report potential implications of changing situations.	Report all channels used, the means to verify channels (e.g., asset validation), the credibility of each, and cross-channel inconsistencies and explanations.	Report contextual motive, operational and technical means, and opportunities available to the adversary; report empirical evidence of denial and deception.
		Report summary judgments and basis of judgment; report multiple perspectives and alternative analyses, including deception factors, gaps, and contradictions.		

detect incongruities in raw data (e.g., inconsistencies across channels, changes, outlying observations, and suspicious trends) that generate automated cues for analysts to review their relevance to counterdeception analysis.

- *Analysis and production* integrates and evaluates all incoming data, in context, and synthesizes alternative explanations or hypotheses to explain reality. Counterdeception is a component of the overall analytic process, introducing a heightened sensitivity to the possibility of deception and synthesizing hypotheses that include that possibility. The process (explained in greater detail in Section 7.5) integrates inferential analysis (moving by logical inference from empirical evidence to hypothesis) and exploratory analysis (moving from hypothetical models to expected evidence) with an emphasis on properly explaining and attributing value to incongruities (contradictions) that may be indictors of deception. The analytic process results in requests to adapt and refine the collection process to improve the diagnostic value of evidence that will support or refute hypotheses. Analysts are also called upon to weigh tactical indicators (new empirical information) over strategic assumptions (preexisting contextual beliefs), challenge alternative hypotheses, and prepare to revisit prior reported judgments.
- *Dissemination of reporting* provides decision-makers with summary judgments and the basis of the judgments regarding deception activities; the reports should explain the multiple perspectives of assessment and the alternatives analyzed, including deception factors, gaps, and contradictions. The *Commission on the Intelligence Capabilities of the United States Regarding Weapons of Mass Destruction* emphasized that alternative analysis is important in dealing with deception, but it is also critical that these independent views reach policymakers in disseminated reports [16]. Where deception is involved, reporting should include information in four areas of the counterdeception principles:
    - *Self:* Report own policy positions (desires) and beliefs; identify potential biases relevant to these positions that may produce policy, operational or analytic vulnerabilities, and the approaches used to mitigate those effects.
    - *Situation:* Report all situational elements that influence the deception analysis; report the potential implications of changing situations.
    - *Channels:* Report all channels that are used, the means to verify those channels (e.g., validation of HUMINT assets, calibration of technical collections, and so forth.), the credibility of each and cross-channel inconsistencies and explanations. The gaps in collection must also be reported, with a rationale for the gaps, and potential approaches to close the gaps (e.g., active probes and tripwires).
    - *Adversary:* Report motive, operational and available operational-technical means, and opportunities available to the adversary; report the specific empirical evidence of denial and deception, as well as evidence that supports alternative hypotheses of the real situation.

It is important to notice that collection is necessary, but not sufficient for countering sophisticated deception. Unless there is a rare silver-bullet source of penetrating information, improvements in collection generally provide added channels, more frequent or accurate coverage, and limited penetration of some covers. Avoiding the tendency to focus on collection to find a silver bullet source, emphasis on analysis is required. Former CIA analyst Richards Heuer has wisely noted that [17]: "Any systematic counterdeception program must focus primarily on problems of analysis, only secondarily on collection."

7.3 Counterdeception Planning and Collection Strategies

The counterdeception process begins with the process of planning for collection, processing, and analysis. The process includes a *target development* stage where collection priorities and collection gaps (especially those that prohibit deception penetration) are defined, and integrated collection strategies are defined to address those gaps, a *collection management* stage where the integrated collection strategy is implemented across all channels of collection, and the *data management* stage that oversees the processing and analysis of data that is collected across the different collection channels.

Planners (or intelligence *mission managers*) must consider strategies that coordinate (or integrate) collection, processing, and analysis to:

- *Resist deceptive reinforcement:* To reduce vulnerability to deceiver attempts to reinforce the analyst or policymaker mental models or expectations and condition the analyst to reduce sensitivity to target phenomena and changes.
- *Recognize or mitigate the impact of misdirection:* To reduce seductive reactions when events or object are presented by the deceiver to gain sensor or source attention and force the collector to make resource allocation decisions that minimize detection of deceptive activities.
- *Counter multiple-channel deception integration:* By increasing channels of information beyond the deceiver's ability to fully coordinate the transmission of deception information simultaneously or consistently across multiple channels to create a high-fidelity deception.
- *Enhance collection breadth:* To effectively tailor all resources to minimize vulnerabilities and limitations of information access to the target and close collection gaps to penetrate possible deceptions.

The planner must strategically develop seek to develop and enhance the diagnostic value of collected data (to distinguish between hypotheses or lines of analytic inquiry) in at least four primary dimensions of collection:

- *Time:* Increase the temporal persistence and dwell on target or frequency of repeated sampled observation of a target.
- *Space:* Increase the coverage of the target space or expanse; this includes the expanse in physical space, phenomenological space (e.g., dimensions of physical phenomena sensed), information space (e.g., dimensions of network access), or cognitive space (e.g., dimensions of human perspectives or access by agents).
- *Channel:* Increase the number and diversity of channels of information with access to the target directly or via secondary sources.

- *Type and mode:* Increase the types and modes of collection (active-passive, standard-surprise, probative-seductive, and so forth).

Counterdeception planning strategies must develop an integrated set of collection tactics and techniques—with associated processing techniques also tailored to the situation. Example collection tactics and techniques for these four areas are listed in Table 7.3 to illustrate the wide range of options that the analyst and collection manager may consider to expose and penetrate a targeted deception activity.

The importance of developing, tailoring and increasing multiple channels of information, and keeping them covert cannot be understated. R. V. Jones, the former head of the U.K. Scientific Intelligence and award-winning author of *Reflections on Intelligence*, noted the fundamental importance of developing, comparing, and exploiting multiple channels to counter deception based on his early experience at Bletchley Park (United Kingdom) in World War II [18]:

> As I started to analyze what I was doing in building up an intelligence system to cover scientific and technological developments, I came to realize that just as a human head depends on sight, sound, smell, and touch as channels for gathering data about the external world for processing and interpretation by the brain, so an

Table 7.3 Collection Tactics and Techniques for Counterdeception Enhancement

Dimension of Enhancement of Collection		*Example Collection Tactics and Techniques*
Time	Increase the persistence and dwell on target or frequency of observation.	Increase satellite or aircraft revisit rate to observe target activities. Maintain continual orbit by unmanned air vehicles over target to maintain persistent surveillance of target during critical periods. Coordinate collection by multiple simultaneous sensors during an active probe of a computer network.
Time-space and channel	Reduce predictability of collection.	Conduct collections at random times and in unusual locations that exclude accurate prediction and minimize effectiveness of movements of targets.
Space	Increase the coverage of the target space or expanse.	View physical facility from multiple spatial perspectives. Increase number of ports and network sensors to monitor a targeted computer net.
Channel	Increase the number and diversity of channels of information.	Increase the spectral bandwidth of collection (e.g., multiple discrete spectra, hyperspectral collection, foliage penetration radar). Add duplicate human agents; check technical collection results with agent reports. Perform multi-INT collections designed to confirm simultaneous existence of evidence of static structures and dynamic processes. Develop specifically tailored MASINT sensors to discriminate diagnostic phenomena for a given high-value target.
Type and mode	Increase the types and modes of collection.	Increase number, scale, or scope of passive collection sensors or sources. Augment passive observation with coordinated probes to distinguish decoys, protective actions. Initiate misdirection to perform covert or surprise active collection. Conduct a seductive collection (present A as a source, collect against B as the source is exploited), as in a computer network honeypot or agent dangle operation.

> intelligence system depends on spies, electronic and photographic reconnaissance, and so forth. So I came to see the battle between intelligence and deception as the efforts on one side to establish as many channels as possible through which to observe the opponent, in the hope that he may fail to block at least some of these channels, while the opponent may in addition try to send false, and preferably consistent, signals in as many channels as possible. To succeed in any such exchange, you should therefore aim to establish (and, if possible, multiply) your channels of observation, and to deepen the sophistication in each individual channel so that if your opponent tries to send false signals in that channel he may fail to match a genuine signal in its sophistication.

The vulnerability of U.S. intelligence to Iraqi concealment and deception about its WMD program in 2002–2003 was largely attributed to the lack of channel diversity and the inappropriate confidence attributed to a single HUMINT channel [19]. The U.S. Commission studying the difficulties in penetrating the concealment of WMD programs recommended new emphasis on innovation in the area of collection [20]: "The [Director of National Intelligence, DNI] should also assist collectors in developing and operationalizing the most promising innovations, while redoubling efforts to improve *existing* means of countering and reducing the distorting effects of denial and deception... To aid him in the latter effort, the DNI will inherit a commendable roadmap previously developed by the [Director of Central Intelligence]. Among other things, this strategy establishes efforts to counter-denial and deception by our adversaries as "a top priority for the Intelligence Community." (Throughout this chapter, we cite numerous comments from the U.S. Commission report relevant to countering and reporting deception; hereinafter references to the *Commission on the Intelligence Capabilities of the United States Regarding Weapons of Mass Destruction* will cite *the Commission.*)

7.4 Counterdeception Information Processing

Automated processing of collected data is generally performed to translate raw data for analysis, applying processes of conversion (e.g., image formation, signal calibration, and language translation), filtering (selecting relevant data and detecting specific patterns), and organization (indexing data by characteristics). In some cases, the filtering process may be used to perform detection or discovery of within-channel or cross-channel ambiguities and provide cues to the analyst for further investigation. In tactical applications (e.g., real-time electronic warfare systems), automated processing may perform the complete detection of some deceptions where known deceptive signatures (e.g., spoofed IFF signatures, aircraft radar emission signatures, jamming patterns known to support misdirection and concealment) can be directly detected and used for tactical response.

In strategic intelligence applications confronting sophisticated operational D&D, processing more often serves the function of screening massive volumes of data (streaming and archived) and tentative detections are directed to analysts for further multi-INT analysis. Processing filters are tailored to the target and channel characteristics and include a wide range of detection or discovery attributes, illustrated by the categories of deception filters listed in Table 7.4 with representative examples across the intelligence disciplines (INTs).

Channel processing flows depend upon the knowledge of the target and the context; three representative processing architectures that cover the three target-context classes described earlier in Section 7.1 are illustrated in Figure 7.3. In the first case, where target and context are well known, a data fusion process is appropriate to perform detection by correlation of data across channels, followed by deductive logic, matched filter detection, or other pattern recognition methods.

The second category applies to domains where target characteristics are known but the context is not fully defined. These processing flows integrate the discovery and detection processes to extract, transform, and load (ETL) data to maintain a data store that can be analyzed by an ongoing data mining process to search for and discover new contexts and target descriptions for correlation and discrimination in the data fusion process.

The third process adds a simulation capability to expand the envelope of situations explored by both the fusion and mining processes. The simulation allows the analyst to run computation experiments to explore complex phenomena for emergent (surprising) behaviors not apparent to the analyst. Detected cues from data fusion may be fed back to set the context to adapt the mining and simulation processes.

To illustrate a conceptual implementation of a category 2 semiautomated counterdeception processing flow, consider the processing pipeline depicted in Figure 7.4. This system compares three text reporting streams (S1, S2, S3) for detection of known deception patterns and discovery of incongruities in observations about a

Table 7.4 Representative Deception Processing Filters

Filter Category	*Description*	*Intelligence Example*
Change detection	Detect a temporal change in spatial, temporal or attribute pattern that is not expected by the normal model of behavior.	IMINT: by comparison of two images over a 24-hour period, detect an uncommon change in the combination of military vehicles in a parking area.
Method detection	Detect a known deception practice by matched filter comparison with signature or behavior pattern reference templates.	ELINT: detect a known radar return "range-walk-off" delay deception technique; detect a false radar cross section signature of a decoy.
Cross-channel inconsistency detection	Detect a known form of contradiction of data between two or more channels that support opposing hypotheses.	COMINT-IMINT: the imaged pattern of vehicles in a surface-to-air missile battery of a known type does not correspond to the emissions of the associated fire control radar.
New pattern discovery	Discover a pattern (e.g., correlation of characteristics or linking of relationships among a set of entities forming a cluster) not previously observed.	COMINT: discovery of a new sequence of COMINT traffic over a specific channel; this may be evidence of previously unrecognized concealment of communication.
Cross-channel incongruity discovery	Discover subtle inconsistencies in data between two or more channels that are expected to report consistently; discover outlying data that may be in error or support a new hypothesis revealing a previously unknown deceptive technique.	EO-SAR GEOINT: discovery of a heretofore unrecognized difference between the electro-optical and synthetic aperture radar signatures for a known mobile missile launcher type; this *may* be the discovery of a new decoy type.

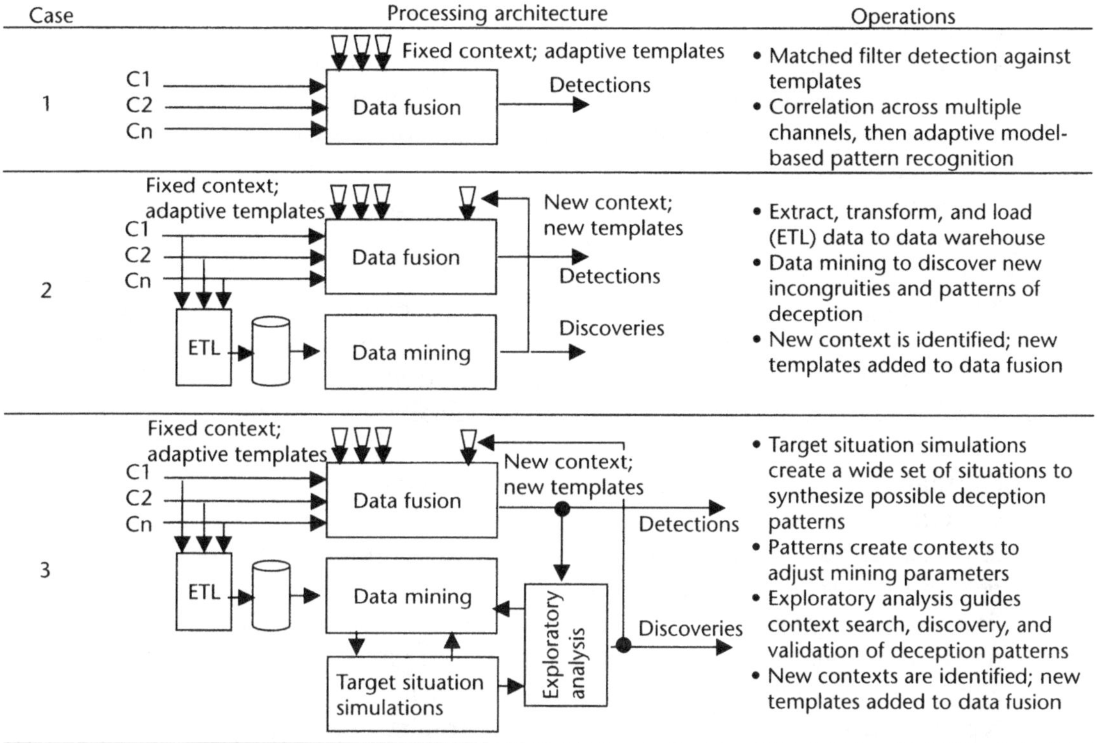

Figure 7.3 Alternative integrating architectures.

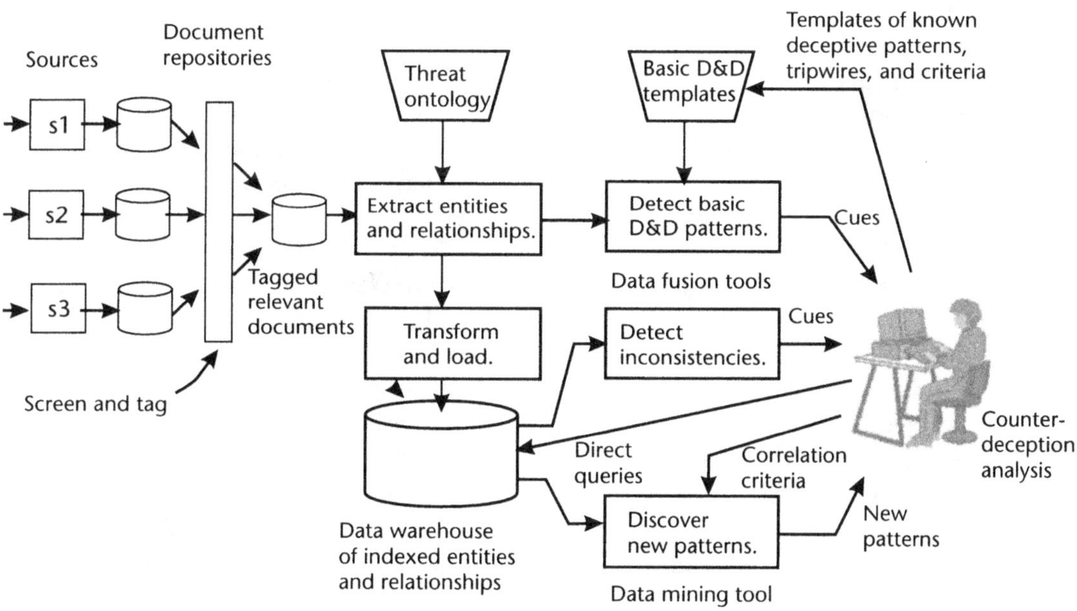

Figure 7.4 Counterdeception processing in a conceptual message-screening system.

foreign organization believed to employing deception tactics, techniques, and procedures (TTPs) [21]. The channels include including the S1 HUMINT stream (representing four different sources or channels), S2 open source reporting channel, and S3 public statements attributed to the organization. The flow accepts text documents from the distinct channels, which are screened, tagged, and translated to a common reference repository; relevant named entities and relationships are extracted from the documents according to reference ontology for the domain. (The ontology defines named entities and relationships for the domain, as well as expected the reference relationships that describe concepts within the domain [22].) The extracted data are continually compared to a range of templates that represent known organizational deception TTPs (e.g., multiple route shipping, multiple aliases for certain employees, linkages with entities on watch lists, and so forth). In addition, selected entity-relationship data are transformed and loaded into a data warehouse for long-term accumulation and analysis by a data mining process that searches for patterns of relationships not previously recognized as deceptive TTPs, but that meet a more abstract correlation property. Patterns that match these general criteria are cued to the analyst for review and assessment to determine if they are indeed a heretofore undiscovered evidence of deception. In addition, inconsistencies between reports are detected to cue the analyst to incongruities. Santos et al. have described one approach to such a message comparison system using similarity functions to compare directed graph representations of documents [23]. In that approach, concepts (entities) and relationships within each document are represented as a directed acyclic graph, and graph comparisons are used to compute similarity metrics to detect discrepancies across documents.

7.5 Counterdeception Analysis, Decision Support, and Production

While the planning, collection, and processing must acquire and make available raw observations, it is only the analyst that has the synoptic perspective, and perhaps the greatest opportunity to detect or discover the presence of the most sophisticated deception. As we have pointed out in earlier chapters, deception is the effect of the human mind—and it is the mind of the analyst that is the focus on concealment and deception.

Whaley and Busby offer encouragement to the feasibility of deception detection and understanding in analysis [24]: "The possibility of detecting deception, is inherent in the effort to deceive. Every deception operation necessarily leaves at least two clues: incongruities about what is hidden; and incongruities about what is displayed in its stead. The analyst requires only the appropriate sensors and mind-set (cognitive hypotheses) to detect and understand the meaning of these clues."

As a result of the failure of U.S. intelligence to penetrate and fully understand the state of the Iraq weapons of mass destruction (WMD) program in 2003, *the Commission* noted four key implications of denial and deception for WMD analysts (Table 7.5) [25].

Notice that the four bullets in the table address the principles cited earlier; in sequence the bullets address knowing the adversary and context, knowing self (and clearly reporting what is known and what is not), knowing the limitations of collection channels, and applying technical methods that address all four principles. *The Commission* noted, for example, that WMD analysts did consider the adversary

Table 7.5 Analytic Implications of WMD Denial and Deception

What Denial and Deception (D&D) Means for Analysis
State and nonstate actors either with or seeking to develop WMD materials and technologies all practice robust denial and deception techniques against U.S. technical collection. We must significantly reduce our vulnerability to intelligence surprises, mistakes, and omissions caused by the effects of denial and deception (D&D) on collection and analysis. To do so, the community must foster:
• *Greater awareness of D&D among analysts,* including a deeper understanding of what other countries know about our intelligence capabilities, as well as the D&D intentions, capabilities, and programs of those countries;
• *Greater specification by analysts of what they don't know and clearer statements of their degree of certainty.* Analysts should also work more closely with collectors to fully exploit untapped collection opportunities against D&D targets and to identify and isolate any deceptive information;
• *Greater appreciation for the capabilities and limitations of U.S. collection systems;*
• *Greater use of analytical techniques that identify the impact of denial and the potential for deception;* Analysts must understand and evaluate the effects of false, misleading, or even true information that intelligence targets may have injected into the collection stream to deceive the United States.

(Iraq's prior deceptions), the situation (Iraq's strategic benefits of maintaining a WMD capability in the region), and U.S. self-limitations in collection channels, yet still misjudged incongruities and the absence of empirical evidence. *The Commission* also observed that [26]: "Analysts' discounting of contradictory information reflected, in part, an awareness of Iraq's sophisticated denial and deception efforts and of Iraq's past success in hiding the extent of its WMD programs. Reacting to that lesson, analysts understandably (if not wholly defensibly) began to view the absence of evidence of WMD as evidence of Iraq's ability to deceive the United States about its existence."

7.5.1 Deception Warning

The basic deception warning signs taught in U.S. analytic tradecraft for alerting the analyst to the *potential* for deception are summarized in Table 7.6 [27]. Note that the first category of warning indicators is contextual in nature (inferences that are based on the overall situation and independent of any specific current observation), while the second category deals with specific empirical evidence of deceptive activities.

Contextual indicators require a general knowledge of the deceiver's potential motive (considering the gain through deception and risk of being caught), an assessment of the means to carry out a deception and opportunities (often the opportunities are produced by the target's exposures and vulnerabilities). These fundamental criteria form the basis for circumstantial evidential standards in criminal case development and they similarly are the basis for an awareness of the potential for deception [28]. Empirical indictors are based on current and historical evidence. Over time, the trend of these indicators can become contextual evidence (e.g., suspicious confirmations that an adversary indeed has the ability to jam or insert false information in an intelligence channel may demonstrate that the adversary has acquired a new technical means). Notice also that observed evidence includes Harris' two

Table 7.6 Warning Indicators of Deception

Warning Sign Categories	*Warning Signs (Indicators)*	*Characteristics of the Intelligence Target Being Assessed*
Contextual information (likelihood that the target will attempt to distort the analysts' perception)	Motive	Motive to deceive is believed to be present due to the high payoff potential for the target
	Opportunity	Has knowledge of collection, processing, or analytic vulnerabilities Known to have previously countered the collection channels Collection process has provided access for manipulation.
	Means	Has experience to undertake deception operations Has methods and channels to convey deception information; also has methods to conceal information from channels
Empirical information (based on observed information available to the analyst)	Suspicious gaps	Suspicious gaps occur in collection where or when critical information is not available, important channels close at critical times, or gaps occur across channels that confirm a conclusion. Gaps prevent the necessary range and volume of information expected unless manipulation was present.
	Contradictions	Observations that contradict carefully researched models or patterns Observations that are unexpected changes, trends, or deviations from known models of behavior.
	Suspicious confirmations	Confirmations from multiple channels that are reinforcing, yet suspicious in their timing, degree of confirmation, precision, or specificity. Multiple channel confirmation alone does not confirm authenticity—it may be an indicator of deception, depending upon the context.

Source: [27].

categories of empirical incongruities (e.g., suspicious gaps and contradictions) and sprignals (detected confirmations of known deceptive behaviors).

7.5.2 Considering Deception in Alternatives Analysis

In addition to being cued by warning indicators, any analytic process must provide for the consideration of alternative perspectives, and alternative explanations of the evidence. In the absence of evidence (often the case where concealment is employed or access is severely limited), the analyst must conjecture alternative hypotheses of the hidden reality to guide collection and analysis. This process of *alternative analysis* has received significant attention since *the Commission* recommended integral community-wide application [29].

> The DNI should encourage diverse and independent analysis throughout the Intelligence Community by encouraging alternative hypothesis generation as part of the analytic process and by forming offices dedicated to independent analysis.... We thus recommend that the DNI give particular "red-team" or "devil's advocate" assignments to individuals or offices on a case-by-case basis, rather than trying to produce all alternative analysis through a separate office. By doing so, no individual or office would constantly bear the brunt of criticizing other analysts' work, nor would such alternative analysis be thought to be the sole responsibility of a single, stand-alone office. And while the DNI is statutorily required to assign an individual or entity responsibility for ensuring that the Community engages in alternative analysis, this should not in our view artificially limit the locations in which such analysis occurs.

The analysis of alternatives has long been recognized as a method to overcome the limitations of a single mindset, the distillation of the intelligence analyst's cumulative factual and conceptual knowledge into a framework for making estimative judgments on a complex subject [30]. The analytic sensemaking process leads to mindsets as valuable frameworks for organization of evidence and explanation, but the convergence on a single, exclusive mindset can become a the framework of intelligence failure when it dominates all others. Such a dominant mindset excludes incongruities that do not fit the frame, reduces the search for evidence outside the frame, and narrows the analysis to a single perspective and line of reasoning that bars the consideration of alternatives; such a mindset is the ideal target of deception. Alternative analysis is strategic in nature, maintaining the consideration of independent perspectives and optional hypotheses, requiring the kind of imaginative analysis called for by the 9/11 Commission. Responding to the commission's requirements, former CIA Deputy Director for Intelligence Jami Miscik, noted that there is "...no one single solution or method that will ensure creativity, imagination, or detailed questioning of inherited assumptions." She encouraged a diversity of approaches to challenge the analysts, suggest the out-of-the-box approaches to problems, perform contrarian analysis, to maintain competing centers of analysis, and occasionally suggest the farfetched [31]. Imaginative analysis of parallel lines of reasoning comes with a cost; Mary McCarthy (National Intelligence Officer for Warning 1994–1996) acknowledged the need for a high level of rigor to overcome the limitations of the single mindset in warning [32]:

> Rigorous analysis helps overcome mindset, keeps analysts who are immersed in a mountain of new information from raising the bar what they would consider an alarming threat situation, and allows their minds to expand other possibilities. Keeping chronologies, maintaining databases and arraying data are not fun or glamorous. These techniques are the heavy lifting of analysis, but this is what analysts are supposed to do.

Roger George has enumerated the principal techniques to practically implement alternative analysis (summarized in Table 7.7); these methods seek to expand the envelope of analytic thinking and maintain multiple frameworks against which to evaluate cumulative evidence [33].

In each case the methods provide analytic discipline and rigor to imagine and synthesize a wider range of hypotheses of reality than a single dominant frame. Of course, the potential for acts of denial and deception must be considered across alternatives, not lumped in a single D&D hypothesis, as described in the table. Considerations of deception in the alternatives must include:

- The basis for deception-sensitive linchpins in each alternative, for example, assume that the reason A maintains a impenetrable concealment program to hide WMD activities is because: (1) there exists a viable capability, (2) there is no capability but a perception of capability is desired, (3) the capability is vulnerable, and (4) the development of a capability is plagued with mismanagement and technical failures.
- Alternative states of an adversary's deception capability. Capability may range from a sophisticated and effective deception program to an adversary

Table 7.7 Alternative Analysis Techniques and Deception Analysis Applications

Alternative Analysis Method	*Approach*	*Application to Deception Alternatives Analysis*
Key assumption checks	Identify key linchpin assumptions; consider the range potential implications to subsequent analysis if the linchpins are not correct.	Identify sensitivity of deception considerations (e.g., collection and analysis) to linchpins that preclude effective deception analysis.
Devil's advocacy: contrarian analysis	Develop an argument in direct opposition to a prevailing line of analysis; reject assumptions and key drivers to develop a contrived analysis of alternative opposing views.	Where analyses presume or preclude deception, consider the opposite.
Team A–Team B competitive	Assign analytic teams to fully develop each of the alternatives (A, B, and so forth) to present their cases to policymakers for judgment; this is similar to trial case development.	Assure that deception effects are considered across all teams; consider the potential role of deception in each alternative; allow red cells to consider the benefits and risks of deception from their cultural perspectives and behavior.
Red cell exercises	Assemble a cell of individuals to role-play adversary actors; conduct an exercise in which the red cell develops the cultural perspective and applies the norms and decision-making style to produce results that approximate the adversary behavior [34].	
Contingency what-if analyses	Focus analysis on causality of arguments—the causes and effects (consequences) of alternative analyses.	Consider the alternative causes for an adversary to choose deception; consider the consequences of both successful and failed deception actions.
Contingency high-impact/ low-probability (HI/LP) analyses	Focus a contingency analysis on specific large-consequence events; identify the potential factors and indicators.	
Scenario development	Identify factors and drivers associated with a key issue; then develop a range of future scenarios that encompass the option space created by the factors-drivers [35].	Narratives of alternative futures may consider deception as one axis of the option space—from highly deceptive to no or ineffective deception.

whose programs are fraught with internal distrust, confusion, and even self-deception.

- Alternative operational means available to conduct deception applying different methods across channels to a variety of targets.
- Alternative effects of deception on intelligence, the public, and policymakers.

7.5.3 Deception Analytic Flow

We can now move beyond the warning guidelines that cue the analyst to deceptive situations and the general principles of alternatives analysis to develop a conceptual analytic flow that proceeds from collection and preprocessing (described in prior sections) to the development and evaluation of alternative hypotheses about the adversarial target. It is important to note that while our emphasis here is on countering deception, the analytic method is not unique to counterdeception—we describe a general method that highlights the detection and discovery activities necessary to deal with the D&D target. The method we describe includes five elements, or stages, that move from evidence to hypothesis and judgment, described in the following. Figure 7.5 shows the process flow beginning with collection and proceeding through reporting and dissemination:

1. *Channel testing:* Occurs first in intelligence processing to screen and detect known deception patterns and incongruities to provide cueing for further analysis. Intelligence analysts further analyze channel data to identify deception-relevant indicators. The known patterns and incongruities are provided by contextual knowledge as well as supporting exploratory models.
2. *Inferential analysis:* Occurs when evidence is decomposed and hypotheses are synthesized; evidence is marshaled to construct, by inference, structured arguments that reveal linchpin assumptions, deception factors, and gaps.
3. *Alternatives analysis:* Proceeds by comparing the set of alternative explanations of the evidence; evidence to support the hypotheses is assessed on the basis of diagnosticity and vulnerability to deception. Both qualitative and quantitative methods are employed to assess alternatives.

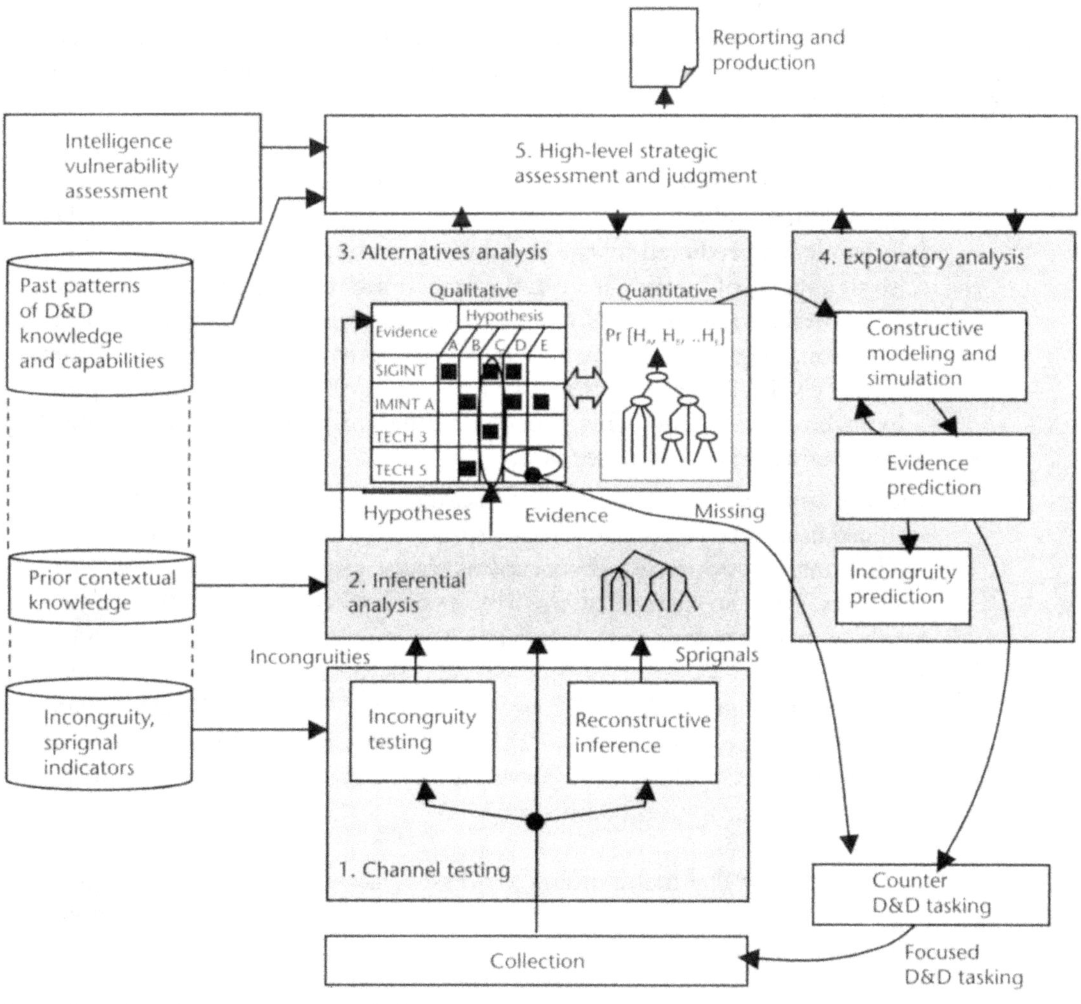

Figure 7.5 Counterdeception analytic flow.

4. *Exploratory analysis:* Continues in parallel with the empirically-based inferential analysis, using contextual knowledge to explore envelopes of possible deceptive behaviors, while predicting the expected incongruities and *sprignal* patterns they would produce.
5. *Strategic assessment:* Above the entire process is the strategic oversight that assures the appropriate focus on structure, and exploratory assessment of alternatives; this assessment must also remain vigilant for planning, collection, cognitive, and judgmental shortcomings.

The five elements, or stages, that move from evidence to hypothesis and judgment are now detailed in the following.

Stage 1 Channel Analysis

We have already introduced the analysis of channels in the previous section—where the automated processing of raw channel data may be used to discover or detect incongruities or known patterns of deception. While the automated processing described earlier may screen and detect some channel deception cues, further analysis is often required to validate or understand the cues or even to discern more subtle cues not easily recognized in the processing stage. The analyst performs two categories of screening of the channel data that were defined by Harris (described earlier in Chapter 5) [36]:

- *Reconstructive inference:* This analyst seeks to detect the presence of spurious signals (Harris called these *sprignals*) that are known indicators of D&D—the faint evidence predicted by the simulation of conjectured D&D activities, the false signatures of known decoys, the inaccurate replication of a known signal, and so forth. Such sprignals can be positive evidence confirming a deceptive simulation, negative evidence that refutes a hypothesis (leakage from the adversary's dissimulation effort), or missing evidence that should be present if a hypothesis were true. This process is inherently deductive, reasoning from know characteristics of deception.
- *Incongruity testing:* This analyst searches to discover subtle deception-induced inconsistencies (not seen before) in the data due to cross-channel contradictions, inconsistent observations from similar sensors, measurement "outliers," and so forth. The possible explanation of these incongruities may reveal a new context that attributes the incongruities to deception. Once incongruities are located, the analyst then synthesizes (conjectures) alternative explanations that attribute the incongruities to D&D (i.e., D&D explains the incongruity of evidence for more than one reality in simultaneous existence) or other influences, and develops methods to test the deception explanation (e.g., additional collection and active probe).

Notice that these channel analysis processes perform the detection and discovery processes, complementing and refining the less rigorous filtering processes in the processing pipeline.

Stage 2 Structuring Hypothetical Arguments

Data are screened to identify relevant elements (evidence) that can be assembled (or marshaled) into hypotheses to explain the evidence. Inspired by the evidence and contextual knowledge, a multidisciplinary team of analysts synthesizes alternative hypotheses and then focuses collection to search for and marshal evidence to support or refute the hypotheses before objectively evaluating the alternatives. *Argumentation* refers to the ability to explain the hypothesis; it structures propositions to move from premises to conclusions. We illustrate a directed acyclic graph format to represent intelligence arguments introduced by Schum in his foundational work, *Evidence and Inference for the Intelligence Analyst* [37], and his subsequent text, *The Evidential Foundations for Probabilistic Reasoning* [38]. The use of graph theory to describe complex arguments allows the analyst to represent two crucial aspects of an argument:

- *Argument structure:* The directed graph represents evidence (E), events or intermediate hypotheses inferred (i) by the evidence, and the ultimate, or final hypotheses (H) as graph nodes. The graph is *directed* because the lines connecting nodes include a single arrow indicating the single direction of inference. The lines move from a source element of evidence (E) through a series of inferences ($i_1, i_2, i_3, \ldots, i_n$) toward a terminal hypothesis (H). The graph is *acyclic* because the directions of all arrows move from evidence, through intermediate inferences to hypothesis, but not back again: there are no closed loop cycles.
- *Force of evidence and propagation:* In common terms we refer the *force*, *strength*, or *weight* of evidence to describe the relative degree of contribution of evidence to *support* an intermediate inference (i_n), or the ultimate hypothesis (H). The graph structure provides a means of describing supporting and refuting evidence, and if evidence is quantified (e.g., probabilities, fuzzy variables, or other belief functions), a means of propagating the accumulated weight of evidence in an argument. Like a vector, evidence includes a direction (toward certain hypotheses) and a magnitude (the inferential force).

The process of reasoning to the best explanation (abduction) introduced earlier in this chapter and a number of approaches to explicitly structure evidence to support such reasoning have been offered to aid the analyst.

We can illustrate the structure of an intelligence hypothesis by examining the structure of an actual intelligence assessment of Iraq's chemical weapon program in a declassified 2002 U.S. National Intelligence Estimate (NIE) on the Iraq WMD program. The following declassified assessment (a hypothesis believed and asserted as an intelligence judgment) is based on an argument that includes three lines of inference identified as supporting bullet points [39]:

> **We assess that Baghdad has begun renewed production of mustard, sarin, GF (cyclosarin), and VX;** its capability probably is more limited now than it was at the time of the Gulf war, although VX production and agent storage life probably have been improved.
>
> - An array of clandestine reporting reveals that Baghdad has procured covertly the types and quantities of chemicals and equipment sufficient to allow limited CW

[chemical weapons] agent production hidden within Iraq's legitimate chemical industry.

- Although we have little specific information on Iraq's CW stockpile, Saddam probably has stocked at least 100 metric tons (MT) and possibly as much as 500 MT of CW agents—much of it added in the last year.
- The Iraqis have experience in manufacturing CW bombs, artillery rockets, and projectiles. We assess that they possess CW bulk fills for SRBM [short-range ballistic missile] warheads, including for a limited number of covertly stored Scuds, possibly a few with extended ranges.

We can describe this example assessment by diagramming the underlying argument structure as an inference diagram that relates the supporting evidence and inference structure to the hypothesis (Figure 7.6). Notice that diagram is organized to explicitly describe the supporting evidence, the three main lines of inferences, and their relationships. For illustrative purposes, the figure has extrapolated beyond the words in the earlier assessment to illustrate the following kinds of information that are found in the structure to support the argument:

1. *Evidence:* Data that are relevant are at the root of the graph and are arbitrarily assumed for this example to be 10 specific elements of data (E1 to E10) that form the basis for subsequent inferences. E9 and E10 are corroborative evidence that support the credibility of E8 and enhance the force of the inference i32.
2. *Linchpin assumptions:* The key factors underlying the argument; these are factors that are likely to drive the inference, especially where there is little hard information available, such as in knowledge of intentions and specific plans [40].
3. *Deception factors:* The factors related to evidence or inferences that are vulnerable to denial or deception, the potential methods of deception, and vulnerabilities to channels of information.
4. *Inference structure:* Proceeding from the evidence at the roots of the graph are the inferences (arrows) that lead to propositions (circles); the terminal proposition is the summary hypothesis. Each proposition is numbered (e.g., i23); propositions and the top hypothesis are summarized in text. Note that the structure shows the three major lines of inference, and the convergent nature of the three propositions that enhance the final proposition when they all occur together.

This argument structure, while not a formal logic, provides greater insight into the basis for the hypothesis and the relative roles of linchpin assumptions, evidence, inference, and deception factors. The structure provides a means for explanation, examination, and the development of metrics for use in the next stage of hypothesis comparison. It also illustrates the complexity of the argument structure for even a relatively simple set of propositions asserted as judgments in a high-level intelligence document [41].

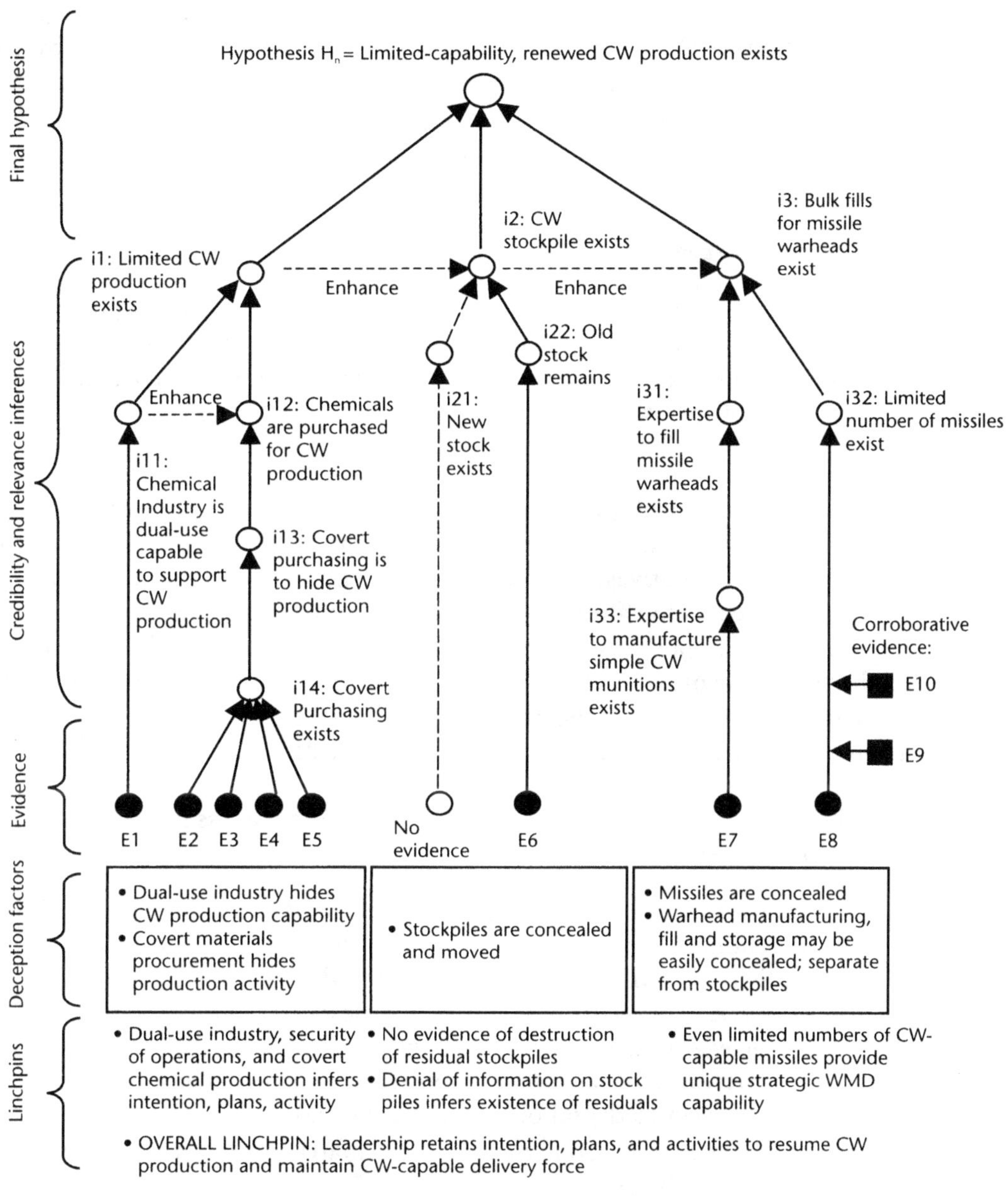

Figure 7.6 Example WMD argument structure considering deception.

Stage 3 Analyzing Alternative Hypotheses

Hypotheses are synthesized as *alternative* explanations of available empirical evidence, and as conjectures of possible realities that are based on contextual considerations. In the following we consider complementary qualitative and quantitative methods to compare alternatives.

Stage 3a Qualitative Assessment of Alternatives

Once synthesized, these alternatives can be comparatively evaluated using the qualitative method of alternative competing hypothesis (ACH) described by Richards Heuer [42]. It is important to note that while ACH is a general analytic method developed to overcome cognitive shortcomings, it is applicable to counterdeception analysis because it is a systematic analytic process that allows objective comparison of alternative hypotheses [43]:

> The ideal is to generate a full set of hypotheses, systematically evaluate each hypothesis, and then identify the hypothesis that provides the best fit to the data... The simultaneous evaluation of multiple, competing hypotheses permits a more systematic and objective analysis than is possible when an analyst focuses on a single, most-likely explanation or estimate. The simultaneous evaluation of multiple, competing hypotheses entails far greater cognitive strain than examining a single, most-likely hypothesis.

The ACH approach provides a methodology to assess multiple explanations of reality—and all hypotheses may include elements of deception. (In most real cases, the simplified alternatives, *without* deception and *with* deception are not at all realistic; in many cases the alternatives will consider multiple possible modes of deception—including, perhaps, the analyst's own possible self-deceptions!) The methodology focuses on explicit representation and objective evaluation to overcome many of the analytic shortcomings introduced in Chapter 5. The ACH method assembles evidence in a matrix to organize and describe the relationship between evidence and alternative hypotheses [44].

The sequence of the ACH process (Figure 7.7) to assess hypotheses synthesized in the prior stage:

1. *Evidence analysis:* Available data is reviewed to locate relevant evidence and inferences that can be assigned to support or refute each of the hypotheses. Explicitly identify the assumptions regarding evidence and the arguments of inference. Following the processes described in the last stage, list the evidence–argument pairs (or chains of inference) and identify, for each, the intrinsic value of its contribution with a particular not to the potential for being subject to denial or deception (D&D).
2. *Matrix synthesis:* Construct an ACH matrix that relates evidence-inference for each of the competing hypotheses.
3. *Matrix analysis:* Assess the diagnostic value of each evidence-inference component to each hypothesis. *Diagnosticity* is the significance or diagnostic value to support, refute or distinguish between hypotheses; evidence that supports multiple hypotheses is less diagnostic than that which uniquely supports a single hypothesis. This process proceeds for each item of evidence-inference *across* the rows, considering how each item may contribute to each hypothesis. An entry may be supporting (consistent with), refuting (inconsistent with), or irrelevant (not applicable) to a hypothesis; a contribution notation (e.g., +, –, or N/A, respectively) is marked within the cell. Where possible, annotate the likelihood (or probability) that this evidence would be observed if the hypothesis is true. Note that the diagnostic

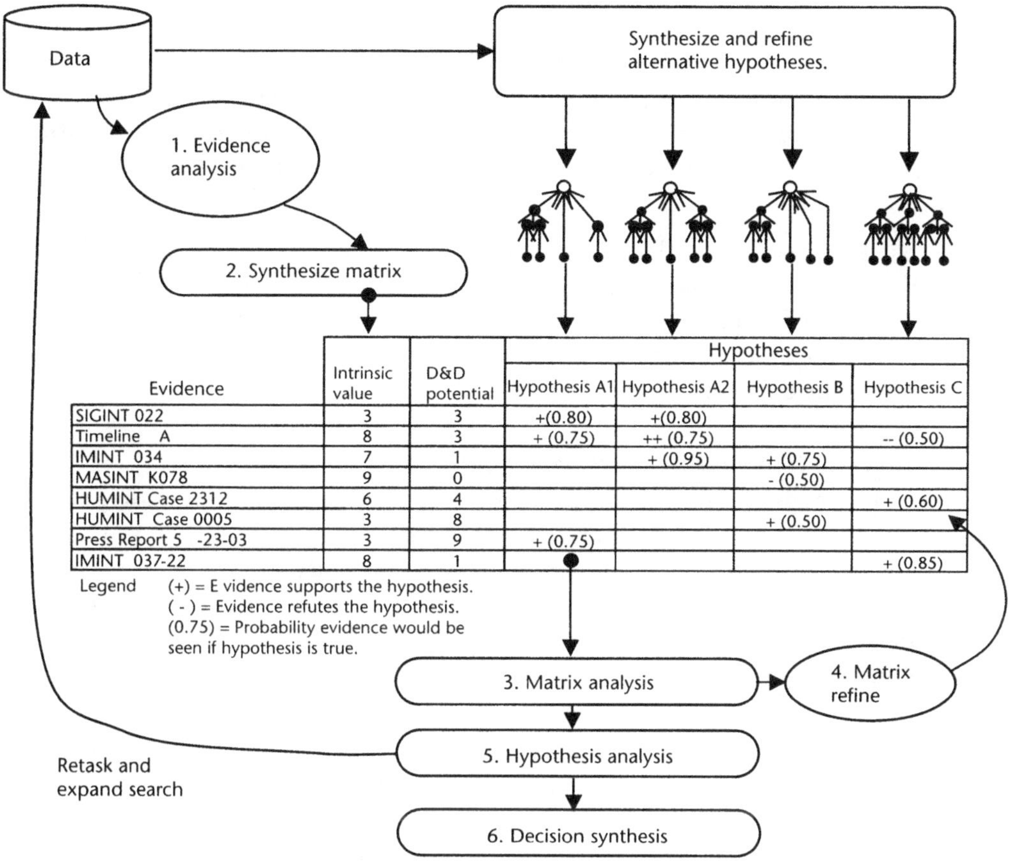

Figure 7.7 Alternative competing hypothesis (ACH) process flow.

significance of an item of evidence is reduced as it is consistent with multiple hypotheses; it has no diagnostic contribution when it supports to any degree, all hypotheses.

4. *Matrix synthesis (refinement):* Evidence assignments are refined, eliminating evidence and inferences that have no diagnostic value.
5. *Hypotheses analysis:* The analyst now proceeds to evaluate the likelihood of each hypothesis by evaluating entries *down* the columns. The likelihoods of each hypothesis are estimated by the characteristics of supporting and refuting evidence (as described in Chapter 6). Inconsistencies and missing gaps in expected evidence provide a basis for retasking; a small but high-confidence item that refutes the preponderance of expected evidence may be a significant indicator of deception. The analyst also assesses the sensitivity of the likely hypothesis to contributing assumptions, evidence, and the inferences; this sensitivity must be reported with conclusions and the consequences if any of these items are in error. This process may lead to retasking of collectors to acquire more data to support or refute hypotheses, and to reduce the sensitivity of a conclusion.

6. *Decision synthesis (judgment):* Reporting the analytic judgment requires the description of the alternatives (not just the most likely), the assumptions, evidence, and inferential chains. The report must also describe the gaps, inconsistencies, and their consequences on judgments. The analyst must also specify what should be done to provide an update on the situation, and what indictors might point to significant changes in current judgments.

Notice that the ACH approach deliberately focuses the analyst's attention on the contribution, significance, and relationships of evidence to all hypotheses, rather than on building a case for the most plausible single hypothesis. The analytic emphasis is first on evidence and inference across the rows, before evaluating hypotheses down the columns.

Stage 3b Quantitative Assessment of Alternatives

While the ACH matrix comparison method is qualitative in nature, focusing on the assessment of the contribution of evidence to arguments (hypotheses), there exist complementary quantitative methods that quantify the uncertainty in evidence and inferences to provide a relative ranking of the likelihood of each hypothesis. Most prominent among the quantitative methods is the use of probabilities to express uncertainty:

- To define a priori probabilities of each hypothesis (a contextual measure of belief independent of experience—prior to accounting for empirical evidence);
- Apply Bayesian inference to compute the a posterior probability (a measure of belief in a proposition after consideration of empirical evidence—literally "after experience") of each hypothesis to rank the likelihood of each.

CIA analyst Jack Zlotnick argued for the benefits of Bayesian methods to complement traditional verbal logic, providing a means to cross-check logical reasoning quantitatively. Zlotnick noted three specific benefits of the Bayesian approach to quantitative analysis [45]:

1. The method requires the analyst to explicitly quantify statements (judgments) about evidence and inference, rather than hiding them in the vagaries of words. Rather than being a difficulty, quantification forces the analyst to consider and reveal.
2. The method further draws the analyst's attention to likelihood that each element of evidence would be observed if each hypothesis were true individually, rather than immediately focusing on a comparison of the hypotheses.
3. Finally, the comparison of hypotheses is performed objectively—as Zlotnick noted, by the "incorruptible logic of a dispassionate mathematics." The objective results also reveal the sensitivity of the posterior probabilities to the analyst's appraisal of the elements of evidence.

The Bayesian approach provides a means of estimating the analysts subjective degree of belief (expressed as a probability) in a hypothesis, H_0; the estimate is based on the a priori probability of H_0 and some evidence, E, for which there exists an estimate of the probability that E would be present if H_0 were true. The method is based on the standard development of Bayes' theorem, which relates these measures of belief [46]:

$$P(H_0|E) = \frac{P(E|H_0)P(H_0)}{P(E)} \tag{7.1}$$

where:

H_0 is the *hypothesis* expressed as an assertion to be estimated true or false.

E is an element of evidence that is related to the belief in H_0.

$P(H_0|E)$ is the computed *a posteriori probability* that H_0 is true, conditioned on (given that) evidence E is present.

$P(H_0)$ is the *a priori probability* that H_0 is true, independent of the evidence.

$P(E|H_0)$ is a *conditional probability*; the probability of observing the evidence E conditioned on (given that) hypothesis H_0 is true.

$P(E)$ is the *marginal probability* that E will be observed at any time; given no other information.

Notice that $P(E|H_0)/P(E)$ is an evidence scaling factor that quantifies the sensitivity of belief in the hypothesis to E. For example, if $P(E|H_0)$ is large (E is strong evidence of H_0), yet $P(E)$ is small (natural occurrence of E is unlikely apart from H_0), the evidence scaling factor is large—and E is a strong contributor when it occurs. The theorem then computes $P(H_0|E)$ as the product of this scaling factor and $P(H_0)$. It must be noted that the method presumes that: (1) the set of hypotheses considered ($H_0, H_1, \ldots, H_N$) are mutually exclusive and exhaustive, and (2) observations of evidence are not interdependent—and the conditional probabilities are therefore independent. The critical issue in applying this method is in estimating the scaling factor for any element of evidence, especially considering the conditional probabilities that relate the occurrence of evidence to a hypothesis. Most deception situations occur at a low base rate, and the estimate of scaling factors must consider all possible alternative explanations for the presence of E, $P(E|H_0)$, and the counterfactual explanations for $P(H_0|E)$.

When the basic theorem is applied to estimate probabilities along the directed acyclic graph of a structured argument, the resulting structure is referred to as a Bayes or inference network that computes conditional probabilities at every node in the net—including the terminating node which provides the posterior probabilities for (H_0, H_1, ..., H_N). The complexity of such a network requires a sophisticated means of updating all nodes while accounting for new evidence at any root, and changes in priors as evidence accumulates [47]. While the Bayesian method is generally applied to estimate a posteriori probabilities for each hypothesis accounting for all evidence accumulated at a point in time, it may also be applied in a sequential manner, estimating a posteriori probabilities as evidence evolves over time.

McLaughlin and Paté-Cornell have demonstrated the sequential Bayesian updating method; in this approach, as observations and evidence are sequentially received, Bayesian updates are computed over all accumulated evidence, and the posteriori probabilities for observation n become the a priori probabilities for the subsequent observation $n + 1$ [48]. Pope and Jøsang have described an alternative approach to Bayesian analysis that employs subjective logic to complement the qualitative ACH method; the method has the benefit of producing diagosticity measures within the quantitative method [49]. In the next chapter, we illustrate how a commercial Bayes network tool can be used to perform the quantitative estimates of posteriori probabilities of mutually exclusive hypotheses.

CIA's Sherman Kent proposed approaches to express the results of estimative intelligence in a classic essay that detailed the challenge of applying a consistent, unambiguous mapping of quantitative probabilities to verbal expressions [50]. Kent noted that while many judgments in life may be made citing odds (subjective probabilities), it is most difficult in intelligence. He noted [51], "... in the world that intelligence estimates try hardest to penetrate—a world of closed covenants secretly arrived at, of national business conducted behind walls of all but impenetrable security, of skillfully planned deceptions, and so on such evidence [on which to base probabilities] is by no means invariably at hand." Kent recognized the cultural differences between the CIA's "poets" (e.g., verbal–logical-oriented analysts) and the quantitative-oriented "mathematicians"; to resolve the disparity, he proposed a mapping of probabilities to five categories of expressions (Table 7.8).

Kent's advice was to estimate and report with precision *both* qualitatively and quantitatively [52], "Let us talk of it in terms of odds or chances, and when we have made our best judgment let us assign it a word or phrase that is chosen from one of the five rough categories of likelihood on the chart. Let the judgment be unmistakable and let it be unmistakably ours."

Stage 4 Exploratory Analysis

In parallel with the prior three stages of logical evidence-to-inference, an exploratory process may be conducted to explicitly model and examine the static relationships and dynamic behaviors of the deceiver's processes that underlie the hypothetical alternatives. This exploration allows the analyst to investigate the expected structure and behavior of each hypothesis—to provide greater insight into the deceiver's planning options, constraints, and required actions and to project the expected evidence (present and missing). Whether performed in the analyst's

Table 7.8 Sherman Kent's Mapping of Probabilities to Expressions

Probability	*Region*	*Estimative Expression*
100%	Certainty	Certain
93% give or take about 6%	The general area of possibility	Almost certain
75% give or take about 12%	The general area of possibility	Probable
50% give or take about 10%	The general area of possibility	Chances about even
30% give or take about 10%	The general area of possibility	Probably not
7% give or take about 5%	The general area of possibility	Almost certainly not
0%	Impossibility	Impossible

imagination (mental models and simulations), verbal exercises performed by multidisciplinary red teams who play the deceiver, or by explicit computer simulations, this process expands the analytic frame of reference beyond a set of narrow and limited hypotheses to support them. Where the inferential process of the earlier stages focus on *empirical* evidence, the exploratory process applies *contextual* knowledge; exploration beyond the current evidence complements the logical process with experts' contextual knowledge and imagination. Such contextual analyses consider:

- The adversary's goals, plans, and possible actions, and the range of courses of action they may consider;
- The potential contribution of deception to those plans, and the relative benefit or risk of both denial and deception;
- Excursions and extrapolations from the current hypotheses, considering alternate perspectives of motive (e.g., *Why else might they be making covert transactions?*), means (e.g., *Suppose the production is twice as much? Half as much? Stopped?*), and opportunities (e.g., *Suppose they are unaware of the opportunity? Or they perceive an opportunity that does not exist?*).

A summary finding of *the Commission* specifically noted the need for such analytic imagination to cope with limited and deceptive information [53]: "The Intelligence Community, because of a lack of analytical imagination, failed even to consider the possibility that Saddam Hussein would decide to destroy his chemical and biological weapons and to halt work on his nuclear program after the first Gulf War."

While analytic teams traditionally perform this function, independent multidiscipline red teams can be formed to conduct exploratory analyses. Red team exercises can be supported by facilitators, observers, and computer simulation to focus the exercise, guide the exploration, and capture the envelope of considerations [54]. Beyond expert red cells, tailored models and simulations may be used by individual analysts as tools, or by analytic teams as games to conduct ongoing refinement and exploration of their hypotheses. A number of such models and simulations that can describe deceptive behavior and effects have been reported in the literature, for example:

- *Strategic deception:* Brams has illustrated the use of the theory of moves to explore the effects of deception in strategic negotiation [55].
- *Organizational behavior:* Carley has demonstrated an agent-based organization simulation that can explore the dynamics of covert organizations, including behaviors associated with deception [56].
- *Military operations:* Military simulations of battlefield movements have long been capable of exploring the effects of deception by modeling camouflage, concealment, and deception; recent research is developing exploratory simulations that explicitly synthesize an adversary's range of feasible deception actions in a complex urban environment to support real-time counterdeception analysis [57].

Over three decades ago, Barton Whaley envisioned the use of computers to explore the option space of an adversary's deception plans [58]: "...it should be possible to adapt certain existing techniques to enable the intelligence analyst to escape the bias of the preconceptions that obscure most stratagems. Such a serendipity machine (computer or manual) would, I presume involve a two-step process: a random (i.e., preconception-free) search for patterns in military posture followed by a comparison of such patterns with an array of the theoretically <u>possible</u> military actions (i.e., capabilities). Those with the best fit would be candidates for closer scrutiny and verification by conventional intelligence procedures."

Stage 5 Assessment of the Integrated Analytic Process

A continual and strategic high-level assessment oversees the process, providing the synoptic view of the analysis, including considerations of the state of its conclusions (or indecision), the breadth and depth of coverage of the target, analytic mindsets, strengths and vulnerabilities, weaknesses, and gaps. Even as the intelligence cycle (introduced earlier in Section 7.2) was an organizing model of the entire intelligence process, this sequential methodology is one perspective of a process that is performed in practice as a continuum.

The five stages of the information flow in this methodology (Figure 7.8) might imply that that the process is data-driven, because we have emphasized the linkage from data, through inferences to hypotheses, as if a relatively firm model of the target reality exists and the data are refining that model. But analysis includes a concurrent concept-driven process that deals with uncertainty in data available and in the concept of the object of study (the intelligence target); this process synthesizes and compares conceptual (mental and explicitly represented) models and drives collection and analysis to refine a model that is coherent (logical consistency of propositions in the model) and corresponds to the data [59]. This largely conceptually driven cognitive process has been described as *sensemaking*—the tacit process of "retrospective rationality" by which the analyst seeks to rationally account for things by structuring events and explanations holistically to create conceptual models [60]. By this process, analysts "make sense" of the empirical data in the context of their tacit and conceptual domain knowledge [61]. While the five stages of the figure illustrate the bottom-up logical flow from evidence to alternative hypotheses and judgment, the entire process is guided by the top-down sensemaking oversight that provides the context, imagination, and agility to frame the logical process.

The high-level strategic oversight must also monitor the cognitive vulnerabilities (identified earlier in Chapter 5) to self-deception as well as adversary deceptions. Analysts are inclined to create mental models of the alternative hypotheses that may distort their perception of the significance of evidence or derived inferences, and then attribute undeserved support for those models. Strategic assessments must consider the emergence of dominant mindsets (the cumulative mental models noted earlier in the chapter) and apply analytic strategies to mitigate their effects. In the case of the Iraq WMD analysis cited earlier, a mindset regarding the deceitful intentions behind all activities caused incongruities to be misused [62]: "... in some instances, analysts went even further, interpreting information that contradicted the prevailing analytical line as intentional deception, and therefore as *support* for the prevailing

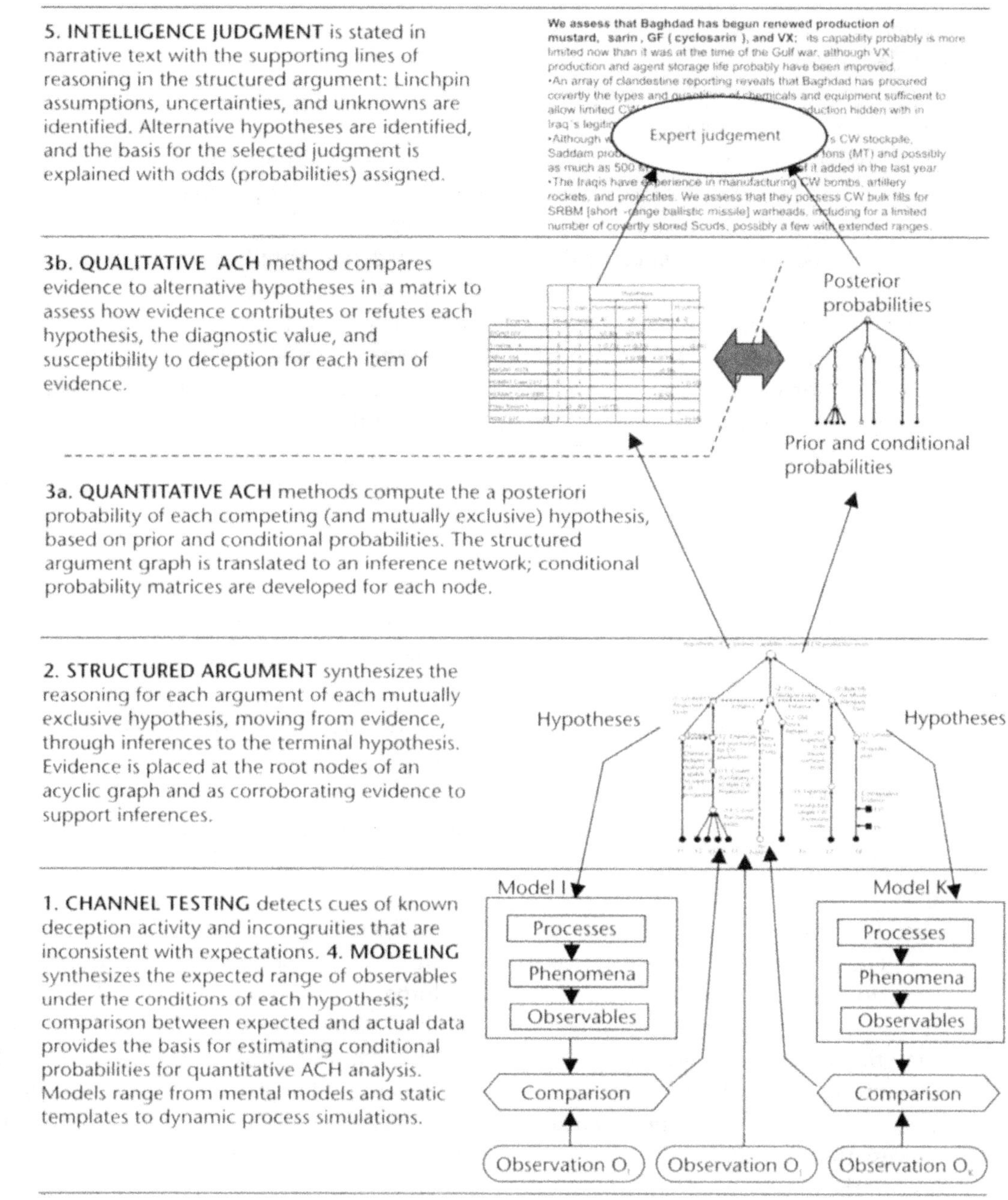

Figure 7.8 Counterdeception analytic flow.

analytical view." Ernest Mays has summarized the three basic vulnerabilities of the intelligence analyst [63]: "[Analysts] are vulnerable in the first place because they follow an almost unavoidable rule of trying to fit the evidence they have into some coherent, rational whole.... They are vulnerable in the second place because, partly perhaps from awareness of the power of prejudice and preconception, they have a preference for data which are quantifiable and therefore appear comparatively objective.... And thirdly they are vulnerable to deception because, after having to judge hard issues, they are prone to look for confirming rather than disconfirming evidence." The strategic oversight must be vigilant of the potential for such analytic self-deception.

Reporting and Production

The reporting of intelligence judgments include the summary judgments and the basis of the judgment. The report should include all relevant perspectives, linchpins, the analysis of alternatives, deception factors, gaps in information, and contradictions. *The Commission* specifically recommended that intelligence reporting provide the basis for judgments to consumers [64]: "We recommend forcing analysts to make their assumptions and reasoning more transparent by requiring that analysis be well sourced, and that all finished intelligence products, either in paper or in digital format, provide citations to enable user verification of particular statements... Intelligence customers should be able to question judgments, and analysts should be able to defend their reasoning." Transparency in reporting situations employing sophisticated D&D may include the following supporting considerations, as appropriate:

- Policy positions (desires) and beliefs; potential biases relevant to these positions that may produce policy, operational, or analytic vulnerabilities;
- Situational elements that influence the deception analysis; potential implications of changing situations;
- Identification of channels used, the means to verify channels (e.g., asset validation), the credibility of each and cross-channel inconsistencies and explanations;
- Contextual motive, operational, and technical means, and opportunities available to the adversary; report all empirical evidence of denial and deception.

Case Study 7A: Applying the Method to Fraud Detection We can now illustrate the general analytic methodology by comparison to a semiautomated deception detection process applied in an alternative domain. Johnson et al. have developed and demonstrated a semiautomated process that follows the general processing and analytic stages developed in the prior sections for application to the diction of accounting fraud (deception) in financial reports [65]. The process, called a *competence model*, was developed to evaluate accounting records and follows a four-step process that matches the methodology developed here (Figure 7.9, with the exception of the exploratory component):

1. Activation is similar to a single-channel testing process. It compares the financial reports to financial models of normal business performance; identifies inconsistencies between reported data and the expected range of values for these values (based on the magnitude of deviation) and logs them with their characteristics.
2. Hypothesis generation is the inferential analysis stage that uses the detected inconsistencies to select hypotheses that explain the inconsistencies as if they are the results of accounting tactics that are functional to the goals of deception. This process identifies potential actions of the fraudulent accountant that are associated with one (or more) of the basic manipulations

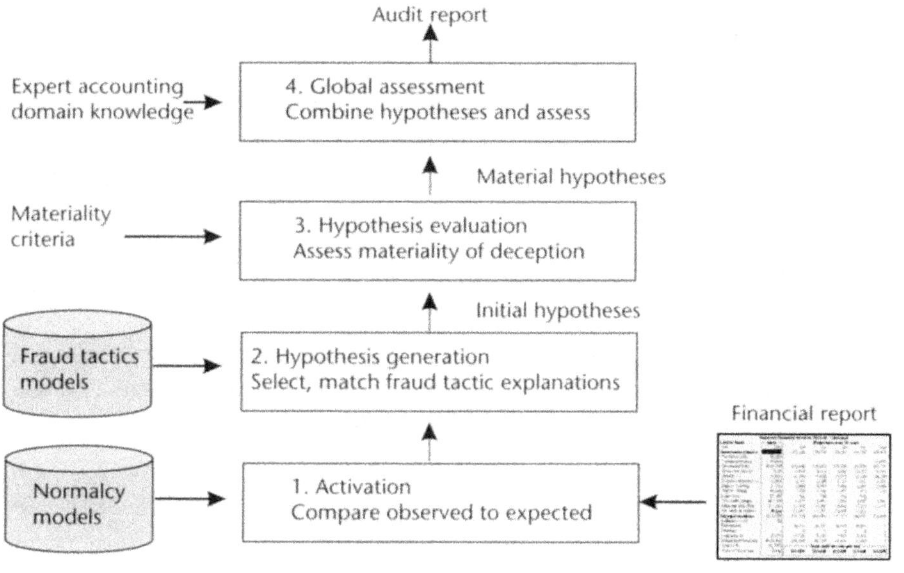

Figure 7.9 Accounting fraud deception detection process.

of the reporting to create the observed inconsistencies in two hypothesis categories: deception or error.

3. Hypothesis evaluation assesses the materiality of the hypothesis generated in the prior step (a matter is material if knowledge of the matter would be likely to influence the user of the financial statements). Two alternative hypotheses are considered for each inconsistency: attributable to unintentional error or attributable to intentional deception (fraud). The hypothesis testing logic establishes a materiality criterion based on the effect of the error (e.g., magnitude of error effect on net operating income).
4. Global assessment performs the strategic assessment over all material hypotheses; individual and aggregate criteria are applied to derive a final judgment on the financial statement, reporting it as "unqualified" (accepted with no qualifications), "unqualified with explanation" (overall inconsistencies are material), or "misleading" (a single hypothesis is material).

This process was implemented as a forward-chaining rule production system that accepts financial reports in a standard format and produces automated assessments. The system maintains prior models of expected incongruities in fraudulent accounting reports. Underlying this expectation, the authors cite Daniel Dennet's concept of the "intentional stance" where the presence of inconsistency implies intention to deceive, and VanLehn's "bug" explanation of inconsistency—as an erroneous repair of knowledge in the process of deception [66]. It is important to note that this example is more limited that a typical intelligence deception problem, because this accounting example considers only simulation in a fully disclosed financial report. It does not deal with the compounding problems of dissimulation (e.g., as if certain critical entries were not revealed) and misdirection (e.g., as if spurious additional financial data were introduced to distract the process).

7.6 Summary

The methods for countering deception described in this chapter demand a severe discipline for those who plan and direct, collect, process, and analyze intelligence. The counterdeceiver's regimen demands technical methods to support:

- An *inquisitive passion* to ever understand the deceptive adversary, with a humility that acknowledges the potential for imminent surprise and a revision of all that has been believed before;
- A most critical *impatience* with the limits of collection, balanced by a creative involvement in conceiving new, unexpected, and innovative means to coordinate collections and invent new collection means to counter concealment and discover deception;
- The greatest *attention* to detail, without losing a synoptic or strategic perspective of the situation;
- The highest level of *attentiveness*, without succumbing to the negative irrational effects of hypervigilance and panic;
- A *careful regard* for logical inference and justification of conclusions from available observations, while retaining the balancing virtues of creativity, intuition, and curiosity when considering incongruities;
- The healthiest *suspicion* of everything, while retaining an ability to make judgments and accurately explain what is believed in the presence of uncertainty;
- A most *creative contemplation* of alternative conjectured contexts and their hypothetical implications for reinterpreting evidence, while basing judgments on the weight of solid evidence and justified inference.

The challenge of these demands is the reason why so many have cautioned against placing overconfidence in a reliable counterdeception methodology. We began this chapter citing Caddell's dire caution against hope in a comprehensive method. We conclude with more of his wise caution about the state of counterdeception after several millennia of its use in competition, crime, and conflict:

> What is known about deception in the past is of considerable, if general, use in the present. We have developed terms to describe the different methods and levels of disinformation. This is useful. We know the dangers inherent to mirror imaging and cognitive dissonance. This is important. We can appreciate the need for the synthesis of intelligence methodologies. This is vital. However, despite these realizations, we can never be confident we are not being deceived. These observations may seem self-evident to even a casual student of deception. Therefore, one might wonder why these obvious statements need repeating. The answer is simple. In successful deception operations, the perpetrator hopes that one or several of these self-evident observations will be overlooked [67].

The methods in this chapter and the tools to implement them that are introduced in the next chapter provide an edge to the counterdeceivers by helping them merely to reduce their vulnerability to overlooking that which is critical.

Endnotes

[1] Caddell, J. W., *Deception 101—A Primer on Deception*, Carlisle, PA: Strategic Studies Institute, U.S. Army War College, December 2004, p. 15.

[2] Whaley, B., *Strategem: Deception and Surprise in War*, Cambridge, MA: MIT, 1969, pp. 146–147. Here, Whaley refers to a "decisional model" (methodology) to support counter deception and mitigation of surprise that is analogous to a decision model he presents earlier (pp. 139–145) to support the development of a deception strategy to achieve surprise.

[3] Ibid., pp. 139–145.

[4] Johnson, R., "Developing a Taxonomy of Intelligence Analysis Variables," *Studies in Intelligence*, Vol. 47, No. 3, 2003, accessed online July 25, 2005, http://www.cia.gov/csi/studies/vol47no3/article05.html.

[5] Statement by Special Assistant to the DCI for Nonproliferation John A. Lauder on the Worldwide Biological Warfare Threat to the House Permanent Select Committee on Intelligence, March 3, 1999.

[6] Koestler, A., *The Act of Creation*, New York: Macmillan, 1964, pp. 105–109. Also see Koestler, A., *Janus*, New York: Random House, 1978, Chs. 6 and 7.

[7] For a description of these reasoning processes in the intelligence context, see Waltz, E., *Knowledge Management in the Intelligence Enterprise,* Norwood, MA: Artech House, 2003, Ch. 5.

[8] Waltz, E., *Knowledge Management in the Intelligence Enterprise,* Norwood, MA: Artech House, 2003, pp. 170–171.

[9] Gerwehr, S., and R. W. Glenn, *Unweaving the Web: Deception and Adaptation in Future Urban Operations*, RAND, MR-1495, 2002, Summary, p. xiii.

[10] A more formal definition of context is: C is a context for a target T, if: C constrains or influences the behavior of T, but C is not a constituent of T.

[11] Waltz, E., "Integrating the Data Fusion and Mining Processes," *Proc. of the National Symp. on Sensor and Data Fusion*, 2004.

[12] Brézillon, P. P., and J. C. Pomerol, *Is Context a Kind of Collective Tacit Knowledge?*, Paris, France: University of Paris, CSCW, 2001.

[13] Whaley, B., and J. Busby, "Detecting Deception: Practice, Practitioners, and Theory," in Godson, R., and J. Wirtz, (eds.), *Strategic Denial and Deception: The Twenty-First Century Challenge,* New Brunswick, NJ: Transaction Publishers, 2002, pp. 200–204.

[14] Boykin, Lt. Gen. W. G. (Deputy UnderSecretary for Intelligence and Warfighting Support), "Intelligence Support to Allied and Coalition Operations," *Proc. 16th Annual SO/LIC Symposium Strategic Environment for Coalition Warfare*, March 3, 2005. See also Boykin, W. G., "Remodeling Defense Intelligence," *Proc. of Annual Meeting of the Association of the U.S. Army,* Washington, D.C.: Assoc. of U.S. Army, October 26, 2004.

[15] While the intelligence process, in practice, is a continuum rather than a cycle, the intelligence cycle is a useful model to describe the basic activities and logical flow from planning to reporting. For a description of the intelligence cycle, see Waltz, E., *Knowledge Management in the Intelligence Enterprise,* Norwood, MA: Artech House, 2003, pp. 33–48.

[16] *The Commission on the Intelligence Capabilities of the United States Regarding Weapons of Mass Destruction,* Washington, D.C., March 31, 2005, p. 171.

[17] Heuer, Richards, "Cognitive Factors on Deception and Counterdeception," in Daniel, D. C., and K. L. Herbig, (eds.), *Strategic Military Deception*, New York: Pergamon, 1982, p. 61. A prevision version of the chapter was published as "Strategic Deception and Counterdeception," *International Studies Quarterly*, Vol. 25, No. 2, June 1981, pp. 294–327.

[18] Jones, R. V., "Some Lessons in Intelligence," *Studies in Intelligence*, Vol. 38, No. 5, 1995. This article quoted Jones' remarks at a symposium at CIA headquarters on October 26, 1993. For a technical description of the activities at Bletchley Park, see Hinsley, F. H., and A. Stripp, *Codebreakers*, Oxford, U.K.: Oxford University Press, 1993.

[19] *The Commission,* op. cit., pp. 367, 372, 558–559.

[20] *The Commission,* op. cit., March 31, 2005, p. 374.

[21] For an example of alternative algorithms and architectures to implement such a system that performs linkage detection and discovery, see Berry, P. M., et al., *Link Analysis Workbench*, AFRL-IF-RS-TR-2004-247, SRI International, September 2004; for the representative requirements for such a systems, see *Rapid Processing of Text Intelligence Data*, BAA-04-09-IFKA, Air Force Research Laboratory (AFRL)/Information Directorate, September 24, 2004.

[22] For a description of state-of-the-art approaches to extract evidence and discovery linkages, see Kargupta, H., et al., (eds.), *Data Mining: Next Generation Challenges and Future Directions*, Menlo Park, CA: AAAI Press, 2004.

[23] Santos Jr., E., et al., "A Cognitive Framework for Information Gathering with Deception Detection for Intelligence Analysis," *Proc. of 2005 International Intelligence Analysis Conference*, McLean, VA, May 2005.

[24] Whaley, B., and J. Busby, "Detecting Deception: Practice, Practitioners, and Theory," in Godson, R., and J. Wirtz, (eds.), *Strategic Denial and Deception: The Twenty-First Century Challenge,* New Brunswick, NJ: Transaction Publishers, 2002, p. 191.

[25] *The Commission,* op. cit., p. 410.

[26] Ibid., p. 169.

[27] This table is based on "Tradecraft and Counterintelligence," Note 10 in *A Compendium of Analytic Tradecraft Notes*, CIA/DDDI, February 1997.

[28] The circumstantial standard for securities fraud, for example, requires evidence of only motive and opportunity to prove *scienter*, a mental state that is characterized by an intent to deceive, manipulate, or defraud. Scienter means the defendant acted with knowledge of the truth, and can be proved by showing: (1) motive and opportunity or (2) strong circumstantial evidence of conscious misbehavior or recklessness. Means can be demonstrated by either contextual evidence (e.g., the defendant possessed requisite technical skills) or by empirical evidence (e.g., a tool was found in the defendant's possession).

[29] *The Commission*, op. cit., pp. 406–407.

[30] Davis, J., "Combatting Mindset," *Studies in Intelligence*, Vol. 36, No. 5, 1992, pp. 33–38.

[31] "Counterterrorism Analysis and Collection/The Requirement for Imagination and Creativity," statement of Jami Miscik, Deputy Director for Intelligence, to House Permanent Select Committee on Intelligence, August 4, 2004, p. 3.

[32] McCarthy, M., "The Mission to Warn: Disaster Looms," *Defense Intelligence Journal,* Vol. 7, No. 2, 1998, p. 21.

[33] George, R. Z., "Fixing the Problem of Analytical Mind-Sets: Alternative Analysis," *International Journal of Intelligence and Counterintelligence*, Vol. 17, No. 3, Autumn 2004, pp. 385–404.

[34] For an example of an adversary perspective analysis, see Kent, S., "A Crucial Estimate Relived," *Studies in Intelligence*, Vol. 36, No. 5, Spring 1964, pp. 117–118.

[35] See Schwartz, P., *The Art of the Long View: Planning for the Future in an Uncertain World*, New York: Currency Doubleday, 1991.

[36] Harris, W. R., *On Countering Strategic Deception*, R-1230-ARPA, November 1973, Ch. III, "Counter-Deception Planning Methodologies," pp. 33–50.

[37] Schum, D. A., *Evidence and Inference for the Intelligence Analyst*, Vols. I and II, Lanham, MD: University Press of America, 1987; this text was authored while Schum was a scholar in residence at the CIA.

[38] Schum, D. A., *The Evidential Foundations for Probabilistic Reasoning,* Evanston IL: Northwestern University Press, 2001. The brief introduction to inferential networks in this section is based on Schum's exhaustive treatment, but does not approach the many critical nuances of the theory developed by Schum.

[39] *Key Judgments from the National Intelligence Estimate on Iraq's Continuing Programs for Weapons of Mass Destruction*, October 2002, Director of Central Intelligence, accessed October 22, 2003, http://www.ceip.org/files/projects/npp/pdf/Iraq/declassifiedintellreport.pdf.

[40] For an overview of linchpin analysis process, see Krizan, L., *Intelligence Essentials for Everyone,* Occasional Paper 6, Joint Military Intelligence College, June 1999, p. 34. In the case of the Iraq WMD example, a major analytic shortcoming was the linchpin assumptions about Iraq's leadership intentions, and the reliance on old assumptions and inferences drawn from Iraq's previous behavior and intentions (see *The Commission,* op. cit., pp. 3 and 9).

[41] With regard to the example argument, the commission noted, "After the war, the [Iraq Survey Group] concluded—contrary to the Intelligence Community's pre-war assessments—that Iraq had unilaterally destroyed its undeclared CW stockpile in 1991 and that there were no credible indications that Baghdad had resumed production of CW thereafter. The ISG further found that Iraq had not regained its pre-1991 CW technical sophistication or production capabilities.... Finally, the ISG noted that the only CW it recovered were weapons manufactured before the first Gulf War, and that after 1991 only small, covert labs were maintained to research chemicals and poisons, primarily for intelligence operations. The ISG did conclude, however, that 'Saddam never abandoned his intentions to resume a CW effort when sanctions were lifted and conditions were judged favorable,' and that Iraq's post-1995 infrastructure improvements 'would have enhanced Iraq's ability to produce CW' if it chose to do so." *The Commission*, op. cit., p. 112.

[42] Heuer, R. J., *Psychology of Intelligence Analysis*, Washington, D.C., CIA, 1999.

[43] Ibid., Ch. 4 "Strategies for Analytic Judgment."

[44] This process is adapted from the eight-step process in Heuer, Jr., R. J., *Psychology of Intelligence Analysis*, Washington, D.C., CIA, 1999, Ch. 8 "Analysis of Competing Hypotheses." See also Sawka, K., "Competing Hypothesis Analysis," *Competitive Intelligence*, Vol. 2, No. 3, July–September 1999, pp. 37–38.

[45] Zlotnick, J., "Bayes' Theorem for Intelligence Analysis," *Studies in Intelligence*, Vol. 16, No. 2, Spring 1972, pp. 43–52; also see the earlier article, Zlotnick, J., "A Theorem for Prediction," *Studies in Intelligence,* Vol. 11, No. 4,Winter 1967, pp. 1–12.

[46] The brief description here only introduces the basic concept of Bayesian inference. For more complete descriptions of the application to analysis, see Charniak, E., "Bayesian Networks Without Tears," *AI Magazine*, Winter 1991, No. 12, Vol. 4, pp. 50–63; Sticha, P., D. Buede, and R. L. Rees, "APOLLO: An Analytical Tool for Predicting a Subject's Decision Making," *Proc. 2005 International Intelligence Analysis Conf*, McLean VA, May 2005; and Nixon, M., "Inference to the Best Next Observation in Probabilistic Expert Systems," *Technology Review Journal*, Spring/Summer 2005, pp. 81–101.

[47] Pearl, J., *Probabilistic Reasoning in Intelligent Systems: Networks of Plausible Inference*, 2nd ed., San Mateo, CA: Morgan Kaufmann, 1991.

[48] McLaughlin, J., and M. E. Paté-Cornell, "A Bayesian Approach to Iraq's Nuclear Program Intelligence Analysis: A Hypothetical Illustration," *Proc. 2005 International Intelligence Analysis Conf.*, McLean, VA, May 2005; also see McLaughlin, J., "A Bayesian Updating Model for Intelligence Analysis: A Case Study of Iraq's Nuclear Weapons Program," Stanford University Center for International Security and Cooperation, May 20, 2005.

[49] Pope, S., and A. Jøsang, "Analysis of Competing Hypotheses Using Subjective Logic," *Proc. 10th International Command and Control Research and Technology Symp.*, McLean, VA, June 2005. See also Pope, S., A. Jøsang, and D. McAnally, "Formal Methods of Countering Deception and Misperception in Intelligence Analysis" *Proc. 11th Intl Command and Control Research and Technology Symp.*, Cambridge U.K., September 2006; and Pope, S., and A. Jøsang, "Analysis of Competing Hypotheses Using Subjective Logic," *Proc. 11th Intl Command and Control Research and Technology Symp.*, Cambridge U.K., September 2006.

[50] Kent, S., "Words of Estimative Probability," *Studies in Intelligence,* Vol. 8, No. 4, Fall 1964, pp. 49–65. See also the earlier article, Wark, D. L., "The Definition of Some Estimative Expressions," *Studies in Intelligence,* Vol. 8, No. 4, Fall 1964, pp. 67–80. For a similar study of expressions of uncertainty outside the intelligence domain, see Karelitz, T. M., and D. V. Budescu, "You Say 'Probable" and I Say 'Likely': Improving Interpersonal Communication with Verbal Probability Phrases," *Journal of Experimental Psychology*, Vol. 10, No. 1, 2004, pp. 25–41.

[51] Ibid., p. 53.

[52] Ibid., pp. 64–65.

[53] *The Commission,* op. cit., p. 410.

[54] For an example of a counterterrorism red cell game using computer simulation support, see: Moore, J., "Hypothesis Generation and Management," *KDD Conference*, Sandia National Laboratories Advanced Concepts Group, November 21, 2003, accessed July 25, 2005, http://www.sandia.gov/ACG/docs/presentations_other/KDDconference.ppt. See also Murray, W., "Thoughts on Red Teaming," Hicks and Assoc, Working Paper #03-2, May 2003, and Murdock, C. A., "The Role of Red Teaming in Defense Planning," Hicks and Assoc., Working Paper #03-3, August 2003.

[55] See, for example, Brams, S. J., "Deception in 2 × 2 Games," *Journal of Peace Science*, Vol. 2, Spring 1977, pp. 171–203, and Brams, S. J., and F. C. Zagare, "Double Deception: Two Against One in Three-Person Games," *Theory and Decision*, Vol. 13, March 1981, pp. 81–90.

[56] Carley, K. M., J. Reminga, and N. Kamneva, "Destabilizing Terrorist Networks," *Proc. NAACSOS*, Pittsburgh, PA, 2003.

[57] *Real-Time Adversarial Intelligence and Decision-Making (RAID)*, Defense Advanced Research Agency, DARPA BAA 04-16, March 1, 2004.

[58] Whaley, B., *Strategem: Deception and Surprise in War*, Cambridge, MA: MIT, 1969, pp. 186–187; Whaley further envisioned the value of simulation (p. 150): "A more fruitful line of further development of a theory of stratagem might be to subject it to the discipline of programming for a decision-making computer simulation."

[59] The distinctions between data- and concept-driven approaches to analysis are described by Heuer, Jr., R., *The Psychology of Intelligence Analysis*, Washington, D.C.: CIA Sherman Kent Center, 1999, Ch. 5.

[60] Weick, K., *Sensemaking in Organizations,* Thousand Oaks, CA: Sage Publications, 1995.

[61] For a survey of intelligence sensemaking models, and an interesting counterfactual perspective, see Moon, B. M., and R. R. Hoffman, "How Might Transformational Technologies and Concepts be Barriers to Sensemaking in Intelligence Analysis?" *Proc. of the Seventh International NDM Conference*, Amsterdam, the Netherlands, June 2005.

[62] *The Commission*, op. cit., p. 73.

[63] May, E. R., "Capabilities and Proclivities," in *Knowing One's Enemies: Intelligence Assessment Before the Two World Wars*, E. R. May, (ed.), Princeton, NJ: Princeton University Press, 1984, pp. 537–538.

[64] *The Commission*, op. cit., pp. 412–413.

[65] See Johnson, P. E., et al., "Detecting Deception: Adversarial Problem Solving in a Low Base Rate World," *Cognitive Science*, Vol. 25, No. 3, May/June 2001, pp. 355–392.

[66] See Dennett, D. C., *The Intentional Stance*, Cambridge, MA: MIT Press, 1989; and VanLehn, K., *Mind Bugs: The Origins of Procedural Misconceptions*, Cambridge, MA: MIT Press, 1990.

[67] Caddell, J. W., *Deception 101—A Primer on Deception*, Carlisle, PA: Strategic Studies Institute, U.S. Army War College, December 2004, p. 16.

CHAPTER 8

Counterdeception Architectures and Technologies

Counterdeception, implemented across an intelligence community or within a special component or cell of the organization, requires the integration of *people* (a diversity disciplines—from planning and collection to analysis and production), their *processes* that coordinate activities, the flow of information and analytic reasoning, and the *technologies* to support them. These three elements form the standard definition of an *enterprise* dedicated to implementing the counterdeception function as a practical operational capability. While we do not imply that an intelligence organization must construct a dedicated counterdeception enterprise, we use an enterprise architecture as a suitable model to illustrate the implementation of the methods developed in previous chapters. Furthermore, the architecture we introduce here is a structure suitable for general intelligence operations or for a dedicated counterdeception cell.

We first must recognize two perspectives of the role that counterdeception should play in an intelligence organization. In the first view, counterdeception is not a special discipline, organization, or function; it is a critical and integral element woven into good intelligence planning, collection and analysis. In this view, counterdeception is performed by everyone using carefully integrated methods, with some special collection—to penetrate concealment. Counterdeception in analysis requires a ubiquitous awareness of the threat of deception, supported by a comprehensive training program for all. In contrast, an alternative view calls for a special and dedicated counterdeception process—staffed by deception specialists that are focused on "hard targets" that employ concealment and are supported by active deception activities. In this view, counterdeception is performed by specialist teams devoted to probe *and* penetrate the deception process, employing unique collection to penetrate the concealment. In this view, counterdeception is performed by special people, using special methods and tools. These views are not mutually exclusive; indeed, counterdeception at some level must be a daily activity across the entire enterprise, while there are situations that call for a dedicated element of the organization to focus on the deception threat.

The United States maintains a Foreign Denial and Deception Committee (FDDC) that is an interagency effort to coordinate the understanding of how foreign adversaries learn about and try to defeat U.S. intelligence collection activities, and to develop strategies to counter deception activities across the intelligence community. The FDDC also leads the effort to provide community-wide awareness of the D&D threat, via briefings and formal counterdeception training programs [1]. In addition, elements of the community maintain experts with a dedicated focus on denial and deception issues [2]. In addition, the United States maintains a strategic plan to develop and deploy processes and technologies to counter deception; the 2005 Commission on the Intelligence Capabilities of the United States Regarding Weapons of Mass Destruction recommended increased emphasis on research, development, and deployment of these capabilities [3]:

> The DNI should also assist collectors in developing and operationalizing the most promising innovations, while redoubling efforts to improve *existing* means of countering and reducing the distorting effects of denial and deception... To aid him in the latter effort, the DNI will inherit a commendable roadmap previously developed by the DCI. Among other things, this strategy establishes efforts to counter-denial and deception by our adversaries as "a top priority for the Intelligence Community."

In this chapter, we introduce the organizational, systems, and technical architectural views of a counterdeception enterprise, illustrating the implementation of the processes (methods) introduced in the last chapter within an architecture using appropriate tools (technologies) necessary to coordinate collection, processing, analysis, and reporting against a determined intelligence target. While the previous chapter focused on counterdeception methodologies, here we focus on practical implementations of those methods in a counterdeception enterprise of people, processes and technologies.

We introduce three major descriptive views of intelligence architecture in Section 8.1 before developing the operational view of implementing the methodology developed in the last chapter (Section 8.2), the interconnecting system view (Section 8.3), and the component technology tools that support planners, collectors, and analysts (Section 8.4). To illustrate a small enterprise, we describe a representative counterdeception cell in Section 8.5.

8.1 Architecture Considerations

The counterdeception process is ultimately practiced by subject matter experts (from planners and collectors to analysts and operators) within an intelligence enterprise employing operational processes, information networks, and technical tools. Throughout this chapter, we illustrate the implementation of counterdeception in an enterprise by describing its *architecture*: the structure of components, their relationships, and the principles and guidelines governing their design and evolution over time [4].

The first consideration for implementing counterdeception across an enterprise, or for implementing it within a dedicated counterdeception cell is the description of the architecture. We adopt the DoD Architecture Framework (DoDAF) as the approach to describe the architecture in multiple *architectural views*, where each view is one representation of a set of system elements that also describes the relations between elements [5]. The following sections are organized by two of the three major views defined in DoDAF:

Operational architecture is a description (often graphical) of the operational elements, intelligence business processes, assigned tasks, workflows, and information flows required to accomplish or support the intelligence function. It defines the type of information, the frequency of exchange, and what tasks are supported by these information exchanges.

Systems architecture is a description of the systems and interconnections providing for or supporting intelligence functions. The system architecture defines the physical connection, location, and identification of the key nodes, circuits, networks, and users and specifies system and component performance parameters. It is constructed to satisfy operational architecture requirements per standards defined in the technical architecture. This architecture view shows how multiple systems within a subject area link and interoperate and may describe the internal construction or operations of particular systems within the architecture.

The third view, not necessary to be described in this section, is the *technical architecture* that describes the services, interfaces, standards, and other technical guidelines for implementing a system. For example, these standards include the selection of Web services (e.g., .NET or J2EE platform standards) and exchange content languages (e.g., eXtensible Markup Language XML, dedicated protocols, and metadata standards [6]), and application package standards or versions.

In subsequent sections we tailor the description of the elements to emphasize the functions supporting counterdeception (Table 8.1) that implement the methods introduced in the prior chapters.

The second consideration in implementing an architecture to perform counterdeception is the development of a means to measure the performance of the elements of the collection to analysis process and the overall effectiveness in countering D&D threats.

8.1.1 Performance Measures

The enterprise requires a means to measure quantifiable performance of the internal activities within the workflow, from planning through collection to analysis. Metrics are required to measure the end-to-end accuracy, timeliness, and rate of each activity. Collection metrics measure collection performance against priority

Table 8.1 Architecture Views and Counterdeception Elements

View	*Section*	*Counterdeception Elements Described*
Operational: business processes	8.2	General workflow of counterdeception planning, collection, processing, analysis, and dissemination; specific representative "threads" through the system illustrated as use cases or scenarios
		User policies and procedures
Operational: supporting tools	8.3	Manual and electronic procedural checklists
		Software tools to navigate, search and retrieve source data, identify and log potential incongruities, generate alternative hypotheses, and simulate hypothetical target behaviors for comparison with observations
		Software tools to quantitatively and qualitatively compare alternative hypotheses, and the diagnosticity of contributing evidence
		Software tools to structure arguments representing judgments and provide traceability to supporting evidence
System architecture	8.4	System network: structure and attributes of processing nodes, storage, and communication links
		Collaboration mechanisms for sharing data and models (shared thinking) across counterdeception teams

information requirements, processing metrics measure the ability of processing to deliver converted data to analysts. Analytic metrics assess the performance of analysts and their tools; Table 8.2, for example, enumerates process metrics adopted by the U.S. intelligence community to measure the performance of analytic tools in support of all-source analysts scanning a massive volume of data to locate relevant evidence [7]. The metrics encompass analyst-directed searches (pull) as well as the delivery of automatically screened data (push). Of particular interest to the counterdeception problem is the ability to detect subtle warning cues and identify incongruities that lead to the discovery and creation of hypotheses that expose alternative deceptive explanations.

8.1.2 Effectiveness Measures

While performance measures address internal component-level activity, effectiveness measures assess overall contribution to enterprise operations (e.g., coverage of D&D targets and rate of penetration) and the intelligence mission (e.g., mitigating surprise by countering D&D, explaining concealed capabilities by penetrating concealment). Examples of such high-level effectiveness measures metrics include:

- Timeliness of delivery of intelligence to consumers (e.g., time from data collection to judgment, reporting, time from hypothesis or argument formulation to first issue of a warning product, time from consumer query to custom report delivery).
- Accuracy, relevance, breadth and completeness of reporting on D&D targets (e.g., number of source types contributing to report, degree of validation of sources and assets, breadth and completeness of alternatives explored, post hoc assessments of reporting accuracy on D&D targets).

Table 8.2 Analytic Tool Performance Metrics' Relevance to Counterdeception Analysis

<table>
<tr><th>Metric Area</th><th>Representative Metrics</th><th>Counterdeception Relevance</th></tr>
<tr><td>Search efficiency</td><td>Time/search for data
Time/data reviewed</td><td rowspan="2">For a given amount of effort, these metrics measure the expanse of potentially relevant data that may be scanned (number of alternative channels, alternate methods) to locate confirming or refuting data (revealing incongruities, changes, and so forth).</td></tr>
<tr><td>Effort</td><td>Number of data items accessed
Number of data items reviewed (e.g., documents read, data exploited)
Relevant data (evidence) repository growth rate</td></tr>
<tr><td>Accuracy</td><td>Evidence used in analysis
Number of hypotheses considered
Average value ranking of data reviewed</td><td>Measure the degree to which potential evidence of deception is explored and explanations of incongruities are developed into hypotheses</td></tr>
<tr><td>Confidence</td><td>User confidence ratings in evidence based on the reliability of sources, diagnostic value, and completeness</td><td>Measure the degree of belief that is justified in hypotheses that account for deception, especially in the absence of direct evidence</td></tr>
<tr><td>Intelligence report quality</td><td>Quality of intelligence report based on correspondence to evidence and coherence of argument
Subjective ranking of report by users</td><td>Measure the value of content describing deception threat, vulnerabilities, available evidence, alternative hypotheses, and judgment—relative to policymakers' interests</td></tr>
</table>

Source: [7].

- Cost and investment in delivery of intelligence to consumer (e.g., collection, processing, and analytic assets allocated to penetrate targets, relative contributions of assets to target penetration by deception methods, and so forth).

Steven Rieber, scholar-in-residence at the Sherman Kent Center for Analytic Tradecraft, has argued for the development of an *evidence-based tradecraft* approach that evaluates the effectiveness of community-wide analytic methods, even as the medical community monitors the long-term effects of surgical procedures and pharmaceutical treatments to quantify effectiveness. In such a process, the actual measured performance of alternative analytic methods, measured post hoc over a range of problems using a large-sample, statistical analysis would provide an assessment of enterprise effectiveness [8]. The operational collection of the metrics described above would permit just such an analysis of the utility of counterdeception processes.

8.2 Operational Architecture: Methodology and Workflow of Counterdeception

The operational architecture describes the set of practices, procedures, and rules applied by intelligence practitioners; it is their applied counterdeception methodology. We distinguish between the specific *tools* of counterdeception investigation (also referred to as specific *methods*) and the system of methods or *methodology* that determines how such tools are deployed and interpreted. This section focuses on the applied methodology that implements the formal methodology introduced in Chapter 7; Section 8.3 describes the tools of implementation.

The methodology must consider the *vertical* cognitive processes that move from simple observations to complex analytic reasoning about situations, and the *horizontal* workflow that moves across many participants in the intelligence counterdeception process.

8.2.1 Individual Analyst's Methodologies

Consider two complementary high-level models of the cognitive process employed by individual intelligence analysts, a prime target of deception. These models attempt to describe the elements of an individual analyst's cognitive activities from an application perspective to understand the inherent methodology performed by an analyst. (These perspectives focus on applying the cognitive vulnerability mitigating processes introduced earlier in Chapter 6.)

First, we consider a structured model of analysis developed by Lambert to describe the effects of deception and to develop methods to understand, simulate, and counter deception, developing a cognitive model relevant to the analytic process [9]. Lambert described a typical unified cognitive model with distinct levels of abstraction (of representation and reasoning) and mapped a generic problem-solving system process (Figure 8.1) into the cognitive model to identify the causes and effects of deception on the analyst. [The model follows accepted approaches that represent cognition as an interaction between units of procedural knowledge

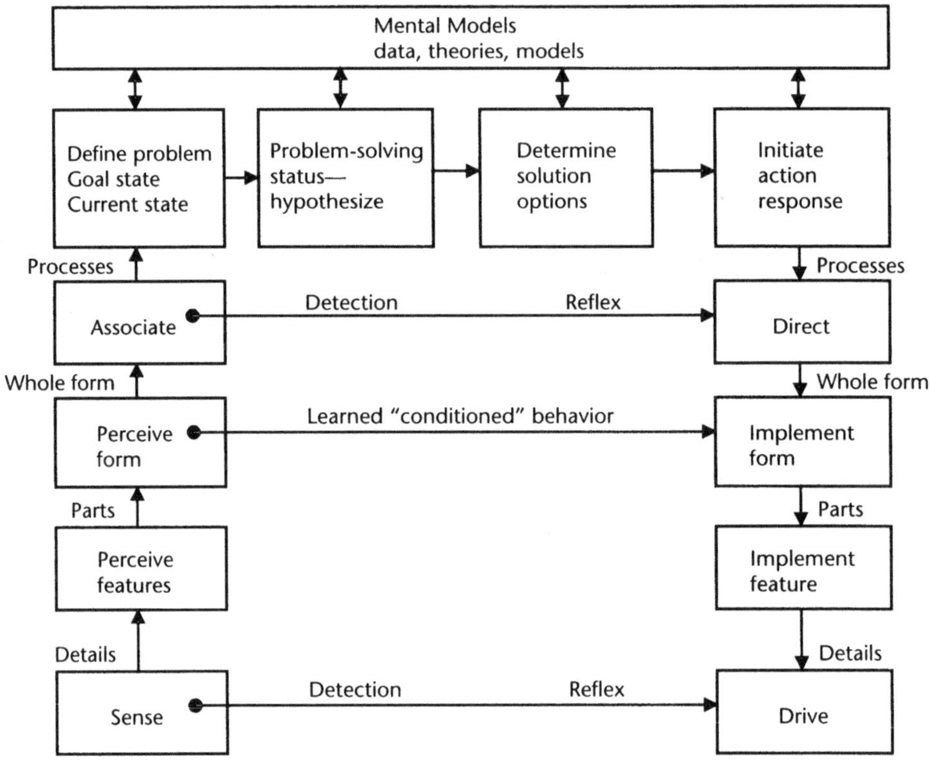

Figure 8.1 System processes of cognitive model. *Source:* [9].

(productions) and units of declarative knowledge (chunks) to achieve goals. Two popular computational models based on corresponding theories of cognition include SOAR; an agent model of the cognitive process is based on a unified approach to cognitive processes described by Newell and ACT-R; and a symbolic production system is organized to allow the construction of large cognitive processes from individual modules [10].)

This model distinguished three levels below the problem definition-to-solution action functions that include levels of sensing and perception (on the left) and then synthesis of component actions to develop a response (on the right). The model highlights the hierarchical and synthetic nature of perception of intelligence that moves from primitive details to synthesize features, then to forms (patterns), and finally to associated patterns. At the highest level, strategic problem solving occurs as the evidence received by perception is marshaled toward hypothesized mental models. The results of analysis are high-level decisions and plans that are then implemented by analytic decomposition into discrete actions. The research developed a simulation of the system process to explore approaches to simulate RED deceptions, then enable the BLUE analyst (the target of deception) to simulate approaches to counter deception effects. The model was then applied to representative naval deception tactics. The reductionist model enabled the researchers to decompose representative and historical naval deceptions into their detail, feature, form, and process components to simulate and understand deception scenarios and opportunities to recognize the potential for deception or related incongruities. Such a model aids in understanding that an analytic methodology must allow for recognition of deception patterns or incongruities at different levels of abstraction (e.g., a discrepancy in an expected signal waveform feature, a discrepancy in a set of signals that make up a traffic pattern, or a discrepancy in an entire process or timeline of events).

Kline et al. [11] have described a more holistic (naturalistic) model to describe the behavior of analysts and decision-makers in both crisis and deliberate analysis and planning processes. Such *metacognition* models are characterized by a more holistic high-level pattern matching process where analysts search for typical patterns (archetypes) of prior situations; from these matches, the analyst may identify relevant solutions (based on past outcomes and consequences) and tailor them to the current situation. The depth and breadth of prior experience (tacit knowledge) are paramount. In this recognition-primed decision-making (RPD) mode, analysts focus on adequate "satificing" solutions, rather than optimizing ones; there is not an emphasis on exhaustive options or optimal selection. This process relies on the analysts application of dynamic mental models (mental simulation) based on extrapolation from prior experience, where the analyst images or envisions the likelihood of alternative explanations of evidence, the likely outcomes of actions. The focus of this mode is on action rather than analysis and judgment. Kline's data-frame model is a state transition model that distinguishes the roles of external *data* and organizing mental *frames* (or, hypotheses) used by analysts to make sense of situations and develop a state of situation awareness over time [12]. This model (Figure 8.2) distinguishes the following activities in the sensemaking process:

1. *Frame representation.* The analyst first represents the situation by forming an initial representation of a situation using a frame (a tacit or explicit framework within which evidence is coherently organized, for example, a narrative, logical flow, graphical structure, and so forth) that expresses the belief in an explanation of the situation.
2. *Frame elaboration.* Next, the frame is detailed, expanded, refined, and more completely elaborated as new data are compared and inserted into the frame.

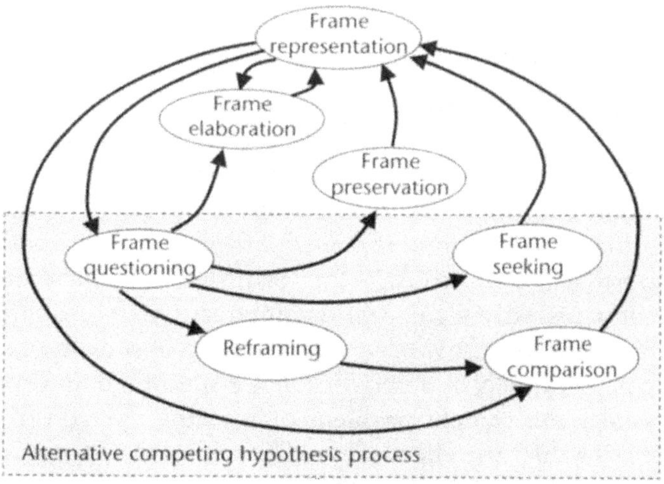

Figure 8.2 Data-frame model of sensemaking. *Source:* [12].

3. *Questioning, reframing, or preserving.* As data are entered, the analyst questions inconsistent data—and is confronted with changing the frame, discarding the data and preserving the frame, or forming a new alternative frame while maintaining the current frame. If the analyst reframes to accommodate new data, there is the possibility that the frame will be distorted or corrupted; in the presence of deception, this may include the error of distorting an initial incorrect hypothesis to fit an incongruity, rather than creating a new frame that may reveal an alternative—and accurate—explanation of the situation.
4. *Seeking a frame.* Newly received data may cast doubt on the validity of a frame and cause the analyst to seek a new frame to explain the complete set of data.
5. *Comparing frames.* When maintaining alternative frames (hypotheses), the analyst sharpens distinctions between data—evaluating the diagnostic value to distinguish between frames.

Note that in the figure, the states that perform the alternative competing hypothesis process introduced in Chapter 7 are apparent; the continual reassessment of the framing hypothesis, the creation of alternatives, and assessment of data to compare hypotheses represent that process.

Both models provide insight into the cognitive processes behind an entire intelligence team's activities to search for data and frameworks to explain available observations—and to conjecture about the hidden things that are not be observable. The process occurs at multiple levels of abstractions—frames are formed at signal, object, and multiple-object pattern levels, and the framing process is a continual reassessment of belief driven by the comparison of observations with conceptual frames.

Beyond the methodology of a single analyst's reasoning process is the collaborative effort of a complete intelligence team, dedicated to focusing on a difficult intelligence target. The process of coordinating such a team is described by the flow of information among team members as they seek, construct and evaluate framed data (hypotheses).

8.2.2 Intelligence Team Workflow

The *workflow* is a narrative and/or graphical description of the "general" or "typical" process steps of a business cycle; the description articulates the actions of people and their associated automated processes. The analytic workflow particularly describes the steps of analysis, the actions and decisions at each step, alternate paths, and the flow of information that moves from problem to solution. It is important to recognize that the workflow is an abstract tool to illustrate the flow of information—not necessarily the day-to-day interaction among analysts. In practice, all of the steps of the workflow occur concurrently by a team of individuals, often interacting collaboratively as a network, not a smooth, data-driven flow.

Consider the sample problem of tracking the construction and operational activities of a dual-use chemical facility employing aggressive D&D methods, such as the Libyan Pharma 150 facility described earlier in Chapter 4. We illustrate the role of counterdeception activities to understand a potential chemical weapons (CW) program in an intelligence workflow across three typical intelligence (INT) sources: IMINT, SIGINT, and HUMINT. The graphical depiction of the intelligence workflow (Figure 8.3) describes the actions performed by the distributed team, from a single-source IMINT, SIGINT, and HUMINT collection, processing, and analysts, as well as those performed by the all-source analysts who place this information in context and integrate all sources.

Note that the workflow implements the five states of the methodology developed in Chapter 7, numbered in correspondence with those stages. The predominant information flow (solid lines) proceeds from collection to reporting; lines of coordination are dashed. The elements of the workflow in the figure include:

- *Target development and coordination of distributed collection and analysis:* At the side of the flow the mission manager is responsible for coordinating target development and the distributed collection and analysis process. The role includes developing strategies for all aspects of intelligence relating to the potential CW organization, resources, facilities, and products, including coordinating collection against the target organization and facilities, as well as related contextual targets. The manager also monitors the effectiveness of collection strategies, oversees analysis to develop strategic analysis plans, fosters the objective analysis of alternatives, monitors the gaps in existing knowledge and develops strategies to fill those gaps [13].
- *Collection and data management:* Collection managers develop integrated collection strategies across the collection disciplines to provide the information identified inn target development. In particular, current collection capabilities are compared to potential D&D strategies available to the target (e.g., physical security and concealment, use of front companies, complex dual-use operations interactions, and so forth) to identify collection gaps and potential new methods to fill intelligence needs. Data managers coordinate the processing setup to exploit technical data sources, guide relevant data to the appropriate analysis cells, set up dedicated portals and knowledge bases, and set filter parameters for automated "push" searches.
- *Single-source collection, processing, and analysis:* The single-source analysts (e.g., IMINT, SIGINT, and HUMINT) perform independent screening of data using their own models to detect deception indicators and incongruities. [All source analysts perform a separate screening for indictors and incongruities across all channels and maintain their independent alternative hypotheses on their component targets of the potential CW program (e.g., IMINT focuses on facilities, while SIGINT and HUMINT focus on organizations that operate the facilities).]
- *GEOINT analysis:* Analysts trained in geospatial intelligence (GEOINT) analysis receive processed geospatial data (imagery, extracted features, and merged geospatial products) to build a geospatial knowledge base of the targeted chemical facilities and temporal pattern of activities. Data accumulated in this knowledge base are exploited to identify features and indicators for comparison with models of expected operations and signatures for a range of commercial pharmaceutical facilities—and chemical weapons facilities. The

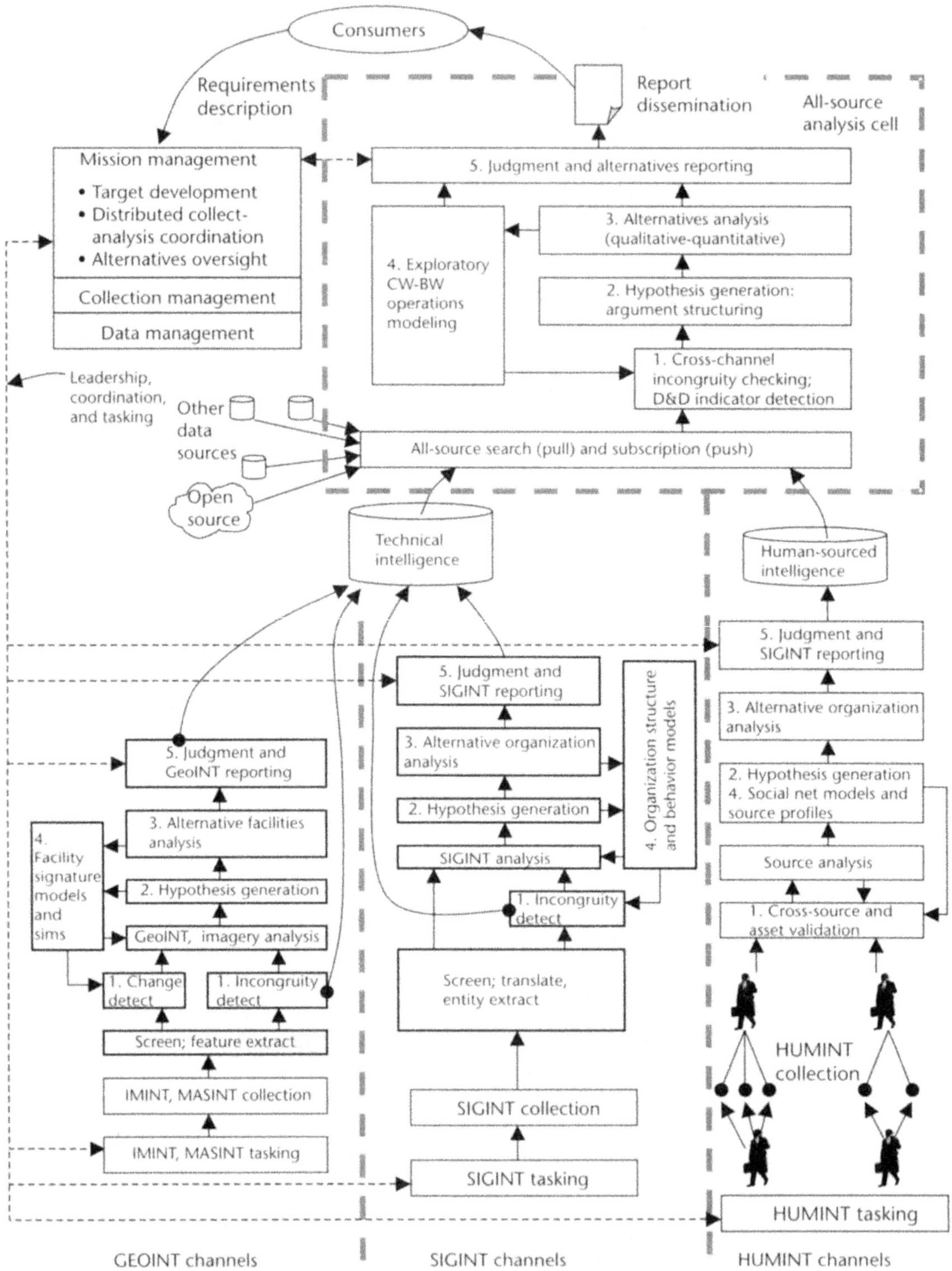

Figure 8.3 Intelligence workflow emphasizing counterdeception activities.

GEOINT analyst maintains alternative facilities hypotheses on the capability, and temporal activity of the facilities. Incongruities in facility construction, behaviors, or signatures of effluents are reported with the alternatives analysis.

- *SIGINT analysis:* Analysts trained in the translation and interpretation of signals data receive information on the facility operating organization, comparing activity and traffic data to models of behavior expected for alternative organization types, levels of activity, and capabilities. The alternative organizational hypotheses are reported, with discovered incongruities across signal sources.
- *HUMINT operations:* A HUMINT ops manager coordinates clandestine case officer efforts to secure information on the potential CW program from multiple assets (human agents) and perspectives, while overseeing the maintenance of an asset database and a program for active validation of assets. Incongruities due to reporting inconsistencies (in a single asset), discrepancies (across different assets), or unrealistic consistencies (too good to be true?) are reported with an alternative analysis of the meaning of asset reports, their estimated veracity, and incongruities. As described in Chapter 4, asset validation includes particular attention to the potential susceptibility to doubled agent operations.
- *All-source analysts:* An all-source analytic cell accepts the reports from the single-source channels that include evidence, alternative hypotheses, and current judgments. In addition to these focused collection sources, the all-source team conducts concentrated "pull" searches for relevant gap-filling data, and receives regular data "pushed" to them by automated filters set to characteristics for the targeted facility and organization (e.g., geocoordinates, keywords, and so forth). This data comes from across open and community-wide sensitive sources. The analytic team maintains top-level alternative hypotheses that integrate organizational and facilities alternatives to consider the possible existence, state of capability, and intent of a CW capability at the targeted pharmaceutical facility.

While this particular workflow perspective highlights the "stovepipe," "information flow," and "vertical fusion" (or data-driven) aspects of the process, it is but one perspective. The flow does not highlight the conceptually driven activities, the horizontal interaction among participants (e.g., opportunistic cross-cueing between the SIGINT and GEOINT analysts), or the critical collaborative and feedback aspects of the process that are covered next, in the use case [14].

8.2.3 Intelligence Team Use Case

While the workflow focuses on the flow of information from collection to judgment, it does not explain the interaction among the mission, collection, and data managers and the analytic teams, or their interaction with their supporting tools and information system. This description is provided by narrative *use cases* that complement the workflow by explaining user interaction. Each use case is a detailed narrative description of a single, specific activity in the counterdeception process from an end-user perspective. Use cases describe how end-users will conduct their day-to-day activities; they identify preconditions, data inputs and outputs, performance/timing requirements, and interfaces with external applications. Because an enterprise may have many different paths (or "threads") through the workflow, multiple-use cases are used to describe the many different ways that users interact to counter a deception target [15].

To illustrate the use case, we consider jut one situation in which a tip-off is received that an existing foreign pharmaceutical facility is undergoing construction changes that may indicate a conversion to provide a dual-use capability for chemical or biological weapons. The use case for a "new deception target development" is formatted (Figure 8.4) to describe an entire scenario from beginning to end, showing how users interact among each other, with their tools, and their information system.

8.3 Operational Architecture: Tools of Counterdeception

The *methodology* of the operational architecture is implemented by mission, collection and data managers, and analysts using *tools*, the instruments or devices used to perform or facilitate the administrative and cognitive processes involved in the counterdeception methodology [16]. Often referred to as cognitive or decision support tools, these devices enable analysts to assemble and explore knowledge constructs to enhance complex learning activities and critical thinking. Cognitive tools support and augment the functions of memory, attention, problem structuring, comprehension, and explicit representation of concepts for sharing, exploration and manipulation (e.g., dynamic simulation of concepts) [17].

In intelligence applications, these tools augment learning or reasoning, providing the following kinds of support to explicitly represent analytic knowledge, enable collaborative analysis, and practically implement the methodology in tangible ways [18]:

- Intelligence mission management, to provide visibility and traceability from requirement creation to collection, through processing and analysis, to intelligence judgments and reporting. Such tools support the allocation and management of resources and workflow [19].
- Requirements decomposition to collection and processing requirements, planning, and performance tracking.
- Evidence organization, evidence marshalling to generate and maintain alternative hypotheses, evidence tracking, and reporting.
- Structured argumentation to support and explain analysis; structured analysis of alternative hypotheses and assessment of probabilistic assessments.
- Target simulation for exploratory analysis to predict behaviors and evidence for comparison with actual observations.

The accepted method for developing tool concepts and evaluating their cognitive contribution is the application of cognitive task analysis (CTA). This process first studies user patterns, then develops a set of candidate concepts to aid the task and a means to evaluate those concepts individually, and then conducts tests of prototype tools within an objective evaluation methodology [20]. The U.S. intelligence community has sponsored research to an extensive set of qualitative and

1. **SCENARIO:** New Deception Target Development

2. **Summary:** Mission manager receives a tip-off that an existing pharmaceutical facility PH23 in KHOUTON is undergoing significant construction changes; the activities are being protected by heavy security measures. The conversion may provide a dual-use capability for chemical or biological weapons.

3. **Preconditions**	4. **Postconditions (Results)**
· Baseline GEOINT data exists for the facility prior to changes	·Periodic target development reports released to critical target portal · Assessment of capabilities provided for National Intelligence Estimate annually

5. **Basic Flow**

1. **Mission manager** establishes a target development board using **collaboration tools** to coordinate rapid response planning.
2. **Mission manager** chairs and coordinates the tasks of target development board:
   - 2.1 **Customer representatives** identify any policy issues, decision points, and intelligence needs.
   - 2.2 **Collection manager** identifies relevant collection capabilities, gaps, and shortfalls, deception vulnerabilities, and tentative collection strategies; **collection planning tools** define integrated collection plan.
   - 2.3 **Data manager** identifies the processing, knowledge bases, workflow, and security approach.
   - 2.4 **Analysis manager(s)** identify distributed, multidiscipline analytic needs and assign team members.
   - 2.5 **Mission manager** establishes security requirements, schedule, and reporting-dissemination requirements.
   - 2.6 **Mission manager** prioritizes the needs and approves target development strategy.
3. **Mission manager** issues target development strategy.
   - 3.1 **All mangers** assign tasking to the distributed team collectors and analysts.
   - 3.2 **Data manager** issues keys to participants and establishes local and community-accessible data repositories, establishing virtual collaborative workspaces and workflow.
   - 3.3 **Collection manager** issues collection plan and tasking across intelligence disciplines (INTs).
   - 3.3 **Data manager** creates "push" subscriptions and filter parameters to forward processed and filtered data to appropriate analysts in the workflow.
4. **Single source analysts** receive "pushed" data and conduct searches to retrieve relevant data to develop the target.
   - 4.1 **System** creates virtual workspaces, identifies existing relevant holdings, and begins to "push" data to populate the workspace with data relevant to the target, PH23.
   - 4.2 **GEOINT analytic team** accumulates and analyzes PH23 facility and related data; **IMINT tools** perform change detection as construction processes and **feature extraction tools** are set to detect incongruities from **modeling tools** that describe normal pharmaceutical and dual-use hypotheses. The team uses a **qualitative alternative hypothesis tool** to compare extracted feature evidence against the two hypotheses.
   - 4.3 **SIGINT analytic team** accumulates and analyzes relevant translated signals traffic to track construction, financing, shipping, and operations planning activities. The team compares information with **organizational and traffic modeling tools** that consider normal pharmaceutical organizational-operational behaviors and concealed high-security behaviors; indicators of concealment and incongruities in organization behavior are compared against pharmaceutical and dual-use CW/BW hypotheses in a **qualitative alternative hypothesis tool.**
   - 4.4 **HUMINT ops manager** coordinates activities of tasked case officers and performs cross-source checking of all received reports; and performs asset validation procedures to monitor veracity of HUMINT channels.
   - 4.5 **System** maintains the technical and human-sources intelligence repositories with data and alternative analyses from the GEOINT, SIGINT, and HUMINT teams.
   - 4.6 **All analysts** provide time critical cross-cues to their counterparts across INTs using **collaboration tools;** when appropriate, collection alerts are issued using **collection planning tools** to request urgent collection at cued events of opportunity.
5. **All-source analysis cell** integrates technical and human-sourced intelligence, and open-source intelligence.
   - 5.1 **Analysts** search ("pull") across all sources for information on the target and receive "pushed" subscription data using **scanning tools**.

Figure 8.4 New deception target development.

<table>
<tr><td colspan="2">
5.2 Analysts perform cross-channel checks to identify incongruities in reporting for potential deception indicators or concealment flaws.
5.3 Analysts develop structured arguments for the "normal pharmaceutical expansion" and "dual-use for CW-BW" hypotheses using argument construction tools.
5.4 Analysts develop models of the "normal pharmaceutical expansion" and "dual-use for CW-BW" hypotheses using operations modeling tools.
5.5 Analysts compare all evidence with the two hypotheses using alternative competing hypothesis (ACH) tools.
5.5.1 Analysts usea qualitative ACH tool to compare evidence diagnosticity and assess the relative credibility and relevance of each item.
5.5.2 Analysts use a quantitative ACH tool to determine the likelihood of each hypothesis and the relative contribution of all evidence and inferences.
5.6 Analysts provide guidance and cueing to single source analysts to focus on special issues and resolve gaps in knowledge about the target via collaboration tools.
5.7 Analysts apply judgment and integrate results into narrative summary assessment of PH23, with citation of all sources, analysis, and methods; gaps and deception vulnerabilities are noted.
5.8 Analytic manager posts approved intermediate results in the community-shared workspace for the team to review and for preliminary review by the mission manager.
6. Mission manager assesses the overall quality of the developing intelligence.
6.1 Mission manager reviews intermediate analytic products, breadth of alternatives analysis, and credibility of all evidence.
6.2 Mission manager uses collaboration tools to convene target development board review.
6.3 Mission manager approves and releases, or tasks further collection (e.g. higher-risk collection is approved) to be conducted before release.
6.4 Mission manager approves and distributes intermediate status reports; report is released to portal.
6.5 System maintains configuration management of analysis as refinements and ongoing updates are issued.
7. The scenario ends.
</td></tr>
<tr><td>5. Alternative flows: The target development flow may require a broad area search when less specific information is provided on the target.</td><td>6. Revision: 1.0 dated 12-27-05</td></tr>
</table>

Figure 8.4 (continued)

quantitative measures of analytic effectiveness, specifically for comparing the effectiveness of tools in enhancing the cognitive functions of analysis [21]. While these measures apply to analysis in general, they may be applied to deception in particular by focusing on the mitigation of cognitive shortcomings, described earlier in Chapter 3, that render analysts vulnerable to deception.

While support tools include a wide range of devices, in the following we focus on those categories that particularly contribute to countering deception: procedural and criteria of merit checklists, automated processing filters, knowledge bases, and computational analytic support tools.

Procedural sequence checklists may be implemented as mnemonics to support recall (e.g., analyst's remember MOM as means, opportunity, motive), hardcopy checklists, or software checklists integrated as dialogue panels within analytic or report-writing tools. Such checklists may also be implemented as guided checklists (evoked by software agents) that appear, for example, when potential incongruities are detected that require further scrutiny. A representative procedural checklist tool developed by the Sherman Kent School to assess the lack of evidence for a WMD program (Table 8.3) illustrates the considerations of concealment and deception factors in the overall assessment (see activities 2–4) [22].

Table 8.3 Information Gap Procedural Checklist

Illustrative Methodology to Assess an Information Gap
Hypothetical Intelligence Challenge
To test the analysts' judgment that Country X probably does not have a robust nuclear weapons program by examining the absence of specific information needed to confirm existence of the program.
Analytic Team Activities
1. Identify three to five essential factors on which analysts have little or no reliable information but that would have to be present if Country X has a robust nuclear weapons program (for example, an ample foreign or domestic source of weapons-grade fissile material).
2. Evaluate Country X's assumed ability to use denial and deception (D&D) to block effective intelligence collection against each essential factor.
3. List plausible non-D&D explanations, however unlikely, for all-source collection to miss each of the essential factors.
4. Evaluate U.S. ability to collect information on each essential factor, if the program existed, taking into account D&D and other barriers.
5. Calculate the team's collective intuitive estimate of the probability that all-source analysis would miss obtaining information on each essential factor, if the program existed (for example, *greater than 90%*, *greater than 50%*).
6. Calculate the team's collective intuitive estimate of the probability that all-source analysis would miss collecting hard information on *all* of the essential factors (that is, the likelihood that a robust weapons program indeed exists).
7. Commission individual team members or supporting contractors to list all anomalous information that has been collected but not credited as authentic or diagnostic and explain the reason for discrediting in each instance.
8. Commission a similar group to prepare a devil's advocacy assessment that seeks to justify analytically a greater likelihood that a robust nuclear weapons program exists
9. On the basis of Steps 1–8, reassess the team's estimative judgment of the likelihood that a robust nuclear weapons program exists.

Such checklists are an example of one method of task restructuring to mitigate cognitive biases and break up mindsets, as described earlier in Chapter 6.

Criteria of merit lists (ComList) include forms that require the analyst to enter data in a format that allows scoring of the data against standard objective criteria. The ACH method introduced in the prior chapter is essentially a ComList form, providing a standard means to enter and evaluate the diagnosticity of evidence and completeness of alternative hypotheses against an objective criterion. Similarly, special ComList forms might be created by imagery analysts, for example, to assess the merit of critical features or indictors of physical target sites that employ concealment.

8.3.1 Automated Processing Filters and Knowledge Bases

Automated filtering tools may be set to detect and forward potentially relevant data from incoming high-volume sources (e.g., incoming open source reports, collected imagery, and signals), based on "subscription" parameters identified by collection and analysis teams. Detected incongruities or spurious signals (see Table 7.4 in Chapter 7) are identified and "pushed" to the user for further review. Knowledge bases supporting counterdeception analysis should maintain information on adversary knowledge of capabilities-vulnerabilities, adversary capabilities versus channels, and candidate adversary deception plan hypotheses.

8.3.2 Computational Analytic Support Tools

A wide range of computer-based analytic support tools have been developed to support individual analysts and collaborative analytic teams more effectively *interact with information* to find relevant data, form hypotheses, and marshal evidence to those hypotheses to arrive at intelligence judgments. These tools are designed to support analysts in numerous ways:

- *Overload:* To cope with data overload by searching massive volumes of data and extracting relevant information to focus the analysts attention of candidates of relevance,
- *Hypothesis generation and evidence marshaling:* To aid in generating explicit hypotheses and structured arguments, then organizing evidence to support or refute them; these explicit arguments can be shared to explain evidentiary reasoning (and can expose gaps and shortcomings),
- *Situation modeling:* To aid in explicit modeling and tracking the dynamics of complex hypotheses about situations (physical or social processes); models may be used to represent the dynamics of targets or situations and their alternative behaviors.
- *Collaborative analysis support:* To enhance collaborative analysis that encourages alternative perspectives of the context and data, alternative lines of analysis and competing hypotheses.

Each of these support areas contributes to a more robust analytic capability because they enable socialization and sharing of concepts, explicit representation of information, combination of information, in internalization (conceptual thinking) [23]. Of particular interest to the application of computational tools to aid in discovery processes for counterdeception, the U.S. intelligence community has acknowledged "a long history of commissioning the development of knowledge engineering and knowledge discovery techniques to address the issue of "strategic surprise," but little of this work has seen actual service." The difficulties with applying such tools fall in the categories of performance and methodology [24]:

> (a) *Tool Performance.* The techniques fail to acquire or to use the prior knowledge —the "thread of logic"—that analysts bring to their tasks. As a result, discoveries made by machines prove to be trivial, well-known, irrelevant, implausible, or logically inexplicable; and
> (b) *Incompatible Methodologies.* The techniques fail to respect analytic work habits. Many analysts have neither the production incentive nor the introspective bent to interrupt their workflow in order to teach algorithms (or researchers) about analytic tradecraft—particularly when that tradecraft may be undergoing rapid change to suit a new domain or information demand.

In spite of these application challenges, numerous tools have been developed and evaluated by analytic teams to support the basic steps the analytic methodology developed in this and the prior chapter; the use of these tools are now illustrated in a practical workflow.

8.3.3 An Analytic Tool Workflow

We can now demonstrate the integration of representative analytic tools to support analysis in a workflow that implements the general analysis and counterdeception methodology introduced in Chapter 7 (compare with Figure 7.8) and applied by the all-source analysis cell in the top-level workflow introduced in Section 8.3. This tool workflow (Figure 8.5) illustrates the use of a representative variety of tools, integrated as independent applications within a system architecture that provides a means to share data among applications and a repository for relevant evidence retrieved from massive data sources, alternative hypotheses (in the form of structured arguments, models, and dynamic simulations), alternative hypothesis comparisons, and intelligence reports (intermediate and final products). The following, numbered by the corresponding element in the figure, describe the use of the tools by a single analyst, although a shared repository and collaborative tools allow collaborating analysts to acquire and share evidence, models and hypothesis—as well as report authoring.

1. Scanning and channel testing is performed as an analyst receives pushed (or subscription) data, and searches to "pull" data from sources based on situation-relevant concepts or keywords using a search tool such as the Oculus nSpace TRIST (The Rapid Information Scanning Tool) [25]. The analyst uses TRIST (Figure 8.6) to examine a large space of data, organizing the results of queries across multiple search dimensions and allowing the analyst to see the associations across a large number of documents. Entity-extraction and document-clustering dimensions are provided. A retrieved set of data (documents, images, and so forth) are represented by type as an array of icons, and the analyst can scan across the icons, using the dimensions of interest to rapidly review and abstract, or click to open the item for detailed review. Relevant data (contextual information or specifically pertinent evidence) identified by the analyst are captured in local relevant data (evidence) storage for subsequent stages of analysis. While reviewing data, the analyst can capture snippets, images, documents, or extracted entities with references and then construct a *conceptual model* of this evidence in the associated nSpace Sandbox tool in the window below TRIST. The Sandbox is an evidence-marshalling environment, and it allows hypothesis structures to be constructed. For example, the analyst can construct entity-relationship networks or other conceptual maps—dragging data from TRIST in the flexible visual thinking space provided by Sandbox.

   The conceptual models created in the Sandbox start as informal descriptions of the linked entities and relationships of important actors, events, topics or objects; the form of the concept map may be a simple list, concept map, link diagram, process diagram, timelines, annotated maps, or other graphical representations of, time, space or causality, or noncausal associations. The conceptual model explicitly captures the analyst's emerging understanding of the structure of the intelligence target, its potential deception strategies and modes, and even its temporal behavior. The model also captures a basic ontology of target-relevant concepts to refine automated processing filters and guide future searches. As the

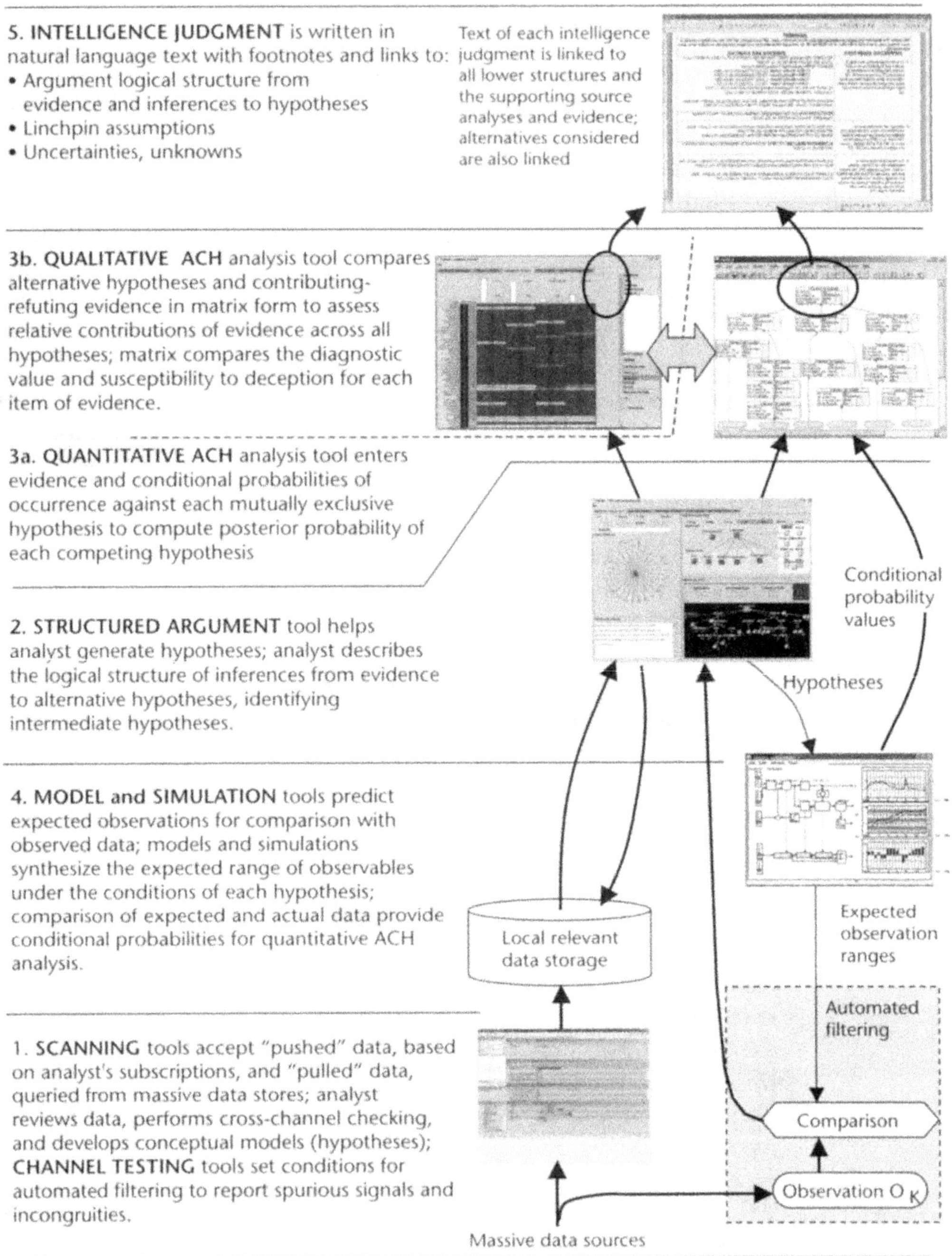

Figure 8.5 A representative workflow of analytic tools.

conceptual models mature, the analyst can translate them into *structured arguments* that logically represent alternative explanations of the data, and *computational models* that represent the internal structure and dynamics of the target.

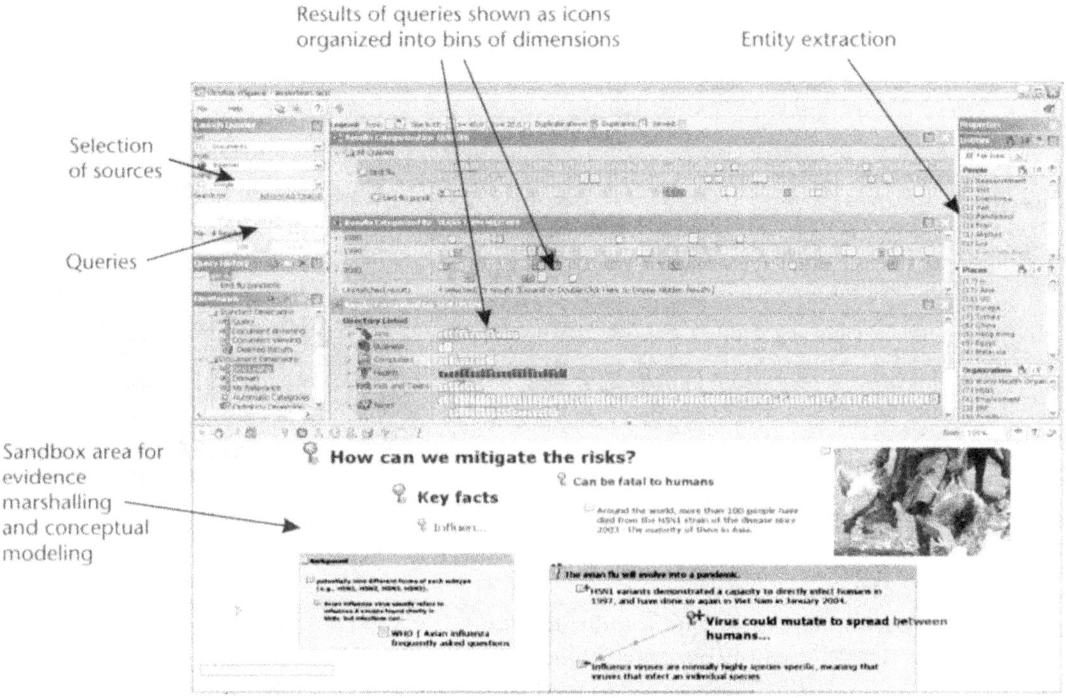

Figure 8.6 Oculus nSpace scanning and conceptual modeling. (©2006 Oculus Info Inc.)

2. *Structured argument.* In the figure, the analyst uses the SSS Research DECIDE tool to structure accumulating evidence into alternative argument structures [26]. The tool enables the analyst to organize the evidence accumulated in the local storage, and assign credibility (relative to sourcing) and relevance (relative to argument) parameters to each element of evidence. The analyst can then construct graphical hypothesis structures using either Wigmore or Toulmin argument forms that explicitly describe the relationships between evidence, inferences, and hypotheses [27]. Evidence is associated with the directed acyclic graphs that form the inference networks, allowing the analyst to see the entire argument structure and drill down to the detail of the contributing evidence at the roots of the graphs. In addition to the logical structure of argument, the tool also provides alternative views of the evidence and their relationships:

   1. *Timelines* that array evidence by time sequence of occurrence;
   2. *Networks* that graphically structure the relationships between events and entities contained in evidence;
   3. *Interactive lists* that can organize evidence by other arbitrary factors relative to a particular problem.

   The view of DECIDE (Figure 8.7) shows the "Hypothesis Visualization" tab that allows the analyst to view evidence in the form of "snippets" in the local store, and structure hypotheses. Other tabs allow the analyst to view the other relationships between evidence, and to translate the argument to an inference network to perform a quantitative comparison of alternative hypotheses. (While DECIDE can directly translate alternative hypotheses to

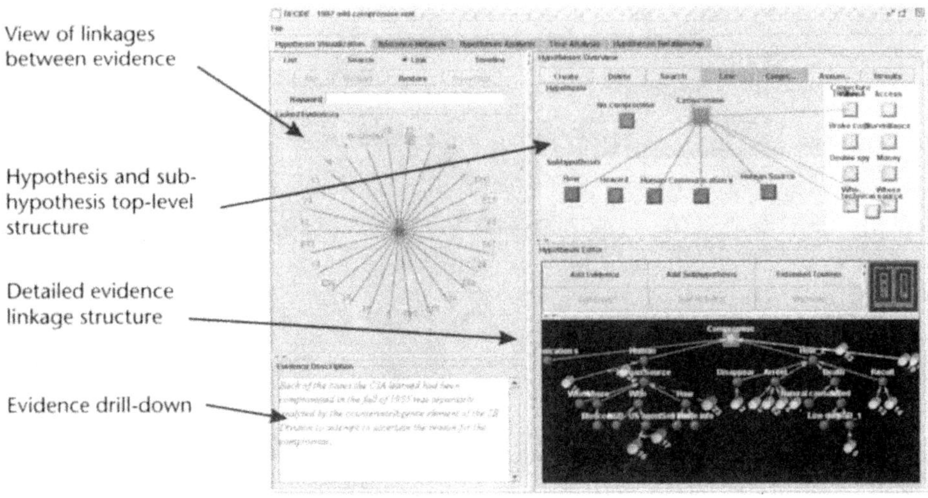

Figure 8.7 SSS Research DECIDE hypothesis generation: argument structuring.

both quantitative and qualitative analyses within the tool, we illustrate these capabilities in separate tools to illustrate a variety of approaches.)

3. *Alternative competing hypothesis analysis tools.* As the analyst constructs the arguments for alternative hypotheses, these hypotheses can be evaluated using the PARC ACH tool that first compares hypotheses using the method of alternative competing hypotheses [28]. The tool helps the analyst array all evidence and identify a complete set of mutually exclusive hypotheses (including those for which structured arguments are being developed, and other less compete hypotheses); it forces the analyst to recognize that evidence may support more than one hypothesis to mitigate the potential for confirmation bias. Elements of evidence, assumed independent, are numbered and arrayed in the first column of the spreadsheet format; the consistence ("I") or inconsistence ("C") with each hypothesis is entered in each corresponding cell under the Hypothesis (Hn) columns (Figure 8.8). A

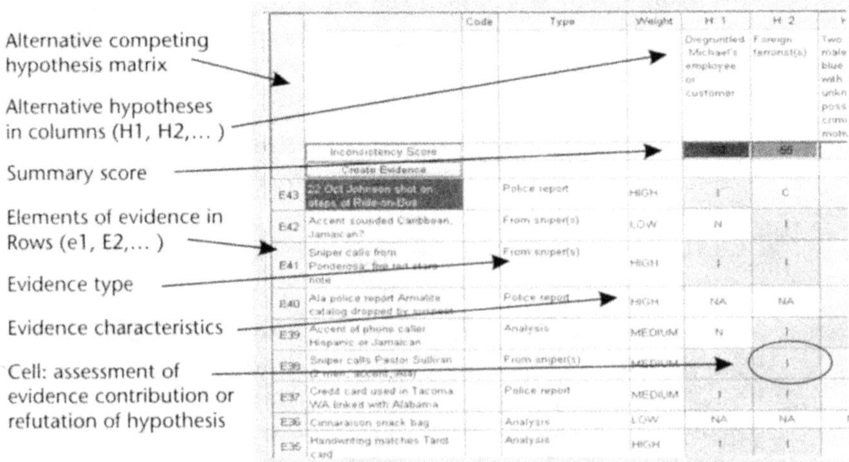

Figure 8.8 Alternative hypotheses compared in the PARC ACH tool. (Screenshot courtesy PARC.)

heuristic weighting may be applied to evidence to grade the relative credibility and relevance of each item. A summary inconsistency score is computed for each hypothesis column.

To complement the qualitative ACH tool, a quantitative assessment of alternatives can be performed using a Bayesian analysis using the Norsys Netica tool (Figure 8.9). This tool allows the structured arguments developed in the prior stages to be compiled into a graphical Bayesian belief net structure. The analyst assigns a priori probabilities to hypotheses, conditional probabilities at nodes (based on conceptual and computational models that provide output probabilities as a function of input conditions). Conditional probabilities are entered in a matrix form, where conditional probability cells are defined across all possible input states (e.g., states of evidence) versus the node output states (e.g., inferred beliefs as a result of the evidence). The Netica graphical display provides bar graph representations of the intermediate node and top-level posteriori probabilities. As new evidence is obtained and the argument refined, the network can be modified to enter the evidence at root nodes, the overall argument structure as well as the conditional probabilities at nodes.

4. *Computational modeling and simulation tools.* The analyst's conceptual models of a target (or situation) may be explicitly modeled using a variety of modeling and simulation tools to represent the static structure and dynamics of the target. *Models* refer to physical, mathematical, or otherwise logical representations of systems, entities, phenomena, or processes, and *simulations* refer to those methods to implement models over time (i.e., a simulation is a time-dynamic model) [29]. Models and simulations are inherently collaborative; their explicit representations (versus mental models) allow analytic teams to collectively assemble and explore the accumulating knowledge that they represent. They support the analysis-synthesis process in multiple ways:

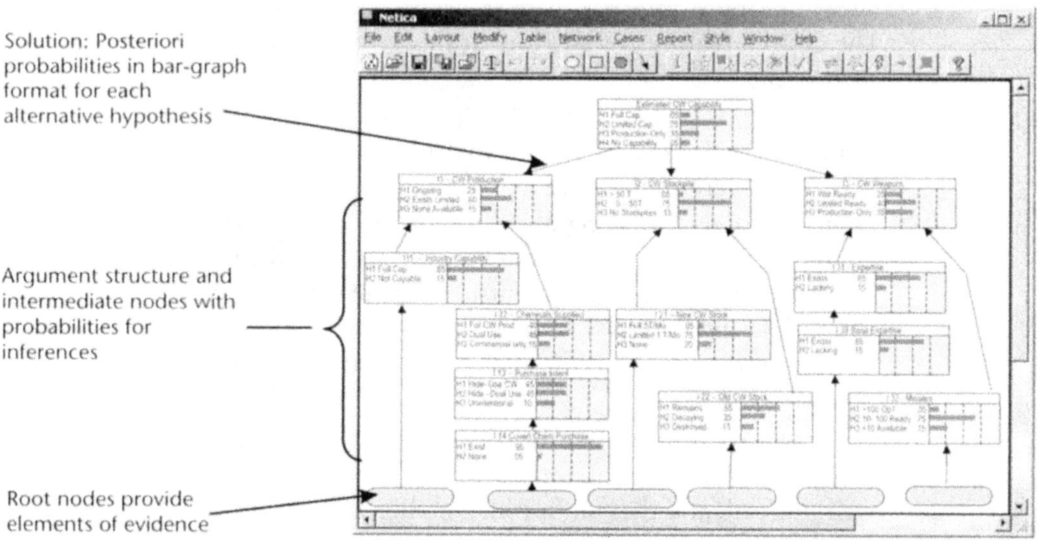

Figure 8.9 Argument represented in a Bayesian net in Netica.

Evidence marshalling: Models and simulations provide the framework on which inference and evidence is assembled; they provide an audit trail of the analyst's reasoning.

Exploration: Models and simulations also provide a means for analysts to be immersed in the modeled situation, its structure and dynamics. It is a tool for experimentation and exploration to provide deeper understanding to determine necessary confirming or falsifying evidence, to evaluate potential collection strategies, and to examine the effects of potential denial and deception efforts being employed by the target.

Dynamic process tracking: Simulations model the time-dynamic behavior of targets, to forecast future behavior, compare with observations and refine the behavior model over time. In particular, models and simulations provide a reference to detect spurious signals, as well as incongruities—relative to the model.

Explanation: Finally, the models and simulations provide a mechanism, locally and visually, for presenting alternative hypotheses, final judgments, and rationale.

A variety of modeling approaches are available to the analyst (Table 8.4) depending on the type of situation being modeled and the level of granularity of the model representation.

5. *Intelligence reporting support tools.* The preparation of reports requires the analyst to summarize, in narrative text, the results of the levels of detailed analysis that have been performed in prior stages of analysis. The application used in this simple example (Figure 8.10) is Microsoft Word with a simple table format that organizes the narrative judgments to be reported and supporting assertions with the cited sources of analysis, evidence (both supporting and refuting), and alternatives considered. This tabular format allows the analyst to structure narrative construction—then rapidly write straight narrative text with a clear link to support. Alternative approaches to proving this structure include footnoting of source reverences and hyper-linking to directly view the source materials stored in local storage. The desired features of any tool at this level include the capabilities for:

   Authoring: Support narrative judgment authoring, editing, and tracing judgments to all related reports.

   Drill-down: Enable the author to drill-down to successive layers of analysis to directly reported source materials.

   Tracing: Enable tracking of the use of any item of evidence across its use in all reports to enable immediate identification of the impact of an element of evidence on multiple judgments. (In the event a source is found to be corrupt, data incorrectly interpreted, or a linchpin assumption is found to be incorrect, the effects of the change must be traced across multiple previous reports [30].)

These capabilities provide the ability to for analysts, "to make their assumptions and reasoning more transparent by requiring that analysis be well sourced, and that all finished intelligence products, either in paper or in

Table 8.4 Representative Target Modeling and Simulation Tools

Modeling Approach	*Description and Characteristics*	*Application to Intelligence Analysis*
General causal modeling	Static Bayes' networks represent chains of actions to nodes and resulting effects; dynamic Bayes nets add a representation of complex states and transitions at nodes to represent the aggregate dynamics of a causal networks	Model expected causal relationships within physical, information and social networks Example tools: Norsys Netica; Bayes' Net Toolbox for Matlab
Continuous or discrete-time simulation	Time-based simulation of continuous or time-discrete processes defined by differential equations; represent continuous processes by state-machine simulation of all processes for each discrete-time increment	Simulate physical processes (e.g., production) and phenomena to compare with sensor data Example tools: Imagine That Inc., Extend
Discrete event simulation	Simulate event-based systems using queuing models of queues-servers, Petri nets, Markov, and other models that define nodes, links, and resources to simulate process interactions, synchronization and scheduling of discrete events	Simulate stochastic flow within sequential information processes (e.g., telecom, C2 systems, and so forth) to compare with observed traffic flow patterns. Example tools: MathWorks MATLAB SimuLink and SimEvents; University of California at Berkeley Ptolemy
System dynamics simulation	System dynamics flow models are based on the principle of accumulation, representing the flow of resources to accumulate stocks of products. System dynamics causal models account for circular feedback across processes and represent nonlinear behavior in complex systems	Simulate integrated physical-information-social systems to understand causal interactions and nonlinearities; compare with observed dynamic behaviors. Example tools: ISEE Systems iThink; Powersim Software Powersim; Ventana Vensim
Agent-based simulation	Agents represent rational cognitive actors, their goals, beliefs and autonomous behavior to study social behavior of individuals, groups or populations; goal-seeking adaptation produces realistic emergent behavior not predictable from the underlying models	Simulate leadership decision-making and social population behaviors to compare with observed rhetoric, decision-making behaviors. Example tools: University of Chicago's Social Science Research RePast; Santa Fe Institute SWARM, SOAR

digital format, provide citations to enable user verification of particular statements," as recommended by a U.S. commission [31].

The preceding tool workflow provides an illustration to one conceptual use of a variety of tools to implement the methodology introduce in Chapter 7. Alternative and subsets of this approach have been applied to counterdeception analysis. Stech and Elsässer have developed a counterdeception process that integrates modeling (adversarial reasoning) and quantitative analysis (Bayesian belief network implemented in Netica), and have conducted detailed validations of the process using well-documented strategic deceptions at Normandy [32] and Midway [33]. Their alternative competing hypothesis–counterdeception (ACH-CD) process: (1) detects incongruities related to deception behaviors, (2) generates hypotheses that link the incongruities to deceptive behaviors (generated by models of adversarial reasoning), (3) links the evidence to deception hypotheses in an ACH framework, and (4) assesses the sensitivity of hypotheses to indicators—and guide collection to reduce uncertainty in hypotheses of deception that account for incongruities. The

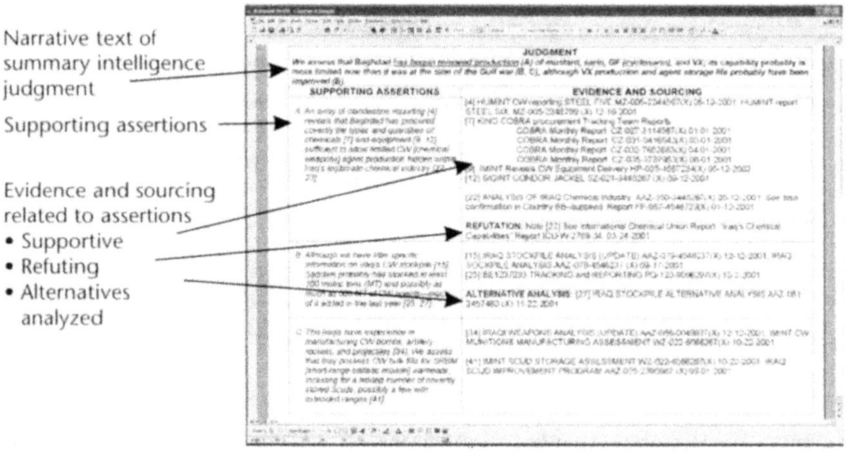

Figure 8.10 Text report structuring in Microsoft Word.

process carefully adapts the standard ACH process to account for the inclination to incorrectly estimate conditional probabilities due to the low base rate of occurrence of specific deceptions. The ACH-D process explicitly requires the analyst to consider the conditional Pr (Hypothesis i | Evidence j) as well as the false positive rate of evidence, expressed by the conditional Pr (Evidence j | NOT Hypothesis i). This modification to ACH sensitizes the analyst to the possibility of the deceiver synthesizing evidence (simulation to deceive) as well as protects the analyst from overestimating the value of evidence that may have many explanations other than a deception.

8.4 System Architecture to Support Counterdeception

The system architecture includes the physical and logical description of the information network structure and services that are required to implement the collaborative workflow of Section 8.2 and tool applications of Section 8.3. Of particular interest to the counterdeception methods introduced in this chapter, the system must enable:

- Collaborative planning, collection, and analysis for a distributed team focusing on the structure and behavior of a deceptive target system.
- Sharing of source information and intelligence products, as well as hypotheses and emerging analysis to allow intelligence teams and mission mangers to have complete visibility into emerging collection-analysis process.
- Immediate cross-cueing of time-sensitive discoveries (e.g., changes that briefly expose concealments) to enable coordinated collection; ad hoc and emergent creation of collaborative teams ("communities of interest") to respond to collection and analysis opportunities.

The system architecture describes the supporting communication infrastructure that includes a physical layer to interconnect major distributed nodes (e.g., fiber optical cables with wavelength division multiplexing, WDM), a data link layer (e.g., bulk data transport and dedicated communication channels applying asynchronous transfer mode, ATM), and network and transport layers of dynamically switched networks (e.g., TCP/IP networks) that support the application services at the top layer.

These capabilities can be implemented in a *service-oriented* system architecture that provides business (support and application) functions as services that may be invoked by client workstations across the network. Available services are registered and exposed to users to allow the services to be composed into flexible workflows like those introduced earlier. The system must dynamically provide trusted access to resources, including posted data and applications. The typical system services required to support such operations are summarized in Table 8.5.

The U.S. Intelligence Community System for Information Sharing (ICSIS) is a system architecture that defines layers of secure communications networks and an agreed set of databases and application services hosted within shared virtual spaces. It is a representative system architecture that provides agile and shared information access across a large community of collaborating users [34]. A representative intelligence enterprise system architecture based on the ICIS architecture (Figure 8.11) defines virtual collaboration workspaces internal to each intelligence organization (e.g., CIA all-source analysis, NSA signals processing and analysis, NGA geospatial intelligence processing and analysis, and so forth) and a common workspace accessible across the community. The internal space provides collaboration at Special Compartmented Intelligence (SCI) levels within each organization (or cell within an organization); owners within the unit may tightly control their data holdings (that

Table 8.5 Typical Services Provided in the System Architecture

Service Categories	*Service Functions*	
System support	Security	Access controls for multiple security compartments, public key infrastructure (PKI), certificate authorities for key distribution, firewall protection between enclaves, intrusion and insider threat detection
	Storage, mediation, and knowledge basing	Metadata and taxonomy management, local and shared repositories, storage area network management, archiving
	Collaboration	Messaging (e-mail, instant messaging), synchronous and asynchronous collaboration environment, portal support, expert directory, and finder
Intelligence application services	Planning	Collection and production supply chain management, performance tracking and reporting
	Search, navigate, query, and retrieval	Multilingual text and audio search and translation; image, audio, and video search
	Processing, fusion, and mining	Image and signal processing, data correlation and combination (data fusion), automated induction (data mining), change detection; automated processing filters (to detect incongruities and spurious signals)
	Analysis, detection, and discovery	Automated source data link analysis, temporal-spatial-causal analysis, hypothesis generation, evidence marshaling, structured argumentation support, alternative hypothesis analysis
	Modeling and simulation	Hypothesis structure modeling tools; dynamic behavior simulation tools to emulate observable phenomena
	Visualization	Scientific data visualization, network link and structure visualization, argument structure visualization

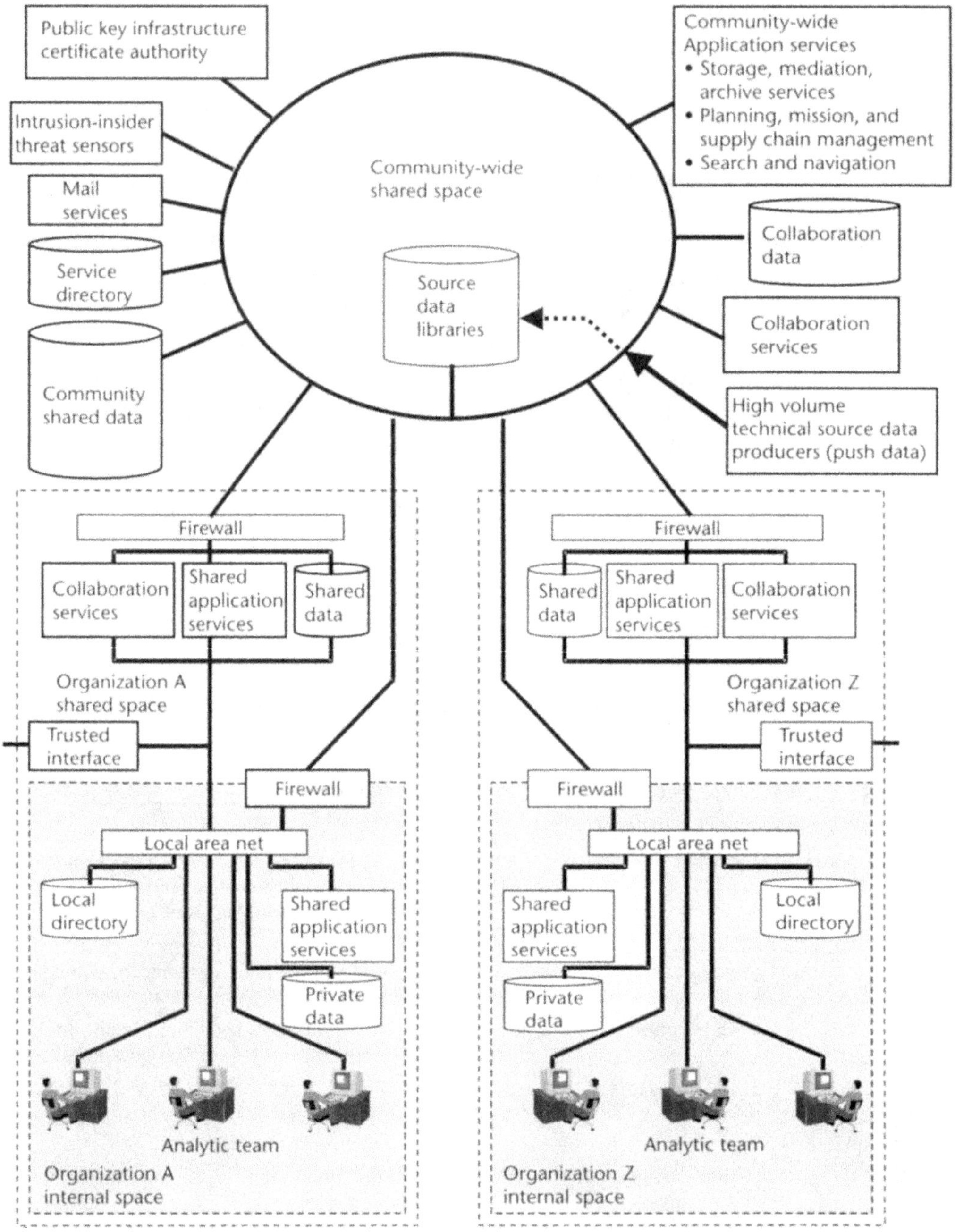

Figure 8.11 Representative top-level system architecture.

are sensitive due to sources and methods). The separate community space enables community-wide collaboration across organization units at the SCI level, providing resource protection and control by a central security policy. Separate community spaces provide a workspaces for data shared with other organizations (e.g., the Department of Defense and other federal agencies) at collateral levels of classification that are below SCI. This is provided through trusted interfaces (certified "guards" that enable bidirectional transfer between dissimilar security levels) that enable approved flow of collateral information between workspaces while assuring that SCI information is not release to collateral network spaces.

Workflows are virtually and rapidly implemented in this system architecture, allowing a distributed community of interest to be rapidly assembled to focus on a difficult target. The workflow described earlier in Figure 8.3 is realized in this architecture in the following manner:

- The mission manager assigns the distributed community of interest (the team that makes up the virtual workflow) to the target of analysis; the data manger enables the workflow by providing access to the team (inviting participation and providing keys to access shared workspace available only to those in this workflow), and setting processing and subscription parameters to push data to the appropriate users.
- Mission, collection, and data mangers use community-wide applications to administer the intelligence mission; they place planning and tasking directions in the common workspace repositories for access by all collaborators on the team.
- Each single-source organization (e.g. the SIGINT, GEOINT, and HUMINT organizations in Figure 8.3 with associated collection, processing, and analysis) resides in separate workspaces and maintains private repositories of data that contain information on sources and methods. These analysts push their intermediate products to the designated all-source analysis cell in yet a separate repository.
- All-source analysts develop hypotheses, and interact with source analysts using community-wide collaboration tools. They use the community-wide directory services to locate experts outside of the community of interest and to invite participation in the analytic effort.
- Approved products are placed in the shared workspace for limited or community-wide access.

Security firewalls protect each organizational enclave; intrusion and insider threat behavior sensors are distributed throughout the network and are centrally administered to monitor for suspicious incongruities. The architecture provides the agility to adapt to targeting needs, rapidly assembling and disbanding communities of interest and associated workflows to focus on emerging targets or situations.

8.5 Summary

This text has progressively developed counterdeception principles, then implementing technical methods and in this chapter, the means to implement them in an enterprise—a single intelligence cell, or across a larger organization. This provides the approach called for by CIA scholar in residence Rob Johnson, who recommended a combined approach to analysis that includes formal thematic teams operating on structured organizational principles, a cadre of analytic methodologists, and supported by a system architecture that enables experts across different domains to share the perspectives of the heuristics of their own domains [35]. This chapter has illustrated the implementation of the counterdeception process within such an enterprise, and it has emphasized the necessity to develop and portray the process in appropriate views (e.g., operational, system views) to include explicit descriptions of:

- The *organization and role* of planners, collectors, and analysts to create an awareness of deception, define the prioritization for collection and analysis, and sustain a coordinated and collaborative counterdeception activity that is tailored to the threat.
- The *required skills and training* to achieve the level of organizational awareness and preparation to counter the level of deception sophistication, and breadth of deception employment posed by intelligence threats.
- The *methods* by which intelligence targets strategically developed (i.e., identifying and nominating critical target system elements for counterdeception investigation), and the means by which aggressive and innovative collections are planned and executed, and results analyzed.
- The *flow of information and workflows of user actions* proceeding from planning and collection to processing, analysis, and dissemination to increase the likelihood that critical incongruities and the leakage of spurious signals will be detected, deception patterns discovered, potential stratagem hypotheses explored and appropriately reported.
- The *structure, capabilities, and capacity* of enterprise systems (e.g., information networks, processing, data structures, and storage) to permit information sharing among participants, and enable collaborative counterdeception planning, collection and analysis.
- The *specific analytic methods* that support constructive synthesis and exploratory analysis of target models to penetrate hard targets; descriptions of all process methodologies by which incongruities are detected, deception patterns are discovered, identified and tracked over time, to reveal stratagems.
- The *manual and technical tools* that support planners, collectors, and analysts to conduct a comprehensive and coordinated focus on deception targets, exchange cues and incongruities, model target structure and behavior, explore alternative explanations, and trace intelligence judgments to cumulating evidence.
- The *reporting methods* by which intelligence judgments containing deception uncertainties inform decision makers; the means by which alternative hypotheses and analyses are described and supported, and assertions about deceptive and concealed targets are supported by source evidence.

The architect of a counterdeception process must describe, document, and implement each of these elements to coordinate the diverse set of people, processes, and technologies to provide a comprehensive snare for stratagem. William Harris, in his classic *On Countering Strategic Deception*, distinguished between genuine counterdeception systems and "seat-of-the-pants deception efforts" that are characterized by uncoordinated and sporadic activities performed by overconfident and self-appointed deception experts [36]. Harris cautioned that [37]: "Those who still cling to the hope that the 'well-rounded' intelligence professional can, by the seat-of-the-pants method, reverse the tide of deceptively induced misestimates..." must revisit the evidence of Barton Whaley's *Stratagem* to heed its warnings. Harris then appealed to a discipline of coordinated collection, vigilant analysis, and a carefully planned organization of people and their tools. A thorough and explicitly documented counterdeception enterprise architecture will provide the necessary attention to detail to ensure that Harris' discipline and planning is achieved.

Endnotes

[1] Bruce, J. B., "The Consequences of Permissive Neglect: Laws and Leaks of Classified Intelligence," *Studies in Intelligence*, Washington, D.C.: Center for the Study of Intelligence, Vol. 47, No. 1, 2003; Also in the *CIA Annual Report 2002*, see "Support to Countering Foreign Intelligence."

[2] For example, the National Geospatial Intelligence Agency (NGA, formerly NIMA) maintains imagery analysts with counterdeception expertise. See NIMA Announcement Number: 035225, January 21, 2003, for Imagery Intelligence Analyst "focusing on worldwide denial and deception (D&D)."

[3] *The Commission on the Intelligence Capabilities of the United States Regarding Weapons of Mass Destruction* March 31, 2005, p. 374.

[4] Definition by *DoD Integrated Architecture Panel, 1995, based on IEEE STD 610.12*; An alternate definition of architecture is provided by IEEE STD 1471-2000, *IEEE Recommended Practice for Architectural Description of Software-Intensive Systems*. An architecture is the fundamental organization of a system embodied in its components, their relationships to each other, and to the environment, and the principles guiding its design and evolution.

[5] Department of Defense Architecture Framework Working Group, "DoD Architecture Framework Ver. 1.0.," Washington, D.C.: Department of Defense, November 2003.

[6] The U.S. intelligence community maintains a metadata working group to enable cross-community data interoperability and information discovery applying XML standards. See https://www.icmwg.org/index.asp (accessed November 7, 2005).

[7] Morse, E., M. Potts Steves, and J. Scholtz, "Metrics and Methodologies for Evaluating Technologies for Intelligence Analysts," *Proc. of 2005 International Intelligence Analysis Conference*, McLean VA, May 2–5, 2005.

[8] Rieber, S., "The Scientific Study of Intelligence Analysis: Why We Need a National Institute for Intelligence Analysis" *Proc. of International Studies Association*, Honolulu, HI, March 5, 2005.

[9] Lambert, D. R., "A Cognitive Model for Exposition of Human Deception and Counterdeception," Naval Ocean Systems Center, TR-1076, October 1987; See a refined model in Cohen, F., et al., "A Framework for Deception," Livermore, CA: Fred Cohen and Assoc., 2001, accessed online December 20, 2005, http://all.net/journal/deception/Framework/Framework.html

[10] For a comparison of the two architectures, see Johnson, T. R., "Control in Act-R and Soar," in Shafto, M., and P. Langley, (eds.), *Proc. of the 19th Annual Conference of the Cognitive Science Society,* Mahweh, NJ: Lawrence Erlbaum, 1997, pp. 343–348. For the basis of SOAR, see Newell, A., *Unified Theories of Cognition*, Cambridge, MA: Harvard University Press, 1990. For the basis of ACT-R, see Anderson, J. R., and Lebiere, C., *The Atomic Components of Thought*, Mahwah, NJ: Lawrence Erlbaum, 1998. Anderson, J. R.,

and C. Lebiere, *The Atomic Components of Thought*, Mahwah, NJ: Lawrence Erlbaum, 1998.

[11] Kline, G. A., J. Orasanu, and R. Calderwood, (eds.), *Decision Making in Action*, Norwood, NJ: Ablex, 1993.

[12] Klein Associates Inc., *Macrocognition: Year One Final Report High-Level Cognitive Processes in Field Research*, Report 02TA1-SP1-RT1 for U.S. Army Research Laboratory, October 14, 2002, and Moon, B. M., and R. R. Hoffman, "How Might 'Transformational' Technologies and Concepts be Barriers to Sensemaking in Intelligence Analysis?" *Proc. of 7th Intl. NDM Conf.*, Amsterdam, the Netherlands, June 2005.

[13] Here, we adopt the term mission manager from the report of *The Commission on the Intelligence Capabilities of the United States Regarding Weapons of Mass Destruction*; we do not refer to national-level mission mangers, but middle-level managers that focus on specific hard target entities—facilities, organizations, programs, and so forth.

[14] We do not imply that workflows cannot capture horizontal and collaborative characteristics; indeed many workflows are captured as wall-size diagrams that encompass information, control, and collaboration flows.

[15] For a high-level example of an intelligence use case narrative, see "Targeting in an Integrated Fashion" in *The Commission on the Intelligence Capabilities of the United States Regarding Weapons of Mass Destruction*, March 31, 2005, pp. 360–361.

[16] We specifically limit our definition here to devices, not activities. In other contexts, activities such as counterdeception awareness training may be described as tools of policy to enhance organizational counterdeception performance.

[17] *Cognitive tools* encompass a wide spectrum of capabilities from learning to decision making support; we limit our discussion to those that enhance planning and analysis.

[18] For an assessment of the functional categories of tools needed to support analysis, see Badalamente, R. V., and F. L. Greitzer, "Top Ten Needs for Intelligence Analysis Tool Development," Proc. of the 2005 International Conference on Intelligence Analysis Methods and Tools, Office of the Assistant Director of Central Intelligence for Analysis and Production, McLean VA, May 2005.

[19] We refer here to desktop tools to manage an individual analyst's or a team's counterdeception activities and materials. These tools may access larger enterprise supply chain management capabilities such as the U.S. intelligence community's large-scale programs to perform mission management, such as the intelligence community's Multi-Intelligence Acquisition Program (IC-MAP) and Cryptologic Mission Management (CMM). These programs provide enterprise-wide system management, customer service, and operations management.

[20] For an example of a CTA applied to an intelligence analysis process under data overload, see Patterson, E. S., et al., "Using Cognitive Task Analysis (CTA) to Seed Design Concepts for Intelligence Analysis Under Data Overload," *Proc. of the Human Factors and Ergonomics Society 45th Annual Meeting*, Minneapolis, MN, October 8–12, 2001. Also see Elm, W. C., et al., "Designing Support for Intelligence Analysis," Proceedings of the Human Factors and Ergonomics Society 48th Annual Meeting, New Orleans, LA, September 20–24, 2004.

[21] Greitzer, F. L., "Toward the Development of Cognitive Task Difficulty Metrics to Support Intelligence Analysis Research," Proceedings of the 4th IEEE International Conference on Cognitive Informatics, Irvine, CA, 2005; and Greitzer, F. L., Methodology, Metrics and Measures for Testing and Evaluation of Intelligence Analysis Tools, Technical Report PNWD-3550, Richland, WA: Battelle-Pacific Northwest Division, 2005.

[22] Davis, J., "Sherman Kent's Final Thoughts on Analyst-Policymaker Relations," *CIA Sherman Kent School Occasional Papers*, Vol. 2, No. 3, June 2003, p. 51.

[23] These are the four fundamental stages of the collaborative knowledge creation spiral model identified in Nonaka, I., and H. Takeuchi, *The Knowledge-Creating Company: How Japanese Companies Create the Dynamics of Innovation*, New York: Oxford University Press, 1995.

[24] Novel Intelligence from Massive Data (NIMD) R&D Program, Broad Agency Announcement NMA401-02-BAA-0004, National Imagery and Mapping Agency, May 22, 2002, Part II, p. 2.

[25] Wright, W., Schroh, D., Proulx, P., Skaburskis, A., and Cort, B., "The Sandbox for Analysis—Concepts and Methods," *Proc. AMC CHI,* 2006. Wright, W., et al., "Information Triage with TRIST," and Wright, W., et al., "Advances in nSpace—The Sandbox for Analysis" (Poster), both in Proc. of the 2005 International Conference on Intelligence Analysis Methods and Tools, Office of the Assistant Director of Central Intelligence for Analysis and Production, McLean VA, May 2005. Screenshot of nSpace in Figure 8.6 used by permission of Oculus Information, Inc. nSpace TRIST™ and nSpace Sandbox™ are Oculus trademarks.

[26] Cluxton, D., and S. G. Eick, "DECIDE™ Hypothesis Visualization Tool," Proc. of the 2005 International Conference on Intelligence Analysis Methods and Tools, Office of the Assistant Director of Central Intelligence for Analysis and Production, McLean VA, May 2005. Screenshot of DECIDE in Figure 8.7 used by permission of SSS Research Inc.

[27] For a description of structured argumentation applied to intelligence analysis, see Waltz, E., *Knowledge Management in the Intelligence Enterprise*, Norwood, MA: Artech House, 2003.

[28] Screenshot of ACH tool in Figure 8.8 used by permission of Palo Alto Research Center (PARC). The software may be downloaded from PARC online at http://www2.parc.com/istl/projects/ ach/ach.html.

[29] Definitions from the Defense Modeling and Simulation Office (DMSO) Modeling & Simulation Glossary.

[30] *The Commission on the Intelligence Capabilities of the United States Regarding Weapons of Mass Destruction,* March 31, 2005, p. 413.

[31] Ibid., p. 412.

[32] Stech, F. J., and C. Elsässer, "Detecting Deception by Analysis of Competing Hypotheses," Proc. of the 2005 International Conference on Intelligence Analysis Methods and Tools, Office of the Assistant Director of Central Intelligence for Analysis and Production, McLean VA, May 2005.

[33] Stech, F. J., and C. Elsässer, "Midway Revisited: Detecting Deception by Analysis of Competing Hypothesis," *Proc. 72nd MORS Symposium*, Monterey, CA, June 2004.

[34] Dawson, W. F., "Intelligence Community Communications Architecture," *Proc. National Defense Industrial Assoc. Interoperability and Systems Integration Conf.*, April 2, 2003.

[35] Johnston, R., "Reducing Analytic Error: Integrating Methodologists into Teams of Substantive Experts," *Studies in Intelligence*, Vol. 47, No. 1, 2003, pp. 57–65.

[36] Harris, W. R., *On Countering Strategic Deception*, R-1230-ARPA, November 1973, pp. 33–34.

[37] Ibid., p. 34.

CHAPTER 9

Speculations About the Future of Deception and Counterdeception

We introduced this book acknowledging that deception has been with us as long as nations, organizations, and individuals have competed and engaged in conflict. While the motives for deception, rooted in human nature, will not change, the opportunities and methods of deception will change as technology enables new technical means and global dynamics open new deception channels for delivery. Nineteenth-century French historian Alexis de Tocqueville noted that it is easier for the world to accept a simple lie than a complex truth; in this chapter we show that the future will continue to bring convincing deceptions that are more powerful and seductive, enabled by increasingly diverse channels and complex means. In this chapter we introduce the factors that will certainly change the future expression of deception and speculate on the prospect of their implications for counterdeception.

9.1 The Future, Changing Factors, and Implications for Deception

It is important for the deception planner and the counterdeception analyst alike to recognize the changing global landscape on which the webs of deception are spread. The landscape is changing and dynamic; a strong deception method or channel today, may be defeated by changes that tip in favor of the counter deceiver tomorrow. A number of factors, ranging from policy and global dynamics to technology will influence the roles and capabilities of deception in the future.

Deception and counterdeception disciplines are not static; those engaged in the art and science of counterdeception must consider the following five top-level factors and influences as they look to the future impact on the national security landscape.

1. Human Nature and the Presence of the Threat of Deception Will Not Change

Deception is here to stay as a significant component of human competition and conflict. As we have indicated in earlier chapters, the deceiver holds a significant advantage over the naïve and the sophisticated alike; the attractive benefits of stratagem to gain advantage will remain powerful, especially for those at a disadvantage to their adversary. The U.S. National Intelligence Council has identified deception as an expected asymmetric response to the information superiority of a superpower [1]: "As noted earlier, most adversaries will recognize the information advantage and military superiority of the United States in 2015. Rather than acquiesce to any potential US military domination, they will try to circumvent or minimize US strengths and exploit perceived weaknesses. Information technology-driven globalization will significantly increase interaction among terrorists, narcotraffickers, weapons proliferators, and organized criminals, who in a networked world will have greater access to information, to technology, to finance, to sophisticated deception-and-denial techniques and to each other."

2. The Role and Moral Basis for Stratagem Will Be Considered

As democratic institutions spread, and deception from increasingly powerful asymmetric adversaries emerge (e.g., those able to threaten the use of WMD), the moral grounds for nation states to conduct deception as an operational capability will be continue to be considered and debated. Democratic governments will struggle to assess the tension between the openness and integrity expected of governments, and the secrecy and deception required by stratagem. While nonstate actors, rogue states, transition regimes, and authoritarian regimes apply deception a routine tool, democracies shun deception as a moral evil, inconsistent with legitimate governance [2]. In democracies, deception may be tolerated in time of war, but only in military operations; the roles of military deception and honest strategic information (diplomacy, public affairs, PSYOP, civil affairs, and so forth) are clearly delineated. Walter Jajko has summarized the controversial moral and policy implementation challenges that confront the implementation of any deception operation by the U.S. government [3]:

> The advent of information warfare offers unprecedented opportunities for deception operations, in scope, effect, and imagination. However, establishing a national political deception program in the United States might be well nigh impossible. Some foreign governments and people are convinced that the United States already practices deception in its foreign policies, but confusion, not dissimulation, is the more probable cause of this misimpression.... Inattention, indiscipline, incompetence, ignorance, and self-absorption, reinforced by domestic interests, often impel American self-deception in policy. Of course, the conduct and sustainment of a political deception program, necessarily covert, would require extraordinary skill and secrecy if it were not to subvert the credibility, viability, and legitimacy of high-minded and principled policy and diplomacy. Even a successful program probably could not repay the cost of its revelation; the loss of the good name of the United States would not be worth even long term successes. In any case, America's vaunted open society seems to militate against a comprehensive deception program. The American polity proclaims a high value on honesty, equity, and publicity in its public, and even private, institutions and their policies and practices, and usually in official dealings with foreign institutions... These operative conditions make it almost impossible to maintain the secrecy of any governmental activity. Nevertheless, a modest and judicious effort might not only be possible but even worthwhile.

A recent strategic conference on the ethical, domestic and international legal implications of strategic deception summarized the general issues that challenge deception as a capability of democratic institutions in an open world [4]. Conferees agreed that modern democracies have the tools (channels and techniques) to employ strategic deception, but have no liberal-democratic theory or doctrine to justify their employment. Philosopher Emmanuel Kant's (1724–1804) *Categorical Imperative*, for example, asserted that trust is a fundamental and universal requirement for any community of rational beings to exist [5]: "To be truthful (honest) in all declarations is a sacred and unconditionally commanding law of reason that admits of no expediency whatsoever." However, abstract principles such as these have not been translated to doctrine for practice in international politics and ethical concerns render the employment of deception problematic. Professor Elizabeth Kiss of the Kenan Institute for Ethics, Duke University, further enumerated the four fundamental aspects of strategic deception that specifically make it morally problematic for democracies [6]:

1. It is increasingly difficult to focus a deception on adversaries alone; there exists the inadvertent potential for collateral deception of friends, allies, and the public because of the diversity and reach of global information channels. Deception of friends undermines intergovernment trust relations; deception of the public undermines democratic legitimacy.
2. Institutional deception requires individual actors to establish patterns of behavior that have been shown throughout history to lead to human corruption and abuse.
3. Deception requires institutions to employ OPSEC at a level that prevents critical, independent assessments of prudent and ethical behavior.
4. Deception, at its core, exploits in the short term the inherent human "expectation of truth" and in the long term undermines the core human value of trust.

Where the value of truth and transparency is held high, the role of deception by governments in any area but military conflict is abhorred. The short life of the U.S. DoD's Office of Strategic Influence in 2002 was attributed to the *perceived* danger of the potential for strategic deception by the office, though the intention for deception was explicitly denied and the purpose of public diplomacy was specifically distinguished from military deception [7]. Where strategic survival or ideological values supersede the values of truth and transparency, deception can become an accepted tool of government. Strategic deception in the former Soviet Union, for example, was viewed as a moral imperative, a legitimate tool to enhance the Marxist-Leninist belief in the dialectic change toward the state of Communism [8]. Similarly, some Islamic understandings of the Koran adopt the practices of *taqiyya* (precautionary dissimulation to keep one's convictions secret) and *kitman* (maintaining a mental reservation or concealing malevolent intentions) as appropriate for all operational practice beyond military conflict, as adopted in the Al-Qaeda terrorist training manual [9].

3. The Channels for Deception Will Continue to Grow

The channels for transferring information to deception targets (leaders, analysts, civil populations) continue to grow as sensors, communication networks, and media outlets expand in global coverage. Not only are the independent channels expanding in scope, but also the effectiveness of information transfer is improving by the convergence of video, voice, and text in digital formats. The implications of this expansion and convergence for deception include:

- Deceivers will be afforded more channels with easier access to large public populations and national targets; they may use these channels to provide multiple, supporting elements of apparently independent information to targets.
- Deceivers will also be able to use these channels to more precisely target populations, organizations, and individuals with culturally tailored and contextually timed deceptive information.
- Counterdeception analysts will also benefit from the expansion of open source channels, because they also provide greater breadth of context, and additional independent means to validate information, increasing the likelihood of detecting the presence of both sprignals and incongruities that may tip off a deception.

The growth and impact of global media channels on the deception of individuals and populations are further discussed in Section 9.2. Beyond media reporting channels, the future will bring greater surveillance of society at large via ubiquitous video coverage (e.g., online Web cameras) and numerous other data and sensors online (e.g., real-time stock market data, weather sensors, and traffic sensors). As society becomes more transparent, individuals will grow more vulnerable because of the potential access by others to their channels (e.g., e-mail, cell phone, and bank account) and the availability of information about them. Author David Brin, in *The Transparent Society*, has speculated about the range of implications of ubiquitous access to both government and private information and the potential misuse, including deception. Brin frames the issue of accountability for knowledge in a matrix that considers four potential uses of future technology: (1) tools that help me see what others are doing; (2) tools that prevent others from seeing what I am doing; (3) tools that help others see what I am doing; and (4) tools that prevent me from seeing what others are doing. Loss of a balance of transparency can result in abuse by some individuals (e.g., criminals controlling 1 and 2) or others (e.g., the government controlling 3 and 4); all abuses enable those who are least accountable the deceptive edge. Brin speculates, for example, on the potential impact of the definitive future counterdeception tool (the ultimate transparency tool: a truly effective lie detector) [10]: "If a truth machine ever did appear, it would have tremendous potential, either for beneficial use or wretched abuse." As the sensors, sources, and channels grow, so do the means for deception and for counter deception (via transparency), and the potential for imbalance and abuse.

4. The Available Methods for Employing Deception Will Likewise Grow

Even as the channels to transfer information from deceivers to targets grow, technology will also enable new capabilities (technical methods) to exploit those channels for deception. Evan as magicians have continuously integrated new technologies (e.g. mirrors, plastics, pyrotechnics, and electromagnetism) and methods (art) to introduce new effects, emerging technologies will be coupled with new methodologies to produce new deceptive effects. The Chinese military, for example, have recognized this potential for lifelike deception when new technologies are *combined* with art to produce new operational methods [11]:

> Technology and Art in Operational Methods: Operational methods have never been just the passive adoption of new technology, but are created by new operational art. Applying new technology in the operational field means that instead of rejecting or degrading the role of operational art, conditions are created for combining military technology and operational art. For example, the advancement of simulation will even more forcefully promote the merging of *deception technology and art in operations, which will thus cause deception warfare to be more lifelike and have a more important role* [emphasis added]. Future methods of operation will be the product of closer combinations of military technology and operational art.

A survey of emerging and potentially disruptive technologies that may influence future deception methods and channels are further discussed in Section 9.3.

5. Deception Will Increase in Both Global Reach and Degree of Influence

The combined effect of increased *motives* for strategic deception, increased *opportunities* afforded by channels, and new *means* enabled by technology will be an increase in the reach and influence of deception in world affairs. This does not mean that deception must become pervasive—influencing every aspect of life; it does imply that the future world may have domains such as global politics, weapons proliferation, and organized crime that will see a rise in the power and perversity of deception. A recent National Intelligence Council futures study noted the ubiquitous effect of globalization as a megatrend shaping all other trends (economic, demographic, and scientific changes); we can expect it to likewise influence the spread of deception's role in competition and crisis [12]:

> We see globalization—growing interconnectedness reflected in the expanded flows of information, technology, capital, goods, services, and people throughout the world—as an overarching "mega-trend," a force so ubiquitous that it will substantially shape all the other major trends in the world of 2020. But the future of globalization is not fixed; states and nonstate actors—including both private companies and NGOs—will struggle to shape its contours.

In the same study, the NIC noted the contradictions of globalization's dynamics: Rising powers will change the geopolitical landscape, bringing new challenges to governance and the potential for a more pervasive sense of insecurity. Continued proliferation of WMD will sustain the potential for an event of catastrophic terrorism—an event that will punctuate any sense of global security and linear trend in global affairs. The competition of rising powers and the asymmetric conflicts they may spawn will include a competition between the planners of deception and the analysts of counterdeception. Evidence of this competition is illustrated in the deceptive practices employed by the nonstate network of A.Q. Khan, the Pakistani scientist who orchestrated the proliferation of Pakistan's nuclear enrichment technology and weapons design information to North Korea and Iran. The private entrepreneurial network (versus a state-run intelligence service) hid transactions within legitimate businesses, and recipient countries hid their nuclear WMD programs inside legitimate dual-use industries, employing a variety of deceptive methods to hide facilities, financing, and relationships [13].

While these general factors are based on likely trends to influence deception, we have labeled this chapter "speculations," recognizing that forecasting complex systems, technology development, and social systems is fraught with danger—even the danger of self-deception. We heed the advice of Professor Colin Gray, reporting to the U.S. National Intelligence Council on a study of future conflict [14]: "Even the most accurate identification and analysis of recent and current trends cannot offer a reliable guide to the future. Trends come in bunches, they interact both with each other and with their contexts, and it is their consequences, rather than they themselves, which make the future... The future has not happened. Beware of those who are addicted to the use of the thoroughly misleading concept, the foreseeable future. The future is not foreseeable, period." Indeed the future of deception is driven by the consequences of the trends and factors that we have described earlier, and the interaction of these factors can be the triggers of nonlinear developments that we cannot now imagine.

9.2 Global Information Flows and Mass Media

The world is experiencing a global expansion of digital information channels (e.g., telecommunications networks, direct satellite broadcast, the Internet, radio, television and film), while technology is enabling a convergence of the media to common digital channels (e.g., voice over Internet Protocol, high-definition digital video, and so forth). In addition to these technology-driven changes, the media content is also changing, blurring earlier distinctions between news coverage (objective reality) and entertainment (subjective romanticism).

The expansion of channel types, convergence into common transmission media, and transformation of content will provide two unprecedented capabilities to governments, commercial companies, ideological groups, and individuals alike who seek to find the truth, present the truth or to deceive:

- *Broadcast* capabilities to allow broad and sustained global multimedia access to large public segments as well as to carefully selected groups, identified by demographics.
- *Pointcast* or *narrowcast* capabilities enabling the precision targeting of regions, interest groups, and individuals (and their immediate families, friends and peer groups, and so forth) with information purposely tailored to their perceptions and interests (or vulnerabilities).

Both of these capabilities today are utilized by commercial businesses to conduct market demographic analysis, to search and identify potential customers, and to target the delivery of tailored information (e.g., special offers, tailored sales, incentives, product pairing by customer interest, and so forth) to likely customers. Similarly, the capabilities offer greater regional and global access to those who seek to deceive at all levels. Three trends illustrate the potential channels for deception planners. First, clandestine radio stations and associated Internet sites are providing a global outlet for overt, covert, and subversive political organizations as well as subnational groups (e.g., Russian Mafia, Columbian FARC, and Al Qaeda). These black propaganda sources conceal and change transmitter and server locations to avoid detection. The second accessible channel includes community and "people's media" (public access and community access television, community and independent nonprofit radio, and so forth) that are providing alternatives to the mainstream global media—and are more accessible to NGOs, small organizations, and individuals. The third channel includes Web log ("Blog") sites that provide alternative journalistic outlets for individuals and organizations to provide daily commentary from particular perspectives—addressed to ideological and sympathetic recipients. Blogs received significant attention in 2004 when they demonstrated the influence and power of distributed analysis (conducted by ad hoc experts across the Internet) against the traditional centralized news media analysis of CBS News regarding a flawed story on the military service record of a presidential candidate [15].

This media reaches across society to influence public opinion, while it can also be a direct channel to policymakers (especially the news media). While intelligence organization used to the most important source of news to policymakers (providing analyzed information, screened for deceptive content), the global media now provides immediate, unscreened information to policymakers; intelligence organizations necessarily lag behind raw media feeds for appropriate analysis to add counterdeception value. While global media access may be the source of individual, short-lived deceptions with tactical impact, they may more effectively be used by deception planners to *support* strategic deception operations in several ways:

- To *set a context* for subsequent deception, by desensitizing, overloading, or otherwise creating a situation that aids a deception activity. Because global news sets a background context for current events, even a context of "hope for peace talks," "imminent merger," or "reduction in forces" can set the stage for a surprise.
- To *reinforce* the existing beliefs of a population that are supportive of a deception activity or story. Many propaganda channels provide sustained reinforcement of racial, ethnic, and nationalistic beliefs that incite hatred and violence. Audiences are subject to frequent exaggeration, distortion, and deceit (e.g., conspiracy stories) that reinforce prior beliefs.
- To *misdirect* attention from a deception operation by drawing news attention to a diversionary news event diversion or by creating a brief information overload sufficient to prevent critical activities from being reported.

While these trends in the mass media increase the potential access for deception, they have likewise brought a greater skepticism of the content of the media, evidenced by public cynicism and declining trust in mass media sources. In spite of this, even discredited sources of information can have an impact on perception and judgment, as noted earlier in Chapter 5.

9.3 Deception and Counterdeception Technologies

As we have emphasized throughout, deception is a cognitive phenomena, created by channeling information to induce errors in sensors, automated agents, and ultimately human decision-makers. Emerging technologies in the areas of sensing, communications, computation, presentation (virtual reality), and cognition therefore provide the potential for evolutionary changes in current deception practices, as well as revolutionary new methods. Similarly, technologies in these same areas hold the potential to enable new counterdeception sensing and analysis methods to thwart the deceiver. Sustaining technologies enhance current deception capabilities, while disruptive technologies hold the potential for significant strategic surprise, disrupting the balance between deceiver and counterdeceiver.

In the business environment, disruptive technologies have shown the potential to disturb an entire market, change the business paradigm, and create whole new markets that drive out incumbent leaders [16]. Similarly, disruptive deception technologies may disrupt a surveillance capability, changing an entire operational concept, creating a new information environment that subordinates those who formerly held a position of information superiority. The U.S. Special Operations Forces (SOF) [17] are actively seeking such disruptive technologies, for example, to allow forces to become "cultural chameleons," remaining "*invisible in all media* (air, land, sea), from all senses, from all sensors, in any environment" and able to "blend with any environment so as to be *undetected in plain view* while conducting sensitive core task assignments." Technologies to provide outline and full spectrum signature masking are being developed by the SOF, as well as nanofabrics that adopt the color and texture of surroundings.

While Section 9.2 emphasized changes in media channels to *deliver* deception effects, afforded by improvements in information technology, in this section we provide a cross section of the technologies that hold the potential to enable new methods of *creating* deception effects themselves, as well as new methods to *counter* those effects. The primary contributions to deception are in the areas of altering physical phenomena and information, while contributions to counterdeception are in the areas of new and enhanced sensing, information channels, and information processing to support cognition. A representative range of science-technology categories is enumerated in Table 9.1, with specific technology capabilities that may enable to introduce new deception capabilities. The table, though not comprehensive, illustrates the breadth of sciences, resulting applied technologies and potential impacts in terms of deception enhancements (e.g. degrade-disrupt sensors or analysis, create more realistic decoys, and so forth) or entirely new modes of deception. The following introduce the key areas where disruptive technology breakthroughs may have the potential to introduce new modes of deception are enabled by new technologies to manipulate materials at the atomic scale, capabilities to manage information at the quantum scale, and capabilities to influence biological and cognitive processes; the table is organized in this sequence, from material sciences, to information and then biological sciences.

Nanoscience research is developing capabilities to construct materials, devices, and systems at atomic and molecular scales (approximately the 1–100-nanometer range) with fundamentally new properties. This research, coupled with materials and electromagnetic sciences will provide refined material properties to control signatures of physical objects across the electromagnetic spectrum, reducing observables while transforming signatures to appear as different objects. The research holds the long term potential to create materials and deceptive "smart

Table 9.1 Deception-Relevant Science and Technologies

Science Category	*Enabling and Emerging Applied Technologies*	*Potential Deception or Counterdeception Applications*
Materials science and nanoscience	Electrochromic materials and adaptive signature laminates, nanofabrics	Smart skin camouflage materials will allow coatings and nets to adapt to surroundings.
	Acoustic absorbent or responsive materials	Frequency selective acoustic signature control
	Controllable conductive materials and tailored dielectrics	Radar frequency selective absorbent or responsive radar materials
	Tailored and adaptive spectral (visible, IR, and multispectral) electroactive polymers, films	Low observable absorbent and reflectivity-emissivity tailored paints and coatings
	Nanoscale sensors and sensor networks; nanoscale robotics; self-replicating nanoscale systems	Dispersed microscopic sensing of denied targets by adaptive, mobile, and self-replicating sensor networks
Electromagnetic sciences	Electromagnetic signature adaptive materials	Signature reduction and automatic adaptation to backgrounds
	Optical materials and detectors; hyperspectral and active laser sensing; foliage penetration and 3D radar, nuclear sensing.	Remote sensing and discrimination of CC&D; camouflage detection and penetration; decoy discrimination
	Plasmonic light scattering materials and control of scattering to background	"Cloaking" of an object in the visible spectra to make an object appear transparent
	Plasma and directed energy technologies	Remote probing and exploitation of CC&D systems (e.g., active decoy attack)
Information and quantum sciences	Agent-based learning, autonomy and intelligence; machine-to-machine collaboration	Automated real-time computer network deception, attack and adaptation (agent lying); agent counterdeception (agent deception detection) and response
	Digital data embedding; steganography	Concealment of messages and data within public information sources
	Digital imaging and image processing	Creation of virtual imagery (still and video with audio) of a deception that is indistinguishable from reality
	Quantum computing	Exponentially enhanced cryptography and cryptanalysis; tamper-proof cryptography for antideception information protection
	Quantum sensing	Remote discrimination of CC&D; detection of nanoscale sensor networks
Psychological and social sciences	Human behavior modeling and analysis	Human deception detection
	Computational social science–based simulation and analysis	Predictive analysis of social populations to manage perceptions; large-scale deception
Biological sciences	Genetic engineering and cloning	DNA evidence spoofing
	Genetic probes and biosensors for specialized detection of biological materials in samples, vapors, and so forth	Chemical-biological materials and weapon detection and discrimination; human discrimination

skins" (e.g., fabrics with embedded sensors to sense surroundings, signature computers to actuate electromagnetic illuminators, and power sources). Furthermore, these materials and devices, coupled with nanoelectromechanical systems (NEMS) for robotic deployment, may offer new capabilities to enhance the scope and scale of decoy deployment and direct attacks on sensors to disrupt, misdirect and deceive sensors. The research also provides numerous capabilities to support nanoscale sensing and tagging to enable a new covert capability to detect, track and uniquely identify physical objects to counter deception. Microscopic sensors and senor networks will revolutionize the ability to covertly deploy unattended ground sensors (UGS) in both scope and scale. Sensor networks at this scale will provide a disruptive ability to counter conventional CC&D of physical objects (by paint, nets, and active signature measures). Such covert sensing and networking capabilities may be developed at a larger, yet invisible, scale in the near term by microelectromechanical systems (MEMS). These "smart dust" sensing networks will be produced by integrating conventional integrated circuit fabrication (for RF and signal processing components) with "micromachining" etching processes to form mechanical and electromechanical devices [18].

Quantum science will provide revolutionary new sensing capabilities to enable greater discrimination of camouflaged and concealed targets and computing capabilities to increase the power to perform cryptanalysis (e.g., by factoring large numbers to break the keys of cryptosystems). Quantum sensing will exploit the entangled properties of photons to form a coincidence image (based on one entangled particle alone) that do not require a specific interaction between the detector and the target, providing the potential for greater discrimination or penetration of CC&D [19].

Biological sciences that allow genetic engineering of life forms hold the potential to enable the reduction and transformation of some biometric signatures to enable human physical changes to support deception and human biological tagging to support counterdeception. The integration of biology, nanoscience, and computation may allow the development of artificial nanosystems with biometic functionality but without biological fragility; such systems could enable covert biological tagging, tracking, or even reporting from individuals (to support deception or counterdeception activities) [20].

While the potential implications of some of these technologies approach well-known science fiction themes, they are seriously considered by policymakers. In testimony before the U.S. Congress, Gregory Treverton of RAND identified biotechnology, nanotechnology, and materials technologies as the primary drivers that will bring genomic profiling, biomedical engineering, and genetic modification to provide revolutionary new sensors and tagging to aid tracking both items and people worldwide (countering deception) while simultaneously aiding deception [21].

These tables provide an illustration of the categories in an assessment of core and emerging technologies that may provide incremental or revolutionary changes, respectively, in deception-counterdeception capabilities. Ongoing assessments of these capabilities are necessary for the deceiver and the counterdeceiver alike to maintain awareness of technology impacts on the practice—and to be alert for disruptive technologies that may upset the balance of knowledge between competitors. An example of such an assessment is that conducted by the Western European

Armament Organisation (WEAO), which identifies many potential deception-related technologies within its Armament Technology Taxonomy [22].

9.4 Summary

As the fundamental principles of deception remain unchanged and the human inclination to employ deception will endure, the classic means of implementing deception will be augmented by new technology-enabling means, conducted over more diverse and changing information channels. The targets of deception may include effective large-scale public deceptions—if even for brief periods—to achieve the effects of public shock, surprise, misdirection or to set the context for other deception operations, all to influence public policy, and support to military operations.

The sophistication of methods to deceive intelligence will be enhanced by emerging technologies to deny and deceive technical means of reconnaissance (detection, identification of capabilities) as well as surveillance (ongoing monitoring of activities and status). The role of deception in computer network operations will also increase the rate at which automated deception and counterdeception exchanges are conducted; this cycle may occur as system trust and security vulnerabilities are discovered and exploited, the attacks are detected and attackers are located by trace back and then reattacked. And the biological sciences will enable the most revolutionary capabilities, enabling the competition between deception and counterdeception to occur at the biological level; agents will seek to spoof their biometric signatures while counterintelligence will seek to tag agents with covert biometric tags.

These capabilities will place increasing demands on those who protect decision and policymakers—analysts who seek to counter deception operations and prevent surprise. These analysts must ever be alert to the adversary, who seeks new ways and channels to put into practice Sun Tzu's age-old advice: "I make the enemy see my strengths as weaknesses and my weaknesses as strengths while I cause his strengths to become weaknesses and discover where he is not strong... I conceal my tracks so that none can discern them; I keep silence so that none can hear me."

Endnotes

[1] *Global Trends 2015: A Dialogue About the Future with Nongovernment Experts*, National Intelligence Council, NIC 2000-02, December 2000, p. 9.

[2] Godson, R., and J. J. Wirtz, "Strategic Denial and Deception," *International Journal of Intelligence and Counterintelligence*, Vol. 13, 2000, pp. 427–430.

[3] Jajko, W., "Deception: Appeal for Acceptance; Discourse on Doctrine; Preface to Planning," *Comparative Strategy*, Vol. 21, 2002, pp. 351–363.

[4] "Strategic Deception in Modern Democracies: Ethical, Legal and Policy Challenges," Conference Cosponsored by the United States Army War College, The Center for the Study of Professional Military Ethics at the United States Naval Academy & Duke University's Kenan Institute for Ethics, October 31–November 1, 2003.

[5] Appendix, Part I of Kant's Critique of Practical Reason and Other Works on the Theory of Ethics, trans. T. Kingsmill Abbott, B. D., Fellow and Tutor of Trinity College, Dublin, 4th revised ed., London, U.K.: Kongmans, Green and Co., 1889.

[6] Kiss, E., "Strategic Deception in Modern Democracies: The Ethical Dimension," *Proc. of Conference on Strategic Deception in Modern Democracies: Ethical, Legal, and Policy Challenges*, Chapel Hill, NC, October 31–November 1, 2003.

[7] Rumsfeld, D. H., Secretary of Defense, Defense Department News Briefing, February 20, 2002, accessed online August 6, 2005, http://www.defenselink.mil/transcripts/2002/t02202002_t0220sd.html.

[8] Glantz, D. M., *Soviet Military Deception in the Second World War*, London, U.K.: Frank Cass & Co., Ltd., 1989, p. 3.

[9] Shultz, R. H., Jr., and R. M. Beitler, "Tactical Deception and Strategic Surprise in Al-Qai'da's Operations," *Middle East Review of International Affairs*, Vol. 8, No. 2, June 2004, p. 59.

[10] Brin, D., *The Transparent Society: Will Technology Force Us to Choose Between Privacy and Freedom?*, New York: Perseus, 1999, p. 290. Research continues in developing more effective human deception-detection methods; the CIA has collaborated with RAND, the American Psychological Association, and the FBI to hold workshops to assess the integration of theory and practice to further the state of the art for a variety of intelligence and law enforcement scenarios. See "APA Works with CIA and RAND to Hold Science of Deception Workshop," *APA's Science Policy Insider News*, American Psychological Association, July 2003, accessed online July 5, 2005, http://www.apa.org/ppo/spin/703.html.

[11] Major General W. Guoqing, "Future Trends of Modern Operations," cited in Pillsbury, M., (ed.), *Chinese Views of Future Warfare*, rev. ed., Washington, D.C.: National Defense University, Strategic Studies Institute, 1998, pp. 350–351.

[12] *Mapping the Global Future*, National Intelligence Council, Washington, D.C., NIC 2004-13, December 2004, p. 10.

[13] Tenet, G. J., "The Worldwide Threat 2004: Challenges in a Changing Global Context," Testimony of Director of Central Intelligence before the Senate Armed Services Committee, March 9, 2004. See also Tenet, G. J., "Iraq and Weapons of Mass Destruction," remarks as prepared for delivery by Director of Central Intelligence at Georgetown University, February 5, 2004.

[14] Gray, C. S., "How Has War Changed Since the End of the Cold War?" *Conference on the Changing Nature of Warfare*, in support of the Global Trends 2020 Project of the U.S. National Intelligence Council, University of Reading, England, May 2004, pp. 2–3.

[15] Johnson, P., M. Memmott, and G. Levin, "Rather: 'Time for Me to Move On,'" *USA TODAY*, November 23, 2004, accessed February 13, 2005, http://www.usatoday.com/life/television/news/2004-11-23-tv-rather_x.htm. See also Kurtz, H., "After Blogs Got Hits, CBS Got a Black Eye," *Washington Post*, September 20, 2004, p. C01, http://www.washingtonpost.com/wp-dyn/articles/A34153-2004Sep19.html.

[16] Christensen, C., *The Innovator's Dilemma*, New York: HarperBusiness, 2000.

[17] Wattenbarger, J. F., "The SOF Warrior: A Disruptive Force in A Complex Environment," *Proc. NDIA 2005 SOLIC Conf.*, February 2005.

[18] The U.S. Defense Advanced Research Projects Agency (DARPA) is conducting research to develop MEMS to enhance levels of perception, control, and performance of systems in battlefield environments; MEMS project areas include: (1) fluid sensing, control, and transport; (2) mass data storage; (3) optics and imaging; (4) inertial instruments; (5) radio frequency components and communication; and (6) sensor and actuator networks or arrays; accessed August 6, 2005, http://www.darpa.mil/mto/mems/. See also Culler, D. E., D. Estrin, and M. Srivastava, "Overview of Sensor Networks," *IEEE Computer*, August 2004, pp. 41–49.

[19] Razeghi, M., and G. J. Brown, (eds.), "Quantum Sensing: Evolution and Revolution from Past to Future," *Proceedings of SPIE*, Vol. 4999, July 2003, and "Quantum Applications," accessed July 27, 2005, http://veridian.com/offerings/suboffering.asp?offeringID=189.

[20] Williams, E., et al., *Opportunities at the Intersection of Nanoscience, Biology and Computation*, JASON Report JSR-03-300, MITRE, November 2002.

[21] Treverton, G. F., "Emerging Threats to National Security," RAND CT-234,

Testimony presented to the House of Representatives Permanent Select Committee on Intelligence on February 2, 2005, p. 12.

[22] WEAG Technology Taxonomy Codes, Western European Armament Organisation, November 24, 2004, http://www.weao.weu.int/site/frameset.htm.

About the Authors

Michael Bennett works as a consultant in northern Virginia. He has experience in both the government and private sectors as a principal investigator and project manager in a variety of intelligence-related disciplines, including research and development, technical operations, and analysis. The focus of his expertise over the past 20 years has been in developing and applying advanced technologies to the most difficult problems of intelligence collection and analysis. He has conceived and managed projects in the areas of product and image security, steganography, imaging sensors, signal processing, communications receivers, direction finding, and advanced technical collection systems. His work in the counterdeception field began in 2000 when he conceived and managed a research study investigating cognitive aids for counterdeception. He holds a B.S.E.E. from Purdue University and an M.B.A. from the University of Connecticut. He is the author of "Using Hypergames for Deception Planning and Counterdeception Analysis" (*Defense Intelligence Journal*, 2007).

Edward Waltz is the chief scientist in the Intelligence Innovation Division of BAE Systems Advanced Information Technologies, where he leads intelligence analysis and information operations research for the U.S. Intelligence Community and the U.S. Department of Defense. For the past decade, his research has focused on modeling human systems, including foreign leadership, organizations and social populations. He holds a B.S.E.E. from the Case Institute of Technology and an M.S. in computer, information, and control engineering from the University of Michigan. He has over 35 years of experience in developing and deploying signal processing, data fusion, and intelligence analysis capabilities. He is the author of *Knowledge Management in the Intelligence Enterprise* (Artech House, 2003), *Information and Warfare Principles and Operations* (Artech House, 1998), and *Multisensor Data Fusion* (Artech House, 1990). He was the cochair of the 2000 NATO Summer Study on Data Fusion and is an editor of the results in *Multisensor Data Fusion* (Kluwer, 2001). In 2004 he was a recipient of the Department of Defense's Joseph Mignona Data Fusion Award. He became a Veridian Technology Fellow in 2002.

Index

The Artech House Intelligence and Information Operations Library

Concepts, Models, and Tools for Information Fusion, Éloi Bossé, Jean Roy, and Steve Wark

Counterdeception Principles and Applications for National Security, Michael Bennett and Edward Waltz

Electronic Intelligence: The Analysis of Radar Signals, Second Edition, Richard G. Wiley

Electronic Warfare in the Information Age, D. Curtis Schleher

Electronic Warfare Target Location Methods, Richard A. Poisel

Information Operations Planning, Patrick D. Allen

Information Warfare and Organizational Decision-Making, Alexander Kott, editor

Information Warfare Principles and Operations, Edward Waltz

Introduction to Communication Electronic Warfare Systems, Richard A. Poisel

Knowledge Management in the Intelligence Enterprise, Edward Waltz

Mathematical Techniques in Multisensor Data Fusion, Second Edition, David L. Hall and Sonya A. H. McMullen

Statistical Multisource-Multitarget Information Fusion, Ronald P. S. Mahler

Stratagem: Deception and Surprise in War, Barton Whaley

Target Acquisition in Communication Electronic Warfare, Richard Poisel

Printed in the USA
CPSIA information can be obtained
at www.ICGtesting.com
BVHW021930280723
667856BV00002BA/5

9 781580 539357